Knowledge–Based Processes in Software Development

Saqib Saeed
Bahria University Islamabad, Pakistan

Izzat Alsmadi
Prince Sultan University, Saudi Arabia

A volume in the Advances in Systems
Analysis, Software Engineering, and High
Performance Computing (ASASEHPC)
Book Series

Information Science
REFERENCE
An Imprint of IGI Global

Managing Director:	Lindsay Johnston
Production Manager:	Jennifer Yoder
Publishing Systems Analyst:	Adrienne Freeland
Development Editor:	Christine Smith
Acquisitions Editor:	Kayla Wolfe
Typesetter:	Lisandro Gonzalez
Cover Design:	Jason Mull

Published in the United States of America by
Information Science Reference (an imprint of IGI Global)
701 E. Chocolate Avenue
Hershey PA 17033
Tel: 717-533-8845
Fax: 717-533-8661
E-mail: cust@igi-global.com
Web site: http://www.igi-global.com

Library of Congress Cataloging-in-Publication Data

Knowledge-based processes in software development / Saqib Saeed and Izzat Alsmadi, editors.
    pages cm
Includes bibliographical references and index.
    Summary: "This book focuses on the inherent issues to help practitioners in gaining understanding of software development processes aimed at software professionals,students and researchers in the domain of software engineering in order to successfully employ knowledge management procedures"--Provided by publisher.
    ISBN 978-1-4666-4229-4 (hardcover) -- ISBN (invalid) 978-1-4666-4230-0
(ebook) -- ISBN (invalid) 978-1-4666-4231-7 (print & perpetual access) 1. Computer software--Development. 2. Software engineering. 3. Knowledge management. I. Saeed, Saqib, 1970- II. Alsmadi, Izzat, 1972-
    QA76.76.D47K575 2013
    005.1--dc23
                              2013010142

This book is published in the IGI Global book series Advances in Systems Analysis, Software Engineering, and High Performance Computing (ASASEHPC) (ISSN: 2327-3453; eISSN: 2327-3461)

British Cataloguing in Publication Data
A Cataloguing in Publication record for this book is available from the British Library.

For electronic access to this publication, please contact: eresources@igi-global.com.

Advances in Systems Analysis, Software Engineering, and High Performance Computing (ASASEHPC) Book Series

Vijayan Sugumaran
Oakland University, USA

ISSN: 2327-3453
EISSN: 2327-3461

MISSION

The theory and practice of computing applications and distributed systems has emerged as one of the key areas of research driving innovations in business, engineering, and science. The fields of software engineering, systems analysis, and high performance computing offer a wide range of applications and solutions in solving computational problems for any modern organization.

The **Advances in Systems Analysis, Software Engineering, and High Performance Computing (ASASEHPC) Book Series** brings together research in the areas of distributed computing, systems and software engineering, high performance computing, and service science. This collection of publications is useful for academics, researchers, and practitioners seeking the latest practices and knowledge in this field.

COVERAGE

- Computer Graphics
- Computer Networking
- Computer System Analysis
- Distributed Cloud Computing
- Enterprise Information Systems
- Metadata and Semantic Web
- Parallel Architectures
- Performance Modeling
- Software Engineering
- Virtual Data Systems

IGI Global is currently accepting manuscripts for publication within this series. To submit a proposal for a volume in this series, please contact our Acquisition Editors at Acquisitions@igi-global.com or visit: http://www.igi-global.com/publish/.

Titles in this Series

For a list of additional titles in this series, please visit: www.igi-global.com

Communication Infrastructures for Cloud Computing
Hussein T. Mouftah (University of Ottawa, Canada) and Burak Kantarci (University of Ottawa, Canada)
Information Science Reference • copyright 2014 • 583pp • H/C (ISBN: 9781466645226) • US $195.00 (our price)

Organizational, Legal, and Technological Dimensions of Information System Administration
Irene Maria Portela (Polytechnic Institute of Cávado and Ave, Portugal) and Fernando Almeida (Polytechnic Institute of Gaya, Portugal)
Information Science Reference • copyright 2014 • 321pp • H/C (ISBN: 9781466645264) • US $195.00 (our price)

Advances and Applications in Model-Driven Engineering
Vicente García Díaz (University of Oviedo, Spain) Juan Manuel Cueva Lovelle (University of Oviedo, Spain) B. Cristina Pelayo García-Bustelo (University of Oviedo, Spain) and Oscar Sanjuán Martinez (University of Carlos III, Spain)
Information Science Reference • copyright 2014 • 424pp • H/C (ISBN: 9781466644946) • US $195.00 (our price)

Service-Driven Approaches to Architecture and Enterprise Integration
Raja Ramanathan (Independent Researcher, USA) and Kirtana Raja (Independent Researcher, USA)
Information Science Reference • copyright 2013 • 411pp • H/C (ISBN: 9781466641938) • US $195.00 (our price)

Progressions and Innovations in Model-Driven Software Engineering
Vicente García Díaz (University of Oviedo, Spain) Juan Manuel Cueva Lovelle (University of Oviedo, Spain) B. Cristina Pelayo García-Bustelo (University of Oviedo, Spain) and Oscar Sanjuán Martínez (University of Oviedo, Spain)
Engineering Science Reference • copyright 2013 • 388pp • H/C (ISBN: 9781466642171) • US $195.00 (our price)

Knowledge-Based Processes in Software Development
Saqib Saeed (Bahria University Islamabad, Pakistan) and Izzat Alsmadi (Prince Sultan University, Saudi Arabia)
Information Science Reference • copyright 2013 • 318pp • H/C (ISBN: 9781466642294) • US $195.00 (our price)

Distributed Computing Innovations for Business, Engineering, and Science
Alfred Waising Loo (Lingnan University, Hong Kong)
Information Science Reference • copyright 2013 • 369pp • H/C (ISBN: 9781466625334) • US $195.00 (our price)

Data Intensive Distributed Computing Challenges and Solutions for Large-scale Information Management
Tevfik Kosar (University at Buffalo, USA)
Information Science Reference • copyright 2012 • 352pp • H/C (ISBN: 9781615209712) • US $180.00 (our price)

www.igi-global.com

701 E. Chocolate Ave., Hershey, PA 17033
Order online at www.igi-global.com or call 717-533-8845 x100
To place a standing order for titles released in this series, contact: cust@igi-global.com
Mon-Fri 8:00 am - 5:00 pm (est) or fax 24 hours a day 717-533-8661

Editorial Advisory Board

Table of Contents

Preface xv

Section 1
Introduction

Chapter 1
Using KMS as a Tool to Improve Decision Making Process 1
Rawan Khasawneh, Yarmouk University, Jordan
Emad Abu-Shanab, Yarmouk University, Jordan

Chapter 2
KM and Global Software Engineering (GSE) 12
Sameer Abufardeh, North Dakota State University, USA

Chapter 3
Knowledge Management and Semantic Web Services 35
Izzat Alsmadi, Prince Sultan University, Saudi Arabia
Sascha Alda, Bonn-Rhein-Sieg University, Germany

Chapter 4
Knowledge-Based Code Clone Approach in Embedded and Real-Time Systems 49
Anupama Surendran, Cochin University of Science and Technology, India
Philip Samuel, Cochin University of Science and Technology, India

Section 2
Knowledge Management in Software Process

Chapter 5
Using Knowledge Management and Aggregation Techniques to Improve Web Effort Estimation 64
Emilia Mendes, Blekinge Institute of Technology, Sweden
Simon Baker, Cambridge University, UK

Chapter 6
Effort, Time, and Staffing in Continually Evolving Open-Source Projects 86
Liguo Yu, Indiana University – South Bend, USA

Chapter 7
Understanding Requirement Engineering Practices: An Empirical Study of the Pakistani
Software Industry 109
Saqib Saeed, Bahria University, Pakistan
Ashi Iram, Bahria University, Pakistan
Kiran Nazeer, Bahria University, Pakistan
Tayyaba Ayub, Bahria University, Pakistan

Chapter 8
The Distribution of Testing Activities in Web Services and SOA Environment 119
Izzat Alsmadi, Prince Sultan University, Saudi Arabia
Sascha Alda, Bonn-Rhein-Sieg University, Germany

Chapter 9
Managing Knowledge in Open Source Software Test Process 135
Tamer Abdou, Concordia University, Canada
Peter Grogono, Concordia University, Canada
Pankaj Kamthan, Concordia University, Canada

Section 3
Applications

Chapter 10
Feature Extraction through Information Sharing in Swarm Intelligence Techniques 151
Lavika Goel, Delhi Technological University, India
V. K. Panchal, Defence and Research Development Organization, India

Chapter 11
A Software System for Grading Diabetic Retinopathy by Analyzing Retinal Images 176
M. Usman Akram, Bahria University, Pakistan
Shehzad Khalid, Bahria University, Pakistan

Chapter 12
Demonic Fuzzy Relational Calculus 194
Fairouz Tchier, King Saud University, Saudi Arabia
Huda Alrashidi, King Saud University, Saudi Arabia

Chapter 13
ONTO-KMS-TEC: An Ontology-Based Knowledge Management Framework to Teach
Engineering Courses 226

    C. R. Rene Robin, Jerusalem College of Engineering, India

    D. Doreen Hepzibah Miriam, Loyola-ICAM College of Engineering and Technology, India

    G. V. Uma, Madras Institute of Technology, India

Compilation of References 250

About the Contributors 270

Index 276

Detailed Table of Contents

Preface xv

Section 1
Introduction

Chapter 1

Using KMS as a Tool to Improve Decision Making Process 1
Rawan Khasawneh, Yarmouk University, Jordan
Emad Abu-Shanab, Yarmouk University, Jordan

Knowledge plays a central role in the decision making process, and it provides a better foundation for managers to make high quality decisions. On the other hand, having the right knowledge at the right time to make the right decision is becoming a competitive weapon utilized by organizations to achieve sustained competitive advantage and other strategic goals. Based on that, it is important for organizations to manage their knowledge (organization intellectual asset) in a more effective and efficient way in order to gain such benefits. This chapter explores knowledge management and decision-making processes and its general concepts, reviews several conceptual frameworks of knowledge management that affect the decision making process proposed in the literature, and demonstrates several knowledge-management practices in software development processes. Conclusions and proposed future work are stated at the end of the chapter.

Chapter 2

KM and Global Software Engineering (GSE) 12
Sameer Abufardeh, North Dakota State University, USA

In the last decade, we have witnessed a dramatic transformation of software development processes. Outsourcing and offshore development has become the norm in current software development because of the many benefits organizations and people can have by adapting such strategy. Benefits include reduced cost, reduced time to market, availability of skilled people, proximity to market and customers in various locals, etc. Furthermore, the transformation from single-site, mostly English-based into a multi-site, multilingual, multicultural, and globally distributed endeavor has marked the birth of Global Software Engineering (GSE). This transformation increases the complexity of GSE when compared to traditional co-located Software development. GSE involves knowledge intensive activities, different people, different teams, and globally dispersed software organization. While there are many benefits in adapting GSE, the new strategy created several challenges/issues for the organization, practitioners, and researchers. Challenges include language and culture, communication, coordination and collaboration, team building, etc. Knowledge Management (KM) is considered fundamental and an essential asset of an organization because it enables organizations to efficiently create, store, and share knowledge, and it helps in resolving many of the current GSE issues. KM tools and techniques has been successfully used in effective management of who knows what, which helps in learning, problem solving, and innovation. This chapter discusses in general the challenges of culture in Global Software Engineering (GSE). However, the main focus of the discussion in this chapter is on the challenges of culture in global software application. For many years, KM literature has focused on the cultural issues of teams, processes, types of knowledge, etc. This chapter's goal is to stimulate and encourage more research on how KM tools and practices can help in overcoming these challenges. Furthermore, it emphasizes the issues of language, which are mostly marginalized.

Chapter 3
Knowledge Management and Semantic Web Services 35
    Izzat Alsmadi, Prince Sultan University, Saudi Arabia
    Sascha Alda, Bonn-Rhein-Sieg University, Germany

Information reliability and automatic computation are two important aspects that are continuously pushing the Web to be more semantic. Information uploaded to the Web should be reusable and extractable automatically to other applications, platforms, etc. Several tools exist to explicitly markup Web content. The Web services may also have a positive role on the automatic processing of Web contents, especially when they act as flexible and agile agents. However, Web services themselves should be developed with semantics in mind. They should include and provide structured information to facilitate their use, reuse, composition, query, etc. In this chapter, the authors focus on evaluating state-of-the-art semantic aspects and approaches in Web services. Ultimately, this contributes to the goal of Web knowledge management, execution, and transfer.

Chapter 4
Knowledge-Based Code Clone Approach in Embedded and Real-Time Systems 49
    Anupama Surendran, Cochin University of Science and Technology, India
    Philip Samuel, Cochin University of Science and Technology, India

Even though human beings are using computers in their day-to-day activities, the terms embedded and real-time systems have received much attention only in the last few years, and they have become an inevitable part of our daily activities. The most evident and highlighted feature of embedded systems is the consideration of time. The significance of time constraints in designing each and every feature of embedded systems has made the software and hardware of embedded systems more complicated and entirely different from ordinary systems. Due to these reasons, several challenges exist in developing and maintaining embedded and real time software. Increase in complexity of the embedded system code increases the chance of occurrence of defects in the embedded software. Failure to deliver the software within the stipulated time, economic constraints faced during the development and the maintenance phase, inadequate testing, design of improper code and its reuse are some of the issues faced during the embedded system software development phase. In this chapter, the authors suggest a knowledge-based approach in managing the issues that arise during the coding and testing phase of embedded and real-time software. Program slicing is used to detect the code clones present in the embedded software, and a knowledge repository of code clones is created. This code clone knowledge repository is utilized during the coding and testing phase of real-time and embedded software, which in turn improves the whole software development process.

Section 2
Knowledge Management in Software Process

Chapter 5

Using Knowledge Management and Aggregation Techniques to Improve Web Effort Estimation 64

Emilia Mendes, Blekinge Institute of Technology, Sweden
Simon Baker, Cambridge University, UK

Effort estimation is one of the main pillars of sound project management as its accuracy can affect significantly whether projects will be delivered on time and within budget. However, due to being a complex domain, there are countless examples of companies that underestimate effort, and such estimation error can be of 30%-40% on average, thus leading to serious project management problems (Jørgensen & Grimstad, 2009). The contribution of this chapter is twofold: 1) to explain the knowledge management methodology employed to build industrial expert-based Web effort estimation models, such that other companies willing to develop such models can do so and 2) to provide a wider understanding on the fundamental factors affecting Web effort estimation and their relationships via a mechanism that partially aggregates the expert-based Web effort estimation models built.

Chapter 6

Effort, Time, and Staffing in Continually Evolving Open-Source Projects 86

Liguo Yu, Indiana University – South Bend, USA

Scheduling and staffing are important management activities in software projects. In closed-source software development, the relationships among development effort, time, and staffing have been well established and validated: the development effort determines the development time and the best number of developers that should be allocated to the project. However, there has been no similar research reported in open-source projects. In this chapter, the authors study the development effort, development time, and staffing in an open-source project, the Linux kernel project. Specifically, they investigate the power law relations among development effort, development time, and the number of active developers in the Linux kernel project. The authors find the power law relations differ from one branch to another branch in the Linux kernel project, which suggests different kinds of management and development styles might exist in different branches of the Linux kernel project. The empirical knowledge of software development effort obtained in this study could help project management and cost control in both open-source communities and closed-source industries.

Chapter 7

Understanding Requirement Engineering Practices: An Empirical Study of the Pakistani
Software Industry 109

Saqib Saeed, Bahria University, Pakistan
Ashi Iram, Bahria University, Pakistan
Kiran Nazeer, Bahria University, Pakistan
Tayyaba Ayub, Bahria University, Pakistan

Requirement engineering is a main task in software process. In Software Engineering literature, many best practices and guidelines are present to construct quality software. However, adoption of such uniform guidelines is not in practice across the globe. In this chapter, the authors discuss requirement engineering practices followed in Pakistani small- and medium-scale enterprises. In order to understand work practices the authors conducted a survey and analyzed the responses. They found that cost and budgeting is one of the major issues of Pakistani industry: higher management is not willing to invest to adopt state-of-the-art standardized practices. This situation can be improved by enhancing public private partnerships to get desired quality software in the local IT industry.

Chapter 8

The Distribution of Testing Activities in Web Services and SOA Environment 119

Izzat Alsmadi, Prince Sultan University, Saudi Arabia

Sascha Alda, Bonn-Rhein-Sieg University, Germany

Testing in Web services and SOA environment can be far more distributed in comparison with testing stand-alone or traditional applications. This is because such systems are composed of several hybrid components. These include Web servers and their related components, server side applications, communication services, and client side Web services. In this chapter, the authors focus on challenges and opportunities for software testing in SOA environment. They divide testing activities based on three classifications: testing activities that are going to be similar to those in traditional software development environments, testing activities that will be less usable or popular in SOA, and testing activities that will evolve significantly to adapt to the new environment. The authors believe that most generic testing activities are going to stay in any new software development environment. However, their importance, significance, challenges, and difficulties are going to be dependent on the subject environment. Some tasks will be easier to implement and test and others will either be un-applicable or difficult to test and implement in comparison with testing in traditional software development environments.

Chapter 9

Managing Knowledge in Open Source Software Test Process 135

Tamer Abdou, Concordia University, Canada

Peter Grogono, Concordia University, Canada

Pankaj Kamthan, Concordia University, Canada

The increasing adoption and use of Open Source Software (OSS) motivates study of its development. This chapter explores the state-of-the art in OSS development processes, in general, and OSS testing processes, in particular. A conceptual model for software Testing Knowledge Management (TKM) that aims to provide an understanding of the testing domain is introduced. The TKM model is informed by earlier studies and guided by international testing standards. Moreover, the TKM model is equipped with different forms of knowledge, reusable across software projects. Using the TKM model as an integrative conceptual model enables understanding of how knowledge life cycle stages are mapped onto the test process of OSS, what type of knowledge is created at each stage, and how knowledge is converted from one stage to another. The chapter is supported by representative examples of OSS that are mature and currently in widespread use.

Section 3
Applications

Chapter 10

Feature Extraction through Information Sharing in Swarm Intelligence Techniques 151

Lavika Goel, Delhi Technological University, India

V. K. Panchal, Defence and Research Development Organization, India

Swarm Intelligence (SI) refers to a kind of problem-solving ability that emerges by the interaction of simple information-processing units. The overall behaviour of the system results from the interactions of individuals through information sharing with each other and with their environment, i.e., the self-organized group behaviour. The chapter details the theoretical aspects and the mathematical framework of the concept of information sharing in each of the swarm intelligence techniques of Biogeography-Based Optimization (BBO), Ant Colony Optimization (ACO), Particle Swarm Optimization (PSO), and Bee Colony Optimization (BCO), which are the major constituents of the SI techniques that have been used for land cover feature extraction of multi-spectral satellite images. The authors then demonstrate the results of classification after applying each of the above SI techniques presented in the chapter and calculate the classification accuracy for each in terms of the kappa coefficient generated from the error matrix obtained. For verification, they test their results on two datasets and also calculate the producer's and the user's accuracy separately for each land cover feature in order to explore the performance of the technique on different features of the satellite image. From the results, they conclude that the concepts of information sharing can be successfully adapted for the design of efficient algorithms that can be successfully applied for feature extraction of satellite images.

Chapter 11
A Software System for Grading Diabetic Retinopathy by Analyzing Retinal Images 176
    M. Usman Akram, Bahria University, Pakistan
    Shehzad Khalid, Bahria University, Pakistan

Medical imaging is very popular and is vital in designing Computer-Aided Diagnosis (CAD) for various diseases such as tumor detection using MRI. Diabetic retinopathy is an eye disease that is caused by the increase of insulin in blood in diabetic patients. It can cause total blindness if not detected and treated in time. The disease affects human retina and shows different signs on retinal surface as time passes. In this chapter, the authors present a software based on novel algorithms for early detection of diabetic retinopathy. It detects dark (Microaneurysms, Haemorrhages) and bright (hard exudates, cotton wool spots) lesions from retinal image. The algorithms consist of retinal image preprocessing, main component extraction, detection of candidate lesions, feature extraction, and finally classification using modified m-mediods based classifier. The proposed system is evaluated using publicly available retinal image databases, and results demonstrate the validity of proposed system.

Chapter 12
Demonic Fuzzy Relational Calculus 194
    Fairouz Tchier, King Saud University, Saudi Arabia
    Huda Alrashidi, King Saud University, Saudi Arabia

In this chapter, the authors categorize methods that are used to formally specify and verify software requirements. They discuss several formal method-related subjects such as calculus fuzzy and relational calculus.

Chapter 13
ONTO-KMS-TEC: An Ontology-Based Knowledge Management Framework to Teach
Engineering Courses 226
    C. R. Rene Robin, Jerusalem College of Engineering, India
    D. Doreen Hepzibah Miriam, Loyola-ICAM College of Engineering and Technology, India
    G. V. Uma, Madras Institute of Technology, India

Knowledge management tools have been used in higher educational institutions for years to improve the effectiveness of teaching methodologies. Knowledge management in pedagogical includes processes of knowledge discovery, capture, storage, retrieval, sharing, and understanding. According to Pundt and Bishr, knowledge management aims at facilitating knowledge flow and utilization across every beneficeiary, such as faculty members and students. An ontology can be used to support knowledge retrieval, store, and sharing domain knowledge. The framework and the case studies described in this chapter detail how the knowledge of an engineering subject can be effectively retrieved, stored, and shared among the teachers and the students.

Compilation of References 250

About the Contributors 270

Index 276

Preface

Knowledge is distilled from large volumes of data and information to serve users' needs. Knowledge management tools have helped different domains to improve the operations. Software development is human intensive activity, and knowledge accumulated through experience from past projects can help in resource optimization for new projects. Software products vary widely by their nature, complexity, size, requirements, etc., and this makes it hard to generalize one specific approach that can successfully be used in developing different software products.

In the first chapter, Rawan Khasawneh and Emad Abu Shanab discuss how to use knowledge management systems to help in improving decision-making. The chapter discusses frameworks that can be used in Knowledge Management (KM) decision-making. The chapter concludes with a section of KM practices related to software development processes and approaches.

Next, Dr. Sameer Abu Fardeh presents a chapter on KM and global software engineering. The chapter elaborates on challenges related to the global software development process. The chapter then discusses KM practices in global software engineering and the different terms and usages of knowledge in such development paradigms. The chapter also discusses how KM helps in solving some of the challenges presented in global software development, especially issues related to cultural and language barriers. The author proposes recommendations on how to improve KM in global software development and future research directions.

In chapter three, Izzat Alsmadi and Sascha Alda discuss KM in Semantic Web services. Semantic Web services are expanded to allow users to make high-level queries with Web services. This is an important component in the Semantic Web in general that aims at making information through the Web more structured and utilizable. While Web services provide important information to a wide range of different users who may use those services in different contexts, it is necessary for users to interact with Web services or make complex queries. The authors also present different KM components developed to help in achieving Semantic Web services.

Chapter 4 by Anupama Surendran and Philip Samuel is focused on the development of embedded systems and major challenges that may arise in the development phase. The authors also discuss how different testing methodologies can be uniquely applied in testing embedded systems.

In the fifth chapter, Emilia Mendes and Simon Baker discussed KM in Web effort estimation. Software projects' effort estimation techniques are traditionally proposed for the development of traditional software products. For development of Websites, the authors present several unique aspects on Web efforts' estimation that may make traditional software effort estimation techniques deficient. The authors discuss how KM can be used to develop Web effort estimation models that can be generalized and used as a dictionary for Website development in general.

In the sixth chapter, Liguo Yu focuses on project management aspects related to open source projects. The author discusses management aspects such as: effort, scheduling, and staffing, and how the agility and flexibility of open source projects pose challenges in handling those projects and their resources. Linux kernel open source is used as a case study in this chapter. The author describes some of the differences in those aspects between closed and open source projects. The author also discusses prediction models that can be used to predict effort and resources in such open source projects.

In the next chapter, Saqib Saeed and his colleagues present a case study where they discuss requirement engineering practices employed by different small- and medium-scale enterprises in Pakistan. They conclude that Pakistani software industry is in its nascent stage and still a lot of effort is needed to improve the work practices.

The eighth chapter by Izzat Alsmadi and Sascha Alda focuses on different testing activities in software development processes of Web services. Unlike Websites or software products, Web services are developed to be generic and can easily be called and used by different clients/users in different environments. Dynamic/real time execution will be far more important in comparison with traditional software products, especially as services are called more often and used by a large number of users' in possibly different contexts. The authors visit all testing activities describing how each testing activity can be different in Web services development.

In the ninth chapter, Tamer Abdou, Peter Grongono, and Pankaj Kamthan discuss KM in testing open source software products. The chapter tries to evaluate testing and quality aspects, especially where open source projects may not go through aggressive testing activities in comparison to typical company type or closed projects. A conceptual model for knowledge in software testing is presented. The authors elaborate on the knowledge management testing model and how to draw traceability between KM components and testing activities.

In chapter 10, Lavika Goel and V. K. Panchal provide a mathematical formulation of the concept of information sharing in each of the swarm intelligence techniques of Biogeography-Based Optimization (BBO), Ant Colony Optimization (ACO), Particle Swarm Optimization (PSO), and Bee Colony Optimization (BCO). The feature extraction results based on the concepts of information sharing are demonstrated on two different datasets for each of the above techniques.

In the next chapter, Usman Akram and Shehzad Khalid present a software solution based on novel algorithms for early detection of diabetic retinopathy. It detects dark and bright lesions from retinal image. The proposed system is evaluated using publicly available retinal image databases and results demonstrate the validity of proposed system. The authors also discuss information related to preprocessing and retinal component extraction.

In chapter 12, Fairouz Tchier and Huda Alrashidi categorize methods that are used to formally specify and verify software requirements. The authors discuss several formal method-related subjects such as calculus fuzzy and relational calculus.

In the last chapter, Rene Robin and his colleagues discuss how knowledge from engineering subjects can be processed, stored, retrieved, and communicated between educators and students.

Saqib Saeed
Bahria University, Pakistan

Izzat Alsmadi
Yarmouk University, Jordan

Section 1
Introduction

Chapter 1
Using KMS as a Tool to Improve Decision Making Process

Rawan Khasawneh
Yarmouk University, Jordan

Emad Abu-Shanab
Yarmouk University, Jordan

ABSTRACT

Knowledge plays a central role in the decision making process, and it provides a better foundation for managers to make high quality decisions. On the other hand, having the right knowledge at the right time to make the right decision is becoming a competitive weapon utilized by organizations to achieve sustained competitive advantage and other strategic goals. Based on that, it is important for organizations to manage their knowledge (organization intellectual asset) in a more effective and efficient way in order to gain such benefits. This chapter explores knowledge management and decision-making processes and its general concepts, reviews several conceptual frameworks of knowledge management that affect the decision making process proposed in the literature, and demonstrates several knowledge-management practices in software development processes. Conclusions and proposed future work are stated at the end of the chapter.

INTRODUCTION

Knowledge plays a central role in decision-making process and it provides a better foundation for managers to make high quality decisions. On the other hand, having the right knowledge at the right time to make the right decision is becoming a competitive weapon utilized by organizations to achieve sustained competitive advantage and other strategic goals. Based on that, it's important for organizations to manage their knowledge (organization's intellectual asset) in a more effective and efficient way in order to gain such benefits.

Knowledge management systems, decision-making systems (DSS) and business intelligence tools are derived from the objectives of organiza-

DOI: 10.4018/978-1-4666-4229-4.ch001

tions, where the literature shows that there are three main approaches in using such systems. These three approaches are: managerial approach, which uses such systems in order to improve the decision making process. The second approach is the technical approach, which focuses on using tools and technologies that can support the processes that require more knowledge and intelligence. The third approach is an enabler approach that focuses on providing value added support capabilities (Rouhani, Asgari & Mirhosseini, 2012).

Integrating knowledge management system with decision support system during decision making process will improve the quality of this process and make it more effective by using an enhanced and required knowledge (Gulser & Badur, 2011). Also, in each phase of the decision making process, knowledge is necessary and has a significant impact on how the process is done based on its availability, usability and quality, especially that poor knowledge will lead to poor quality of decisions and good knowledge will lead to high quality decisions. Based on that, organizations need to support their decision making process with knowledge management system (Jinbo, Xuefeng & Ming, 2011).

This chapter focuses on how knowledge management systems can be used to enhance and improve the decision making process in order to help organizations make the right decision that will lead to short-term and long-term goal achievement. The chapter is divided into four sections. Following is a brief description of each section.

The following section reviews knowledge management and decision making concepts and focuses on the importance of the integration between them. It reviews knowledge management and decision making processes in general, their definitions, and general related concepts. Next, several conceptual frameworks of knowledge management that affect decision making process will be reviewed. The third section will present general discussion of the frameworks reviewed in the previous section with a deep focus on the

importance of integrating knowledge management in decision making during software development process. Finally, several practices of knowledge management in software development process are explored. Conclusions and proposed future work are stated at the end.

KNOWLEDGE MANAGEMENT AND DECISION MAKING

Knowledge is information that is contextual, relevant, actionable and dynamic in nature. It can be classified into two main types: tacit knowledge which is highly personal and difficult to formalize and explicit knowledge which is easily documented, stored and distributed (Raj, 2012; Anand & Singh, 2011; Amine & Ahmed-Nacer, 2011). As presented by Qwaider (2011) and Amine and Ahmed-Nacer (2011), the interaction between tacit and explicit knowledge is known as knowledge conversion which has four modes: socialization (tacit to tacit), externalization (tacit to explicit), internalization (explicit to tacit), and combination (explicit to explicit).

Organizations can obtain knowledge from several resources internally and externally, where it can be named based on the resource it is extract from. For example, acquired knowledge: is knowledge that can be gained from outside the organization; fusion knowledge: is knowledge that can be generated through bringing group of people with different perspectives to work together on the same project; and finally adaptation knowledge: is knowledge that results from the response to new processes or new technologies available in the market (Anand & Singh, 2011).

Knowledge Management (KM) is defined in different ways based on different perspectives that they represent, but most researchers and specialists agreed that it is "a process that helps organizations identify, select, organize, disseminate and transfer important information and expertise that are a part of the organizational memory that typically resides within an organization in an unstructured manner" (Raj, 2012, p. 365). From this definition, the 4 C's of knowledge management that present knowledge management processes can be identified as: knowledge creation, knowledge capturing, knowledge coordination (through the dissemination process), and knowledge consumption (Raj, 2012).

On the other hand, Bjornson and Dingsoyr (2008) proclaimed that working in knowledge management is categorized under three major schools: technocratic school (includes systems school, cartographic school and engineering school), economic school (focuses on how knowledge asset relates to income in organization), and behavioral school (includes organizational school, spatial school and strategic school). Table 1 presents several definitions of KM.

Anand and Singh (2011) indicated that three major factors have a significant impact on knowledge management process that can lead to the success or failure of knowledge management initiatives. These three major factors are: managerial factors, resource factors and environmental factors. On the other hand, implementing knowledge management in the organization helps in achieving better decision making, enhanced learning, smoother collaboration, improved communication, improved business process, and many other things.

According to the knowledge-based perspective of the firm and as a result of the shift from industrial revolution to knowledge revolution, knowledge is an important asset that can be used as a weapon to achieve the strategic goals of the firm in a more effective way in order to gain sustainability, competitive advantage and other long-term benefits (Raj, 2012; Sajeva & Jucevicius, 2010).

It is important for organizations to treat knowledge management not only as a data management process but also as an organizational and social process that leads to leveraging organizational objectives in building knowledge management strategies. Based on that, knowledge strategies focus on how needed knowledge can be obtained, created and shared internally and externally which will leverage organizational focus on the value obtained from the available knowledge. Such step will result in a better and more effective use of knowledge for/during the decision making process, which will has a significant impact on improving organization's operations, products, services and making customers more satisfied (Alrawi & Alrawi, 2011).

Table 1. Knowledge management definitions

KM Definition	Resource
A structured process, through which knowledge can be created, stored, distributed, and applied to decision making.	Alavi & Leidner (2001)
A process that concerned with making sure that the right knowledge is available to the right processors in the right form at the right time for the right cost.	Holsapple & Singh, (2001) as cited in Jinbo, Xuefeng & Ming (2011)
A process in which knowledge is acquired from resources within organizations or outside them in order to turning it into explicit information that can be easily used by employees to increase their organizational knowledge.	Jones (2006)
"A process that helps organizations identify, select, organize, disseminate and transfer important information and expertise that are a part of the organizational memory that typically resides within an organization in an unstructured manner".	Raj (2012, p. 365)
A technique that aims to enhance individuals' and organizations' performance by utilizing the present and future value of knowledge assets.	Shannak (2010)
"systematic approach that provides efficient disciplines and procedures to enable the knowledge to grow and create value to organization"	Matayong & Mahmood, (2011, p. 1)

Knowledge Management Systems (KMS) can be defined as a special type of information systems that can be used to support knowledge management activities that range from acquisition, generation and codification to retrieval, usage and maintenance (Qwaider, 2011). This definition implies that the main goal of KMS is to support knowledge management process in order to increase the efficiency and leverage the performance. On the other hand, KMS is considered as the technological infrastructure that makes KM activities done smoothly in an efficient and effective way (Amine & Ahmed-Nacer, 2011). In addition, KMS has the following essential elements as summarized by Sajeva and Jucevicius (2010): KM process, strategic leadership, organizational infrastructure, technological infrastructure, organizational learning, and knowledge culture.

In order to implement KMS, there are several implementation methodologies that can be adopted and used but, in general, all of these available methodologies include three main phases starting with analysis, then implementation and at the end exploitation. Each of them can be divided into multiple steps based on the chosen methodology (Amine & Ahmed-Nacer, 2011).

Shannak (2010) indicated that organizations should utilize knowledge management capabilities in providing timely and relevant information that will facilitate different organizational activities such as planning, controlling, decision making and performance evaluation. Related to decision-making activities, using knowledge management in decision making process is influenced by four major factors: Capabilities of individuals, availability of required technologies, coordination between departments and acceptance and trust of decision makers. Also, the use of KMS will not replace the current software tools and processes but it will be used as a support tool to enhance KM activities and leverage the quality of decisions made (Amine & Ahmed-Nacer, 2011). Furthermore, KMS can be viewed as a key enabler to effective knowledge management and decision-making (McCall, Arnold & Sutton, 2008).

A survey conducted by Reuters found that 90% of the companies that utilize and use knowledge management solutions have better decision making, and 81% noticed that productivity is increased after such utilization (Raj, 2012). Decision making is a human activity that can be defined as selecting the best alternative from two or more alternatives in order to achieve a specific predefined goal (Anisseh & Yusuff, 2011; Ismail, 2011; Jinbo, Xuefeng & Ming, 2011; Lunenburg, 2010; Hashim, Alam & Siraj, 2010). The previously mentioned definition of decision-making implies that there are three main components of decision making activity. The first one, the existence of several options (alternatives) from which decision makers will choose. The second one, decision making is a process that involves several steps more than making a choice. Finally, a predefined set of goals or objectives exists in the minds of decision makers (Lunenburg, 2010; Liu, 2010).

Decision making as a process includes four main phases: Intelligence phase, in which decision makers search the environment for conditions that call for a decision making situation; design phase, in which alternatives are identified and analyzed; choice phase, in which the best possible alternative is chosen and recommended; and finally, implementation phase, in which selected alternative is implemented through a set of actions (Jinbo, Xuefeng & Ming, 2011).

On the other hand, decision-making seems to be considered by managers as an art that will lead to high quality decisions (Ismail, 2011). Viewing decision making as an art is derived from the existence of three sets of factors that affect decision making and they are: decision features, situational factors, and individual differences (Appelt, Milch, Handgraaf & Weber, 2011).

The availability of variant types methods, techniques and approaches, that will be helpful and useful for decision makers in order to make the right decision at the right time using the right resources utilizing their knowledge and personal experiences, supports such view (viewing decision making as an art) (Ismail, 2011). Table 2 presents several definitions of decision making based on different perspectives and viewpoints.

Decisions can be classified into five main types: First, programmed decisions, which are structured, repetitive and routine in nature; second, non-programmed decisions, which deal with unstructured situations in a dynamic environment; third, strategic decisions taken by high level managers; fourth, organizational decisions, taken on the organizational level; and finally, tactical decisions, which are distilled from the strategic direction. The first two categories of decisions are based on the nature of decisions to be made and the last three categories are based on the level of control in which a decision will be made (Ismail, 2011; Bohanec, 2009).

All kinds of decision support systems have three common components which are: an information store of knowledge, a process by which this knowledge is used and a user interface that provides users with easy way to get the knowledge and information they require. Organizations that used decision support system in order to enhance the decision making process need information and knowledge as a vital component that needs to be managed effectively and efficiently in order to use it during the decision making process (Faiz & Edirisinghe, 2009).

KM DECISION MAKING FRAMEWORKS

Orzano, McInerney, Scharf, Tallia, and Crabtree (2008) introduced a knowledge management model that enhances the decision making and organizational learning process and improves the overall organizational performance in terms of its quality, productivity and satisfaction as a result of the proper usage of the right knowledge to make the right decisions. This significant impact is the outcome of the integration of knowledge management critical processes mentioned in the literature and they are: finding knowledge, sharing knowledge, and developing knowledge. The model depicts eight key enablers, which are: active networks, reflective practice, helpful relationships, robust infrastructure, accessible technology, supportive leadership, effective communication, and trusting climate. Integrating knowledge management systems with decision support systems during the decision making process will improve the quality of decisions made not only by businesses and private sector organizations but also made by public sector.

Arora (2011) presented a basic framework for knowledge management that will help governments (especially e-government) in improving the quality of their decisions. This framework required six main components. These components are: first, executive level leadership that supports e-government initiative and motivates employees. Second, processes and policies that generate, store,

Table 2. Decision making definitions

Decision Making Definition	Resource
"A conscious and human process, involving both individual and social phenomenon based upon factual and value premises, which concludes with a choice of one behavioral activity from among one or more alternatives with the intention of moving toward some desired state of affairs".	Ismail (2011, p. 178)
It is a process that "basically involves selecting the most preferred alternative(s) from a finite set of alternatives in order to achieve certain predefined objectives."	Anisseh & Yusuff (2011, p. 425)
"A knowledge-intensive activity with knowledge as its raw materials, work-in-process, by-products, and finished goods".	Jinbo, Xuefeng & Ming (2011, p. 134)

retrieve, share and manage knowledge. Third, dedicated and well-trained employees that generate, adapt, apply and use knowledge. Fourth, learning and sharing culture that encourages everyone to learn and apply what they learned when making decisions. Fifth, the latest information technology that enables people to connect and share content. Finally, chief knowledge manager to manage the content generated.

Jinbo, Xuefeng, and Ming (2011) proposed a framework of knowledge management system that will enhance decision making process in Web-enabled environment and thus improve business process quality. This proposed framework architecture is a combination of three main modules: unified KM platform, problem solving system and human computer interface. In terms of decision making support, the unified KM platform is the most important one because it has a significant impact on enhancing decision making process not only through making knowledge acquisition happens in a more extensive and convenient way, but also through presenting knowledge in more rule-based way. Such representation decreases the effort and time needed to search for knowledge during decision making process and increases the depth, breadth and accuracy of information received, which will improve the quality of decision making.

Amine and Ahmed-Nacer (2011) proposed a new methodology for the implementation of KMS, which consists of five main phases: initialization phase, domain mapping phase, profiles and policies identification phase, implementation and personalization phase, and validation phase. The proposed methodology that ensures short iterations, intensive customer collaboration, and continuous assessment and integration has a significant impact on the quality of decision-making processes and suitable to be adopted and used by software engineering organizations.

Sandhawalia and Dalcher (2007) presented the dynamic feedback model (DFM) as an example of models that are useful to be used in managing software development process. This model focused on four different functional areas: managerial, technical, quality and decision making, and presented non-linear relationships between them. Such model provides a framework that highlights the importance of knowledge as a valuable resource in supporting the implementation of software development process.

Bal, Bal, and Demirhan (2011) discussed the significant role of data mining in decision making process as a competitive weapon and a very effective tool that can help organizations gain competitive advantage through several areas. As an example, data mining can be used to achieve organizational strategic benefit and facilitate decision making process through the utilization of huge amounts of data. Direct marketing, customer acquisition, customer retention, cross selling and trend analysis are more examples of these areas.

The Industrial Credit and Investment Corporation of India (ICICI) is the second largest bank in India and largest private sector bank by market capitalization which was founded in mid 1950s to provide medium and long-term development finances for Indian businesses and now it has a presence in 18 countries. The ICICI bank has several knowledge management initiatives in order to build a learning organization with knowledge sharing culture that is critical for being competitive and meeting customer expectations. "Wise Guy" portal, "Wise Wednesday," "Brown Bag," "Daily Dose," and "The Learning Matrix" are examples of such initiatives. "Wise Guy" portal contains discussions, queries, edited contributions, books, training calendar, vendors, external and internal reports, captured offline lectures, presentations, and events that were managed using document management system. This portal has helped the bank in the creation of a common storehouse of knowledge and improved the employees' decision-making ability, which resulted in a more competitive position for the bank (Goswami, 2008).

On the other hand, Mohammed and Jalal (2011) conducted an explanatory research to evaluate the knowledge management initiative of the Central Bank of Bahrain (CBB) in order to determine the critical factors that affect decision making process through using a survey distributed among the bank employees. Authors concluded that IT infrastructure, human resources, organizational culture, and knowledge sharing have a significant impact on decision-making process in the bank. On the other hand, research recommended that the bank needs to make more effort to improve the process of knowledge acquisition, knowledge creation and knowledge sharing, which will enhance its employees decision-making abilities.

DISCUSSION OF KM IMPORTANCE IN DECISION MAKING PROCESS

Software engineering is a knowledge intensive work that involves a large number of people, different phases, and diverse activities. Such work needs to be managed using a proper manner and utilizing several KM techniques, approaches, and strategies. Furthermore, knowledge is an important asset that organizations should exploit as a strategic weapon and an effective asset in order to help achieve their short and long term goals using the right knowledge (timely and relevant) at the right time to make the right decisions. Also, it represents an important asset that helps in the decision making process when integrated in the software development process.

Organizational learning in software organization promotes the use of several software tools that are relevant to knowledge management including: tools for managing documents and content, tools for managing competence and tools for collaboration. On the other hand, the literature shows that the majority of studies related to KM in software engineering relate to technocratic and behavioural

aspects of KM with a great focus on reporting lessons learned rather than scientific studies.

Integrating knowledge management system with decision-making system during decision making process and utilizing KMS capabilities especially in software development process will have a significant impact on the quality and efficiency of such process. Knowledge is an integral and essential part of each phase of the decision making process (intelligence, design, choice, and implementation) and for all types of decisions: programmed decision, non-programmed, strategic decision, organizational decision and tactical decision.

KMS integration is important not only for the private sector but also for the public sector, which requires looking at knowledge management not only as a data management tool but also as an organizational and social tool. Such perspective requires building special strategy that focuses on how organizations can benefit from valuable knowledge obtained from managing knowledge to make better decision and achieve strategic goals.

Different decision making systems that utilize the value of knowledge obtained from ideal knowledge management process are available and can be used to leverage the quality of decisions made in different areas such as marketing, trend analysis and customer retention. Also, all proposed frameworks and models are suitable to be adopted and used by software organizations in the software development process.

KM PRACTICES IN SOFTWARE DEVELOPMENT PROCESS

It is important to integrate knowledge within the system/software development, where the success of a software development process depends on the learning experience for both the organization and the team individuals. One of the problems in system development is the evaluation of such experience where many firms do not take the evaluation process for both the system and the knowledge inherent in the process seriously (Ghose & Choudhury, 2010). Based on that existing practices need to be explored to find the success and failure stories reported in the literature.

Kumar, Paul, and Tadisina (2005) conducted an exploratory study that included eight Indian software consultants to investigate their KM practices and concluded that employees perceive KM as a management of intellectual resources. Other perspectives included management of expertise and management of competitors and customers information. Also, some respondents viewed KM from an efficiency perspective, where they thought it improves performance and employees capabilities. The study also looked into the most needed KM capability, where three perspectives prevailed: management of knowledge assets, knowledge sharing culture and KM infrastructure.

Bjornson (2007) reviewed the literature in an attempt to explore different practices in the software industry, where a bias toward two major strategies prevailed: the codification strategy and the personalization strategy. The first depends on a method for tailoring the rational unified process to the software development process, where the author recommended contextualization as a strategy for process workshop improvement. The second strategy discussed was the personalization strategy where the author recommended again contextualization as a method for improving the process. The author proposed also a root-cause analysis for more effective project retrospectives. Finally, a recommendation to increase the level of reflection would increase the learning cycle and increase the learning effect of mentor programs in software engineering.

In a similar study in Australia, and exploiting a sample in two software firms, knowledge sharing utilizing personal networks, informal networks, groupware and third party knowledge was highly appreciated (Aurum, Daneshgar & Ward, 2008).

The authors concluded that the tool, techniques and methodologies used for software development were inadequate to ensure effective knowledge management in both organizations. Finally, in both firms, a uniform framework for KM process did not exist.

Looking into a different perspective (than technical and informational), Chou (2011) proposed an artificial knowledge structure that takes a cognitive approach to system development knowledge management, where three major issues need to be taken into consideration: the first, is an artificial knowledge structure that overcomes the difficulty of cognitive processing because of the remote communication and diversity of knowledge and backgrounds. Second, the proposed framework will decrease the complexity of CASE tools used, where a symbiotic relationship exists. Finally, the proposed model could be complementary to the CMM/CMMI (Capability Maturity Model Integration) implementation method.

When looking into the human side of KM practices in software engineering, research emphasized the importance of human coach who will focus on KM, cyclical assessment, informal learning, and dynamics coaching. Such role is important to ensure team harmony and growth, sound project management practices, and quality software (Jensen et al., 2011). Similarly, Song, Zhang, Wang, and Lin (2009) proclaimed that the complexity of the system development teams is a major factor that determines how knowledge is shared in organizations. As the case of most global companies, diversified and large teams need initial knowledge management strategy and role definition. On the other hand, for teams with highly technical and unstructured task (which is the case of system development) a balance between "people-to-documents" approach and "people-to-people" approach is needed for knowledge management process and at various stages of development (Song et al., 2009, pp. 11-12).

CONCLUSION AND FUTURE WORK

This chapter tried to explore the literature related to knowledge management utilization in the software development process. Firms working in software and system development face difficult task in managing development teams, where they lack a structured view of how knowledge needed and generated from the process can be managed. The literature showed that many frameworks and models exist that depicts how the decision-making process and knowledge management in this process can be improved. Most models revolved around the system development process steps and stages, or the knowledge management phases and how to fulfill each stage to guarantee the success of system and software development process.

Also, previous research paid much attention to the decision making process and how knowledge can be of an advantage. Knowledge represents an important asset that helps in the decision making process when integrated in the software development process. Thus, this chapter reported cases and models that depict how knowledge management is utilized in different cases from the world.

Based on the previous sections, it is important to develop a comprehensive model based empirical evidence, where most of the literature in this area lacked the sample size requirements or reported KM practices based on interviews and simple case analysis. Future work also needs to establish a common ground that validates the concepts related to this domain like knowledge management, decision-making, and the learning process.

REFERENCES

Alavi, M., & Leidner, D. (2001). Knowledge management and knowledge management systems: Conceptual foundations and research issues. *Management Information Systems Quarterly*, 25(1), 107–136. doi:10.2307/3250961.

Alrawi, K., & Alrawi, W. (2011). Managers' perception of potential impact of knowledge management in the workplace: Case study. *American Journal of Social and Management Sciences*, 2(1), 188–195. doi:10.5251/ajsms.2011.2.1.188.195.

Amine, M., & Ahmed-Nacer, M. (2011). An agile methodology for implementing knowledge management systems: A case study in component-based software engineering. *International Journal of Software Engineering and Its Applications*, 5(4), 159–170.

Anand, A., & Singh, M. (2011). Understanding knowledge management: A literature review. *International Journal of Engineering Science and Technology*, 3(2), 926–939.

Anisseh, M., & Yusuff, R. (2011). A fuzzy group decision making model for multiple criteria based on Borda count. *International Journal of the Physical Sciences*, 6(3), 425–433.

Appelt, K., Milch, K., Handgraaf, M., & Weber, E. (2011). The decision making individual differences inventory and guidelines for the study of individual differences in judgment and decision-making research. *Judgment and Decision Making*, 6(3), 252–262.

Arora, E. (2011). Knowledge management in public sector. *International Refereed Research Journal*, 2(1), 165–171.

Aurum, A., Daneshgar, F., & Ward, J. (2008). Investigating knowledge management practices in software development organizations: An Australian experience. *Information and Software Technology*, 50(6), 511–533. doi:10.1016/j.infsof.2007.05.005.

Bal, M., Bal, Y., & Demirhan, A. (2011). Creating competitive advantage by using data mining technique as an innovative method for decision making process in business. In *Proceeding of Annual Conference on Innovations in Business & Management*. London, UK: CIBM.

Bjornson, F. (2007). *Knowledge management in software process improvement*. Retrieved from idi.ntnu.no/grupper/su/publ/phd/bjornson-thesis-final-26sep07.pdf

Bjornson, F., & Dingsoyr, T. (2008). Knowledge management in software engineering: A systematic review of studied concepts, fiKnowle and research methods used. *Information and Software Technology, 50*(11), 1055–1068. doi:10.1016/j.infsof.2008.03.006.

Bohanec, M. (2009). Decision making: A computer-science and information-technology viewpoint. *Interdisciplinary Description of Complex Systems, 7*(2), 22–37.

Chou, S. (2011). Management of system development knowledge: A cognitive approach. *Behaviour & Information Technology, 30*(3), 389–401. doi: 10.1080/0144929X.2010.528451.

Faiz, R., & Edirisinghe, E. (2009). Decision making for predictive maintenance in asset information management. *Interdisciplinary Journal of Information, Knowledge, and Management, 4*(1), 23–36.

Ghose, D., & Choudhury, D. (2010). Information system evaluation and information system development process. *The IUP Journal of Systems Management, 8*(4), 19–32.

Goswami, C. (2008). Knowledge management in India: A case study of an Indian bank. *The Journal of Nepalese Business Studies, 5*(1), 37–49.

Gulser, G., & Badur, B. (2011). Developing a framework for integrating knowledge management and decision support systems: Application to time series forecasting. *Communications of the IBIMA, 1*(1), 1–15. doi:10.5171/2011.137658.

Hashim, F., Alam, G., & Siraj, S. (2010). Information and communication technology for participatory based decision-making-e-management for administrative efficiency in higher education. *International Journal of Physical Sciences, 5*(4), 383–392.

Ismail, S. (2011). The role of marketing information system on decision making: An applied study on royal Jordanian air lines (RJA). *International Journal of Business and Social Science, 2*(3), 175–185.

Jensen, R., Smullin, F., Peters, J., Thompson, K., & Gordon, D. (2011, May/June). Improving software engineering through holistic project coaching. *Cross Talk Magazine,* 9-15.

Jinbo, W., Xuefeng, L., & Ming, D. (2011). A framework of knowledge management system for support decision making on web-enabled environment. *Journal of Convergence Information Technology, 6*(7), 133–139. doi:10.4156/jcit.vol6.issue7.17.

Jones, K. (2006). Knowledge management as a foundation for decision support systems. *Journal of Computer Information Systems, 46*(4), 116–124.

Kumar, M., Paul, S., & Tadisina, S. (2005). Knowledge management practices in Indian software development companies: Findings from an exploratory study. *Asian Academy of Management Journal, 10*(1), 59–78.

Liu, G. (2010). Spontaneous group decision making in distributed collaborative learning: Toward a new research direction. *MERLOT Journal of Online Learning and Teaching, 6*(1), 279–296.

Lunenburg, F. (2010). The decision making process. *National Forum of Educational Administration And Supervision Journal, 27*(4), 1-12.

Matayong, S., & Mahmood, A. (2011). KMS innovation decision making: The case study of oil and gas industry in Malaysia. In *Proceeding of* National Postgraduate Conference (NPC). Malaysia: NPC.

McCall, H., Arnold, V., & Sutton, S. (2008). Use of knowledge management systems and the impact on the acquisition of explicit knowledge. *Journal of Information Systems, 22*(2), 77–101. doi:10.2308/jis.2008.22.2.77.

Mohammed, W., & Jalal, A. (2011). The influence of knowledge management system (KMS) on enhancing decision making process (DMP). *International Journal of Business and Management, 6*(8), 216–229. doi:10.5539/ijbm.v6n8p216.

Orzano, A., McInerney, C., Scharf, D., Tallia, A., & Crabtree, B. (2008). A knowledge management model: Implications for enhancing quality in health care. *Journal of the American Society for Information Science and Technology, 59*(3), 489–505. doi:10.1002/asi.20763.

Qwaider, W. (2011). Integrated of knowledge management and e-learning system. *International Journal of Hybrid Information Technology, 4*(4), 59–70.

Raj, P. (2012). Knowledge management – A road map for winning organization. *International Journal of Research in Economics & Social Sciences, 2*(2), 363–373.

Rouhani, S., Asgari, S., & Mirhosseini, S. (2012). Review study: Business intelligence concepts and approaches. *American Journal of Scientific Research, 50*, 62–75.

Sajeva, S., & Jucevicius, R. (2010). Determination of essential knowledge management system components and their parameters. *Social Sciences, 1*(67), 80–90.

Sandhawalia, B., & Dalcher, D. (2007). Knowledge support for software projects. In *Proceeding of IRMA International Conference*, (pp. 936-940). Vancouver, Canada: IRMA.

Shannak, R. (2010). Knowledge-based systems support for strategic decisions. *European Journal of Economics, Finance and Administrative Sciences*, (21), 7-20.

Song, L., Zhang, C., Wang, Y., & Lin, L. (2009). Knowledge Management in multi-party IS development teams: A case study at Fudan University. *International Journal of Management Innovation Systems, 1*(2), 1–14.

Chapter 2
KM and Global Software Engineering (GSE)

Sameer Abufardeh
North Dakota State University, USA

ABSTRACT

In the last decade, we have witnessed a dramatic transformation of software development processes. Outsourcing and offshore development has become the norm in current software development because of the many benefits organizations and people can have by adapting such strategy. Benefits include reduced cost, reduced time to market, availability of skilled people, proximity to market and customers in various locals, etc. Furthermore, the transformation from single-site, mostly English-based into a multi-site, multilingual, multicultural, and globally distributed endeavor has marked the birth of Global Software Engineering (GSE). This transformation increases the complexity of GSE when compared to traditional co-located Software development. GSE involves knowledge intensive activities, different people, different teams, and globally dispersed software organization. While there are many benefits in adapting GSE, the new strategy created several challenges/issues for the organization, practitioners, and researchers. Challenges include language and culture, communication, coordination and collaboration, team building, etc. Knowledge Management (KM) is considered fundamental and an essential asset of an organization because it enables organizations to efficiently create, store, and share knowledge, and it helps in resolving many of the current GSE issues. KM tools and techniques has been successfully used in effective management of who knows what, which helps in learning, problem solving, and innovation. This chapter discusses in general the challenges of culture in Global Software Engineering (GSE). However, the main focus of the discussion in this chapter is on the challenges of culture in global software application. For many years, KM literature has focused on the cultural issues of teams, processes, types of knowledge, etc. This chapter's goal is to stimulate and encourage more research on how KM tools and practices can help in overcoming these challenges. Furthermore, it emphasizes the issues of language, which are mostly marginalized.

DOI: 10.4018/978-1-4666-4229-4.ch002

INTRODUCTION

Global Software Engineering (GSE) or Global Software Development (GSD) is a software development that involves teams from multiple geographic locations. The team's locations are commonly referred to as sites or development sites. In general, both traditional and GSE software development are complex, knowledge intensive and rapidly changing activities. However, in a traditional, co-located project, coordination between teams is considered a trivial issue since people working together naturally built up a number of ways to coordinating their work (Herbsleb, 2007). They plan ahead how the work will proceed and usually they follow a defined process adapted by the organization. Furthermore, development team members have a clear idea of who has what sort of expertise and how responsibilities are allocated. While this view is somewhat accepted by many researchers, we can argue that, even in a co-located project, culture is not truly homogenous because individuals working in the same organizations mostly come from different cultures and have different backgrounds.

In today's global economy, the majority of the software development companies have already made the shift towards Global Software Engineering (GSE). It has been reported that more than 80% of software projects are being globally distributed and distributed development continues to grow (Forrester, 2010). The major benefits of this shift include, involving skilled people from different locals, increased customer satisfaction, reduced development process cost and time to market, increased productivity, and quality (Herbsleb, 2001, Conchúir, 2006) . However, despite the benefits it provides, it has also brought many challenges to the GSE such as, physical distance, trust, culture and language differences, loss of communication, time-zone differences, and so on (Damian et al., 2003).

From the literature, and many published case studies we find strong evidence to the fact that KM practices and tools can be used to mitigate the problems of complexity in global software development. Furthermore, KM literature in the last decade focuses on two perspectives of the field – taxonomic and process (Orlikowski, 2002). Taxonomists have proposed various classifications of organizational knowledge. The process perspective of KM literature focuses on organizational knowledge flows. Research in this stream identifies a dynamic set of activities, called KM processes, which improve firm's knowledge flows. In addition, KM literature continues to focused on the issues of explicit knowledge and very little discusses the issues of tacit knowledge especially those directly related to culture. Furthermore, most of the research we reviewed was focused on the cultural issues of the teams and/or the organization, and occasionally included the software development processes. However, very few were concerned with issues of culture in the software product itself (Noll et al., 2010). Furthermore, there are many solutions introduced in KM literature to overcome the cultural challenges in GSE. The proposed solutions emphasized that GSE involve the exchange and transfer of huge amounts of knowledge between all software stakeholders and the success of GSE is dependent on proper and timely decimations and sharing of knowledge. However, these solutions did not address or provide techniques and strategies to overcome many of the cultural challenges in the software product itself. Furthermore, many of the techniques and tools proposed and used were designed to work for co-located individuals.

This chapter is structured as follows. The first section discusses the concept of Global Software Engineering (GSE) and the unique challenges present in GSE. The second section discusses the types of Knowledge in GSE. In the third section discusses the cultural aspects of global software. The fourth section discusses how Km help GSE benefit from culture diversity. The fifth chapter discusses the proposed solution and recommendations which are the focus of this chapter. The sixth section discusses future research directions, and the last section discusses conclusions and final remarks.

GLOBAL SOFTWARE ENGINEERING (GSE)

Definition of Global Software Development

Global Software Engineering (GSE) or Global Software Development (GSD) is a software development that involves teams from multiple geographic locations. The team's locations are commonly referred to as sites or development sites. Global Software Engineering (GSE) has been adopted widespread and gaining fame with the passage of time. The fact that GSE development teams are dispersed geographically has its advantage. The most important is closeness to market/customer. In addition, GSE acceptance by major organizations is driven mainly by an economical factor where the product is developed in less time and resources used (Damian and Moitra, 2006, Herbsleb, 2007). Furthermore, GSE offers many benefits like cost effectiveness, shorter development time, skilled people and less use of resources (Holmstrom, Conchúir, et al., 2006).

The main difference between GSE and traditional, co-located software development is that, the development teams in GSE are spread out into multiple geographic locations. This creates new challenges to the organization as a whole and more specifically to the software development teams involved in a project. In the following section, we briefly discuss the unique challenges facing global software development teams.

GSE Unique Challenging

The adaption of GSE provides many benefits to the organization and to the product. However, it also introduced many new challenges to the software development process and to the development teams. The most critical of these challenges are culture differences, geographical dispersion, loss of communication richness, coordination breakdown, and loss of teamness (Carmel, 1999). The following is a brief discussion to the challenges:

Culture Differences

In GSE different teams from different countries cooperate to develop a new product. Consequently, teams from different countries have different cultures and hence differences in style of communication, response time, attitudes, commitment, ways of thinking and ways of solving problems and so on. These differences require close cooperation among different individuals from different culture backgrounds to ensure successful process and high quality products. Extensive research done by (Herbsleb, 2007; Hofstede, 2001; Hall, 2001; Del Galdo and Nielsen, 1996; Myers et al., 2002) and many others examined cultural challenges and identified the impact of culture on software development. They all reported that people with different cultural backgrounds behave differently and that will have a direct impact on software engineering practices in a GSE.

Geographic Dispersion

Geographic dispersion simply means the allocation of different units of an organization through some physical distance. And hence a product will be developed by the coordination and thorough communication of different members of such dispersed organization. People involved in such dispersed organizations are called virtual teams. Further, "the greater the team's dispersion (distance, time-zone, national, language, etc.) the greater the challenges the team will face" to (Smith and Blanck, 2002; Komi-Sirvio and Tihinen, 2005). Hence, virtual (dispersed) teams may fail to perform, because of lack of trust, less-coordination and communication.

Loss of Communication Richness

The farther the distance between organizational units, the more challenging and problematic communication becomes. Furthermore, developing teams located across boundaries makes the situation more complex because of differences in culture, language, and availability of good technology infrastructure which affects the communication among different units of an organization (Komi-Sirvio and Tihinen, 2005).

Coordination Breakdown

According to (Herbsleb, 2007), "The fundamental problem of GSD is that many of the mechanisms that function to coordinate the work in a co-located setting are absent or disrupted in a distributed project". Coordination in GSE is the activity where different tasks of each organizational unit are integrated so that the units contribute for setting goals and objectives (Carmel and Agarwal, 2001). Hence, close coordination and collaboration is critical for reaching on consensus about a specific issue or problem throughout the development cycle of a product. In GSE the means of coordination are different from collocated. For example, visiting a teammate in the next office room personally or corridor talks to resolve an issue is easier and less complex than communication across geographically distant teams. Furthermore, unique and different dimensions have been identified for coordination in globally distributed units such as shared processes, shared and detailed project management, shared past experiences and background knowledge (Herbsleb et al., 2005). Therefore, distributed units increase the burden on the mechanism of coordination.

Loss of Teamness

Software development involves different teams such as, requirements engineers, architects, developers, testers, etc. Therefore, teamness is a fundamental issue that must be resolved because it provides benefits to any organizations whether the organization operate in an offsite or in onsite environment.

Time Zone Difference

Time zone is a critical issue and can have negative impacts on GSE activities (Conchuir et. al, 2006). Furthermore, organizations working in many of time zones face more problems than organizations working in one or two time zones. For example, arranging meeting time between units in many time zones is more challenging because a selected time may be suitable for one unit and problematic for other unit. Furthermore, time zones create serious problems when some urgent meetings or interaction is necessary.

KM IN GLOBAL SOFTWARE DEVELOPMENT (GSD)

Today, most software products are developed for global market. Hence, the process of software globalization requires deep understanding to the diverse cultural aspects of the product and the diverse customer and market cultures. On one hand, the realization of the benefits of global software development requires effective information and knowledge sharing mechanisms. On the other hand, indentifying and applying the proper knowledge sharing mechanisms introduces many challenges to GSD itself (Desouza et al., 2006).

In KM literature we find several types of knowledge are being identified and studied. The most common types are "Tacit vs. Explicit" and "Individual vs. Group/Social" knowledge. The diversity of knowledge and the distinction between its types produced a plethora of definitions which added more challenges to GSD. For that, we leave the particularity of the various definitions to the reader and we briefly explain what each type means:

Tacit Knowledge vs. Explicit Knowledge

Explicit Knowledge

Explicit knowledge refers to codified knowledge available in form of documents, books, figures, maps, diagrams, manuals, etc. (Hislop, 2005). Explicit knowledge can easily be shared, communicated, stored and manipulated, and mostly easily understood. Hence, explicit knowledge is impersonal (Hislop, 2005; Koskinen et al., 2003). In addition, explicit knowledge is representational and can live and be manipulated manually or digitally. Further, it is general easy to make it publically available using Information Communication Technology (ICT) tools.

Tacit Knowledge

Tacit knowledge is the more challenging and it's considered a critical asset for any organization. Polanyi (Nonaka, 1994) was the first to introduce and define the term tacit knowledge. Tacit knowledge is very hard to communicate or share and it is generally considered personal i.e. deeply rooted in actions. Further, tacit knowledge is very hard to articulate in words and requires some metaphors and drawings (Koskinen et al., 2003). According to (Hislop, 2005) tacit knowledge resides in human minds so therefore it is subjective and personal in nature. Using the words of Polanyi, "we have more knowledge and know-how than ours ability to convey" (Nonaka, 1994), shows that often people know more but they cannot express in words which represents the tacit nature of knowledge they have.

Tacit knowledge in GSE is made up of best practices, experience, wisdom and un-recordable intellectual property that live within individuals and teams. Since tacit knowledge exists within minds, it cannot be reduced to the digital domain as a material asset, or be manipulated directly. However, it expresses in the social realm as the response ability of individuals (productivity, innovation and initiative), and teamwork (communication, coordination and collaboration) (Nonaka and Takeuchi, 1995). Furthermore, cultural aspects of software application are generally classified as tacit and hence the difficulty of accommodating and implementing cultural requirements in the software product increases. For that, cultural and language issues of the product are the focus of our discussion in rest of this chapter.

Individual Knowledge vs. Group/Social Knowledge

Individual Knowledge

Individual knowledge is the knowledge possessed by individual in their minds. This knowledge can be in the form of experiences, abilities, and skills of individuals. According to Nonaka and Takeuchi knowledge is initially created by individuals and that the knowledge created by individuals becomes organizational knowledge through a process described by the authors. For details of the process the reader can refer to Nonaka and Takeuchi work (Nonaka and Takeuchi, 1995). This concept of individual knowledge by Nonaka and Takeuchi has several critics and who argued that "in addition to individual knowledge there is also knowledge present in the work environment" (Hislop, 2005).

Group Knowledge

Group knowledge is the kind of knowledge, which is present or possesses in working groups.

Furthermore, group knowledge can be either tacit or explicit depending on nature. For example, collective explicit knowledge is documented system of rules and formalized organization routines and collective tacit knowledge includes informal organization routines, stories, and methods of doing work.

Culture in Global Software

Culture continues to be a challenging issue to all professionals in all research areas. Today we have more than 164 definitions for the word 'Culture'. Therefore, the validity of data collected about culture regardless of the collection instruments can become subject to interpretation. In the area of software, the culture issues are among the most critical for the success of the software. Hence, the culture and the cultural influences of the target customer must be carefully studied and considered throughout the software development lifecycle (Abufardeh and Magel, 2008, 2010). Furthermore, GSE involve different teams from different countries with different cultures and that magnify the challenges of culture. Therefore, developers must take a holistic approach to issues of culture and should take into account the cultural and the linguistic requirements of the target countries and local groups including developers, customers, clients, and end-users. In addition, developers must take into account the cultural differences between teams and also the cultural differences within the same team. Differences include style of communication, response time, attitudes, values, behavior, commitment, beliefs, traditions, dealing with stress, ways of thinking and ways of solving problems, etc. (Herbsleb, 2007). According to Carmel (Carmel, 1999), culture have several dimensions like national, organizational, ethics and bodies of manners, ideologies, strategies, tactics, technical, professional, etc. The key to understanding culture is keep in mind that Culture is not "holidays and celebration or food festivals". Culture encompasses a way of life to its members and it defines and provides both technical and social norms and guidance to its members. Furthermore, culture difference can be found between cities within the same country as well as between countries. (Smith and Blanck, 2002) identified four types of culture:

- **Individual Culture:** This type is the most critical and the most challenging of all types. It encompasses the individual values, beliefs, outlook, style, ethics, etc.
- **Functional Culture:** This represents the outlook of a specific department way of working.
- **Organizational Culture:** This represents the characteristics differences between companies.
- **National Culture:** This represents the differences which are related to nationality. This type also influences directly the individual culture.

As we mentioned earlier, culture encompasses a way of life accepted and shared by its members. We must also emphasize that "the key term in any definition to culture is sharing". Furthermore, the idea that culture has many types can be misleading because we and many others believe that culture is one (we will call it base or core culture) and from that we can have different levels or different sub-cultures (Huang, and Trauth, 2006, 2005; Leung et al., 2005; Myers and Tan, 2002; Straub, 2002). Furthermore, culture is directly influenced by religion which an issue the majority of researches avoids to discuss. Therefore, understanding the issues of culture should start by identifying the issues of the core culture and then move to the sub-cultures. Furthermore, from KM literature and the many case studies reported in the last decade, we found that success is somewhat common in dealing with explicit knowledge; however the real and continued challenge remains in dealing with tacit knowledge. These successes as it has been reported were due to the fact that explicit knowledge can be codified, easily shared, communicated, stored and manipulated, and mostly easy to understand. However, the more challenging to GSE and to KM is that most of the knowledge in software engineering can be classified as tacit and mostly remains tacit.

Why Culture Is Challenging In GSE?

There is amble evidence in the literature to support the fact that culture issues have profound influence and relevance to the success or failure of global software (Komi-Sirvio and Tihinen, 2005; Nicholson and Sahay, 2001; Desouza et al., 2006; Herbsleb et. al, 2005). There are many studies that identified culture difference as a problematic issue and that culture differences have negative impact on project activities. Cultural issues are directly related to and influence how software is built, managed, marketed, and maintained.

Knowledge Management (KM) practices and tools were successfully used to deal with some of the GSE challenges. The lion share of the research focus was directed towards the cultural issues of GSE regarding process and teams, but the cultural issues of the product itself were rarely mentioned or discussed. Among the four types of culture identified above we believe that individual and national cultures are the most difficult to capture using the current KM practices and tools. Such difficulty can be contributed to the following:

1. Culture knowledge is mostly classified as tacit (i.e. subjective) and it's hard to transform to explicit knowledge. This true for most of the tacit knowledge in GSE and in any other context. Reported reasons for such difficulty can be attributed to people mistakenly think tacit knowledge is explicit, or not important, or it is difficult to codify and transform to explicit, or we don't have the time to make it explicit.

2. Global Software processes and the software involve complex context specific knowledge generally classified as tacit. Furthermore, the wide spread of agile development methods relies heavily on tacit knowledge because agile methods focuses more on social team interaction and customer collaboration and less on documentation and codification of knowledge.

3. Culture knowledge is naturally contextual which make it hard to disseminate without loss of meaning using traditional information systems. Current approaches and tools for turning tacit knowledge into explicit knowledge are very rare and if they exist they are directed towards processes and teams and almost none to the software product itself.

4. Current cultural aspects and terms in GSE literature mostly reflect Hofsted's framework of cultural dimensions which is the subject of extensive critique for many years (Hofsted's, 1997, 2001). Consequently many cross-cultural information systems studies often treat culture as a static concept and use Hofstede predefined cultural dimensions which are not enough to provide in-depth understanding of the complex aspects of culture.

5. The lack of systematic processes and coding schemes to record and share cultural knowledge. This is due to the fact that many of the KM tools and technologies available were built for co-located software development environment.

6. People have different attitudes and behavior with respect to knowledge sharing. Therefore, people may be unwilling to share their knowledge with other for variety of reasons, for details the reader can refer to (Lindvall et al., 2003).

7. Culture have different levels or contexts and that can create problems of misinterpretations or misunderstanding because culture issues can be understood and/or interpreted differently even within the same organization.

Despite the negative impacts or problems generated by culture diversity in GSE, when it's understood and dealt with properly it has positive impacts as well. Culture diversity provides organizations involved in GSE with opportunities to diversify their functional and organizational culture to meet their own and their customer's customs and values. This will have positive impact on the development team and the product being developed. Furthermore, culture diversity enhances the teams understanding to the system requirements and the client customs and values. It creates a more cooperative relationship within the team members and with their clients and customers. The issue is that when dealing with culture diversity we need to keep in mind that culture has different factors or elements which can be dynamic or static. These factors interact with each other in different ways in different contexts' (Straub et al., 2002).

How KM Help GSE Benefit From Culture Diversity?

Drawing back on many years of working experiences in software industry, research in academia, and the reviewed work of many researchers we believe that the answer to this question has many folds. First, there enough evidence from literature and from practice to claim that "KM somehow did help GSE benefit from culture diversity". Second, the question we have is not intended to simplify the problem and it has intended to focus the attentions to "how" and to "what extent"? Third, we admit that we do not have the magic wand to resolve the many cultural challenges facing GSE. Our goal is that raising such questions will encourage KM future researchers to take a holistic approach to the issues of culture.

KM Holistic Approach to the Issues of Culture

We believe that taking KM holistic approach is key element to resolve many of the challenges of cultural issues in GSE. The KM holistic approach will take into consideration the aspects of culture in (organization and teams) on one side and the aspects of culture in (product and process) on the other side. Figure 1 shows a KM holistic view to the cultural issues of both sides. The view is simple but as the saying goes "the devil is in the details". We will start by explain why this view is critical and then we will show how this approach can succeed.

As we mentioned earlier the holistic view is critical because simply focusing on the cultural issues of one side (organization and teams) most often leads to neglecting these issues in the other side (product and development process). From the literature review we found out that most of the KM research was focused on organization and teams. Furthermore, we believe that many of the cultural challenges facing GSE are directly influenced by language barriers. Language is a common theme issue that emerges in every discussion to the cultural issues of GSE but most often it's being marginalized.

In the case of software, KM software product related research focused on the cultural issue is sporadic. Furthermore, most of the work in this area was focused on the software requirements. Software development involves other activities

Figure 1. A simplified KM holistic view to the cultural issues in GSE

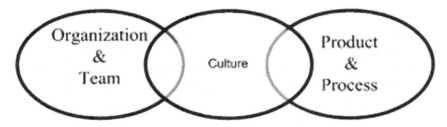

and artifact such as design, coding, and testing (Hofsted, 1997, 2001; Hall, 2001; Del Galdo and Nielsen, 1996; Abufardeh and Magel, 2010, 2008; Myers and Tan, 2002). In addition, the production of global software globally presents many challenges to the development community as we mentioned earlier. Global software development is a two-step internationalization (I18N), then localization (L10N) process. The internationalization process's main objective is separating the software into two components: a culture-independent and a culture-dependent component (Abufardeh and Magel, 2008, 2010). The culture-independent (culture neutral) component, known as the generic core, contains the bulk of the software and is devoid of culture-sensitive elements. Localization is defined as the process of providing the culture-dependent component for a particular target culture (Abufardeh and Magel, 2008, 2010).The product must be adapted to various end users' linguistic and cultural requirements. Translation issues are mostly associated with adapting software for a specific country. However, developing global software goes beyond translation to involve many aspects of the software such as text representation, data formatting, and data processing issues. The most critical are the language and cultural aspects that affect the user interface and the core functionality. Furthermore, the impact of linguistic and cultural requirements on development processes and software usability is often underestimated. Until recently, many of the traditional software models did not adequately address the specific aspects that are uniquely present in global software (Abufardeh and Magel, 2010).

Culture knowledge is tacit in nature and directly affects the quality and the success or failure of the global product. In GSE culture has impact on the requirements understanding, architectural design options, coding, testing, and the evolution of the product. Culture influences interpretation of communication. Culture also affects interpretation of requirements; domain knowledge used to fill in gaps or place requirements in context varies considerably across national culture (Herbsleb et al., 2005). Culture also interferes with collaboration when cultural norms result in conflicting approaches to problem solving. Cultural differences can occur even when teams share a common language and nationality; differences in "corporate culture" can lead to conflicting approaches to problem solving and communication, which in turn might be misinterpreted as rudeness or incompetence (Herbsleb et al., 2005).

Knowledge Management tools promotes and facilitates the creation of knowledge sharing culture within the distant and diverse team members, within the company, and with the outside world. Finding the proper tools for tacit knowledge acquisition continues to be a challenging task in KM. And the need for KM tools and techniques that can enhance our understanding to issues of culture in GSE and to prevent misinterpreting the cultural aspects of the product is paramount.

GSE Cultural Challenges and the Language Barriers

The relationship between language and culture continues to be a subject of debate for many years. Does culture influence language or vice versa? The debate is still going among researchers and in linguistics it is called the "world view problem." It is similar to the popular question "the chicken and the egg question: which came first?" Linguists and anthropologists are divided into two camps. One side claims that language determines how we see the world. Everything we see and do is described using language. The other camp argues that culture determines how we see the world and that language is merely an aspect of culture.

Regardless of what viewpoint the reader may adapt, the issue of language is critical to understand the cultural issues of GSE. Language issues in the context of GSE are complex and should not be marginalized when dealing with GSE challenges. The importance of language skills—especially English—to the success of software exporting countries or outsourcing destinations is evident in many case studies (Carmel, 2003; Li and Gao, 2003; Heeks and Nicholson, 2004; Minevich and Richter, 2005). (Heeks and Nicholson, 2004) considered "people" a component of software related infrastructure. They attributed the success of Ireland, India, and Israel in software exports to the English language skills of the local. On the other hand, when they compared China to India they found that poor English language skills among Chinese workforce gave Indian workers an advantage over Chinese workers when competing for global IT services market (Carmel, 2003; Li and Gao, 2003; Minevich and Richter, 2005).

The language issue is a common concern for all parties involved in GSE. This includes developers, managers, stakeholders, customers, processes, and the product itself. (Haiyan and Eileen, 2007) concluded a study about the issues of langue among Chinese IT professionals. They reported that there are discrepancies regarding the proficiency level of different linguistic skills among Chinese IT professionals. They found that among Chinese IT professionals the reading capability is better than listening comprehension and the listening comprehension capability is better than speaking. They concluded that:

In globally distributed IT work, some communication technologies, such as email which is asynchronous and concerned with reading and writing capabilities, may be more preferred than other communication technologies, such as a teleconference which is synchronous and concerned with listening comprehension and speaking capabilities. (Haiyan and Eileen, 2007)

Therefore, language should put at the fore front and should be an integral component in any proposed solution (Lutz, 2009; Abufardeh and Magel, 2010). Language skills can impede communication in more subtle ways and the lack of proficiency in the chosen language can lead to a preference

for asynchronous communication, which can be an impediment if video and teleconferencing are important communication media. Removing the language barriers will definitely promote and encourage knowledge sharing, improve communication (formal and informal), facilitate coordination, and foster creativity and collaboration among all parties involved in the development of the product. The following section discusses possible solutions and recommendations to the cultural issues of global software applications.

Solutions and Recommendations

There are many KM tools and techniques used to create, store, and share explicit knowledge present in the global software product. However, the challenge of finding tools and techniques to handle the cultural and the linguistic knowledge of global software which considered tacit in nature remains standing. Kellner introduced Electronic Process Guide (EPG) as KM solution to deal with the requirements understanding challenges (Kellner, et al., 1998). EPG is a structured, workflow-oriented and a reference document to all involved in a project. However, the tool was designed to deal with mainly requirement s and for a co-located team. Furthermore, individuals tend to prefer informal ways to express their views, experiences, and opinions, what they like and what they do not? We also believe that the simplicity of the tools will encourage people to use them. For that, we propose the use of two simple existing techniques, concept maps and cultural design patters to deal with the cultural and linguistic knowledge of global software application. These techniques are simple to use and simple to learn and they are successfully used in other fields to solve a wide range of problems. They can be used to capture, store, and sharing knowledge by all people involved and throughout the development life cycle. Adding these tools to KM Tools box can facilitate better understanding and better interpretations to the issues of culture and language in GSE as a whole including product, people, and process. The following is a brief discussion to both techniques.

Concept Mapping a Tool for Codifying and Understanding Culture

Concept mapping technique was developed by Prof. Joseph D. Novak at Cornell University in the 1960s. The idea of concept maps was based on David Ausubel learning theory, which is based on the assumption that meaningful learning occurs when the new concepts are linked to familiar concepts existing in the learner's cognitive structure (Ausubel, 1968). In 1987, Novak and Cañas extended the use of concept mapping to other applications such as knowledge elicitation, organization, and representation (Novak and Cañas, 2008). Today concept maps and many other concept tools are being used in almost every discipline.

A concept map is a graphical way of representing and organizing knowledge (Figure 2). The figure illustrates one important aspect of concept maps, which is their ability to show large amounts of information in a compact format. A concept map is comprised of nodes and links, arranged in some order to reflect the domain information. Nodes symbolize concepts, and links represent relationship between concepts. Both nodes and links are labeled and may be categorized. Concept Mapping is the process of constructing concept maps.

Novak and Cañas emphasized that concept mapping is a powerful tool to promote meaningful learning and it can be used as a form of template or scaffold that helps organize and structure knowledge (Novak and Cañas, 2008). Khamesan and Hammond argue that one of the most promising uses of concept maps is its integration into collaborative learning activities (Khamesan and Hammond, 2004). Interaction and communication between group members not only helps to de-

Figure 2. A concept map showing the key features of concept maps (Novak & Canas, 2008)

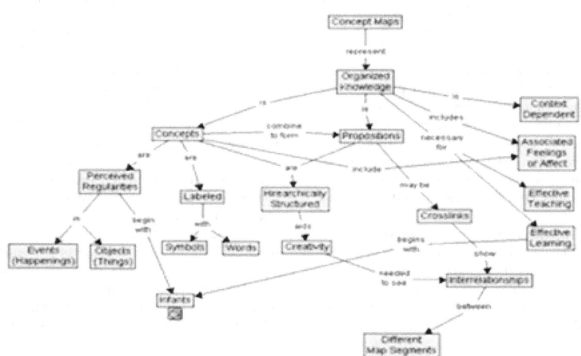

velop the reconstruction of individual's understanding but it also provides some practice in important interpersonal reasoning skills. It is also accepted that concept mapping and collaborative learning techniques complement one another. While concept mapping aids in the external representation of ideas, collaborative learning, with its emphasis on dialogue and discussion, furthers the elaborations of these externalizations so ideas can be shared. Learning environments are most effective when learners are actively involved in constructing their own meanings and doing so within authentic learning situations (Brown et. al, 1989).

As we discussed earlier, concept maps are effective collaborative learning techniques that can be used by users with differing backgrounds. Maps can provide a visual means for people to share their experiences and perspectives in new and unique ways. According to Plotnick (1997), some of the advantages of using concept maps are:

- Visual symbols are quickly and easily recognized.
- Minimum use of text makes it easy to scan for a word, phrase, or the general idea.
- Visual representation allows for development of a holistic understanding that words alone cannot convey.
- A Concept map visually describes the relationships between ideas in a knowledge domain." Representing knowledge in the visual format of a concept map allows one to gain an overview of a domain of knowledge.

Concept mapping is a technique for representing the structure of information visually. There are several uses for concept mapping, such as idea generation, design support, communication enhancement, learning enhancement, and assessment. A wide range of computer software for concept mapping is now available and it is mostly free. Furthermore, similar tools such as mind maps *(mind-mapping.org)*, spider maps can be used too to enhance our understanding to the concepts of culture or any other concepts related to the project. In the case of Software Development Life-Cycle (SDLC) concepts maps can be used to represent and share cultural knowledge about the product by all involved in the development process. Developing a global software usually require the localization of the product to different locals with different cultures. Concept maps can be used as a form of template or scaffold that includes cultural knowledge related to each culture or local. The initial concept map can start with the generic cultural requirements and then the specific cultural elements of the target local are added.

As we pointed out earlier, GSD involves people from different cultures which if managed correctly means a rich source of cultural expertise from various cultures. Concept maps provides participants from different cultural background with a simple platform to freely share and record their own experience and express their view of the cultural aspects of the application being developed instead of relying designated culture experts which is a common practice among large companies.

Concept maps can be simple to create, enhance, and manage by individuals involved. For example, multilingual software being developed to support multiple languages and locales can start with internationalized version of the application say in USA. Localization of the product is carried out by assigning the localization process to the local team of the targeted country or language say, team India for Indian localization, team China for Chinese locations, etc. see Figure 3.

The culture diversity of teams is considered a rich source of expertise to support the localization process of the product. Local teams can use concept maps to document their understanding and their own experiences and share it and discuss it with their local team and with other teams. Furthermore, it minimizes the reliance on individual culture expertise that can lead to misunderstand-

Figure 3. Concept map showing product localization strategy in GSD

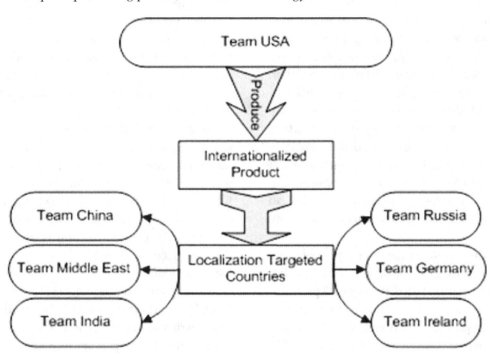

ing and in some case misinterpretation of the local culture requirement. It also eliminates bottlenecks when relying on individual experts to support the development team. Having a team from the same culture which is the target of localization ensure full understanding, and on the spot and on time answer to any cultural issue that may arise during the localization process. Today, most companies rely on what is called culture expertise. Sometimes the only qualification the expertise has is that, he may come or lived in the target country or he just speaks the language of the targeted local. Furthermore, most often culture expertise live countries other than their country of origin. In such cases we can expect misinterpretation and misunderstanding to the local requirements because of the influences of the foreign culture on the cultural expert himself.

Furthermore, local teams in general prefer and tend to use simple and informal tools to communicate. Concept maps are simple and flexible and they are considered informal form of communication. The simplicity, the informality, and the ease of creating concept maps can encourage local teams to document their expertise and share it with other outside the team.

Culture Design Patterns a Tool for Codifying and Understanding Culture

In 1979, Christopher Alexander introduced the concept of design patterns (Alexander, 1979). Design patterns gained popularity in computer science after the book "Design Patterns: Elements of Reusable Object-Oriented Software" was published in 1994 by the so-called "Gang of Four," which is frequently abbreviated as "GOF." Since then, patterns are being used in many disciplines especially in Software development (Gamma et al., 1995), localization (Mahemoff and Johnston, 1999), Pedagogy (Eckstein, 2000). According to Alexander, patterns are good solution to problem in a certain context (Alexander, 1979). They capture best practice in a specific professional domain and they facilitate reuse. They also enhance and support communication among software stakeholders and offer a "lingua franca" for designers (Erickson, 2000). Furthermore, each pattern describes the context, scope, and validity of a design solution, underlining its principles and providing examples. Patterns are interrelated, cross-referenced and organized in collections. This allows the discovery of related problems and solutions in more complex design situations (Erickson, 2000).

Alostath and Wright (2004) and Mahemoff and Johnston (1999) introduced the idea of using pattern to supported cross-cultural usability in globalizing software which involves two processes, internationalization (I18N) and localization (L10N). The patterns identified by the authors offers support for the design process of system internationalization. In 2004, Alostath and Wright proposed using cross-cultural dimensions systematically in design patterns to identify the effect of cultural differences on a design. In general, patterns capture the static and dynamic structures and collaborations of successful solutions to problems that arise when building applications. The benefits of design patterns include:

- While they are originally designed to enable large-scale reuse of software architectures, they can be used for capturing and documenting systems to enhance understanding.
- Patterns can be used to capture expert knowledge and design and make it explicit which make design expertise more widely available.
- Patterns help improve developer communication. Pattern names form a vocabulary that can be used to communicate with people involved in the development of the product.
- Pattern help to improve software quality and reduce development time.

- Patterns ensure consistency across the development of the application.
- Patterns include a description to the context in which the pattern is used, the forces within the context that the pattern seeks to resolve and the suggested solution for the issue in hand.

Today, design patterns are used in software development in many ways and in all development phases. Design patterns originally classified into creational patterns, structural patterns, and behavioral patterns. Other types were added later such as concurrency patterns, architectural design pattern, and cultural patterns. The popular format to documenting patterns includes many sections. In software, the pattern template is somewhat strict and formal consists of a number of sections, each one describing a certain aspect of the overall pattern. For example, pattern name, intent, motivation (forces), applicability, structure, participants, collaboration, ..., related patterns sections. The focus of the pattern is to describe the static and the dynamic aspects of the pattern, and the many ways of using it.

Furthermore, cultural patterns were introduced in recent years followed somewhat similar format and it was intended to describe the explicit cultural requirement of the application such as data formatting, text directionality. Furthermore, the design of such pattern was generally based on existing cultural models such as Hofsted's cultural model which is controversial and in some case considered stereotypical. The type of culture patterns we advocate her are simple patterns that could be created and used by the local development teams to document their understanding and their experience to implement localization cultural aspects of the product in hand. The format include, name of the pattern, context, solution, and a brief description to how it can be used and applied in the targeted culture and in other similar contexts. The pattern focuses on the specific culture element and it can also include cultural similarities with other locals or cultures because some aspects of the software are locally bound and influenced, while other aspects, such as business rules, regulations, would share global characteristics. Furthermore, the pattern format should remain somewhat informal, free format, and flexible to accommodate and capture various culture specifics. In general, individuals tend to prefer informal ways to express their views, experiences, and opinions, what they like and what they don't? The simplistic format of the pattern is being emphasized to encourage all involved in the development of the product to use them.

In summary, concept maps and design patterns are being used for many years and in many fields and for different purposes. We recommend the use of such lightweight tools because of their simplicity, proven record of success in other areas, they work well with agile development processes and most important is that they can facilitate the elicitation and the codification of tacit knowledge such as cultural knowledge.

Recommendations

Based on the literature review concerning the issues of culture and language in GSE we found that the cultural and the linguistic issues of product being developed are rarely discussed in GSE literature. Since the end goal of the process and the team are to develop high quality global software products we should seriously invest in more research efforts towards understanding the cultural and the linguistic issues of the product being developed. Therefore, we recommend the following:

- Invest more in the process of finding new tools to enhance the team understanding to the cultural requirement of the product. We can say with confidence that people normally share what they understand and when they don't want to share communications tools and technology will be the least of their concerns.

- Teams can be motivated to share and codify tacit knowledge by providing them with the proper tools that enable them to do so. Today most of circulated tools were designed to deal with explicit types of knowledge. Many are considered heavyweight, expensive, and have high learning curve.

- Use concept maps, mind maps, simple culture design patterns, and any other available lightweight tools. Concept maps enable the team to put the product requirement in some context and it encourages them to elaborate, discuss, and share what they know with others. Adding diagrams and pictures to concept maps can help with visualization and enhances understanding of the subject or the concept being studied or discussed.

- The use of design patterns and templates can be used to elicit and codify tacit knowledge throughout organization, which then can be shared and reused. However, we should avoid relying on specific cultural model and avoid stereotyping. Culture is dynamic and keeps changing and it varies in the same country.

- Hiring culture consultant/experts/liaisons/ brokers can help in understanding the customer and the product cultural requirements but it is not enough to understand the deep cultural issues of the product being developed. Proficiency in the language issues is critical and it also can help in understanding the customer and the product cultural and linguistic requirements. However, proficiency in the language is not enough to qualify an individual to become a cultural expert.

FUTURE RESEARCH DIRECTIONS

There is a need for more research to address the impact of the cultural and linguistic aspects of global software globally developed. This is more challenging because we have to address the impact of culture and language not only on the GSD process, but also on the product being developed. Furthermore, there is more and more evidence that the Hofstede cultural model—used by the majority of researchers—is not enough to understand the impact of culture on GSE or global software. The need for a new and more comprehensive cultural model is paramount. While Hofstede views culture as homogeneous within national boundaries, we and many researchers find culture to be a dynamic, constantly changing field. The new models must analyze and understand culture in terms of contemporary standards and must keep up with the continuous shifting of cultural boundaries. The GSD can be a golden opportunity for researchers and designers to engage directly with the targeted culture and to create new models.

Another KM area of research that needs to be explored is finding objective measures of knowledge sharing which a core issue in KM studies. Most of the qualitative studies used structured interviews, surveys, and observation. We believe that data mining techniques can be used to study the content of what is being shared (emails, documents, interviews, meeting minutes, blogs, forums, etc.) to understand and measure the level or extent of sharing and the effectiveness of the communication tool.

CONCLUSION AND FINAL REMARKS

Culture continues to be a challenging issue to all professionals in all research areas. In GSD, the culture issues are among the most critical for the success of the software. Hence, the culture and the cultural influences of the target customer must be carefully studied and considered throughout the software development. Furthermore, GSE involve different teams from different countries with different cultures and that magnify the challenges of culture.

The lack of holistic view and comprehensive models to understand the complex issues of culture and language hinders the process of developing effective tools and techniques to manipulate cultural knowledge effectively. Tacit knowledge represents a critical and valuable asset to any organization. Sometimes, the loss of key people from and organization (i.e. leaving the organization) can put at risk the net worth of the entire organization. When people leave the organization they also take with them their tacit knowledge, expertise, skills, etc. In the case of global or international software application, dealing with tacit knowledge is far more critical. Because handing the cultural and the linguistic aspects of the product means the success or the failure of the project.

Furthermore, the issue of language is critical to understand the cultural issues of GSE. Language issues in the context of GSE are complex and should not be marginalized when dealing with GSE challenges. Language issue is a common concern for all parties involved in GSE. This includes developers, managers, stakeholders, customers, processes, and the product itself.

The cultural aspects are very critical to the success of any global system developed by co-located or geographically dispersed teams. These aspects affect directly the quality of the software, the process as well as people and organization. Culture and language influences must be carefully studied and fully understood and should be considered throughout the software development process. Our review to the current KM research we found that it is generally focused on understanding the cultural issues of GSE in terms of process and teams. However, the cultural and the linguistic issues of the product being developed were rarely discussed. Concept maps and design patterns are both simple and easy to create. They can be used to record, share, and codify all types of tacit knowledge especially cultural knowledge.

The proposed tools discussed are not the magic wand that we can wave and all problems will be gone. There are many tools which can be used to deal with the challenging issues of culture and language. We believe that understanding and handling the cultural and the linguistic issues of GSE will not only improve coordination and communication among different team members but also will improve the quality of the software product being developed. We hope our discussion will encourage more research efforts to be directed towards finding solutions to these issues.

REFERENCES

Abufardeh, S. (2009). *A framework for the integration of I18N & L10N activities in the software development process*. (Unpublished doctoral dissertation). North Dakota State University, Fargo, ND.

Abufardeh, S., & Magel, K. (2008). Culturalization of software architecture: Issues and challenges. In *Proceedings of the International Conference on Computer Science and Software Engineering (CSSE 2008)*. Wuhan, China: IEEE.

Abufardeh, S., & Magel, K. (2010). The impact of global software cultural and linguistic aspects on global software development process (GSD), issues and challenges. In *Proceedings of the 4th International Conference on New Trends in Information Science and Service Science*, (pp. 133–138). IEEE.

C. Alexander (Ed.). (1979). *The timeless way of building*. New York: Oxford University Press.

Alostath, J. M., & Wright, P. (2004). Pattern languages towards a tool for cross-cultural user interface design development. In H. M. Khalid (Ed.), *Proceedings of 7th International Conference on Work With Computing Systems*. Kuala Lumpur, Malaysia: Damai Sciences.

Ausubel, D. P. (1968). *Educational psychology: A cognitive view*. New York: Holt, Rinehart and Winston.

Brown, J. S., Collins, A., & Duguid, P. (1989). Situated cognition and the culture of learning. *Educational Researcher*, *18*(1), 32–41. doi:10.3102/0013189X018001032.

Carmel, E. (2003). The new software exporting nations: Success factors. *Electronic Journal of Information Systems in Developing Countries*, *13*(4), 1–12.

Carmel. (1999). *Global software teams collaborating across borders and time zones*. New York: Prentice Hall.

Conchuir, H. Agerfalk, & Fitzgerald. (2006). Exploring the assumed benefits of global software development. In *Proceedings of the IEEE International Conference on Global Software Engineering (ICGSE'06)*, (pp. 159-168). IEEE.

Cusick & Prasad. (2006). A practical management and engineering approach to offshore collaboration. *IEEE Software*, *23*(5), 20–29. doi:10.1109/MS.2006.118.

Damian, & Zowghi. (2003). Challenges in multisite software development organizations. *Requirements Engineering*, *8*(3), 149–160.

Del Galdo, E. M. (1996). Culture and design. In E. M. Del Galdo, & J. Neilsen (Eds.), *International UI*. New York: John Wiley & Sons.

Desouza, K. C., Awazu, & Baloh. (2006). Managing knowledge in global software development efforts: Issues and practices. *IEEE Software*, *3*(5), 30–37. doi:10.1109/MS.2006.135.

Erickson, T. (2000). Lingua francas for design: Sacred places and pattern languages. In D. Boyarski & W. A. Kellogg (Eds.), *Proceedings of the 3rd Conference on Designing Interactive Systems* (pp. 357-368). New York: ACM Press.

Forrester. (2010). Making collaboration work for the 21st century's distributed workforce (White paper). *Forrester Research Inc.* Retrieved Aug. 25, 2012 from http://www.idgconnect.com/view_abstract/6086/making-collaboration-work-21st-century-s-distributed-workforce

Gamma, E. Helm, Johnson, & Vlissides. (1995). Design patterns: Elements of reusable object-oriented software. Reading, MA: Addison-Wesley.

Hall, P. (2001). The cross-cultural web: Designing for global markets. In *Proceedings of the 3rd International Workshop on Internationalizations of Products and Systems*, (pp. 109–113). IEEE.

Heeks, R., & Nicholson, B. (2004). Software export success factors and strategies in follower nations. *Competition and Change, 8*(3), 267–302. doi:10.1080/1024529042000301962.

Herbsleb. (2007). Global software engineering: The future of socio-technical coordination. In *Proceedings of the 2007 Future of Software Engineering (FOSE'07)*, (pp. 188-198). FOSE.

Hislop. (2005). Knowledge management in organizations: A critical introduction. Oxford, UK: Oxford University Press.

G. Hofstede (Ed.). (2001). *Culture's consequences: Comparing values, behaviors, institutions, and organizations across nations* (2nd ed.). London: Sage Publications.

Hofstede, G. (n.d.). *Cultural dimensions.* Retrieved Sep. 2012 from http://www.geert-hofstede.com/index.shtml

Huang, H., & Trauth, E. M. (2006). Cultural diversity challenges: Issues for managing globally distributed knowledge workers in software development. P. Yoong & S. Huff (Eds.), Managing IT Professionals in the Internet Age, (pp. 253-275). Hershey, PA: Idea Group Inc.

Huang & Trauth. (2007). Cultural influences and globally distributed information systems development: Experiences from Chinese IT professionals. [CPR.]. *Proceedings of CPR, 2007*, 36–45.

Kellner, M. I. Becker-Kornstaedt, Riddle, Tomal, & Verlage. (1998). Process guides: Effective guidance for process participants. In *Proceedings of the Fifth International Conference on the Software Process*, (pp. 11-25). IEEE.

Khamesan, A., & Hammond, N. (2004). Synchronous collaborative concept mapping via ICT: Learning effectiveness and personal and interpersonal awareness. In *Proceedings of the First International Conference on Concept Mapping*, (pp. 385–392). IEEE.

Komi-Sirvio & Tihinen. (2005). Lessons learned by participants of distributed software development. *Knowledge and Process Management, 12*(2).

Koskinen, Pihlanto, & Vanharanta. (2003). Tacit knowledge acquisition and sharing in a project work context. *International Journal of Project Management, 21*(4), 281–290. doi:10.1016/S0263-7863(02)00030-3.

Leung, K., Bhagt, R. S., Buchan, N. R., Erez, M., & Gibson, C. B. (2005). Culture and international business: Recent advances and their implications for future research. *Journal of International Business Studies, 36*, 357–378. doi:10.1057/palgrave.jibs.8400150.

Li, M., & Gao, M. (2003). Strategies for developing China's software industries. *Information Technologies and International Development, 1*(1), 61–73. doi:10.1162/itid.2003.1.1.61.

Lindvall, Rus, & Sinha. (2003). Software systems support for knowledge management. *Journal of Knowledge Management, 7*(5), 137–150. doi:10.1108/13673270310505449.

Lipnack & Stamps. (1997). *Virtual teams: Reaching across space, time and organizations with technology.* New York: John Wiley & Sons.

Lutz. (2009). Linguistic challenges in global software development: Lessons learned in an International SW development division. In *Proceedings of the 2009 Fourth IEEE International Conference on Global Software Engineering (ICGSE '09),* (pp. 249–253). Limerick, Ireland: IEEE Computer Society.

Mahemoff, M. J., & Johnston, L. J. (1999). The planet pattern language for software internationalisation. In D. Manolescu & B. Wolf (Eds.), *Proceedings of the 6th Annual Conference on the Pattern Languages of Programs.* IEEE.

Mind Mapping. (n.d.). Retrieved Sep. 2012 from http://www.mind-mapping.org/blog/

Minevich, M., & Richter, F.-J. (2005). *Global outsourcing report.* Retrieved on July 08, 2012, from http://globalequations.com/Global%20Outsourcing%20Report.pdf

Myers, M. D., & Tan, F. B. (2002). Beyond models of national culture in information systems research. *Journal of Global Information Management, 10*(1), 24–32. doi:10.4018/jgim.2002010103.

Nicholson & Sahay. (2001). Some political and cultural issues in the globalization of software development: Case experience from Britain and India. *Information and Organization, 11*(1), 25–43. doi:10.1016/S0959-8022(00)00008-4.

Noll, Beecham, & Richardson. (2010). Global software development and collaboration: Barriers and solutions. *ACM Inroads, 1,* 66–78.

Nonaka, I., & Takeuchi, H. (1995). *The knowledge-creating company.* New York: Oxford University Press.

Novak, J. D., & Cañas, A. J. (2008). *The theory underlying concept maps and how to construct and use them (Technical Report IHMC CmapTools 2006-01 Rev 01-2008).* Boca Raton, FL: Institute for Human and Machine Cognition.

Plotnick. (1997). *Concept mapping: A graphical system for understanding the relationship between concepts.* Retrieved from http://www.mind-mapping.org/seminal-papers-in-information-mapping/concept-mapping-overview.html

Smith & Blanck. (2002). From experience: Leading dispersed teams. *Journal of Product Innovation Management, 19*(4), 294–304. doi:10.1016/S0737-6782(02)00146-7.

Software Design Patterns. (n.d.). Retrieved Sep. 2012 from http://www.oodesign.com/

Straub, D., Loch, K., Evaristo, R., Karahanna, E., & Strite, M. (2002). Towards a theory-based measurement of culture. *Journal of Global Information Management, 10*(1), 13–23. doi:10.4018/jgim.2002010102.

The Theory Underlying Concept Maps and How to Construct and Use Them. (n.d.). Retrieved Aug. 2012 from http://cmap.ihmc.us/publications/researchpapers/theorycmaps/theoryunderlyingconceptmaps.htm

ADDITIONAL READING

Barrett, M., & Walsham, G. (1995). Managing IT for business innovation: Issues of culture, learning, and leadership in a Jamaican insurance company. *Journal of Global Information Management, 3*(3), 25–33.

Borchers, G. (2003). The software engineering impacts of cultural factors on multi-cultural software development teams. In *Proceedings of 25th International Conference on Software Engineering* (pp. 540-545). IEEE.

Briggs, R. O., & Gruenbacher, P. (2002). Easy win win: Managing complexity in requirements negotiation with GSS. In *Proceedings of 35th Annual Hawaii International Conference on Systems Science*. Hawaii, HI: IEEE.

Child, J. (2002a). Theorizing about organization cross-nationally: Part 1–An introduction. In M. Warner, & P. Joynt (Eds.), *Managing across cultures: Issues and perspectives* (2nd ed., pp. 26–39). London: Thomson Learning.

Cramton, C. D., & Webber, S. S. (2005). Relationships among geographic dispersion, team processes, and effectiveness in software development work teams. *Journal of Business Research, 58*(6), 758–765. doi:10.1016/j.jbusres.2003.10.006.

Curtis, B., Krasner, H., & Iscoe, N. (1988). A field study of the software design process for large systems. *Communications of the ACM, 31*(11), 1268–1287. doi:10.1145/50087.50089.

Espinosa, J. A., & Pickering, C. (2006). The effect of time separation on coordination processes and outcomes: A case study. In *Proceedings of 39th Hawaiian International Conference on System Sciences*. IEEE.

Hanisch, J., Thanasankit, T., & Corbitt, B. (2001). Understanding the cultural and social impacts on requirements engineering processes-Identifying some problems challenging virtual team integration with clients. In *Proceedings of the 9th European Conference on Information Systems* (pp. 11-22). Bled, Slovenia: IEEE.

Harrison, G., McKinnon, J., Wu, A., & Chow, C. (2000). Cultural influences on adaptation to fluid workgroups and teams. *Journal of International Business Studies, 31*(3), 489–505. doi:10.1057/palgrave.jibs.8490918.

Hartenian, L. (2000). Cultural diversity in small business: Implications for firm performance. *Journal of Developmental Entrepreneurship*, 209-219.

Hawk, J. (2004). Evolution of offshore software development: From outsourcing to cosourcing. *MIS Quarterly Executive, 3*(2), 69–81.

Hazzan, & Dubinsky. (2006). Can diversity in global software development be enhanced by agile software development?. In *Proceedings of the 2006 International Workshop on Global Software Development for the Practitioner*. Shanghai, China: IEEE.

Henninger, S. (1997). Case-based knowledge management tools for software development. *Automated Software Engineering, 4*, 319–340. doi:10.1023/A:1008679010073.

Holmstrom, H., Conchuir, E. O., Agerfalk, P. J., & Fitzgerald, B. (2006). Global software development challenges: A case study on temporal, geographical and sociocultural distance. In *Proceedings of the IEEE International Conference on Global Software Engineering*, (pp. 3–11). Washington, DC: IEEE Computer Society.

Kakabadse, N., & Kakabadse, A. (2000). Critical review–Outsourcing: A paradigm shift. *Journal of Management Development, 19*(8), 670–728. doi:10.1108/02621710010377508.

Kellner, D. (2002). Theorizing globalization. *Sociological Theory, 20*(3), 85–305. doi:10.1111/0735-2751.00165.

Korkala, M., & Abrahamsson, P. (2007) Communication in distributed agile development: A case study. In *Proceedings of 33rd EUROMICRO Conference on Software Engineering and Advanced Applications*, (pp. 203-210). EUROMICRO.

Krishna, S., Sahay, S., & Walsham, G. (2004). Managing cross-cultural issues in global software development. *Communications of the ACM, 47*(4), 62–66. doi:10.1145/975817.975818.

Kryssanov, V. V., Tamaki, H., & Kitamura, S. (2001). Understanding design fundamentals: How synthesis and analysis drive creativity, resulting in emergence. *Artificial Intelligence in Engineering, 15*(4), 329–342. doi:10.1016/S0954-1810(01)00023-1.

Laplante, P. A., Costello, T., Singh, P., Bindiganaville, S., & Landon, M. (2004). The who, what, why, where, and when of IT outsourcing. *IT Professional, 6*(1), 19–23. doi:10.1109/MITP.2004.1265538.

Larsen, K. R., & McInerney, C. R. (2002). Preparing to work in the virtual organization. *Information & Management, 29*, 445–456. doi:10.1016/S0378-7206(01)00108-2.

Layman, L., Williams, L., Damian, D., & Bures, H. (2006). Essential communication practices for extreme programming in a global software development team. *Information and Software Technology, 48*(9), 781–794. doi:10.1016/j.infsof.2006.01.004.

Luz, M. G. D., & Teófilo, M. (2009). *Challenges on adopting scrum for distributed teams in home office environments*. World Academy of Science, Engineering and Technology.

MacGregor, E., Hsieh, Y., & Kruchten, P. (2005). *The impact of intercultural factors on global software development*. Electrical and Computer Engineering. Jiménez, Piattini, & Vizcaíno. (2009, January). Challenges and improvements in distributed software development: A systematic review. *Advances in Software Engineering*, 1–16.

Miroshnik, V. (2002). Culture and international management: A review. *Journal of Management Development, 21*(7/8), 521–544. doi:10.1108/02621710210434647.

Moe, N. B., & Smite, D. (2007). Understanding lacking trust in global software teams: A multi-case study. *Lecture Notes in Computer Science, 4589*, 20–32. doi:10.1007/978-3-540-73460-4_6.

Moe & ˇSmite. (2008). Understanding a lack of trust in global software teams: a multiple-case study. *Software Process Improvement and Practice, 13*(3), 217–231. doi:10.1002/spip.378.

Nagappan, Murphy, & Basili. (2008). The influence of organizational structure on software quality: An empirical case study. In *Proceedings of the 30th International Conference on Software Engineering (ICSE '08)*, (pp. 521–530). Leipzig, Germany: ICSE.

Olson, J. S., & Olson, G. M. (2003). Culture surprises in remote software development teams. *QUEUE, 1*(9), 52–59. doi:10.1145/966789.966804.

Osland, J. S., & Bird, A. (2004). Beyond sophisticated stereotyping: Cultural sense making in context. In S. M. Puffer (Ed.), *International management: Insights from friction and practice* (pp. 56–66). Armonk, NY: M. E. Sharpe, Inc..

Paasivaara, M., Durasiewicz, S., & Lassenius, C. (2009). Using scrum in distributed agile development: A multiple case study. In *Proceedings of the 2009 Fourth IEEE International Conference on Global Software Engineering*, (pp. 195–204). Washington, DC: IEEE Computer Society.

Pilatti, Audy, & Prikladnicki. (2006). Software configuration management over a global software development environment: Lessons learned from a case study. In *Proceedings of the International Workshop on Global Software Development for the Practitioner (GSD '06)*. Shanghai, China: GSD.

Shrinivasavadhani, J., & Panicker, V. (2007). Remote mentoring a distributed agile team. [Washington, DC: IEEE Computer Society.]. *Proceedings of the Agile, 2008,* 322–326.

Shukla, M., & Sethi, V. (2004). An approach of studying knowledge worker's competencies in software development team. *Journal of Advancing Information and Management Studies, 1*(1), 49–62.

Swart, J., & Kinnie, N. (2003). Sharing knowledge in knowledge-intensive firms. *Human Resource Management Journal, 13*(2), 60–75. doi:10.1111/j.1748-8583.2003.tb00091.x.

Trauth, E. M. (2000). *The culture of an information economy: Influences and impacts in the Republic of Ireland.* Dordrecht, The Netherlands: Kluwer Academic Publishers. doi:10.1007/978-94-010-9836-6.

Walsham, G. (2000). IT, globalization and cultural diversity. In C. Avgerous, & G. Walshem (Eds.), *Information technology in context: Studies from perspective of developing countries* (pp. 291–303). Aldershot, UK: Shgate Publishing Ltd..

Weisinger, J. Y., & Trauth, E. M. (2003). The importance of situating culture in cross-cultural IT management. *IEEE Transactions on Engineering Management, 50*(1), 26–30. doi:10.1109/TEM.2002.808259.

Winkler, J. K., Dibbern, J., & Heinzl, A. (2008). The impact of cultural differences in offshore outsourcing- Case study results from German–Indian application development projects. *Information Systems Frontiers, 10*(2), 243–258. doi:10.1007/s10796-008-9068-5.

Zolin, R., Hinds, P. J., Fruchter, R., & Levitt, R. E. (2004). Interpersonal trust in cross-functional, geographically distributed work: A longitudinal study. *Information and Organization, 14,* 1–26. doi:10.1016/j.infoandorg.2003.09.002.

KEY TERMS AND DEFINITIONS

A Concept Map: Is a diagram showing the relationships among concepts. It is a graphical tool for organizing and representing knowledge.

A Design Pattern: Is a formal way of documenting, capturing, and communicating a solution to a design problem in a particular field.

A Mind Map: Is a diagram used to visually outline information. It is often created around a single word or text, placed in the center, to which associated ideas, wordswords, and concepts are added.

Data: Is a fact that alone is not significant, as is doesn't relate to other data (i.e., without or out of context).

Global Software Engineering (GSE): Is a software development that involves teams from multiple geographic. The team's locations are commonly referred to as *sites* or *development sites*.

Information: Is data that is related and is therefore in context. It can be transformed into a process or procedure, making it useful.

Internationalization (I18N): Also referred to as "Globalization" in the context of software development"— is "the process of generalizing a product so that it can handle multiple languages and cultural conventions without the need for re-design. Internationalization takes place at the level of program design and document development."

Knowledge: Is the application of information. Knowledge addresses how and why, in addition to who, what, where, and when. The knowledge links all the information together to produce a comprehensive policy, processprocess, or procedure.

Locale: Is the collection of features of the user's environment that is dependent upon language, country/region, and cultural conventions.

Localization (L10N): Is "the process of taking a product and making it linguistically and culturally appropriate to the target locale (country/region and language) where it will be used and sold."

Chapter 3
Knowledge Management and Semantic Web Services

Izzat Alsmadi
Prince Sultan University, Saudi Arabia

Sascha Alda
Bonn-Rhein-Sieg University, Germany

ABSTRACT

Information reliability and automatic computation are two important aspects that are continuously pushing the Web to be more semantic. Information uploaded to the Web should be reusable and extractable automatically to other applications, platforms, etc. Several tools exist to explicitly markup Web content. The Web services may also have a positive role on the automatic processing of Web contents, especially when they act as flexible and agile agents. However, Web services themselves should be developed with semantics in mind. They should include and provide structured information to facilitate their use, reuse, composition, query, etc. In this chapter, the authors focus on evaluating state-of-the-art semantic aspects and approaches in Web services. Ultimately, this contributes to the goal of Web knowledge management, execution, and transfer.

INTRODUCTION

In the current information world, the Web is not only an environment for information transfer and communication; it has deeply interfered with all human daily activities. It has greatly impacted and empowered the human civilized way of life.

Through information spread and communicated over the Web, collective efforts can have a significant impact on people and states in the same and in sometimes even more significant impact if compared with real or traditional mechanisms. For different audience, Web semantics can have different expectations and perspectives. In one

DOI: 10.4018/978-1-4666-4229-4.ch003

aspect, adding semantics to Web contents may indicate adding more reliability and authenticity to the information uploaded to the Web in terms of credibility of the information itself and their authors. On another important aspect of Web semantic is the ability for such information to be reused, transferred and applied in a different context whether by humans or more important by agents, or tools with the least amount of human intervention. Working on standards and according to standards then are main procedures to apply and follow to reach the goals of Web semantics. Without common international standards that can regulate and control the different processes and applications throughout the Web, achieving semantics in Web content can stay a dream. Adding semantics to the Web in general and to Web services in particular is seen as the key enabler for future interactive Web. However, only future can tell how much that is true.

Ontology and conceptual modelling are important factors in knowledge management systems. An ontology includes the vocabulary terms and the semantic groundings. At lower levels, data and information are transformed and exchanged between the different group parties. An ontological model can help in information reusability and can help in answering high-level user queries and search through the available information looking for answers. In the Internet world, XML is one of the most popular standards that are used to exchange information. In Web services in particular, XML is the language for several important activities for the Web services architecture. This includes: Web Service Description Language (WSDL), messaging services (SOAP), process presentation (BPEL), and service discovery. While XML provides an important aspect that contributes to Web standards, however, semantic Web includes further standards that in one way or another can extend XML. An intelligent Web semantic system should be able to receive a high level user, or program query and parse through Web pages to find the best answer. In a more realistic approach,

the search engines architecture can be adopted where indexers and crawlers continuously search the Web for data, index and archive such data. One the search engine interface receives a query, such query can be processed using the structured information from the indexers or crawlers.

The Web service has two major life cycles: design and development life cycle, execution and usage life cycle. In the first cycle, Web services can be similar to other software applications where their development process will include a requirement or specification stage, design, coding and testing. All those stages are accomplished in the service provider side without the need to communicate with clients. In traditional software development models, especially when a software product is developed for a specific customer, requirements are collected based on customer needs and clients maybe contacted in later stages for reviewing and verification. However, Web services are usually developed based on high level generic requirements that are not meant to a specific user or company.

In the second life cycle, the dynamic usage life cycle, Web services can be used by different users for different purposes. They can be used alone in one context, or they can be part of an orchestra of services in another context. The usage life cycle is very dynamic and unpredictable. This dynamic usage life cycle is what majorly distinguishes Web services from most other software products. In addition, most semantic Web approaches are developed to ensure that Web services are capable of acting as autonomous agents that can serve different users in different contexts.

Service descriptions should be machine readable. Web Service Description Language (WSDL) XML files hold the Web services metadata that include descriptions of Web service public methods. Those public methods can be called and used by service users or requesters. For each method, WSDL contain information related to the method output and input parameters. For syntactical purposes, traditional WSDL may contain enough information to enable calling the method. However, semantically such enough lacks thorough understanding of method constraints, post-conditions or clear scope of input parameters. Further, WSDL does not include Quality of Service (QoS) requirements or constrains, or service taxonomy. WS-policy framework came to complement WSDL on QoS behaviours asserting service requirements, constraints, and capabilities. WS-policy assertions can describe transactions, security issues, or message reliability constraints.

In typical SOA architectures, service requesters search for possible proper service providers in service registries or third party central directories (Universal Description, Discovery, and Integration Protocol: UDDI). Registry includes information related to providers such as WSDL and policies. It is possible for service requesters to contact service providers without the mediator. The role of UDDI is then somewhat similar to the role of search engines where they can be used to search for Websites. However, if a client knows a specific Website, they don't need a search engine to reach it.

Service composition is a core task in SOA architectures. Applications can perform complex tasks utilizing a team ob Web services.

The Web Services Description Language (WSDL) files usually in XML formats represent the Web service interface. In WSDL, all public Web methods are described. For each method, required inputs or parameters and produced output is also described. WSDL contains the following information about the Web service: The Website of the service, service interface or public methods that are available to users, and for each public method, WSDL include its interface (i.e. input parameters and return type). Major interface relevant information are included in the two element types: <portType>, and <message>. WSDL may include some unstructured information included under (wsdl:documentation) (Figure1) nodes to provide descriptions about the Web methods.

Extensions for WSDL such as WSDL-S try to add more information and semantics to WSDL so that such information can be used in testing, service calls, etc.

BACKGROUND

In this section, we will describe three important standards or applications that contribute to Web semantics in particular focus on Web services.

RDF

Resource Description Framework (RDF) schemas define the data model and provide description about the data. RDF includes three core classes: Root, meta and literals. RDF is an XML based framework for knowledge representation and information exchange on the Web. Each statement in RDF contains three parts: subject, predicate and object. Some research projects and applications try also to transform structured data into RDF data. For querying data in RDF some query lan-

Figure 1. An example of documentation in WSDL

```
<wsdl:operation name="GetCitiesByCountry">
<wsdl:documentation xmlns:wsdl="http://schemas.xmlsoap.org/wsdl/">
      Get all major cities by country name
      (full / part).</wsdl:documentation>
<wsdl:input message="tns:GetCitiesByCountryHttpGetIn" />
<wsdl:output message="tns:GetCitiesByCountryHttpGetOut" />
</wsdl:operation>
```

guages such as SPARQL exist. Many tools exist also to harvest RFD data from Web services and resources. Along with OWL, RDF is considered one of the main components in semantic Web. RDF main goal is to provide unambiguous standard method to create statements about Web resources.

DAML, OWL-S (DAML-S)

DARPA Agent Markup Language (DAML) sponsored by DARPA (http://www.daml.org/services/). It allows creation and instantiation of domain ontologies with expressive semantics. One of its major goals is to allow users to find and communicate with Web services effectively. In addition DAML tries to establish a common framework for Web services description, distribution and discovery. DAML initiates started in 2000. Till 2007, the group released the following standards/applications/ontologies: DAML+OIL, WSDL, DAML-S (later on OWL-S), OWL, WSMO, SWSL, WSDL-S, and SAWSDL.

Web Service Description Language (WSDL) XML files are used to represent services. They are the public interface through which service consumers can see the service details and how to call or use such service. Similar to method headers or signatures in programming languages, WSDL file include all public methods in the subject Web service. For each method, the file also includes information related to the input parameters for the method and the expected output. For a program or a tool, WSDL includes all syntactic information required to call a Web method in a service. However, for users or for semantic purposes, WSDL does not include semantic information that can help understand the service. For example, WSDL does not include any possible required conditions or constraints to call the public method. Input data types are also defined in general (e.g. string, integer, etc.), however, WSDL does not include a description of the actual format of the input. In addition, WSDL does not include expressive information on the expected results.

Web services in particular and Service Oriented Architecture (SOA) in general has one of the founding principles related to service isolation and reusability. Services should be developed without a specific user in mind. They should be as generic as it can be. This encapsulation or separation between service and clients is necessary to ensure that such service can service a wide spectrum of current or even future users. On the other hand, the need to add more semantics to the service maybe seen as scoping down the service to one or more specific users or usages. It is then challenging to achieve or sustain services' high reusability and encapsulation while at the same time improving their semantics.

OWL is an ontology description language. OWL-S is an OWL ontology to describe Web services. It came to enhance WSDL and help in Web services automatic discovery, composition, invocation and execution monitoring. OWL covers RDF and provides the ability to make inferences about data. As mentioned earlier, WSDL provided all syntactic information to programmatically call a service or one of its methods. However, WSDL lacks some of the necessary semantic information that can help machines to communicate with those Web services effectively. OWL-S development goal was not to replace WSDL but rather add a semantic layer to it. With the same goal as OWL-S, WSDL-S is proposed by IBM and the METEOR group to annotate WSDL with semantic information. OWL-S has three main parts: service profile for service discovery and advertisement, process model for service detail description and grounding for service message interactions.

For testing and many other user activities from the client side, the information included in WSDL lacks some important semantics. As such, Web semantics introduced several standards and tools to add semantic information to WSDL. W3 organization (http://www.w3.org/Submission/WSDL-S/) introduced WSDL-S for semantics to add semantic annotations to the content of WSDL. Such semantic information can be added by users or by add-on tools. Figure2 shows an excerpt of WSDL-S based semantic content. For testing purposes, such information can be extremely useful and can help in generating more effective test cases.

The following tags were added to include semantics in service operations (Rajasekaran et al., 2004):

- **Operation Tag:** To include description of the operation.
- **Parameters Tag:** This further consists of two meta-tags: inParam, for input parameters and outParam, for output parameters.

User is expected to provide inputs according to the defined types.

- **Exceptions Tag:** All types of exceptions that maybe thrown through the service call process.
- **Constraints Tag:** Pre- and post-conditions are described in this tag to define requirements to call the particular operation and describe expected results from the service provider.
- **Interface Tag**
- **Service Tag:** To provide service provider specific parameters such as: location, Quality of Service and reliability.

Figure 2. A sample WSDL-S XSD content

```
- <complexType>
   - <complexContent>
       - <extension base="wsdl:documented">
           <attribute type="NCName" use="required" name="categoryname"/>
           <attribute type="anyURI" use="required" name="taxonomyURI"/>
           <attribute type="String" use="optional" name="taxonomyValue"/>
           <attribute type="integer" use="optional" name="taxonomyCode"/>
       </extension>
     </complexContent>
   </complexType>
 </element>
- <element name="precondition">
   - <complexType>
       - <complexContent>
           - <restriction base="anyType">
               <attribute type="string" name="name"/>
               <attribute type="anyURI" name="modelReference"/>
               <attribute type="string" name="expression"/>
           </restriction>
         </complexContent>
       </complexType>
     </element>
- <element name="effect">
   - <complexType>
       - <complexContent>
           - <restriction base="anyType">
               <attribute type="string" name="name"/>
               <attribute type="anyURI" name="modelReference"/>
               <attribute type="string" name="expression"/>
           </restriction>
```

Another example for WSDL-semantic add-on applications is OWL-S. OWL-S tool (http://www.semWebcentral.org) is a tool, based on OWL ontology, developed to add semantics to WSDL files. The tool can be used to extra semantic information of the WSDL and the service that can be useful for testing purposes. Figure3 shows a sample output from OWL-S tool to add semantics to a WSDL file. In addition to the documentation or information included from WSDL, the tool allows users to add information especially for input and output parameters in input fields under (XSLT). Such added information is then saved along with WSDL information into an OWL file. The tool is used in several research papers for generating the data in the test case generation process (e.g. Bozkurt and Harman 2011; Yu and Ning 2008; Ngan et al., 2009). The tool generates an output file with extension (owl) that includes WSDL and semantic information.

OWL-S can define atomic processes that can be invoked directly or composite process from several atomic services.

We will use OWL-S tool and its generated files as an input to the automatic test data generation process.

SWSI and SWSL

Semantic Web Services Initiative (SWSI: http://www.swsi.org/) with teams from DAML and the Europian semantic Web projects to introduce semantic Web services technologies in the current Web. One of the major components in the project is the Semantic Web Services Language (SWSL: http://www.w3.org/Submission/SWSF-SWSL). This is a general purpose logical language with features focused on semantic Web construct. Along with other components proposed by the initiative, SWSL will converge effort from OWL-S with products in this initiative to the goal of automation of service tasks such as: selection, invocation, monitoring, and composition (http://www.w3.org/2004/12/rules-ws/paper/124).

Figure 3. A sample output from OWL-S semantic tool

WSMO

Web Service Modelling Ontology (WSMO) is an extension and refinement of the Web Service Modelling Framework, WSMF. It is a conceptual framework to describe Web services and related aspects. It inherits some of the good software design principles: Strong decoupling and mediation, encapsulation or differentiation interface from implementation, etc. In addition to describing service functional properties, non functional properties or quality aspects (e.g. accuracy, availability, or performance) can be described and specified. WSMO stresses on solving Web services integration and composition problems and try to act as a mediator.

Rule-ML

Rule Markup Language (RuleML) is the de facto open language standard for rule interchange/ markup or the Web. It represents an XML-based rule syntax for the Web. Other tasks that require rule descriptions include: translation, interchange, execution, publication, and/or archiving of services. The rules extended the query language SQL rules. RuleML is based on logic programming with model theoretic semantics. RuleML initial goal was to enable semantic exchange of rules with close connection to relational databases.

UDDI tModel

As an online yellow book for Web services, UDDI acts as a directory where information about Web services can be found. Service providers register their services in the UDDI and then those services can be visible to service requesters. Unlike the search engine models for Web pages, where Websites don't need to register to the search engine, in UDDI, service requesters should made themselves visible to the UDDI first. Service providers need to publish their interfaces (i.e. WSDL) describing in those interfaces their services and how can

they be called. The interface is like the contract between service providers and consumers to define what is a service, how it is provided and used. Interfaces are saved in UDDI using tModel and every interface has an instance of tModel. Those tModel instances are then used when searching for a particular service.

A large number of researchers and developers participate in the Semantic Web Services Interest Group (SWSIG: www.w3.org/2002/ws/swsig), a public forum created in 2003 to discuss the integration of the semantic Web with Web services.

LITERATURE SURVEY

In synchronization with the scope of this book in general (i.e. knowledge management in software engineering environments), we will focus on surveying papers that discussed semantic Web issues particularly in the scope of Web services.

There are several papers that discuss using DAML for semantic Web services (e.g. McIlraith et al 2001, Cost et al. 2001, Paolucci and Sycara 2003). As described in the background section, DAML came to extend XML and describe objects with greater flexibility and semantics.

McIlraith et al 2001 paper titled "semantic Web services" described the roles of DAML in Web services automatic: discovery, execution, composition and interoperation. Authors focused on the automatic composition of Web services as service composition requires several complex activities to accomplish. The first task is to receive a high level service quest from a user or a system and analyze it. Such quest or query maybe unstructured or structured in a different format. The second complex activity is to search and find the best candidate services that can possibly fulfill such request and the third also complex task is how to compose those different services and combine them to response to the query. In the proposed service composition frameworks, agents are proposed to handle such complex tasks.

Agents here work as mediators between service requesters of users and try to analyze their requests, constraints, etc and on the other side deal with service for discovery, execution and composition. An agent needs to do this automatically with the least amount of human intervention. Authors in the paper discussed markup based on DAML to automate Web service activities.

Paolucci and Sycara paper 2003 proposed a model in which Web services act as autonomous goal directed agents. Authors focused on presenting Web services' inference mechanism for representing core Web service concepts. Major semantic Web products that try to make Web content readable and reusable include: Resource Description Framework (RDF) DARPA Agent Markup Language for Services (DAML-S) and Web Ontology Language (OWL). Authors approach focused on using DAML-S in semantic Web services. DAML-S includes semantic descriptions on Web services and provides knowledge level information about those services. DAML-UDDI match maker is proposed to match between service requesters and providers or between different services and also create on-demand services. The successful matching of such algorithms depends on the complexity of the queries and the ability of the algorithms to search through services based on described services for possible matches.

Further on DAML, some papers elaborated on the usage of DAML-S as a semantic extension for DAML (e.g. Martin et al 2004, Ankolekar et al 2002, Wu et al 2003). DAML-S or OWL-S main goal is to automate Web service tasks; discovery, execution, interoperation, composition and monitoring (http://www.daml.org/services/owl-s/).

Wu et al 2003 paper focused on using DAML-S for the automatic composition of Web services using Artificial Intelligence (AI) planning techniques. Service composition is one of the most complex service activities specially to automate. Domingue et al paper 2006 discussed orchestration

activities o combine several Web services. Authors utilized WSMO Web service communication ontology that was developed as an e-commerce enabler for Web services. The adopted the formal Abstract State Machines (ASMs) to represent the guarded transitions executions.

Hepp et al 2005 paper used also WSMO and proposed an architecture to combine Web services with Business Process Management (BPM). BPM focused on managing IT support for the execution of business operations. The reason for using WSMO and Web services is that they can provide machine accessible or readable representation and manipulation of knowledge. Authors discussed two major process activities in the scope on business processing and Web services: querying and manipulating the process space. One problem with the proposed semantic business processes is that in most cases business processes are customized in each company or environment. This means that utilizing semantic standards and ontologies may not be enough to solve business process problems and each business needs to handle their own special cases.

Howard and Kerschberg paper 2004 discussed automating Web services for brokering activities. They proposed a framework for automatically managing and dynamically brokering Web services particularly for virtual organizations. Many papers other papers as well discussed approaches related to building a complete Web application or organization work flow system based on Web services. Such approaches are taken more attention especially in the SOA and cloud computing environments. Similar to the previous papers, Pedrinaci et al 2008 paper discussed semantic Web services in the scope of business process management. They discussed the model in the scope of different business layers: strategic, operational, processes, services, and implementation. They proposed semantic BPM as a mean for increasing tasks automations in business processes life cycle. Khan et al 2006 paper used semantic Web services for domain knowledge presentation. Wu et al in 2008 proposed and developed a tourist service integration system based on semantic Web services and knowledge management. The system use historical data to help tourists plan trips and other related services. Semantic Web services can utilize the automatic collection of data and historical data for building knowledge management or expert systems in general.

Bianchini et al paper in 2009 discussed semantic search issues in Web services particularly in peer systems P2P. The approach is based on recording historical semantic service searching and then search through. This is an approach that is adopted in several research papers in semantic Web services to solve the issue of automatic semantic Web services search. Based on similarity and relevancy measurements or matching algorithms, subject query is compared and matched with existed ones. In their framework, authors proposed two components to be added in semantic Web services architecture that can assist in the semantic search: Knowledge evolution manager to update knowledge and experience based on service usage and semantic search assistant to find best matched services for service requests.

In Dietze et al 2008 paper, authors proposed situation based dynamic Web services' composition. By large, the task of Web services composition is the most complex task to automate that requires semantic understanding and analysis of users' queries, match approaches and processes to find best service or services to fulfill a service request and third algorithms to combine dynamically several Web services to solve the subject request.

In summary of surveyed papers, ontology and common standards are key enablers for automation and semantic Web services. In addition, there are several different tasks that are required to accomplish in a complete semantic Web services framework. Achieving automation in those tasks may vary from one to another and from one scenario to another.

AUTOMATION IN WEB SERVICE ACTIVITIES

Automation is a key symptom that Web services are semantics. Tools, programs, or Websites, should be able to communicate with Web services without user intervention. They should be able to automatically discover those Web services, know their capabilities, and communicate with them. Toward this goal, we developed a tool that takes the standard Web services WSDL as an input and then perform activities automatically on the Web service based on input parameters data analysis, invocation preparation, invocation, logging and analysis of invocation reports. Some search engines for Web services (e.g. http://Webservices. seekda.com/) exist to perform such functions. However, many of the services that were tested failed in the invocation process. Either the invocation client is not working well, or search engine is not updated on the status and any possible changes in those Web services.

Figure 4 depicts our automation framework for discovering and communicating with Web services. The main input to the framework is the service WSDL file.

An OWL-S tool is then used to annotate WSDL file with semantic information. This semantic information is user defined. As described earlier in Figure3, using OWL-S semantic tool, user can annotate inputs and outputs for service Web methods. Each method in the service will have a separate file and so for one WSDL, we can have several OWL-S generated files based on the number of methods.

OWL-S Parser

Part of our developed automation framework, we developed an OWL-S parser that uses the OWL files as input. Those files were previously generated from Web services' WSDL and then annotated by users. The output of the OWL-S parser includes files that contain relevant information

Figure 4. Web Service automation framework

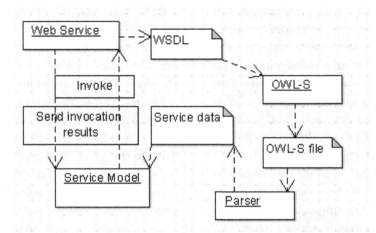

for the process of test cases and data generation. Figure 5 shows a sample from an output file. Three main columns are parsed from OWL files: Subject, predicate and object name. Those are parsed based on OWL files structure. Most of the important data relevant for testing exist under the column: object name, however, information from other columns can be sometime useful as well.

Information about Web operations or methods along with annotated information is then used as an input for the invocation process as depicted by Figure 4. A tool, program, Web application or database can be the receiver of such information in order to communicate with the service.

For a typical invocation with the service, a client or invoker needs to know: 1. The WSDL of the service, 2: the service name, 3: the called method name 4: provide values for all method inputs. Figure 6 shows all those required information for a particular Web service. GetGeoIP method takes one input (an IP address).

A client program or an invoker can then used this message to invoke the Web service. The tool also collects the log of invocation results. Figure 7 shows an except sample log for a set of invoca-

tions. It represents a service that takes the zip code as input and returns geographical longitude and latitude for the location of the zip code.

Log files from service invocations can be utilized to understand the Web service semantics. For example, and based on the invocation results, whether successful or not, users can understand the nature of the service and the constraints or pre-conditions of method input parameters. Knowledge by learning or by examples can be an option to improve users understanding of Web services. Those can be also used for the automatic learning of constraints on Web services based on learning from invocations' results.

Results and analysis showed that automating Web services activities can be divided into two sections. There are some activities such as service publishing, discovery, monitoring and communicating with. Those activities can be automated and generalized relatively with small effort. However, some other activities such as composition and intelligent service queries are still complex to automatically accomplish in the current Web services infra structure.

Figure 5. An excerpt of OWL-S parser

Subject..	Predicate...	objectName...
out0	type	Output
out0	label	GetGeoIPResult
out0	parameterTy	Thing
Grounding	type	WsdlGrounding
Service	type	Service
Service	supports	Grounding
Profile	type	Profile
in0	type	Input
in0	label	IPAddress
in0	parameterTy	string
Profile	hasInput	in0
Profile	textDescript	GeoIPService - G
Profile	serviceName	GetGeoIP
Profile	hasOutput	out0
Profile	presentedBy	Service
Profile	label	GetGeoIP
Service	presents	Profile
ProcessMc	type	ProcessModel

Figure 6. A sample web service call

```
http://www.webservicex.net/geoipservice.asmx?WSDL,
GeoIPService,GetGeoIP,120.230.23.45
```

Figure 7. An excerpt of invocation log for a web service

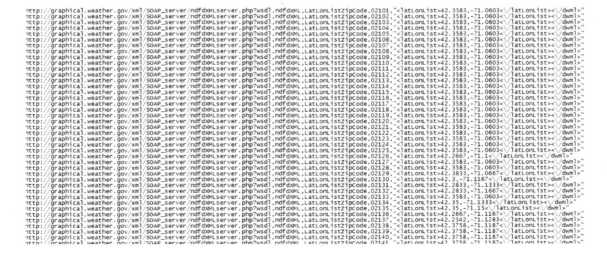

Web Services Expert System

Using data mining and expert system methods, a large amount of data from services' invocations can be used to build an expert system for Web services. Such expert system can be goal oriented specially from some automatic activities such as service composition or monitoring. It can be also quality or testing oriented to analyze successful and failed calls to Web services and build a knowledge system based on that. Using our automation system, we collected a large amount of data from log reports for different service invocations. We hope through studying and mining collected data, we can build a Web services expert system that can contribute in some way or another to improving semantics in Web services.

Automatic Composition in Web Services

As mentioned earlier, a major goal for semantic Web and semantic Web service is automation. Through automation, machines and algorithms, without user intervention should be able to perform service related tasks such as: service discovery, query, invocation, monitoring and composition. By large, for automation, service composition is the most complex and the one that is getting the majority of research focus in this field. Accomplishing service composition in a generic or dynamic structure is not yet available and most approaches in service composition automation focus on a particular domain or system. Reaching the goal of building such a generic dynamic service composition should be proceeded with building semantic search engines that can communicate effectively with Web services. Web services can then act as agents. Each agent should not only contain a Web service and Web service description. It should also contain a knowledge miner that records historical use and experience for the Web service. Knowledge from fields such as: data mining, sensor networks, neural networks

should be utilized to build the orchestration between semantic Web services search engines and Web services.

SUMMARY

Semantic Web services can provide machine readable and accessible knowledge representation and manipulation. In the semantic Web services architecture, all information exchanged is machine readable. Service query, discovery, invocation, composition, and monitoring can be automatically conducted. Many ontological standards are proposed in the scope of Web semantics in general and Web services semantic in particular. The levels of achieved automation in Web services activities vary as the complexity of those activities vary as well. We designed and implemented a system that can interact with Web services automatically. The system can, based on Web services WSDL and user annotations, build a usage profile through sending many service calls to evaluated Web services and collect automatically service response feedback reports. We hope that this can be part of an expert system that can be used in further complex Web service activities such as service composition or knowledge mining.

ACKNOWLEDGMENT

This chapter was conducted as part of postdoc scholarship for AVEMPACE (Erasmus Mundus (EM) Action 2 Strand 2 Lot 5 AVEMPACE) in 2012.

REFERENCES

Adamopoulou, P., Sakkopoulos, Tsakalidis, & Lytras. (2007). Web service selection based on QoS knowledge management. *Journal of UCS, 13*(9), 1138-1156.

Alesso, P. (2012). *Preparing for semantic web services*. Retrieved from www.sitepoint.com/article/semantic-web-services

Ankolekar, A. Burstein, Hobbs, Lassila, Martin, McDermott, … Sycara. (2002). DAML-S: Web service description for the semantic web. In *Proceedings International Semantic Web Conference (ISWC)* (LNCS), (vol. 2342). Berlin: Springer.

Bianchini, D. De Antonellis, & Melchiori. (2009). Service-based semantic search in P2P systems. In *Proceedings of the 2009 Seventh IEEE European Conference on Web Services*. IEEE.

Cob, Z. C., & Abdullah. (2008). Ontology-based semantic web services framework for knowledge management system. In *Proceedings of the International Symposium on Information Technology, 2008*. ITSim.

Cost, R. Finin, Joshi, Peng, Nicholas, Soboroff, … Tolia. (2001). *ITTalks: A case study in the semantic web and DAML*. Retrieved from http://www.semanticWeb.org/SWWS/program/full/paper41.pdf

Darr, T. Benjamin, Mayer, Fernandes, & Jain. (2010). *Semantic services for intelligence preparation of the battlefield (IPB) composition*. Paper presented at the 2010 International Symposium on Collaborative Technologies and Systems. New York, NY.

Dietze, S. Gugliotta, & Domingue. (2008). *Situation-driven processes for semantic web services*. Paper presented at the 5th International Conference on Service Systems and Service Management (ICSSSM'08). Melbourne, Australia.

Diosteanu, A., & Cotfas. (2009). Agent based knowledge management solution using ontology, semantic web services and GIS. *Informatica Economică, 13*(4).

Domingue, J. Galizia, & Cabral. (2006). The choreography model for IRS-III. In *Proceedings of the 39th Hawaii International Conference on System Sciences*. IEEE.

Fu, X. Li, Guo, & He. (2003). Distributed configuration knowledge model. In *Proceedings of the 8th International Conference on Computer Supported Cooperative Work in Design*. IEEE.

Hepp, M. Leymann, Domingue, Wahler, & Fensel. (2005). Semantic business process management: A vision towards using semantic web services for business process management. In *Proceedings of the 2005 IEEE International Conference on e-Business Engineering (ICEBE'05)*. IEEE.

Howard, R., & Kerschberg. (2004). A knowledge-based framework for dynamic semantic web services brokering and management. In *Proceedings of the 15th International Workshop on Database and Expert Systems Applications (DEXA'04)*. DEXA.

Khalili, A. Badrabadi, & Khoshalhan. (2008). A framework for distributed market place based on intelligent software agents and semantic web services. In *Proceedings of the 2008 IEEE Congress on Services*. IEEE.

Khan, M. T. Zia, Daudpota, Hussain, & Taimoor. (2006). *Integrating context-aware pervasive environments*. Paper presented at the 2nd International Conference on Emerging Technologies. Peshawar, Pakistan.

Lo, M., & Gandon. (2007). *Semantic web services in corporate memories*. Paper presented at the Second International Conference on Internet and Web Applications and Services (ICIW'07). New York, NY.

Martin, D. Paolucci, McIlraith, Burstein, McDermott, McGuinness, ... Sycara. (2004). Bringing semantics to web services: The OWL-S approach. In *Proceedings of the First International Workshop on Semantic Web Services and Web Process Composition (SWSWPC 2004)*. San Diego, CA: SWSWPC.

McIlraith, S., Son, & Zeng. (2001). Semantic web services. *IEEE Intelligent Systems*, *16*(2), 46–53. doi:10.1109/5254.920599.

Ni, J., Jiu, Y., & Ni. (2010). A practical development of knowledge management model for petrochemical product family. In *Proceedings of the 2011 International Conference on Information Management, Innovation Management and Industrial Engineering*. IEEE.

Paolucci, M., & Sycara. (2003). Autonomous semantic web services. *IEEE Internet Computing*, *7*(5), 34–41. doi:10.1109/MIC.2003.1232516.

Pedrinaci, C. Domingue, Brelage, van Lessen, Karastoyanova, & Leymann. (2008). Semantic business process management: Scaling up the management of business processes. In *Proceedings of the IEEE International Conference on Semantic Computing* (pp. 546-553). IEEE.

Rajasekaran, P. Miller, Verma, & Sheth. (2004). Enhancing web services description and discovery to facilitate composition. In *Proceedings of SWSWPC 2004*, (pp. 55-68). SWSWPC.

Remli, K., & Deris, B. (2012). *Automated biological pathway knowledge retrieval based on semantic web services composition and AI planning*. Paper presented at the International Conference on Information Retrieval & Knowledge Management. Kuala Lumpur, Malaysia.

Woelk, D., & Lefrere. (2002). Technology for performance-based lifelong learning. In *Proceedings of the International Conference on Computers in Education (ICCE'02)*. ICCE.

Wu, D. Parsia, Sirin, Hendler, & Nau. (2003). Automating DAML-S web services composition using SHOP2. In *Proceedings International Semantic Web Conference (ISWC)* (LNCS), (vol. 2342). Berlin: Springer.

Wu, K. C., & Chiu. (2008). Toward tourist service integration and personalization with semantic web services: A case study in Hong Kong. In *Proceedings of the IEEE International Conference on e-Business Engineering*. IEEE.

Chapter 4
Knowledge–Based Code Clone Approach in Embedded and Real–Time Systems

Anupama Surendran
Cochin University of Science and Technology, India

Philip Samuel
Cochin University of Science and Technology, India

ABSTRACT

Even though human beings are using computers in their day-to-day activities, the terms embedded and real-time systems have received much attention only in the last few years, and they have become an inevitable part of our daily activities. The most evident and highlighted feature of embedded systems is the consideration of time. The significance of time constraints in designing each and every feature of embedded systems has made the software and hardware of embedded systems more complicated and entirely different from ordinary systems. Due to these reasons, several challenges exist in developing and maintaining embedded and real time software. Increase in complexity of the embedded system code increases the chance of occurrence of defects in the embedded software. Failure to deliver the software within the stipulated time, economic constraints faced during the development and the maintenance phase, inadequate testing, design of improper code and its reuse are some of the issues faced during the embedded system software development phase. In this chapter, the authors suggest a knowledge-based approach in managing the issues that arise during the coding and testing phase of embedded and real-time software. Program slicing is used to detect the code clones present in the embedded software, and a knowledge repository of code clones is created. This code clone knowledge repository is utilized during the coding and testing phase of real-time and embedded software, which in turn improves the whole software development process.

DOI: 10.4018/978-1-4666-4229-4.ch004

INTRODUCTION TO REAL-TIME AND EMBEDDED SYSTEMS

As the software industry is improving day by day, the competition among software companies have also increased. Improving the software quality and productivity improves the software development process and this in turn may help the software companies to manage the competition faced in software industry. Embedded systems are influencing our daily life activities due to their unique properties. In other words, it has become almost impossible for human beings to live without using embedded system applications. For example, the working of most of the household applications like television, washing machine etc. are based on the embedded chips present in them. The communication system of the world is also dependent on embedded chips present in them. Similarly in

public transport vehicles like bus, trains etc. embedded processors are present, which controls their working. In effect, embedded systems is having a significant role today's world (Heath, 1991).

Embedded systems are computing systems with tightly coupled hardware and software integration, which are designed to perform a dedicated function. They can be either stand-alone systems or they will be dependent systems. In standalone type of embedded system, they can work as an independent unit whereas in independent embedded systems, they can do the designated task. Nowadays it has almost become impossible to find a real life application which does not involve embedded application. Some household applications which use embedded chips for their smooth working are shown in Figure 1. Figure 2 shows how embedded systems enable communication across various networks.

Figure 1. Household applications using embedded systems

Figure 2. Communication between embedded systems across network

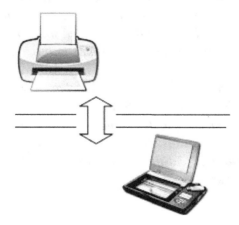

An Embedded system can be defined as a microprocessor based control system, which processes a fixed set of programmed instructions to control the operation of an electromechanical system, which in turn may be a part of a large system. The word 'embedded' itself denotes that the device will be mostly embedded or placed inside a larger device or any industrial equipment.

In real-time systems, the functioning depends not only on the output produced by the system, but also on the time constraints defined by the system. Even if correct output values are produced by real-time after the specified time slot, then their output is considered invalid. There are mainly two types of real-time systems. They are hard real-time systems and soft real-time systems. In soft real-time systems, time is not a critical factor which affects the performance of the system. On the other hand in hard real-time systems, time constraint is a critical factor and the results produced after the specified time slot is considered invalid. In real-time systems the system should respond to a stimulus within the specified time constraint. A periodic stimulus occurs at a predefined time interval and aperiodic stimulus occurs at uncertain time intervals.

In Real-time embedded system a combination of embedded system properties and real-time properties are present. Anyway all embedded systems may not have real-time properties and all real-time systems may not be embedded in

nature. Figure 3 shows the picture of a real-time embedded system. Real-time embedded systems can be processor based, micro-controller based, DSP based or a general processor based embedded system with predefined time constraints. Some of the examples of real-time embedded systems are nuclear control system, aircraft navigation system, defense system, medical equipment etc. (Kopetz, n.d.) The processor used in real-time embedded systems should be easily flexible, upgradeable, and maintainable. During the design of real-time embedded system factors like cost, memory, reliability, power consumption etc. should be considered.

One of the major issues faced during the software development phase of embedded and real time software is the length of the source code (Hennell, Hedley, & Riddell, 1987). This makes difficulty in managing, testing the program code, and understanding the code for re-engineering etc. These problems become more significant during the maintenance phase of the software development life cycle. It may not be practical for the developer to go through the whole source code line by line to understand the whole program. In some situation there may not be even proper documentation present. We have discussed such a situation, where a knowledge based process may be used to alleviate these problems faced by embedded and real time software. Using knowledge based approach during the coding and testing of

Figure 3. Real-time embedded system

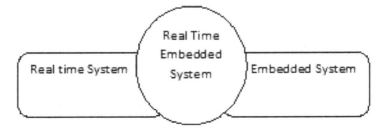

embedded and real time software improves the software development process. We have suggested making a code clone repository which acts as a knowledge base during the coding and testing of embedded and real time software which is discussed in the forthcoming sections.

NEED FOR KNOWLEDGE BASED CODE CLONE REPOSITORY IN REAL TIME AND EMBEDDED SYSTEM APPLICATIONS

Whenever possible, the software developers should not write the program code from the scratch, provided the code already exists. This results in waste of time and effort. In other words, the software developer should try to reuse the existing code, reuse library functions, reuse test cases etc. which is already available. The concept of code clones is derived from this idea. A code clone is defined as a set of program statements which may be contiguous or non-contiguous and this repeats in several other parts of the same program or in different parts of the same program or in different files of the same application program. Some researchers claim that software code clone increases the software maintenance cost. For example, if a programmer makes any slight modification in a code clone, and if the same change is not made in the other code clones present in the program, it may cause inconsistency. Even though there are many issues related with the maintenance of software code clones in a program, proper detection of code clones in each and every stage of software development and utilizing the positive aspects of code clones in an appropriate way may result in marked changes in the field of real-time software development industry (Surendran, Samuel, & Jacob, 2011, pp. 1050-1055). Many of our day-to-day computer applications take advantage of the code reuse property. The main reason behind this code reuse mentality is to make the software development process easier rather than writing the source code from scratch. For example, consider a situation in which a set of program statements repeats in several other parts of source code. The developer may record or store these, so that this knowledge base may be referred by other programmers during the software maintenance, re-engineering phase etc. The set of repeating statement may be converted to a function form or they may be stored as library routines in the knowledge base. When these statements are required in later situations, they may be selected from the knowledge repository. Apart from this point, during the coding phase of embedded and real time system, the length of the program code is a significant factor, which affects the performance of the system. The software developer should make a note of this point because, the size of the embedded chip may not be increased beyond a certain limit and within the specified embedded chip size and capacity, the developer should be able to in cooperate all the required software code. In such situations, repeated program statements may be substituted by calling appropriate functions which contains the concerned functionality. Therefore creating a knowledge repository of code clones is inevitable in embedded software development process. An overview of using knowledge based code clone repository in embedded system is shown in Figure 4.

Definition: Code Clones

Consider a set of program statements 'CLN'. Another set of program statements 'CLNc' can be considered as a code clone of 'CLN', if they contain the same set of program statements or if they have some similar properties up to certain extend. In order to check the degree of similar-

Figure 4. Using knowledge based code clone repository in embedded & real time software deveopment process

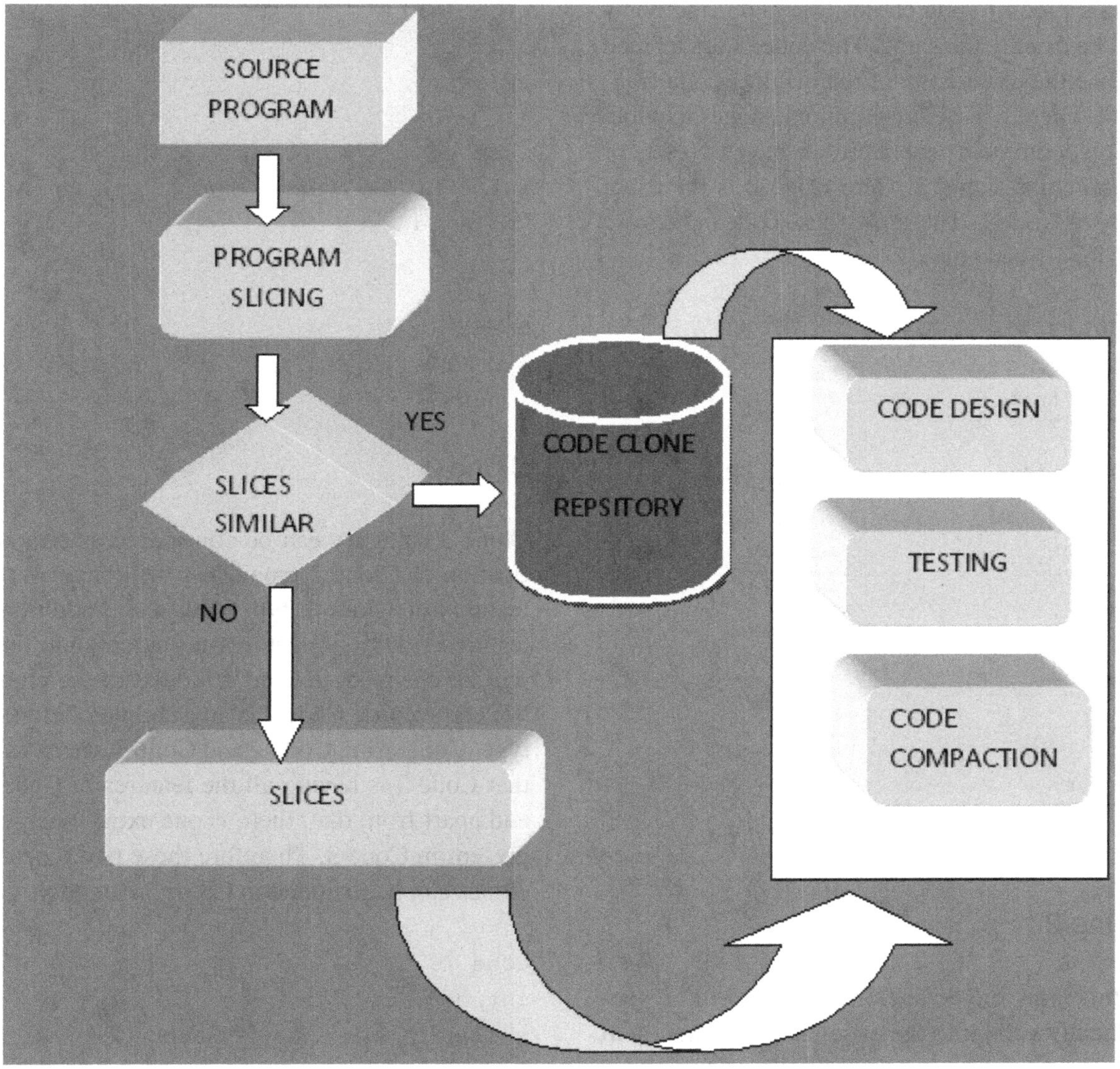

ity which exists between code fragments 'CLN' and 'CLNc', we have to categorize the clones according to their behavioral properties (Roy & Cordy, 2007).

Code Clone Categories

There are mainly four types of code clones. They are Clone 1, Clone 2, Clone 3, and Clone 4. Each of these is explained below (Krinke, 2007).

Clone 1

In this type of code clones, the code fragments will be exactly the same. The code clone formed will be the exact copy of the original code fragment. There will be some minor changes in white spaces, comments etc. Here we have two sets of code named 1 and 2. Here Code 2 is the exact copy of Code 1. Therefore these code clones are in Clone 1 category.

```
Code1:
int p=0, q=1, r=5;
while (r > 0)
{
p= p + r;
q=q* r;
r= r-1;
}
Code 2:-
int p=0, q=1, r=5;
while (r > 0)
{
p= p + r;
q=q* r;
r= r-1;
}
```

Clone 2

In this type, the code clone formed will be syntactically similar to the original code. There will be changes in the name of identifiers, functions, literals etc. along with minor variations in white spaces, comments etc. Here we can see that Code 2 is similar to Code 1. The main difference is the change in the variable names. Therefore, these two types of clones can be included in Clone 2 category.

```
Code 1:
int p=0, q=1, r=5;
```

```
while (r > 0)
{
p= p + r;
q=q* r;
r= r-1;
}
Code 2:
int c=0, b=1, d=5;
while (d > 0)
{
c=c+d;
b=b*d;
d=d-1;
}
```

Clone 3

Clone 3 category can be considered as a modification of Clone 2 type. They will have all the features of Clone 2 type with some additional features. Additional features means that some lines will be changed, deleted or added to the clone. We can see that Code 2 is an example of clone 2 type. Comparing Code 2 and Code 3, we can see that Code 3 is having all the features of Code 2 and apart from that, there is one extra statement present in Code 3. Therefore these two types of clones can be included in Clone 3 category.

```
Code 2:
int c=0, b=1, d=5;
while (d > 0)
{
c=c+d;
b=b*d;
d=d-1;
}
Code 3:
int c=0, b=1, d=5, e=0;
while (d > 0)
{
c=c+d;
```

```
b=b*d;
e=c+d;
d=d-1;
}
```

Clone 4

This type of clones will have entirely different syntax and there will be no similarity between the program text or program lines. Even though they differ syntactically, their functionality remains the same. Here Code 1 and Code 2 are syntactically not similar, but their behavior is the same. Therefore, these two can be considered as Clone 4 type.

```
Code 1:
int x, y, z;
z=0;
while (x>0)
{
z=z+p;
x=x-1;
}
Code 2:
int t, u, v;
v=0;
while (t<0)
{
v= v-p;
t=t+1;
}
```

Using Program Slicing to Construct Knowledge-Based Code Clone Repository

In this section, we have discussed the need of program slicing in detecting code clones in real-time systems. Code clones are to be detected from the program source code. It may not be always practical to check the whole program, which may contain thousands of lines of code to find the presence of code clones or to find the set of similar program statements. The program tester may be interested only in particular parts or function of the source program which is supposed to perform certain important tasks. In such a scenario, it is not advisable to analyze the program lines one by one as this will only cause unnecessary waste of time and effort. Program slicing can be used in such situations (Gallagher & Binkley, 2008, pp. 58-67). Instead of analyzing the whole program, slicing converge the focus to some specific program parts implied by the slicing criterion. The structural similarity of the control flow graphs which are constructed for the various slices in the program are used to identify the code clones. Sliced statements also identify the variable dependencies between the different variables present in the program.

Program Slicing

Weiser introduced program slicing in 1979 and his work encouraged many theoretical and empirical research works in this field (Weiser, 1984, pp. 352-357). Deleting all the statements from a program which cannot affect the values of variable of interest is known as slicing. Program slice does not contain all the statements in a program. So the original program is the superset of the corresponding program slice. Slicing is done with respect to a set of variables in a program and this consists of slice set. This subset of the original program is very useful in the field of testing real-time program. There are mainly two types of slicing. They are static and dynamic slicing.

Static Slicing

A static slice is put up by removing those parts of the program that are unrelated to the list of values stored in a selected set of variables at the selected point (Samuel & Surendran, 2010, pp. 270-274).

The point is usually denoted by a statement number. Therefore the parameters of static slice contain a slice variable and a statement number. This is also known slicing criterion and it is denoted as C= (s, v). If 'v' is a variable and 's' is the statement number or the point of interest, then a slice can be constructed for v at s Consider the set of statements given in Sample 1given below. Here if the value of 'count' is initialized as 5, we can see that the final value or the resultant value of 'total' is correct and the value of 'result' is wrong. The value of result will be always zero. In order to find the defect in the program code we can apply static slicing to the variable 'result'. Since the value of 'total' is correct, there is no need to perform slicing with respect to 'total'. Performing slicing with respect to 'result' will help to find the error and thus we can debug the errors. Here the slicing criterion is specified as C= (11, result).

Sample 1

```
1.  cin>>count;
2.  total=0;
3.  result=0;
4.  while(count>0)
5.  {
6.  total=total+ count;
7.  result= result * count;
8.  count= count -1;
9.  }
10. count<< total;
11. count<< result;
Static Slices for criterion C= (11,
result)
1.  cin>>count;
3.  result=0;
4.  while(count>0)
5.  {
7.  result= result * count;
8.  count= count -1;
9.  }
```

Here we can see that the static slice obtained is smaller and simpler than the source program. The static slice for Sample 1 contains all the statements which affect the value of the variable 'result' at statement number 11. This helps in identifying the potential statements which may contain error and which in turn affect the value of the variable 'result'. The statement 'result=0' is initialized wrongly and because of this wrong initialization, the final value of result was incorrect. Thus the error can be corrected.

Dynamic Slicing

Even though static slices gives all possible executions, the size of static slices obtained are very large and may cause difficulties in some situations. There will not be even any significant reduction in the number of statements present in the static slice compared to the original program. In such situations, performing static slicing causes mere waste of time and effort. Due to this uncertain nature of static slices, Korel and Laski in 1988 introduced the dynamic slicing concept (Korel & Laski, 1988, pp. 155-163). Runtime information about a program is used in dynamic slices. In dynamic slicing criterion there are three parameters. The first two parameters are same which we used in static slicing criterion. The first parameter is the statement number or the point of interest with respect to which the slicing is to be performed, the second parameter is the variable with respect to which the slicing is to be performed and the third and final parameter is the input value for which the program is executed. These three parameters are collectively known as dynamic slicing criterion. It is denoted by C= (s, v, i) where's' is the statement number, 'v' is the variable and 'i' is the input value. Consider the program code given in Sample 2 given below.

Sample 2

```
1. cin>>count;
2. total=0;
3. result=0;
4. while(count>0)
5. {
6. total=total+ count;
7. result= result * count;
8. count= count -1;
9.}
10. count<< total;
11. count<< result;
```

We can construct a dynamic slice of Sample 2 for the variable 'result' and the point of interest can be taken as the end of the program. Here the input value for variable 'count' is taken as zero.

```
Dynamic Slice of Sample 2 for Crite-
rion C = (Result, 11, Count=0)
3. result=0;
```

Detecting Code Clones in Embedded and Real-Time Systems from Slices

In the above section we saw an overview of slicing techniques. After obtaining the slices, the next step is to analyze the slices to detect the presence of code clones. Either static or dynamic slicing is selected and consider that here we are applying static slicing to the real-time program code which results in a set of statements. The next step is to construct the control flow graph of the slices obtained. We are mainly considering the structural similarity present in the CGF to identify the code clones. Figure 5 shows the control flow graph obtained as a result of static slicing on a real time program and it is named as Set I. Figure 6 shows the control flow graph of the obtained as a result of static slicing on the same real time program,

Figure 5. CFG of set 1

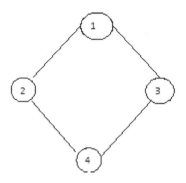

Figure 6. CFG of set 2

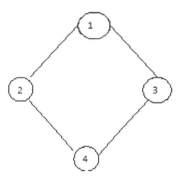

but for a different slicing criteria. This is named as Set II. Here it can be noticed that the control flow graphs of Set I and Set II are the same.

Here we are checking whether the CFG of Set 1 and Set 2 are isomorphic graphs or not. Two graphs, G= {V, E} and G1= {V, E} are said to be isomorphic graphs if there exists one-to-one correspondence between their vertices and between their edges such that the incidence relationship is preserved. Suppose that an edge 'e' has end vertices V1 and V2 in G, then the corresponding edge 'e' in 'G1' must be incident on vertices V11 and V12 that correspond to V1 and V2 respectively. Here both the control flow graphs satisfy these properties. Here both the graphs of Set I and Set II have the same number of vertices, same number of edges and same degree sequence.

Therefore these two control graphs can be regarded as code clones.

After detecting the code clones from the control flow graph, the next step is to check the nodes of each graph. We are checking each and every node of the two code clones. Checking the node contents of the graph to detect code clones is compulsory because, in some scenarios the control flow graph may be similar even though the contents of the node differ. This is due to the presence of false positives in the detection of code clones. If all the nodes of both the graphs are equal, this indicates that the slices are code clones.

Benefits of using Program Slicing-Based Code Clone Detection in Embedded and Real Time Systems

Using program slicing in code clone detection in real-time system has the following benefits:

- Avoids unnecessary program checking.
- Avoids unnecessary coding for similar program statements.
- Gives the relevant parts of the program.
- Slices give dependence information between the program variables.
- Interpreting of node values in Code Clones strengthens the code clone detection technique.

Construction of Knowledge-Based Repository of Code Clones

As we got an idea of identifying code clones from program slices, the next step is to create a knowledge base of code clones. For this the first step is to make a documentation of the available code clones. Search facility for this document should be enabled so as to locate the required clone from document. If the similar program statements are converted to a function form, the documentation should provide a clear explanation of the task performed by the function. Similarly, the program statements which form the library routines should be given proper explanation. The developer may now search the document to find any function or routine which may be applied during the process of new software development, maintenance of software etc.

USING KNOWLEDGE-BASED CODE CLONE REPOSITORY IN EMBEDDED AND REAL-TIME TESTING

In the above section, we saw how to detect code clones using program slicing. In this section, we will have a glance of real time and embedded system testing methods and the advantages of using knowledge base code clone repository in testing. As a real-time embedded system should respond according to the time constraints, a failure to do so can result in a big havoc. It can create even life threatening situations in several scenarios. The only possible solution to avoid real-time system failure is to test it properly. Testing is one of the most difficult tasks in real-time systems and it consumes nearly 50% of the total project development time and effort. Real-time testing differs from ordinary testing because the working of real-time systems is time dependent and the main goal of testing is to find errors, fix the errors so that the overall performance of the system is improved.

Testing Techniques

In real-time systems, we are mainly having two types of testing. They are black-box and white box testing.

Black-Box Testing

In black-box testing, no analysis is made about the nature of the code used to develop the system. The only information available will be the set of inputs and outputs. The programmer will have a set of inputs and the goal is to check whether the outputs are produced correctly according to the input specification.

For example in a car, there will be a fuel indicator. As the level of fuel decreases, some indication should be shown and this is performed at specific time interval. Here the input data is the fuel and time and the output is the warning. In this type of testing, the tester is not supposed to know how the software is programmed to generate the output value for the corresponding input value.

White-Box Testing

In white-box testing the tester should analyze the software code and should check the logic of the program. Usually a path based testing approach is used here. In real-time white box testing, mainly two subdivisions are there. They are static testing and dynamic testing.

Static Testing

In static testing the source code is checked line by line to identify the errors in the program. In this type of testing there is no need of program execution. An example of static testing is a vehicle automation program, where all the lines are checked line by line to identify whether the logic is correct or not.

Dynamic Testing

This type of testing is based on program execution. Here the goal is to check whether the program is working correctly for specific test cases. For example in a vehicle automation program for fuel indication, if there are five options, the programmer has to check whether the program is working correctly for all these five options based on the test case value for each option.

Benefit of using Code Clone Repository in White-Box Testing

As the working of real-time systems is based on strict time constraints, ensuring the quality of real-time systems is a critical task especially in the case of high risk applications like nuclear reactors, rocket propulsion etc. Any failure in the working of such systems may cause danger to human life. Therefore, automated testing of real time deserves a significant role. Among black-box and white-box testing methods, it is always better to use white-box method for testing real-time systems and this is due to the fact that, in black-box testing, an overview of the source code is not revealed. Anyhow, this is not universally established till now.

During the white-box testing of real-time program, one of major problems faced by the tester is the large size of the source code and the program tester should keep this point in mind to develop an effective testing method. In testing, the general strategy is to identify the part source code and to trace the cause of errors. It is a difficult task for the program tester to sit and analyze each and every line of source code to detect the errors present in a program and it may be impossible in some situations if the program is extremely large. Therefore during the testing phase, the programmer may identify the statements of interest using program slicing. The slices are analyzed to get the test sequences from the slices. If the tester finds a test case for a particular loop present in the program, and if this loop repeats in several other program locations, there is no need to design test case again for the repeated loop. For similar loop structures, the same test case may be applicable. The programmer may refer the code clone repository to see whether any code clones are present, so that if a test case is once found for code clone, then there is no need to find the test case for similar code. This in turn simplifies the real time testing process. To conclude, using code clone repository and program slicing in testing may have the following benefits:

- Avoids unnecessary program checking.
- Avoid multiple test case generation for similar code.
- Simplifies testing process.
- Gives relevant parts of the program.

KNOWLEDGE-BASED CODE CLONE REPOSITORY IN CODE COMPACTION OF REAL-TIME SYSTEMS

Real-time embedded systems are hard to design as several factors like cost, power consumption etc. should be considered. According to Moore's Law, the transistor density of semiconductor chips would double roughly every 18 months. This affects the embedded chip design. Therefore while designing the real-time embedded system, care should be taken to reduce the size of the silicon chip used inside the embedded system processor. If the chip size increases, the cost will also increase. We have suggested a solution to this problem by incorporating some features in the embedded system program code. In order to reduce the size of embedded system program code, code compaction is to be performed and procedural abstraction enables code compaction. Moreover, code compaction enables design reuse. Similar statements may be stored as code clones and this collection may be referred as a knowledge base. After identify the code clones present in the program code, they can be replaced by some subroutine or function call in the original program. This in turn reduces

the program size and the required code clones may be selected from the knowledge repository without developing them from the scratch. . In this chapter, we have already discussed how code clones assists in program testing and the method of detecting code clones using program slicing. Program slicing is used to detect the code clones which in turn are used to implement the code compaction process.

BENEFITS OF USING KNOWLEDGE-BASED CODE CLONES IN REAL-TIME AND EMBEDDED SYSTEMS

To sum up, using knowledge based code clone repository in real-time and embedded systems has the following benefits:

1. Optimal design
   a. Code compaction
      i. By procedural abstraction.
   b. Design reuse
2. Program Testing
   a. Identify similar code.
   b. Same test sequence for code clones.
3. Program understanding
   a. Splitting the program into subcomponents using code clone detection and slicing.

CONCLUSION

Real-time and embedded systems have deeply influenced our life activities to a great extent. We have explained some of the basic aspects of real-time and embedded system coding and testing. Some of the major issues involved in real time testing and coding have been discussed and we have explained how to solve these issues using knowledge based repository of code clones. A detailed explanation of creating code clone repository using program slicing is also explained. We have also highlighted the significance of knowledge based approach in embedded and real time software design.

FUTURE WORK AND RESEARCH DIRECTIONS

As discussed in this chapter, embedded and real-time coding and testing is one of the most important phases of real-time software development. Here we have discussed some of the issues involved in testing and coding of real-time system and the need of program slicing in creating knowledge based repository of code clones. Significance of using knowledge based code clone repository is explained. Here we have discussed only the software aspects of real-time and embedded system. In future, we wish to explore the hardware aspects of real-time systems and the role of knowledge based code clone repository to improve the hardware design of embedded and real-time systems.

REFERENCES

Gallagher, K., & Binkley, D. (2008), Program slicing. In Proceedings of Frontier of Software Maintenance, (pp. 58-67). Frontier of Software Maintenance.

Heath, W. S. (1991). *Real-time software techniques*. New York: Van Nostrand Reinhold.

Hennell, M. A., Hedley, D., & Riddell, I. J. (1987). Automated testing techniques for real-time embedded software. In *Proceedings of the European Software Engineering Conference ESEC '87*. Strasbourg, France: ESEC.

Kopetz, H. (n.d.). *Real-time systems, design principles for distributed embedded applications*. Dordrecht, The Netherlands: Kluwer Academic Publishers.

Korel, B., & Laski, J. (1988, October). Dynamic program slicing. *Information Processing Letters*, 155–163. doi:10.1016/0020-0190(88)90054-3.

Krinke, J. (2007). A study of consistent and inconsistent changes to code clones. In *Proceedings of WCRE*. IEEE.

Roy, C. K., & Cordy, J. R. (2007). *A survey on software clone detection research* (Technical Report 541). Kingston, Canada: Queen's University.

Samuel, P., & Surendran, A. (2010). Forward slicing algorithm based test data generation. In *Proceedings of 3rd IEEE International Conference on Computer Science & Information Technology*. IEEE.

Surendran, A., Samuel, P., & Jacob, K. P. (2011). Code clones in program test sequence identification. In *Proceedings of World Congress on Information and Communication Technologies*. IEEE.

Weiser, M. (1984). Program slicing. *IEEE Transactions on Software Engineering*, *10*(4), 352–357. doi:10.1109/TSE.1984.5010248.

KEY TERMS AND DEFINITIONS

Code Clones: A set of program statements which may be contiguous or non-contiguous and which repeats in several other parts of the same program or in different parts of the same program or in different files of the same application program.

Embedded Systems: Embedded systems are computing systems with tightly coupled hardware and software integration, which are designed to perform a dedicated function.

Hard Real-Time Systems: Systems where time is considered as a critical factor and the performance of the system is affected by the time factor.

Program Slicing: Slicing is a process of deleting all the statements from a program, which cannot affect the value of variable of interest.

Real-Time Systems: In real-time systems, the functioning depends not only on the output produced by the system, but also on the time constraints defined by the system.

Soft Real-Time Systems: Systems where time is not considered as a critical factor and the performance of the system is not affected by the time factor.

Testing: Testing is a process of checking the program with an intention of finding errors in the program.

Section 2
Knowledge Management in Software Process

Chapter 5
Using Knowledge Management and Aggregation Techniques to Improve Web Effort Estimation

Emilia Mendes
Blekinge Institute of Technology, Sweden

Simon Baker
Cambridge University, UK

ABSTRACT

Effort estimation is one of the main pillars of sound project management as its accuracy can affect significantly whether projects will be delivered on time and within budget. However, due to being a complex domain, there are countless examples of companies that underestimate effort, and such estimation error can be of 30%-40% on average, thus leading to serious project management problems (Jørgensen & Grimstad, 2009). The contribution of this chapter is twofold: 1) to explain the knowledge management methodology employed to build industrial expert-based Web effort estimation models, such that other companies willing to develop such models can do so and 2) to provide a wider understanding on the fundamental factors affecting Web effort estimation and their relationships via a mechanism that partially aggregates the expert-based Web effort estimation models built.

INTRODUCTION

Effort estimation, the process by which effort is forecasted and used as basis to predict costs and to allocate resources effectively, is one of the main pillars of sound project management, given that

its accuracy can affect significantly whether projects will be delivered on time and within budget (Mendes et al., 2001). However, because it is a complex domain where corresponding decisions and predictions require reasoning with uncertainty, there are countless examples of companies that

DOI: 10.4018/978-1-4666-4229-4.ch005

underestimate effort. Jørgensen and Grimstad (2009) reported that such estimation error can be of 30%-40% on average, thus leading to serious project management problems.

Similarly to software effort estimation, most research in Web effort estimation has to date focused on solving companies' inaccurate effort predictions via investigating techniques that are used to build formal effort estimation models, in the hope that such formalization will improve the accuracy of estimates. They do so by assessing, and often also comparing, the prediction accuracy obtained from applying numerous statistical and artificial intelligence techniques to datasets of completed Web projects developed by industry, and sometimes also developed by students. A recent systematic literature review of Web resource estimation studies is given in (Azhar et al. 2012).

The variables characterizing such datasets are determined in different ways, such as via surveys (Mendes et al. 2005a), interviews with experts (Ruhe et al., 2003), expertise from companies (Ferrucci et al. 2008), a combination of research findings (Mendes et al. 2001), or even a researcher's own consulting experience (Reifer, 2000). In all of these instances, once variables are defined, a data gathering exercise takes place, obtaining data (ideally) from industrial projects volunteered by companies. Except when using research findings to inform variables' identification, invariably the mechanism employed to determine variables relies on experts' recalling, where the subjective measure of an expert's certainty is often their amount of experience estimating effort.

However, in addition to eliciting the important effort predictors (and optionally also their relationships), such mechanism does not provide the means to also quantify the uncertainty associated with these relationships and to validate the knowledge obtained. Why should these be important?

Our experience developing and validating several single-company expert-based Web effort prediction models that use a knowledge management methodology to incorporate the uncertainty

inherent in this domain (Mendes, 2012a) showed that the use of a structured iterative process in which factors and relationships are identified, quantified and validated (Mendes, 2011a; Mendes 2011b; Mendes et al., 2009) leads the participating companies to a much more thorough and deep understanding of their mental processes and their decisions when estimating effort, when compared to just the recalling of factors and their relationships. The iterative process we use employs Bayesian inference, which is one of the techniques employed in root cause analysis (Ammerman, 1998); therefore, it aims at a detailed analysis and understanding of a particular phenomenon of interest.

In all the case studies we conducted, the original set of factors and relationships initially elicited was always modified as the model evolved; this occurred as a result of applying a root cause analysis approach comprising a Bayesian inference mechanism and feedback into the analysis process via a model validation. In addition, post-mortem interviews with the participating companies showed that the understanding companies gained by being actively engaged in building those models led to both improved estimates and estimation processes (Mendes, 2012a, 2011a 2011b; Mendes et al., 2009).

We therefore contend that the aggregation of the diverse factors and relationships from these models into a single knowledge map brings several advantages over a simple compilation of factors from different lists provided by several companies, or the non-aggregation of factors and relationships, as follows:

- The recalling mechanism used in surveys and interviews to elicit the important factors when estimating effort (and also occasionally their relationships) does not provide any means for experts to understand thoroughly their own decision making processes via the quantification of the uncertainty part of that decision process, and the validation of the factors they suggested during the elicitation. This means that the list of factors elicited is based on a superficial process; therefore to compile a set of factors from different lists obtained from experts via superficial processes will simply lead to a set that is unlikely to genuinely portray the phenomenon under interest.

- The non aggregation from different experts of knowledge relating to the same phenomenon has the obvious drawback of missing out the opportunity to amplify and broaden our overall understanding of that phenomenon. For example, none of the four models used herein had individually more than 34 factors and 60 relationships; however, their aggregation led to the identification of 70 different factors and 158 relationships, thus providing a much richer way to understand the phenomenon of Web effort estimation than when only considering each model separately.

- The knowledge map resulting from the aggregation mechanism employed herein uses as input factors and relationships from models that were built and validated using a process based on a root cause analysis technique (Ammerman, 1998); such technique, by requiring a thorough and deep understanding of experts' mental processes and their decisions when estimating effort, provides the means to truly portray the phenomenon focus of this research, i.e. Web effort estimation.

- The use an aggregated knowledge map introduces more structure into the effort estimation process as such knowledge map can be used as a checklist to help improve judgment-based effort estimates (Jørgensen & Grimstad, 2009).

- Anecdotal evidence obtained throughout the elicitation process and post-mortem meetings with several companies revealed that the use of a knowledge map result-

ing from aggregating companies' expert knowledge with regard to factors and relationships relevant for Web effort estimation would be extremely useful to help them elicit factors and relationships when building their own Web effort prediction models; therefore they would like to use such aggregated knowledge map at the start of their elicitation process as means to help their recalling of factors and relationships.

- Our aggregated knowledge map shows graphically not only the set of factors and relationships from the input models, but also a way to identify visually the most common factors and relationships resulting from the aggregation. Such knowledge may also be useful to project managers to revisit the factors they consider when estimating effort for new projects.

- The aggregated knowledge map can be used to provide companies with a starting point to building a single-company expert-based Web effort estimation model. This approach is also suggested in (Jørgensen & Grimstad, 2009; Montironi et al., 1996).

The contribution of this chapter is therefore twofold: 1) to explain the knowledge management methodology that we have employed to build several industrial expert-based Web effort estimation models, such that other companies willing to develop such models can do so too. These models are used as input to the aggregation mechanism also discussed herein; and 2) to provide a wider understanding on the fundamental factors affecting Web effort estimation and their relationships via a mechanism that uses as input the factors and relationships from the expert-based Web effort estimation models.

Note that this research focuses on Web effort estimation because previous work has already shown that, in addition to other cost drivers that are also Web-specific (e.g. Web browser back-compatibility), there are legitimate differences in the way Web applications are sized when estimating effort, compared to conventional software (Mendes 2012b; Mendes et al., 2005a, 2001). A detailed discussion on this issue is provided in (Mendes et al., 2005b).

The remainder of this Chapter is to be organised as follows: the next Section will provide a detailed summary of a recent systematic literature review on Web resource estimation (where 85.7% of the studies are in Web effort estimation), followed by another Section that describes the knowledge management methodology used to build and validate each of the four expert-based single-company Web effort estimation models used in our aggregation. Next, we have two Sections that respectively discuss the aggregation of different structures of factors and relationships, and detail our proposed aggregation mechanism; they are followed by a subsequent Section describing how the aggregation mechanism was employed to combine the four knowledge maps. Finally, another three Sections present our results, threats to validity, and conclusions & comments on future work, respectively.

LITERATURE REVIEW ON WEB EFFORT RESOURCE ESTIMATION

This Section provides a detailed summary of a recent systematic literature review on Web resource estimation (Azhar et al., 2012). The large majority of studies reported in this review (85.7%) focused solely on Web effort estimation; therefore, we assume that the results being presented herein represent mostly the state of the art in the field of Web effort estimation.

To understand effort estimation for Web projects, previous studies have developed models that use as input, factors such as the size of a Web application, and cost drivers (e.g. tools, developer's quality, team size), and provide an effort estimate as output. The differences between these studies were the number and type of size measures used, choice of cost drivers and occasionally the techniques employed to build resource estimation models.

Mendes and Counsell (2000) were the first, back in 2000, to investigate this field by using machine-learning techniques with data from student-based Web projects, and size measures harvested late in the project's life cycle. Mendes and collaborators also carried out a series of consecutive studies (e.g. (Mendes & Kitchenham, 2004; Mendes et al., 2001, 2003, 2005b) where models were built using multivariate regression and machine-learning techniques using data on industrial Web projects. Recently they also proposed and validated size measures harvested early in the project's life cycle, and therefore better suited to resource estimation (Mendes et al. 2005a).

Other researchers have also investigated resource estimation for Web projects, and some examples are as follows: Reifer (2000) proposed an extension of the COCOMO model, and a single size measure harvested late in the project's life cycle. None were validated empirically. This size measure was later used by Ruhe et al. (2003), who further extended a software engineering hybrid estimation technique to Web projects, using a small data set of industrial projects, mixing expert judgement and multivariate regression. Later, Baresi et al. (2002), and Mangia and Paiano (2003) investigated effort estimation models and size measures for Web projects based on a specific Web development method, namely the W2000. Finally, Costagliola et al. (2006) compared two types of Web-based size measures for effort estimation.

Given that Web development is a rapidly growing industry (Azhar et al., 2012), it is important to obtain a detailed account of the state of the art in this field in order to inform interested practitioners and researchers. Motivated by such need, Azhar et al. (2012) have recently carried out a systematic literature review of Web Resource Estimation. They chose to carry out a systematic literature review, as opposed to just a subjective literature review, because a systematic review is a method that enables the evaluation and interpretation of all accessible research relevant to a research question, subject matter, or event of interest (Kitchenham 2007).

A total of 84 studies were selected, after employing 11 different databases/search engines to search for related literature in Web resource estimation.

The systematic literature review addressed three main areas relating to Web resource estimation research, as follows:

1. The techniques used for Web resource estimation.
2. What resource facets have been investigated and the predictors considered.
3. The characteristics of the datasets used in the empirical research.

Tables 1 to 3 provide summaries respectively for each of the main areas abovementioned. Please refer to Azhar et al. (2012) for more detailed tables and results.

A range of techniques have been used, which include expert judgment, various algorithmic and

Table 1. Estimation method/technique used for web resource estimation

Estimation Method/Technique	%
Case based reasoning (CBR)	34.5
Stepwise regression	34.5
Linear regression	23.8
Bayesian networks	10.7
Classification and regression trees (CART)	6.0
Support vector regression	6.0
Expert judgment	4.8
Web-COBRA	4.8
Custom	13.1
Mean estimation	20.2
Median estimation	22.6
Other	16.7
No estimation method/technique	6.0

Table 2. Resource facets and predictors investigated in the studies

Resource Facet Investigated	%	Resource Predictors	%
Design	3.6	Size: Length	50.0
Quality	3.6	Size: Functionality	32.1
Maintenance	6.0	Size: Reusability	21.4
Size	1.2	Complexity	34.5
Cost/Effort	85.7	Cost Drivers	19.0
		Tukutuku	32.1
		Other	4.8
		No predictors investigated	1.2

Table 3. Domain and Type of dataset used in the studies

Domain	%	Type	%
Industry	69.0	Cross-company	53.4
Academia	33.3	Single-company	50.0
Not specified	1.2		

machine learning techniques, as well as those that fall into more than one category. Estimation accuracy forms the basis for evaluating these techniques, and a number of numerical and graphical measures of accuracy were employed most of which using as basis the absolute residual (Mendes & Kitchenham, 2004).

Results showed that within the domain of Web resource estimation, work has been done on effort/cost, design, quality, maintenance, and size estimation, where the main focus has been on development effort/cost estimation with only 14.4% of the primary studies centring on other resource facets. In addition, out of the three studies focusing on quality estimation and out of the five studies dealing with maintenance estimation, only one and two provided an accuracy assessment respectively. Such lack of accuracy assessment limits their usefulness for practitioners looking to undertake quality or maintenance estimation.

Size measures have historically been considered as key predictors of effort. This still holds true with length, reusability, and functionality size measures being seen in 69% of the selected primary studies. In addition, given that size measures are included amongst the Tukutuku variables (Mendes et al. 2005a), results show that, except for one study, every single primary study that investigates resource predictors considered size measures as predictors of resource estimation.

Most of the research done to date in Web resource estimation employed predictors that presented an association with the resource facet being estimated, without assuming that this association was of the type cause and effect. However, there were some exceptions (studies using Bayesian nets and Web-COBRA), which used predictors that had a cause and effect relationship with the resource facet being estimated. These predictors were usually expert-based.

The review also showed that industry datasets were more frequently used than academic datasets, where such industry datasets contained either data from a single company (single company dataset), or from numerous companies (cross-company dataset). Estimates from single company datasets appeared to be superior to those from cross-company datasets, which corresponds to findings from prior research that has been done on single versus cross-company estimates, in both Web and general software resource estimation (Kitchenham et al. 2006). Single company datasets are smaller than their cross-company counterparts, of which the Tukutuku database is the largest and most often used.

The results from the systematic review showed that several estimation techniques have been employed, with no single technique providing the best accuracy results overall. In addition, most work focused on development effort/cost estimation, with little done on areas such as quality or maintenance effort estimation.

The lack of consensus on the best Web resource estimation techniques could be due to a number of reasons, such as (Azhar et al., 2012): choice of resource predictors and accuracy measures, dataset characteristics, and type of cross-validation employed, to name a few.

Overall, none of the previous studies used data to build their predictions models gathered using any form of root cause analysis mechanism. The very few studies that represented in some way or the other the uncertainty inherent to effort estimation did not do so based on experts' tacit knowledge. These two points are two of the main drivers for the research detailed herein.

EXPERT-BASED SINGLE-COMPANY WEB EFFORT ESTIMATION MODELS

The factors and relationships that were aggregated herein are part of four different expert-based Web effort estimation models created using a technique called Bayesian Network (BN). This Section introduces this technique by briefly explaining the process employed to build each of the Web effort estimation models. Further details on this process are given in (Mendes et al. 2009).

A BN is a model that enables the characterization of a knowledge domain in terms of its factors, their relationships, and the uncertainty inherent to that domain. How each is characterized is detailed next.

A BN has two parts (Mendes et al. 2009). The first part, known as the qualitative part of a BN, results in a graphical structure comprised of the factors and causal relationships identified as fundamental in the domain being modelled. This structure is depicted by a Directed Acyclic Graph (DAG) (see Figure 1a). In addition to identifying factors and relationships, this part also includes the identification of the states (values) that each factor should take (e.g. Small [1 to 5], Medium [6 to 15], Large [16+] in Figure 1a).

The second part of a BN is the quantitative part, where the relationships identified in the qualitative part are quantified probabilistically.

Figure 1. Parts of a Bayesian network model

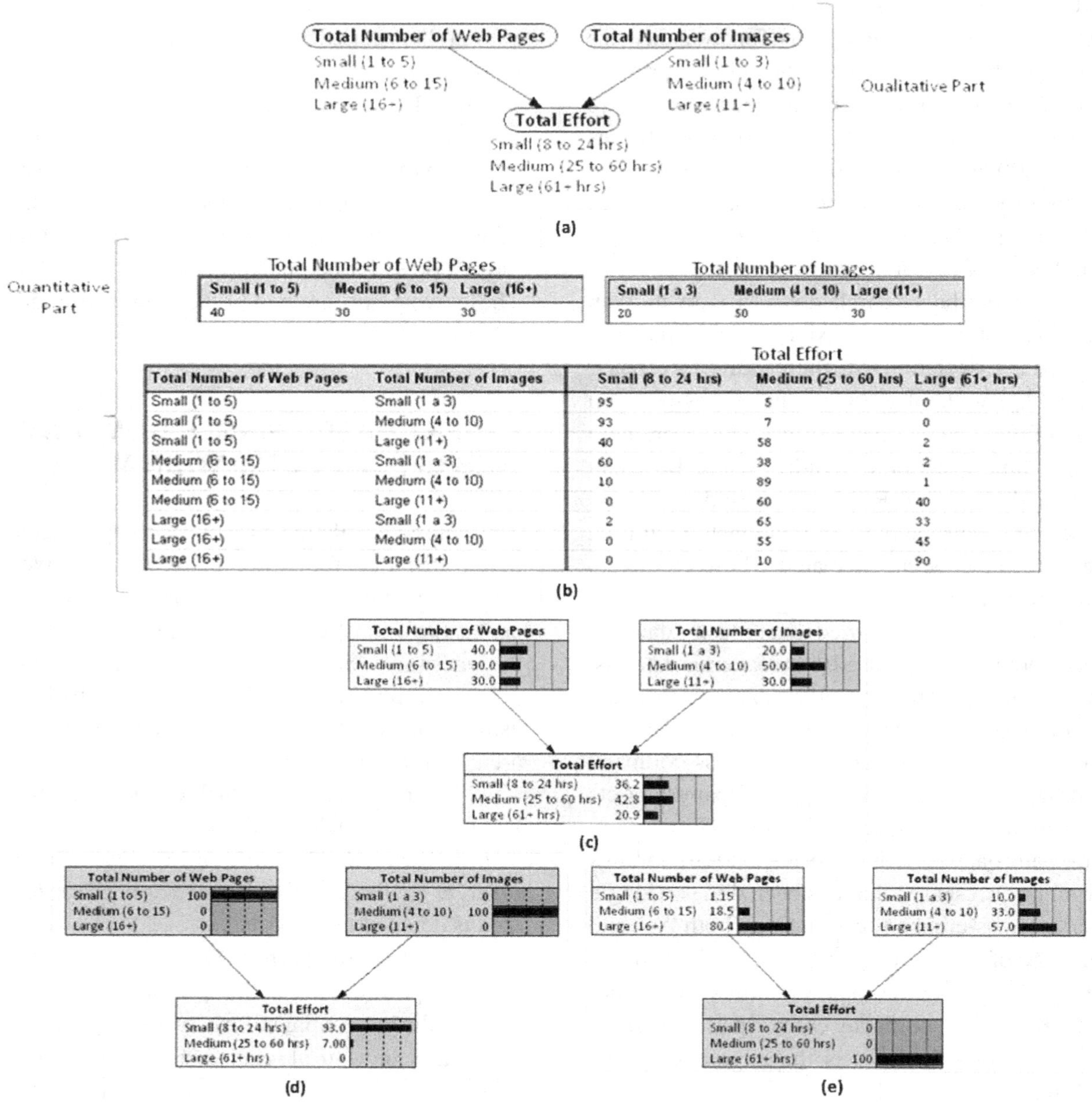

This quantification is represents the uncertainty in the domain being modelled. In order to enable this quantification, a Conditional Probability Table (CPT) is associated to each node in the graph. A parent node's CPT describes the relative probability of each state (value) (Figure 1b CPTs for nodes 'Total Number of Web pages' and 'To-

tal Number of Images'); a child node's CPT describes the relative probability of each state conditional on every combination of states of its parents (Figure 1b CPT for node 'Total Effort'). Each row in a CPT represents a conditional probability distribution and therefore its values sum up to one [3]. Such probabilities can be attained via expert elicitation, automatically from data, from existing literature, or using a combination of these. Within the context of this work all probabilities were obtained via expert elicitation.

Once both qualitative and quantitative parts are specified, the BN is validated using data on past finished projects, where one project at a time is entered as evidence (see Figure 1d) and used to check whether the BN provides the highest probability to a value (range of values) that includes the real actual effort for that project, which is known. If not, then the BN is re-calibrated.

The building of a BN model is an iterative process where one can move between the three different steps of this process – building the BN's structure, or qualitative part, building the CPTs, or the quantitative part, and validating the model.

Once a BN is validated (see Figure 1c), evidence (e.g. values) can be entered into any node, and probabilities for the remaining nodes automatically calculated using Bayes' rule (Jensen, 1996) (see Figure 1d and Figure 1e). This was the method used to validate each of the Web effort BNs used herein.

Therefore BNs can be used for different types of reasoning, such as predictive (see Figure 1d), diagnostic (see Figure 1e), and "what-if" analyses to investigate the impact that changes on some nodes have on others (Jensen, 1996).

The effort required by each company to have their Web effort BN models created and validated, and the characteristics of each completed model, are detailed in Table 4.

All the domain experts who took part in building the models were project managers of four well-established Web companies in Auckland (New Zealand). All four companies were of small size, where all of their project managers had each worked in Web development for at least 10 years. In addition, all four companies developed a wide range of Web applications, from static & multimedia-like to very large e-commerce solutions. They also used a wide range of Web technologies, thus enabling the development of Web 2.0 applications. They were all looking at improving their current effort estimates.

Note that the aggregation that was carried out as part of this research used as input only the factors and relationships from each model's qualitative part. In other words, it used each BN's structure only. The aggregation of both the states that each factor took, and the probability tables was outside

Table 4. Characteristics of the BNs created and the companies involved

BN Models' Characteristics	Companies			
	B	C	G	H
Number of DEs	1	1	2	2
Number of 3-hours elicitation sessions	12	6	8	12
Total hours to elicit & validate model	36	18	24	36
Effort to elicit & validate model (person/hours)	72	36	72	108
Number of factors	14	13	34	33
Number of relationships	18	12	41	60
Number of projects in the validation set	22	8	11	22

the scope of this work given that the aim of this paper was not to build a cross-company Web effort estimation BN model.

PROBLEMS RELATING TO THE AGGREGATION OF STRUCTURES

It is often recommended that a map representing the aggregation of several BN structures be constructed through elicitation from different domain experts in order to derive a comprehensive and accurate map (e.g. Hu et al., 2007; Montironi et al., 1996; Rajabally et al., 2004). However, it is difficult to combine the beliefs of different experts in a coherent and impartial manner.

In order to arrive at a comprehensive map we would need to consult domain experts, many of whom working for different and perhaps competing companies, and thus likely to have a different prospective about the Web development domain. Therefore, the difficulty in combining expert-based BN structures increases for the following reasons:

- **Identifying Common Variables:** Different experts might represent semantically equivalent concepts in their BN structures using different variable names (e.g. *'Number of Developers'* vs. *'Project Human Resources'*). Furthermore, experts might use a different number of variables to represent the same concept.
- **Conflicting Relationships:** Factors might have contradictory relationships according to different experts. Two kinds of relationship conflicts can occur: the first when there is an influence between two factors according to an expert's belief, which is strictly prohibited by another expert's belief. The other type of conflict is the occurrence of cycles (which is ruled out within the context of this work in order to keep the resulting aggregated map consistent

with all the four individual structures being used as input, which were all Directed Acyclic Graphs [DAGs]).

- **Collaboration Constraints:** One feasible way to construct a unified map for Web effort estimation is to elicit a single structure from a group of domain experts from a representative sample of Web development companies. This would need to be done in stages, and such approach might work well with small groups of domain experts but will likely to be impractical when additional structures are included in the unified map. However, within the context of this research, any form of collaboration between domain experts is not feasible because all of the participating companies competed in the same market. This means that, by collaborating with other experts, they would be forced to share sensitive business information that they are not willing to disclose.

Therefore, it was vital to apply a mechanism for combining different expert-elicited BN structures that solved the difficulties abovementioned. We employed the same mechanism we proposed previously to merge different BN structures, which solved many of the affiliated challenges in combining expert-elicited BN structures that have not been sufficiently addressed in prior work (Baker, 2009).

This mechanism is explained in the next Section, and further details are available in (Baker, 2009).

AGGREGATION MECHANISM EMPLOYED

Our aggregation mechanism is a qualitative methodology that pragmatically addresses the shortcomings of previous work (Baker, 2009) by:

1. Introducing a mapping scheme, i.e., a way to identify similar existing factors in the participating companies' BN structures.

2. Instead of using a simple union/intersection, which can only include a common node or edge exactly once, it aggregates the causal structures. Within this context, aggregation implies that all edges and nodes in the original BN structure are preserved. As more BN structures are aggregated, the most common variables and relationships emerge, thereby simulating in our view a form of consensus between the different companies' BN structures.

The output of our proposed mechanism is a map, which we termed Aggregated Knowledge Map (AKMa). Strictly speaking an AKMa is not a unified map, but it is a tool for discovering a consensual map because it represents the cumulative addition of individual knowledge maps according to a node mapping scheme. The aim of a knowledge map aggregation model is to identify commonalties between independently developed knowledge maps that share the same domain. Consider the maps from the three BN models presented in Figure 2. All are used to estimate the total effort required to develop a Web application. Since they all share the same domain, it is possible to assume that the nodes in two different models portray the same factor. For example, nodes A1, B1, and C1 all model the same factor - the number of developers required to develop a Web application, and therefore, it is possible to map those three nodes into a single factor.

Some nodes are more subjective in their definition, e.g., nodes B2 and C2 both attempt to model the effort required to develop a Web application, but the exact details of how to measure this effort might vary between the two companies. However, because both models share the same domain, both B2 and C2 are likely to portray the same underlying concept. By performing this type of mapping between the three BN structures, we can produce the AKMa presented in Figure 3.

The left partition of an AKMa' node represents a factor of interest, while the right partition contains a list of nodes from the original knowledge maps that relate to this factor. All the relationships from the original maps are preserved in the AKMa, i.e., if there is a relationship between two nodes in one of the original maps (for example from A2 to A0), then in the AKMa there must be an edge from every node that contains A2 in its mapping to every node that contains A0 in its mapping. The numbers attached to the edges in the AKMa represent the cardinality of their mapping. For example, the edge from node (1) to node (0) has a cardinality of three; this is because there are three original edges that map to it: A1 to A0, B1 to B0, and C1 to C0. The cardinality of a node is the number of 'original' nodes that it maps to (i.e. the number of nodes listed in its right partition). The example in Figure 3 has a simple one-to-one mapping between the AKMa factors and the nodes from the example maps. It is possible to have a many-to-many mapping to resolve more ambiguous situations.

AGGREGATING THE FOUR KNOWLEDGE MAPS

The goal of this research was to provide a wider understanding on the fundamental factors affecting Web effort estimation and their relationships, and in order to achieve that we built a AKMa by aggregating the knowledge maps from four expert-driven Web effort estimation BNs. The methodology used to combine these maps comprised a six-step process (detailed below) mixing both linear and iterative approaches (see Figure 4).

Formatting of the Companies' BN Structures

The companies' maps were first formatted so they could be handled by the aggregation algorithm (step 4). The formatting consisted of the following steps:

Figure 2. Three examples of very simple web effort estimation models

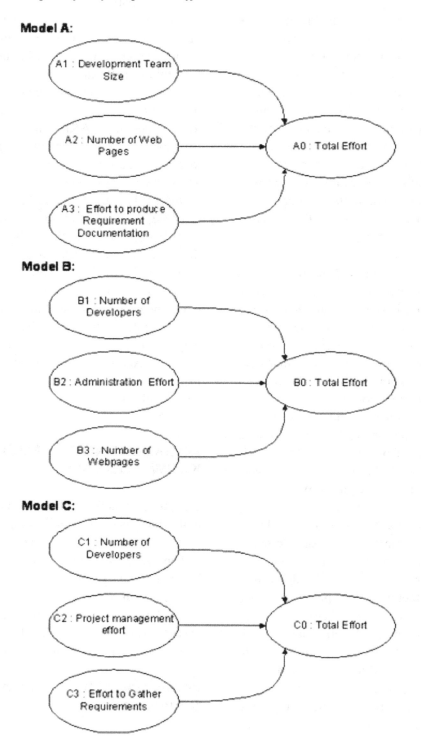

Figure 3. AKMa map

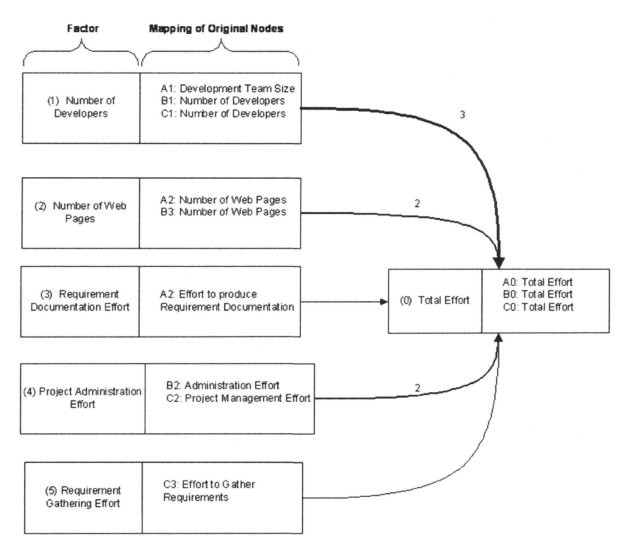

Each node in every map was given a unique Identifier. The identifiers chosen for our research represented a concatenation between a company's map identifier and a unique natural number (a number only valid within the context of a single map). Each map was represented in a parseable format, where the format chosen herein was CSV (Comma Separated Values). The choice relating to the identifiers' representation and parsing format to use was informed by the tool implemented to help with this aggregation process (Baker, 2009).

Removal of Optimisation Nodes

Optimisation nodes are intermediate nodes that were inserted into a knowledge map to partition large CPTs in order to reduce their probability elicitation effort. In general, such nodes are not part of the original map elicited with the domain experts; rather, they are suggested by later the Knowledge Engineer, and approved by the experts. The purpose of our AKMa was to only aggregate the factors and relationships originally modelled

Figure 4. Process flow diagram to produce a MoAS map

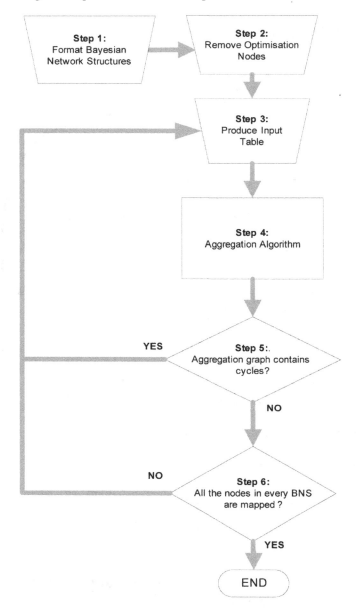

by the experts, and as such, the inclusion of optimisation nodes was deemed inappropriate. Optimisation nodes were first identified from the documentation available for each of the companies' maps. To remove an optimisation node we connected all of its incoming edges (coming from its parent nodes) directly to all of its child nodes, followed by the removal of this optimisation node and all of its outgoing edges (see Figure 5). During this operation BNs' existing graph rules must always hold (note that each BN structure used was part of a larger model – a BN model). For example, only a single edge could have the same source and destination nodes; therefore,

Figure 5. Removing an optimisation node

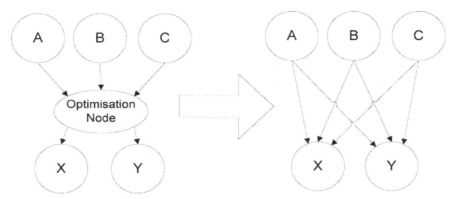

if the removal of an optimisation node resulted in adding an edge between two nodes that were already directly linked, then the resultant edge had to be discarded.

Creation of an Input Table

Each node in our AKMa corresponded to a semantically equivalent node originating from one of more of the knowledge maps used as input. Sometimes different maps would contain the same node however named differently; when carrying out the mapping (as detailed below) we checked for the semantic equivalence between nodes across maps. These mappings were documented using a Table, where each row was used to map a AKMa node to all the other semantically equivalent nodes originating from maps. The table's first column represented an AKMa node (factor), identified by a unique ID; the remaining columns contained node identifiers associated with the nodes contained in the input maps.

Given a company's input map, the first node to be mapped was the most-posterior node, which within our context always happened to be the Total Effort. We chose this node because it was part of all the participating companies' maps, and therefore we believed it to be the easiest node to identify and map. Once Total Effort was mapped, the remaining nodes were mapped according to the following steps:

1. Selection of a node (factor) from a company's knowledge map that had not yet been mapped.
2. Identification of the contextual meaning of the factor selected in (1), which usually involved interpreting the underlying concept that the domain expert employed when that factor was elicited. We first identified the units and quantification used to measure the factor, followed by looking at the supporting documentation from the elicitation sessions, which contained examples and additional commentary about the experts' beliefs. In the rare cases where a factor's contextual meaning was still ambiguous, the experts were contacted for clarification.
3. Attempt to map the factor identified in (1) () to a factor, or set of factors, already present in our AKMa. Whenever there was no corresponding factor(s) clearly mapping to , we created a new factor(s) within our AKMa to match that given factor .

There were no strict rules as to whether an original node was mapped to one or more factors within our AKMa; however, we always aimed to keep as much of the original context as possible through the mapping. Thus the reason why our methodology is iterative and not linear is because mappings often change as new factors are created and old ones are revised.

In order to minimise the effort of constantly changing the mappings as the aggregation map was populated, we decided to map the original nodes in different iterations rather than mapping all nodes at once. This gave us the opportunity to run the aggregation algorithm (see step 4 below) and generate the AKMa several times, containing incomplete aggregation maps, and then to look for faults and inconsistencies (e.g. cycles). The first iteration involved mapping every prior node from all the companies' structures. The second iteration involved mapping all the nodes from all the companies' structures that were directly pointed to by all prior nodes, and so on until the most posterior (the Total Effort Node) was reached.

Aggregation Algorithm

The Table prepared in step 3 was used as input to an aggregation algorithm that produced a graphical representation of the AKMa. The algorithm worked by first merging the prior nodes according to the mapping specified in the Table, and continuing until all nodes in all the companies' maps were processed (Baker, 2009).

Whenever the Table from Step 3 did not include mappings for some of the nodes in the inputted structures, then these nodes were represented in the AKMa by placeholder nodes. The purpose of the placeholder node was so that we were aware of which nodes still required mapping in the next iteration of this process (see Step 6).

Check if the Aggregation Graph Contains Cycles

The aggregation algorithm allowed for the occurrence of cycles since it simply followed what was documented in the Table used as input. Therefore, when the generated AKMa graph contained cycles, the input Table needed to be modified so that all of the documented cycles were broken. Cycles could be broken by changing the mapping of

one or more nodes that made up the cycle, which could be achieved by either removing or adding factors to the input Table. However, because all the companies' maps were independent of one another and yet shared the same domain, it is theoretically possible to have cycles occurring that may not be resolved. This would occur whenever nodes in their original structures did not form cycles, but ended up contributing to a cycle in the AKMa due to conflicting contexts.

Check if All Nodes are Mapped

The final step in the process was to check whether every node (except for optimisation nodes) in all the companies' maps had been mapped in the AKMa. For this we looked for the existence of placeholder nodes in the AKMa outputted by the algorithm. If found, we mapped the map's nodes identified by the placeholder nodes by referring back to Step 3; conversely, if there were no placeholder nodes, we considered that the AKMa was complete according to our mapping.

RESULTS

The AKMa[1] resulting from our 6-step methodology (presented in Section 5) enabled us to identify common patterns amongst the four knowledge maps used as input. This AKMa contains 70 nodes and 158 relationships, encompassing all the factors and relationships identified by the four participating companies via their maps.

Table 2 lists only a subset of these 70 factors[2], which are those with cardinality of at least 3. A factor's cardinality corresponds to the number of knowledge maps that contained that factor, thus it is an indication of how common it was as a predictor amongst the four participating companies.

Apart from Total effort, which was part of all four knowledge maps, there were four factors that were common to three of the four companies:

- Average Project Team Experience with Technology
- Client Personality Difficulty
- Effort to Program Features
- Project Management Effort

These effort predictors represent people issues (project team and clients) and also some processes that are to be carried out throughout a Web development project. Figure 6 provides other factors that represent processes. Although the use of processes as effort predictors is not common, it has already been suggested previously to build software effort predictions models using BNs (Bibi & Stamelos, 2004) (see Table 5).

Figure 6 shows a sub-graph of the resultant AKMa with all edges having cardinality greater than two. Factors were grouped into higher level categories (grey boxes) simply to facilitate their understandability. These categories are: Implementation-oriented factors, User Interface Design-oriented factors, Documentation-oriented factors, and Project-oriented factors. Note that, as previously mentioned, most factors measure the effort required to carry out a particular task (e.g. manage projects, produce requirements documentation);

Figure 6. A sub-graph of the resultant MoAS with all edges having cardinality greater than two

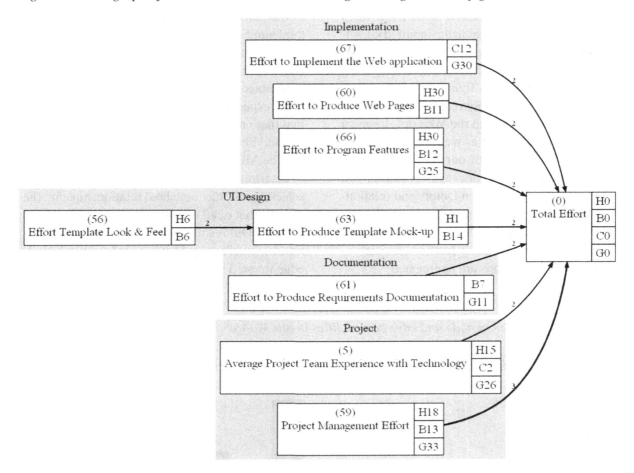

Table 5. Factors with cardinality of at least 3

Label	DataType	Cardinality
Total Effort	Person hours	4
Average Project Team Experience with Technology	Total number of years	3
Client Personality Difficulty	User Defined (e.g. Low, Medium, High; good, normal, bad)	3
Effort to Program Features	Person hours	3
Project Management Effort	Person hours	3

however two of these factors – effort to produce Web pages, and effort template look and feel, and effort to produce template mock-up are quite specific to Web development projects, when compared to more traditional software development projects.

Figure 6 can be described as an aggregated intersection of all the edges in the inputted knowledge maps. The higher the weight value of an edge the more common a relationship is amongst the maps used as input. This figure is therefore very useful as it indicates likely relationships that exist between factors within the Web development domain. We believe that as we further aggregate other knowledge maps to our resultant AKMa, a more informative and decisive consensus will emerge relating to common factors and relationships, thus also strengthening the external validity of this model. In other words, an AKMa is a maturing map, providing further certainty as further knowledge maps are aggregated.

Figure 7 shows the proportion of factors according to their equivalent nodal cardinality. We can see that approximately 67% of all factors appeared in only a single company's BN structure, and 26% of factors were common to at least two BN structures. The percentage of nodes decreased as the cardinality increased, suggesting that the total number of factors available in the target domain significantly outnumbered the factors being considered by individual companies. Likewise, the percentage of causal edges also rapidly decreases with respect to edge cardinality, which suggests that there are many relationships not considered by individual companies.

The AKMa presented 158 edges. We were able to determine the most common relationships by selecting all the matched relationships in the AKMa, that is, all edges with a cardinality of two or more. Our results showed that 26% of all relationships were shared between at least two knowledge maps. The most prevalent relationship was

Figure 7. Distribution of node and edge cardinalities in our MoAS

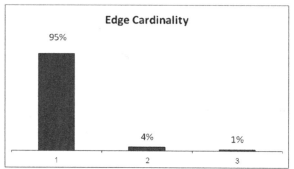
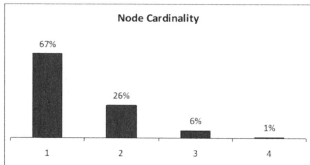

between factors 'Project Management Effort' and 'Total Effort' whereby 66.6% of the participating companies included such relationships in their maps. Other common relationships identified were:

- Relationship from 'Effort to Implement the Web Application' directly influencing 'Total Effort'.
- Relationship from 'Effort to Produce Web Pages' directly influencing 'Total Effort'.
- Relationship from 'Effort to Program Features' directly influencing 'Total Effort'.
- Relationship from 'Effort to Produce Template Mock-up' directly influencing 'Total Effort'.
- Relationship from 'Effort to Produce Requirements Documentation' directly influencing 'Total Effort'.
- Relationship from 'Average Project Team Experience with Technology' directly influencing 'Total Effort'.

Each of the six relationships listed above appeared in 50% of the companies' knowledge

maps. Edges with higher cardinality tended to be closer to the most posterior node ('Total Effort'). Figure 8 shows a falling trend in the mean and median average distances to the Total Effort node. An average mean distance = 0.95 for edges with cardinality of 1, and mean distance = 0.14 for edges with cardinality of 2. This is in our view an important outcome because 'effort' is what all the companies whose maps were used in this research aim to predict; it is therefore advantageous to know which factors were likely to have a direct effect upon effort, since this would be the focal point of any future consensus-based knowledge map.

THREATS TO VALIDITY

There are a few threats to the validity of our work. One is the mapping of original nodes (i.e. creating the aggregation map as part of the third step in our methodology, as detailed previously). The mapping was performed by the authors, not the experts; therefore, there is always the possibility of bias being introduced. However, it is important to note that many steps were undertaken to mitigate this risk. All mappings were based on an extensive

Figure 8. Average distance by edge cardinality to total effort node

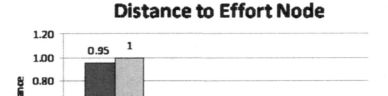

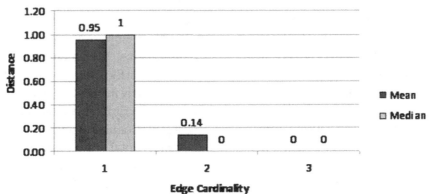

documentation provided by the experts, and for cases where there was still ambiguity, the experts were contacted directly for further clarification.

Another threat is that our methodology does not in any way guarantee that the final AKMa is free of cycles. Although for the four knowledge maps, all potential cycles were resolved by further investigation and remapping, this might not always be the case. It is always possible to have intrinsically contradictory knowledge maps, rendering it impossible to resolve cycles unless at least one edge is omitted from the AKMa.

Finally, for the AKMa to be fully comprehensive in terms of domain factors, it is necessary to aggregate a large number of knowledge maps. For our case, the aggregation of four maps is not enough to argue that they represent all the important factors and relationships that affect the effort for a new project within the Web development domain. However, we note that the resultant AKMa is a maturing map, and we plan to aggregate further knowledge maps as part of our future work.

CONCLUSION AND FUTURE RESEARCH DIRECTIONS

The main goal of this chapter was to obtain a deeper understanding of the fundamental factors affecting Web effort estimation and their relationships via a mechanism that created an aggregated map (AKMa) combining knowledge maps from four expert-based single-company Web effort estimation models, elicited independently with the participation of domain experts from four Web companies in Auckland (New Zealand). This AKMa contained 70 factors and 158 edges.

We also argued that the map resulting from the aggregation mechanism employed herein is more trustworthy than simply compiling lists of factors because it uses as input factors and relationships from models that were built and validated using a process based on a root cause analysis technique;

such technique, by requiring a thorough and deep understanding of experts' mental processes and their decisions when estimating effort, provides the means to truly portray the phenomenon focus of this research, i.e. Web effort estimation.

To build a AKMa presents numerous challenges, namely identifying common factors, resolving relationship conflicts, and company collaboration constraints. However, we believe that one can overcome some of these challenges by applying an aggregation process that can yield the most common patterns shared between single-company knowledge maps.

The resultant AKMa revealed the following patterns: 1) 33% of the AKMa factors were shared between at least 2 single-company knowledge maps; 2) The most common factor was 'Project Management Effort'; 3) The proportion of nodes rapidly decreased as cardinality increased, implying that the total number of factors relevant in the Web effort estimation domain significantly outnumbers the number of factors being considered by individual companies; 4) 5% of all relationships found in the AKMa were shared between at least two single-company knowledge maps; 5) The most common relationship in our AKMa was between factors 'Project Management Effort' and 'Total Effort', included in 66.6% of the single-company knowledge maps; 6) Six other common relationships which were evident were: 'Effort to Implement the Web Application', ' Effort to Produce Web Pages', 'Effort to Program Features', 'Effort to Produce Template Mock-up', 'Effort to Produce Requirements Documentation', and 'Average Project Team Experience with Technology', all of which directly influenced 'Total Effort'; 7) Edges with higher cardinality tended to be closer to the most posterior node, suggesting that most factors influenced total effort directly.

The abovementioned points show that even with a small number of companies we can already see reasonable commonality in terms of factors and relationships. The AKMa is a maturing map, which means that as more knowledge maps are aggregated the more common factors and relationships will emerge, hence providing an improved consensus. The aggregation process presented herein can be used to aggregate other knowledge maps within the Web domain or in another domain.

REFERENCES

Ammerman, M. (1998). *The root cause analysis handbook: A simplified approach to identifying, correcting, and reporting workplace errors*. Academic Press.

Azhar, D., Mendes, E., & Riddle, P. (2012). A systematic review of web resource estimation. [Promise.]. *Proceedings of Promise, 12,* 49–58.

Baker, S. (2009). *Towards the construction of large Bayesian networks for web cost estimation*. (Unpublished Master's Thesis). University of Auckland, Auckland, New Zealand.

Baresi, L., Morasca, S., & Paolini, P. (2002). An empirical study on the design effort for web applications. [WISE.]. *Proceedings of WISE, 2002,* 345–354.

Bibi, S., & Stamelos, I. (2004). Software process modelling with Bayesian belief networks. [IEEE.]. *Proceedings of IEEE Software Metrics, 2004,* 1–10.

Costagliola, G., di Martino, S., Ferrucci, F., Gravino, C., Tortora, G., & Vitiello, G. (2006). Effort estimation modeling techniques: a case study for web applications. In *Proceedings of the International Conference on Web Engineering (ICWE'06)*, (pp. 9-16). ICWE.

Ferrucci, F., Gravino, C., & Di Martino, S. (2008). A case study using web objects and COSMIC for effort estimation of web applications. In Proceedings of EUROMICRO-SEAA, (pp. 441-448). SEAA.

Hu, X.-X., Wang, H., & Wang, S. (2007). Using expert's knowledge to build Bayesian networks. In *Proceedings of the 2007 International Conference on Computational Intelligence and Security Workshops*, (pp. 220-223). IEEE.

Jensen, F. V. (1996). *An introduction to Bayesian networks*. London: UCL Press.

Jørgensen, M., & Grimstad, S. (2009). Software development effort estimation: Demystifying and improving expert estimation. In A. Tveito, A. M. Bruaset, & O. Lysne (Eds.), *Simula Research Laboratory - By Thinking Constantly About It* (pp. 381–404). Heidelberg, Germany: Springer. doi:10.1007/978-3-642-01156-6_26.

Kitchenham, B., Mendes, E., & Travassos, G. H. (2006). A systematic review of cross-company vs. within-company cost estimation studies. In *Proceedings of the Evaluation and Assessment in Software Engineering,* (pp. 89 – 98). EASE.

Kitchenham, B. A. (2007). *Guidelines for performing systematic literature reviews in software engineering (version 2.3). Software Engineering Group*. School of Computer Science and Mathematics, Keele University and Department of Computer Science, University of Durham.

Mangia, L., & Paiano, R. (2003). MMWA: A software sizing model for web applications. In *Proceedings of the Fourth International Conference on Web Information Systems Engineering*, (pp. 53-63). IEEE.

Mendes, E. (2011a). Knowledge representation using Bayesian networks: A case study in web effort estimation. In *Proceedings of the World Congress on information and Communication Technologies (WICT 2011)*, (pp. 310-315). WICT.

Mendes, E. (2011b). Building a web effort estimation model through knowledge elicitation. In *Proceedings of the International Conference on Enterprise Information Systems (ICEIS)*, (pp. 128-135). ICEIS.

Mendes, E. (2012a). Using knowledge elicitation to improve web effort estimation: Lessons from six industrial case studies. In *Proceedings of the International Conference on Software Engineering (ICSE 2012)*, (pp. 1112-1121). ICSE.

Mendes, E. (2012b). An overview of web effort estimation. In M. Zelkowitz (Ed.), *Advances in Computers* (Vol. 78). London: Elsevier Academic Press.

Mendes, E., & Counsell, S. (2000). Web development effort estimation using analogy. In *Proceedings of the 2000 Australian Software Engineering Conference*, (pp. 203-212). ASEC.

Mendes, E., & Kitchenham, B. A. (2004). Further comparison of cross-company and within-company effort estimation models for web applications. In *Proceedings of IEEE Metrics*, (pp. 348-357). IEEE.

Mendes, E., Mosley, N., & Counsell, S. (2001, January-March). Web metrics - Metrics for estimating effort to design and author web applications. *IEEE MultiMedia*, 50–57. doi:10.1109/93.923953.

Mendes, E., Mosley, N., & Counsell, S. (2003). Investigating early web size measures for web cost estimation. In *Proceedings of Evaluation and Assessment in Software Engineering*. EASE.

Mendes, E., Mosley, N., & Counsell, S. (2005a). Investigating web size metrics for early web cost estimation. *Journal of Systems and Software*, 77(2), 157–172. doi:10.1016/j.jss.2004.08.034.

Mendes, E., Mosley, N., & Counsell, S. (2005b). The need for web engineering: An introduction. In E. Mendes, & N. Mosley (Eds.), *Web Engineering* (pp. 1–26). Berlin: Springer-Verlag.

Mendes, E., Polino, C., & Mosley, N. (2009). Building an expert-based web effort estimation model using Bayesian networks. In *Proceedings of the 13th International Conference on Evaluation & Assessment in Software Engineering*, (pp. 1-10). IEEE.

Montironi, R., Whimster, W. F., Collan, Y., Hamilton, P. W., Thompson, D., & Bartels, P. H. (1996). How to develop and use a Bayesian belief network. *Journal of Clinical Pathology*, *49*, 194. doi:10.1136/jcp.49.3.194 PMID:8675727.

Rajabally, E., Sen, P., Whittle, S., & Dalton, J. (2004). Aids to Bayesian belief network construction. In *Proceedings of the Intelligent Systems*, (pp. 457-461). IEEE.

Reifer, D. J. (2000, November-December). Web development: Estimating quick-to-market software. *IEEE Software*, 57–64. doi:10.1109/52.895169.

Ruhe, M., Jeffery, R., & Wieczorek, I. (2003). Cost estimation for web applications. In *Proceedings ICSE 2003*, (pp. 285-294). ICSE.

KEY TERMS AND DEFINITIONS

Bayesian Networks: A Bayesian Network is a model that represents a domain knowledge using a directed acyclic graph structure (to model variables and their causal relationships), and also enables these causal relationships to be quantified using probabilities. These probabilities represent the uncertainty in the domain being modeled.

Domain Uncertainty: Characterises the uncertainty that is inherent to certain domains, and that should be taken into account as part of a decision making process. For example, effort estimation is a very complex domain where the relationship between factors is non-deterministic and has an inherently uncertain nature. E.g. assuming there is a relationship between development effort and an application's size (e.g. number of Web pages, functionality), it is not necessarily true that increased effort will lead to larger size. However, as effort increases so does the probability of larger size.

Effort Estimation: The process by which the amount of effort (in person hours) needed to develop a software application is predicted, in order to be used as basis to predict project costs and to allocate resources (e.g. developers). This estimate is generally derived taking into account the characteristics of the new project, and corresponding application, for which an estimate is needed, and also the characteristics of previous 'similar' projects, and corresponding applications, for which actual effort is known.

Estimated Software Size: A measure that characterizes the size of the problem that is to be solved by developing a software application. In general, in order to obtain this estimate one uses as input a requirements specification document that details what the application is supposed to do.

Expert-Based Effort Estimation: An effort estimate that has been obtained by subjective means, only based on the tacit knowledge of experts, and optionally also some data from past finished projects.

Knowledge Elicitation: The process employed to elicit an expert's tacit knowledge (expertise and experience) so to obtain a tangible representation of this knowledge.

Software Project Management: Process that is employed to plan and control the development and delivery of software applications.

ENDNOTES

[1]   The resultant MoAS is available here: http://www.cs.auckland.ac.nz/~emilia/Theory/CSAM.png

[2]   A description of all MoAS factors is given here: http://www.cs.auckland.ac.nz/~emilia/Theory/Factors.pdf

Chapter 6
Effort, Time, and Staffing in Continually Evolving Open–Source Projects

Liguo Yu
Indiana University – South Bend, USA

ABSTRACT

Scheduling and staffing are important management activities in software projects. In closed-source software development, the relationships among development effort, time, and staffing have been well established and validated: the development effort determines the development time and the best number of developers that should be allocated to the project. However, there has been no similar research reported in open-source projects. In this chapter, the authors study the development effort, development time, and staffing in an open-source project, the Linux kernel project. Specifically, they investigate the power law relations among development effort, development time, and the number of active developers in the Linux kernel project. The authors find the power law relations differ from one branch to another branch in the Linux kernel project, which suggests different kinds of management and development styles might exist in different branches of the Linux kernel project. The empirical knowledge of software development effort obtained in this study could help project management and cost control in both open-source communities and closed-source industries.

DOI: 10.4018/978-1-4666-4229-4.ch006

1. INTRODUCTION

In software projects, scheduling and staffing are important management activities. Over scheduling and over staffing can result in the addition of development cost. Under scheduling and under staffing could result in delays of product delivery. Therefore, in software projects, scheduling and staffing are determined based on the estimated development effort. Several formulas have been proposed and validated to show the ideal relationships among development effort, development time, and the number of developers that should be allocated to a project (Walston & Felix, 1977; Putnam, 1978; Boehm, 1981).

However, most of the published work in this area is performed on closed-source projects. Little work has been done to study the relationship among development effort, development time, and the number of active developers in open-source projects (Koch & Schneider, 2002; Koch 2008). Although open-source projects are loosely organized and managed, it is worth of studying their management styles to understand how open-source projects self-organize to form their own laws about development effort, development time, and staffing in order to help project management and cost control in both open-source communities and closed-source industries.

The remainder of this chapter is organized as follows. Section 2 reviews related work in software effort estimation. Section 3 presents the background knowledge of this study. Section 4 describes the data source and the data representation. Section 5 presents the analysis and the results. Conclusions appear in Section 6.

2. LITERATURE REVIEW

Software effort estimation is to predict the manpower required to develop or maintain a software product. Effort estimation is the basis for cost estimation, time scheduling, and staff allocation.

Extensive research has been performed in this area (Albrecht & Gaffney, 1983; Jeffery & Low, 1990). Basically, there are two types of effort estimation method: expert judgment (Parkinson, 1957) and algorithmic models (Donelson, 1976). In algorithmic models, COCOMO II is considered the most successful approach (Boehm et al., 2000). Since the introduction of these models, a lot of following work has been performed in this area.

Some studies are reported to compare the performance of different effort estimation models. For example, Jorgensen (1995) compared different software maintenance effort prediction models developed using regression analysis, neural networks, and pattern recognition. He found the most accurate estimations were achieved through applying multiple regression and pattern recognition in the prediction models. Jeffery, Ruhe, and Wieczorek (2000) compared the development cost estimation differences of models using ordinary least-squares regression and analogy-based estimation. Menzies, Chen, Hihn, and Lum (2006) applied heuristic rejection rules to comparatively assess effort predictions generated from different models.

Some studies are performed to improve the accuracies of effort estimation models. For example, Chulani, Boehm, and Steece (1999) proposed using Bayesian approach to calibrate and improve cost estimation models, such as COCOMO II. Idri, Kjiri, and Abran (2000) suggested improving COCOMO model with fuzzy logic. Reddy and Raju (2009) recommended using Gaussian Membership Function to determine the cost drivers in order to improve the prediction accuracy. Huang, Ho, Ren and Capretz (2007) proposed improving the COCOMO effort estimation mode using neuro-fuzzy approach.

Building cross-project effort estimation models has been the major line of study in this area. Kitchenham and Mendes (2009) investigated the comparative effort prediction models. Caivano, Lanubile and Visaggio (2001) found that effort estimation models are process-dependent and accordingly cannot be reused for other processes. Maxwell, Wassenhove, and Dutta (1999) suggested that software companies should develop their own cost estimation models based on their own experience in order to generate accurate effort predictions. Menzies, Port, Chen, Hihn, and Sherry (2005) found that effort estimation models should be calibrated to local data using incremental holdout studies and predictions based on the within-company model were not significantly more accurate than those based on the cross-company model.

Software maintenance and evolution is one of the most important phases in software life cycle. Building maintenance effort estimation model is accordingly an important task for software engineering researchers. Sneed (2004) presented an effort model for software maintenance and evolution based on separations of fixed and variable cost. In a different study, Sneed (2005) described an eight-step process for calculating the time and the cost required to reengineer an existing system. De Lucia, Pompella, and Stefanucci (2005) proposed a two-step approach to improving the effort estimation model for corrective maintenance activities. Fioravanti and Nesi (2001) presented an effort estimation model for adaptive maintenance of object-oriented systems. Ramil (2000) studied cost estimation in software evolution by building a set of quantitative models and assessing their predictive powers.

Another line of research in area is to build iterative effort estimation models. For example, Abrahamsson, Moser, Pedrycz, Sillitti, and Succi (2007) proposed a cost estimation model for agile software development. Trendowicz et al. (2006) proposed an enhanced process for developing cost estimation models. This process includes iterative analysis, feedback cycles, and evaluations in a software development.

Open-source software development has become a mainstream in software ecosystem. Some work has been done to estimate the development and maintenance effort of open-source projects. For example, Yu (2006) used the effort model obtained from closed-source projects to predict the maintenance effort in opens-source projects. However, compared with closed-source projects, open-source projects still have many unresolved development effort related issues. This chapter intends to address one of these issues: the relations among development effort, development time, and staffing in open-source projects.

3. BACKGROUND

3.1. Development Time and Staffing

In the algorithmic model proposed for closed-source projects, after the development effort is predicted, it will be used to estimate the development time required for this project. Table 1 summarizes some of the commonly used formulas to determine the development time.

In all the formulas listed in Table 1, E represents development effort in person-months and T represents development time in months. Therefore, the average number of staff that should be assigned to this project could be calculated using the formula $S = E / T$, where S is measured in persons.

Because development time T is only dependent on development effort E, the number of staff S could also be represented as a function that is only

Table 1. Relations between development time and development effort (Van Vliet, 2008)

Model Name	Formula
Walston-Felix	$T = 2.5E^{0.35}$
COCOMO (organic)	$T = 2.5E^{0.38}$
COCOMO II (nominal schedule)	$T = 3.0E^{0.33 + 0.2 \times (b - 1.01)}$
Putnam	$T = 2.4E^{1/3}$

dependent on development effort E. Accordingly, these relations can be summarized in the following two equations.

$$T = A \times E^b \qquad (3.1.1)$$

$$S = C \times E^d \qquad (3.1.2)$$

In Equations 3.1.1 and 3.1.2, A, b, C and d are project dependent constants. The equations indicate the power law relations between (1) development time and development effort; (2) number of allocated staff (developers) and development effort. The development time and the number of staff calculated using Equations 3.1.1 and 3.1.2 are called nominal development time and nominal number of staff, and they are only dependent on development effort. Obviously, if we want to shorten the development time, we need to increase the number of staff in this project. However, studies showed nominal development time and nominal number of staff are the most realistic solutions for a software project [38]. Over scheduling and under scheduling could both reduce individual's productivity, which can result in the addition of development cost.

On the one side, if a project is scheduled to take longer than its nominal development time, the work process will be slowed down and the developers' productivity will be reduced. On the other side, if a project is scheduled to take shorter than its nominal development time, the development team should get larger and the communication overhead will increase and result in the decrease of productivity. Therefore, either over scheduling or under scheduling could result in the decrease of productivity and the increase of development cost. Therefore, in closed-source software development, development time and staffing are determined solely based on development effort estimated for the project.

3.2. Comparisons of Closed-Source Projects and Open-Source Projects

The development styles of both open-source projects and closed-source projects have been intensively studied. In this section, we summarize some major differences between open-source projects and closed-source projects.

- Usually, closed-source projects have clear short-term and long-term objectives; the tasks and activities are well assigned. On the contrary, open-source projects do not assign the tasks mandatorily; instead, voluntary developers take the development tasks for their own interest.
- Closed-source projects have specified due dates for each task or activity. Usually, open-source projects have no firm deadlines for any tasks.
- Developers in closed-source projects are full-time employees; they should spend all their effort on the project during the development period. Most developers in open-source projects undertake development or maintenance tasks during their personal time. They might not spend all their available effort on the project.
- Closed source products are released only after they are intensively tested. Usually, open-source products are tested by the end users. Therefore, open-source projects are released more frequently than closed-source projects.

Due to the management style differences between open-source projects and closed-source projects, the development time and staffing in open-source projects might have different relations with development effort. Therefore, it is worth to study the relationships among development effort, development time, and staffing in open-source projects to see if they follow the similar power law relations as observed in closed-source projects.

4. DATA SOURCE AND DATA DESCRIPTION

Linux kernel[1] is an open-source project. The first release was in 1994. Up to now, there are about 700 releases. Therefore, Linux kernel is considered as a continually evolving software product. The data used in this study is extracted from the Linux kernel repository[2], which is maintained with Git[3] configuration management tool. A Git client is set up and all available versions of the Linux kernel are checked out (copied from the server repository to the client repository). Table 2 shows all the available versions of Linux kernel that are included in this study.

It should be noted that in Table 2, for each branch, the number of versions is one more than the number of revisions, because in this study, we consider the first version in each branch (Version 2.5.0 and Version 2.6.0) as the original release and the rest of the versions as revisions. Specifically, revision is defined below.

Definition: A revision i of a product is defined as a release of version i of a product, which is based on the modification of version $i - 1$ of the same product.

According to this definition, if one branch has n versions (releases), it will have $n - 1$ revisions. For each revision, we extract the following data fields: number of files added (including number of lines of code in these files), number of files deleted (including number of lines of code in these files), number of files modified (including number of lines of code added and number of lines of code deleted in these files), release date, number of commits, and number of committers.

Commit is the operation of updating a file in the server repository with developer's modified local copy. Number of commits represents the amount of changes made to the specific revision. Therefore, file changes and commits can be used to represent development effort. Release dates difference between Version i and Version $i - 1$ can be used to represent the development time of Revision (Version) i. The number of committers represents the staffing (number of active developers) in this revision. As discussed by Nguyen (2010a; 2010b), deleting a file is not considered a major factor of development/maintenance effort. Accordingly, only added files and modified files are used to represent the development effort. Table 3 summarizes the representations used in this study.

Based on the representations in Table 3, we further define our metrics for this study. They are illustrated in Table 4.

5. ANALYSIS AND RESULTS

5.1. Correlations among Effort Measurements

First, we study the correlations among file measurement effort (E_1), code measurement effort (E_2), and commit measurement effort (E_3). Their scatter plots are shown in Figure 1 through Figure

Table 2. The Linux kernel versions included in this study

Branch	Number of Versions	Number of Revisions	First Vision Release Date	Last Version Release Date
2.5	76	75	11/23/2001	7/10/2003
2.6	40	39	12/18/2003	5/19/2011

Table 3. The data retrieved from each revision

Original Data	Representation	Symbol
Number of source code files added and modified	Development effort	E_1
Number of lines of code added in new files	Development effort	E_{21}
Number of lines of code added and deleted in modified files	Development effort	E_{22}
Number of commits	Development effort	E_3
Days between current release and prevision release	Development time	T
Number of committers	Number of staff	S

Table 4. The metrics defined for each revision

Name	Representation
Effort (file measurement)	E_1
Effort (code measurement)	$E_2 = E_{21} + E_{22}$
Effort (commit measurement)	E_3
Development time	T
Number of staff	S

3. The data used in this analysis are taken from Branch 2.5 and Branch 2.6 of the Linux kernel, which means each figure contains 114 pairs of data points.

The correlation tests (Pearson, Kendall, and Spearman) among E_1, E_2, and E_3 are summarized in Table 5, from which we can see that all three effort measurements are strongly correlated at the 0.001 significance level. Therefore, they might all be good candidates to represent development effort and can be used to study the relations to development time and staffing (number of active developers) in the Linux kernel project.

5.2. Prediction Models

5.2.1. Single-Variable Prediction Models

First, we assume that in open-source projects, development time and the number of staff follow similar power law relations with development effort as described in Equations 3.1.1 and 3.1.2

for closed source projects. Applying logarithm on the two sides of Equations 3.1.1 and 3.1.2, we can obtain Equations 5.2.1.1 and 5.2.1.2, where $a = \log(A)$ and $c = log(C)$.

$$\log(T) = a + b \times \log(E) \qquad (5.2.1.1)$$

$$\log(S) = c + d \times \log(E) \qquad (5.2.1.2)$$

Using the metrics defined in Table 4, we can derive three $log(T)$ equations to model the relations between development time and three effort measurements (Equations 5.2.1.3−5.2.1.5). Similarly, we can also derive three $log(S)$ equations to model the relations between number of staff and three effort measurements (Equations 5.2.1.6−5.2.1.8).

$$\log(T) = a_1 + b_1 \times \log(E_1) \qquad (5.2.1.3)$$

$$\log(T) = a_2 + b_2 \times \log(E_2) \qquad (5.2.1.4)$$

$$\log(T) = a_3 + b_3 \times \log(E_3) \qquad (5.2.1.5)$$

$$\log(S) = c_1 + d_1 \times \log(E_1) \qquad (5.2.1.6)$$

$$\log(S) = c_2 + d_2 \times \log(E_2) \qquad (5.2.1.7)$$

Figure 1. The scatter plot of E_1 (file measurement effort) and E_2 (code measurement effort)

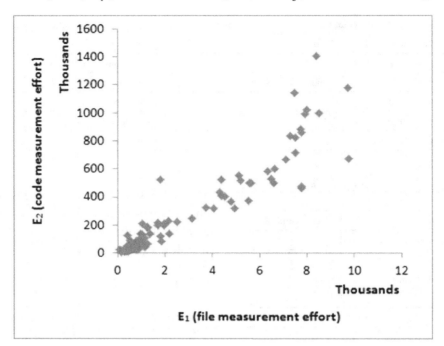

Figure 2. The scatter plot of E_1 (file measurement effort) and E_3 (commit measurement effort)

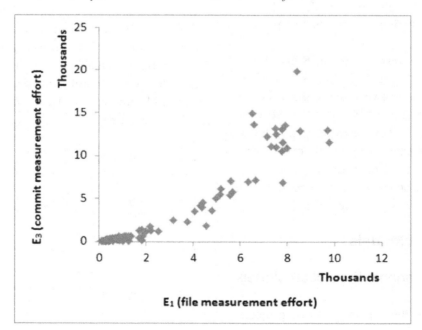

Figure 3. The scatter plot of E_2 (code measurement effort) and E_3 (commit measurement effort)

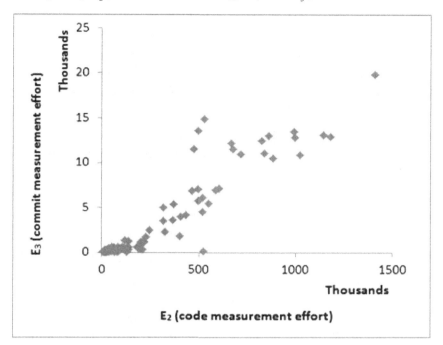

Table 5. The correlation tests among three effort measurements

		Pearson's Test			Kendall's Test			Spearman's Test		
		E_1	E_2	E_3	E_1	E_2	E_3	E_1	E_2	E_3
E_1	r	1	0.937	0.941	1	0.976	0.803	1	0.939	0.925
	p	<0.001	<0.001	<0.001	<0.001	<0.001	<0.001	<0.001	<0.001	<0.001
E_2	r	0.937	1	0.932	0.976	1	0.723	0.939	1	0.876
	p	<0.001	<0.001	<0.001	<0.001	<0.001	<0.001	<0.001	<0.001	<0.001
E_3	r	0.941	0.932	1	0.803	0.723	1	0.925	0.876	1
	p	<0.001	<0.001	<0.001	<0.001	<0.001	<0.001	<0.001	<0.001	<0.001

r: correlation coefficient; p: significance; Number of data pairs: 114

$$\log(S) = c_3 + d_3 \times \log(E_3) \qquad (5.2.1.8)$$

Equations 5.2.1.3 to 5.2.1.8 are called single-variable models, because in each model, there is only one independent variable $log(E)$. We can also see that linear relations exist between $log(T)$ and $log(E)$, $log(S)$ and $log(E)$. Therefore, linear regression analysis could be used to estimate the model parameters. We note here (1) in this study, base 2 logarithm will be applied to these equations; and (2) the number of staff S is measured with the number of committers in each revision, as described in Table 3.

5.2.2. Multi-Variable Prediction Models

Because we have three measurements of development effort, we can combine them together and create multi-variable prediction models.

$$T = A \times E_1^{b_1} \times E_2^{b_2} \times E_3^{b_3} \qquad (5.2.2.1)$$

$$S = C \times E_1^{d_1} \times E_2^{d_2} \times E_3^{d_3} \qquad (5.2.2.2)$$

In these two equations, T, S, E_1, E_2, and E_3 are defined in Table 4. Applying logarithm on the two sides of Equations 5.2.2.1 and 5.2.2.2, we can obtain the following two equations, where $a = log(A)$ and $c = log(C)$.

$$\log(T) = a + b_1 \times \log(E_1) \\ +b_2 \times \log(E_2) + b_3 \times \log(E_3) \qquad (5.2.2.3)$$

$$\log(S) = c + d_1 \times \log(E_1) \\ +d_2 \times \log(E_2) + d_3 \times \log(E_3) \qquad (5.2.2.4)$$

We can also see linear relations between dependent variable $log(T)/log(S)$ and independent variables $log(E_1)$, $log(E_2)$, and $log(E_3)$. Therefore, linear regression analysis could also be used to estimate the model parameters. Again, base 2 logarithm will be applied in these estimations.

5.3. Inner-Branch Predictions

5.3.1. Branch 2.5

Linux kernel Branch 2.5 contains 75 revisions (Version 2.5.1 through Version 2.5.75). In this part of the study, the first 40 revisions (Version 2.5.1 through Version 2.5.40) are used to build prediction models. The remaining 35 versions (Version 2.5.41 through Version 2.5.75) are used to evaluate the predictions models.

First, we analyze the single-variable models. The results of linear regression analysis of Equations 5.2.1.3−5.2.1.5 are summarized in Table 6 and the results of linear regression analysis of Equations 5.2.1.6−5.2.1.8 are summarized in Table 7.

Table 6. Single-variable models of $log(T)$ for branch 2.5

	a_i	b_i	R Square
Model (Equation) 5.2.1.3 ($i=1$)	-4.789	0.813	0.358
Model (Equation) 5.2.1.4 ($i=2$)	-3.630	0.400	0.170
Model (Equation) 5.2.1.5 ($i=3$)	0.423	0.284	0.052

Table 7. Single-variable models of $log(S)$ for branch 2.5

	c_i	d_i	R Square
Model (Equation) 5.2.1.6 ($i=1$)	0.796	0.492	0.321
Model (Equation) 5.2.1.7 ($i=2$)	0.614	0.299	0.233
Model (Equation) 5.2.1.8 ($i=3$)	0.269	0.679	0.731

Accordingly, six power-law models can be established between development time and effort measurements, and number of committers (staff) and effort measurements. We remark here that in these equations, T is measured in days and S is measured in persons.

$$T = 0.036 \times E_1^{0.813} \qquad (5.3.1.1)$$

$$T = 0.081 \times E_2^{0.4} \qquad (5.3.1.2)$$

$$T = 1.341 \times E_3^{0.284} \qquad (5.3.1.3)$$

$$S = 1.736 \times E_1^{0.492} \qquad (5.3.1.4)$$

$$S = 1.530 \times E_2^{0.299} \qquad (5.3.1.5)$$

$$S = 1.205 \times E_3^{0.679} \qquad (5.3.1.6)$$

As described before, these six models are built using the first 40 revisions of Branch 2.5. To evaluate the forward prediction accuracy of these models, they are used to estimate the development time and the number of committers in the next 35 revisions of Branch 2.5. The result is illustrated in Figure 4 where T1, T2, and T3, are the estimated development time based on Model 5.3.1.1, Model 5.3.1.2, and Model 5.3.1.3, respectively; and Figure 5, where S1, S2, and S3, are the estimated number of committers based on Model 5.3.1.4, Model 5.3.1.5, and Model 5.3.1.6, respectively.

Next, we analyze the multi-variable models. The results of linear regression analysis of Equations 5.2.2.3–5.2.2.4 are summarized in Table 8. The corresponding power-law models are given in Equations 5.3.1.7 and 5.3.1.8.

$$T = 0.066 \times E_1^{1.04} \times E_2^{-0.086} \times E_3^{-0.218} \quad (5.3.1.7)$$

$$S = 0.517 \times E_1^{-0.031} \times E_2^{0.119} \times E_3^{0.635} \quad (5.3.1.8)$$

Comparing the R square values of single-variable models (Table 6 and Table 7) with multi-variable models (Table 8), we can see that in general multi-variable models have greater R square values, which means they outperform single-variable models in predicting development time and number of committers in each revision.

It should be noted that the model performance represented by the R square value is a self-assessment of the model with the same data set (Revisions 2.5.1 to 2.5.40) that generated the model. To evaluate the forward prediction accuracy of these two multi-variable models, we use them to estimate the development time and the number of committers in the second data set of Branch 2.5 (Revisions 2.5.41 to 2.5.75). The results are illustrated in Figure 6 and Figure 7.

The average forward prediction accuracies of both single-variable models and multi-variable models are calculated and summarized in Table 9. The prediction accuracy is calculated using the formula:

$$1 - abs(observation - estimation) / observation$$

Figure 4. Estimation of development time in Linux kernel branch 2.5 based on single-variable models

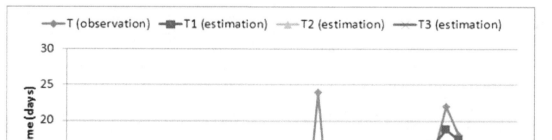

Figure 5. Estimation of number of committers in Linux kernel branch 2.5 based on single-variables

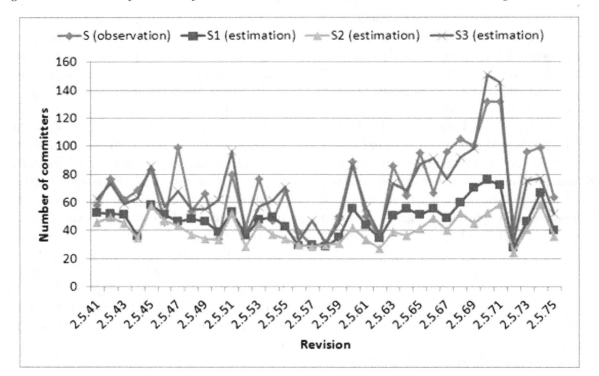

Table 8. Multi-variable models for branch 2.5

Model	a(c)	$b_1(d_1)$	$b_2(d_2)$	$b_3(d_3)$	R Square
log(T) model (Eq. 5.2.2.3)	-3.917	1.040	-0.086	-0.218	0.381
log(S) model (Eq. 5.2.2.4)	-0.952	-0.031	0.119	0.635	0.756

We can see that multi-variable models perform at least as good as the best single-variable model.

5.3.2. Branch 2.6

Linux kernel Branch 2.6 contains 39 revisions (Version 2.6.1 through Version 2.6.39). In this part of the study, the first 20 revisions (Version 2.6.1 through Version 2.6.20) are used to build prediction models. The remaining 19 versions (Version 2.6.21 through Version 2.6.39) are used to evaluate the prediction models.

First, we analyze the single-variable models. The results of linear regression analysis of Equations 5.2.1.3–5.2.1.5 are summarized in Table 10 and the results of linear regression analysis of Equations 5.2.1.6–5.2.1.8 are summarized in Table 11.

Accordingly, six power-law models can be established between development time and effort measurements, and number of committers (staff) and effort measurements.

$$T = 0.027 \times E_1^{0.92} \qquad (5.3.2.1)$$

Figure 6. Estimation of the development time in Linux kernel branch 2.5 based on the multi-variable model

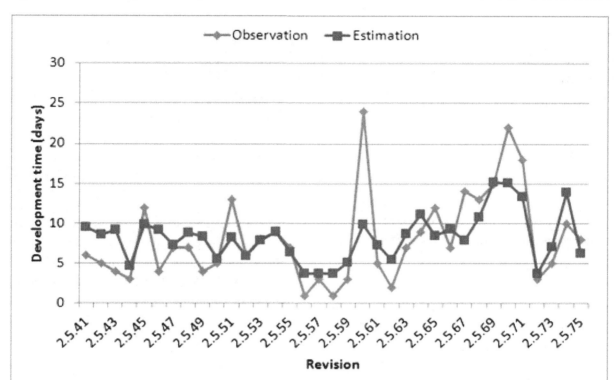

Figure 7. Estimation of the number of committers in Linux kernel branch 2.5 based on the multi-variable model

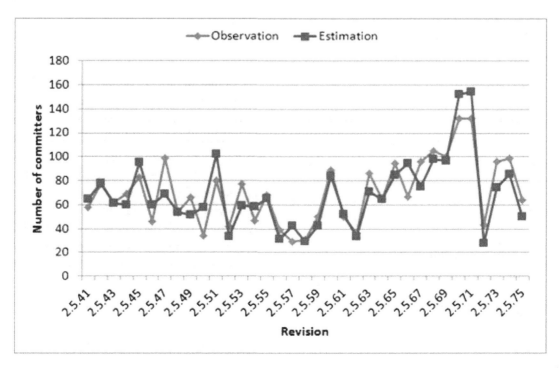

Table 9. Comparisons of the average prediction accuracies of single-variable models (5.3.1.1–5.3.1.6) and multi-variable models (5.3.1.7–5.3.1.8)

	Single-Variable Model			Multi-Variable Model
Independent variable	E_1	E_2	E_3	E_1, E_2, E_3
Dependent variable: Development time (T)	42%	46%	32%	44%
Dependent variable: Number of committers (S)	72%	63%	83%	82%

Table 10. Single-variable models of $\log(T)$ for branch 2.6

	a_i	b_i	R Square
Model (Equation) 5.2.1.3 ($i=1$)	-5.206	0.920	0.772
Model (Equation) 5.2.1.4 ($i=2$)	-8.431	0.772	0.615
Model (Equation) 5.2.1.5 ($i=3$)	-1.871	0.655	0.671

Table 11. Single-variable models of $\log(S)$ for branch 2.6

	c_i	d_i	R Square
Model (Equation) 5.2.1.6 ($i=1$)	-5.485	1.194	0.867
Model (Equation) 5.2.1.7 ($i=2$)	-10.076	1.023	0.723
Model (Equation) 5.2.1.8 ($i=3$)	-2.212	0.942	0.925

$$T = 0.003 \times E_2^{0.772} \qquad (5.3.2.2)$$

$$T = 0.273 \times E_3^{0.655} \qquad (5.3.2.3)$$

$$S = 0.022 \times E_1^{1.194} \qquad (5.3.2.4)$$

$$S = 0.001 \times E_2^{1.023} \qquad (5.3.2.5)$$

$$S = 0.216 \times E_3^{0.942} \qquad (5.3.2.6)$$

As described before, these six models are built using the first 20 revisions of Branch 2.6. To evaluate the forward prediction accuracy of these models, we use them to estimate the development time and the number of committers in the next 19 revisions of Branch 2.6. The result is illustrated in Figure 8 where T1, T2, and T3 are the estimated development time based on Model 5.3.2.1, Model 5.3.2.2, and Model 5.3.2.3, respectively, and Figure 9, where S1, S2, and S3 are the estimated number of committers based on Model 5.3.2.4, Model 5.3.2.5, and Model 5.3.2.6, respectively.

Next, we analyze the multi-variable models. The results of linear regression analysis of Equations 5.2.2.3–5.2.2.4 are summarized in Table 12. The corresponding power-law models are given in Equations 5.3.2.7 and 5.3.2.8.

$$T = 0.092 \times E_1^{1.215} \times E_2^{-0.277} \times E_3^{-0.016} \qquad (5.3.2.7)$$

$$S = 0.338 \times E_1^{0.546} \times E_2^{-0.26} \times E_3^{0.738} \qquad (5.3.2.8)$$

Comparing the R square values of single-variable models (Table 10 and Table 11) and multi-variable models (Table 12), we can see that in general multi-variable models have greater R square values, which means they outperform single-variable models in predicting the development time and the number of committers in each revision. To evaluate the forward prediction accuracy of these two multi-variable models, we use them to estimate the development time and the number of committers in the second data set

Figure 8. Estimation of development time in Linux kernel branch 2.6 based on single-variable models

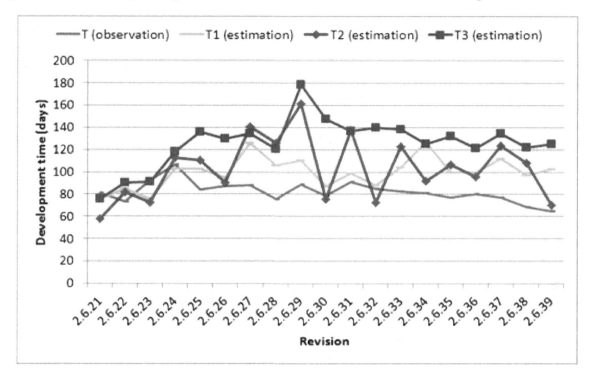

Figure 9. Estimation of the number of committers in Linux kernel branch 2.6 based on single-variable models

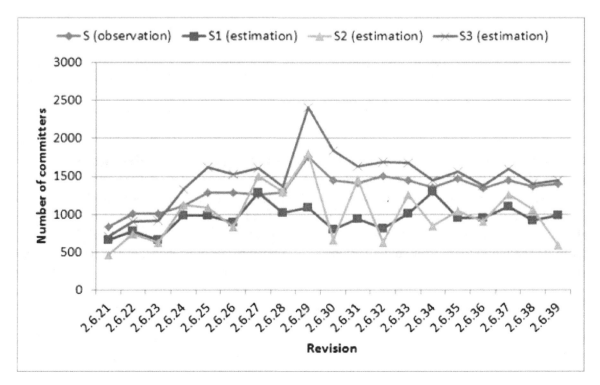

Table 12. Multi-variable models for branch 2.6

Model	a(c)	$b_1(d_1)$	$b_2(d_2)$	$b_3(d_3)$	R square
$log(T)$ model (Eq. 5.2.2.3)	-3.448	1.215	-0.277	-0.016	0.782
$log(S)$ model (Eq. 5.2.2.4)	-1.567	0.546	-0.260	0.738	0.938

Figure 10. Estimation of the development time in Linux kernel branch 2.6 based on the multi-variable model

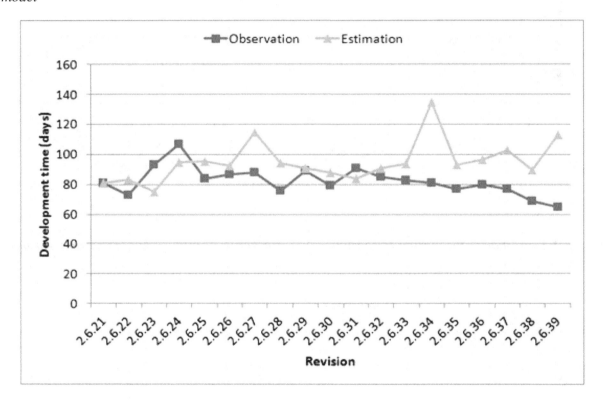

of Branch 2.6 (Revisions 2.6.21 to 2.6.39). The results are illustrated in Figure 10 and Figure 11.

The average forward prediction accuracies of these models are calculated and summarized in Table 13. We can see that multi-variable models perform at least as good as the best single-variable model.

5.4. Cross-Branch Predictions

In this part of the study, the Linux kernel revision data of Branch 2.5 are used to build prediction models. These models are then evaluated on the revision data of Branch 2.6. The results of single-variable models are summarized in Table 14 and

Figure 11. Estimation of the number of committers in Linux kernel branch 2.6 based on the multi-variable model

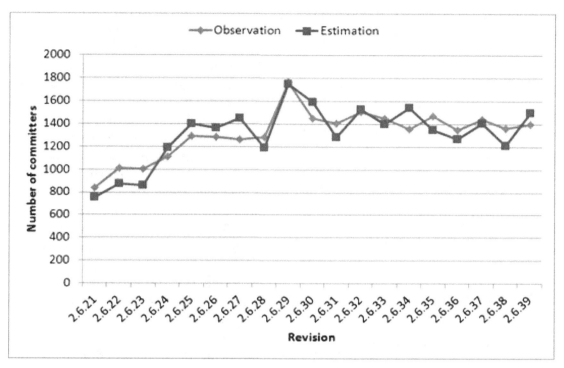

Table 13. Comparisons of the average prediction accuracies of single-variable models (5.3.2.1–5.3.2.6) and multi-variable models (5.3.2.7–5.3.2.8)

	Single-Variable Model			Multi-Variable Model
Independent variable	E_1	E_2	E_3	E_1, E_2, E_3
Dependent variable: Development time (T)	74%	67%	44%	79%
Dependent variable: Number of committers (S)	73%	73%	86%	92%

Table 14. Single-variable cross-branch models of $\log(T)$

	a_i	b_i	R Square
Model (Equation) 5.2.1.3 ($i=1$)	-5.292	0.846	0.442
Model (Equation) 5.2.1.4 ($i=2$)	-5.306	0.508	0.282
Model (Equation) 5.2.1.5 ($i=3$)	-1.042	0.461	0.188

Table 15. The results of multi-variable models are summarized in Table 16.

Accordingly, eight power-law models can be established for development time and number of staff (committers).

$$T = 0.026 \times E_1^{0.846} \qquad (5.4.1)$$

$$T = 0.025 \times E_2^{0.508} \qquad (5.4.2)$$

$$T = 0.486 \times E_3^{0.461} \qquad (5.4.3)$$

$$S = 0.762 \times E_1^{0.644} \qquad (5.4.4)$$

$$S = 0.727 \times E_2^{0.390} \qquad (5.4.5)$$

$$S = 1.295 \times E_3^{0.667} \qquad (5.4.6)$$

$$T = 0.024 \times E_1^{1.008} \times E_2^{-0.005} \times E_3^{-0.173} \qquad (5.4.7)$$

$$S = 0.709 \times E_1^{0.005} \times E_2^{0.08} \times E_3^{0.615} \qquad (5.4.8)$$

Comparing the R square values of single-variable models (Table 14 and Table 15) with multi-variable models (Table 16), again we can see that in general multi-variable models have greater R square values, which means they outperform single-variable models in predicting development time and number of committers in each revision.

Note that these eight models are built based on the revision data of Linux kernel Branch 2.5. To evaluate their cross-branch prediction accuracies, we use them to estimate the development time and the number of committers in the revisions of the Linux kernel Branch 2.6. The results are illustrated in Figure 12 through Figure 15. In these figures, T1, T2, and T3, are the estimated development time based on Model 5.4.1, Model 5.4.2, and Model 5.4.3, respectively, and S1, S2, and S3, are the estimated number of committers based on Model 5.4.4, Model 5.4.5, and Model 5.4.6, respectively.

From these figures, we can see that models built on the revision data of Branch 2.5 could not accurately predict the development time and the number of staff in the revisions of Branch 2.6.

Table 15. single-variable cross-branch models of $log(S)$

	c_i	d_i	R Square
Model (Equation) 5.2.1.6 ($i=1$)	-0.392	0.644	0.523
Model (Equation) 5.2.1.7 ($i=2$)	-0.461	0.390	0.340
Model (Equation) 5.2.1.8 ($i=3$)	0.373	0.667	0.802

Table 16. Multi-variable cross-branch models

Model	$a(c)$	$b_1(d_1)$	$b_2(d_2)$	$b_3(d_3)$	R Square
$log(T)$ model (Eq. 5.2.2.3)	-5.363	1.008	-0.005	-0.173	0.453
$log(S)$ model (Eq. 5.2.2.4)	-0.496	0.005	0.080	0.615	0.812

Figure 12. Estimation of the development time of revisions of Linux kernel branch 2.6 based on cross-branch single-variable models

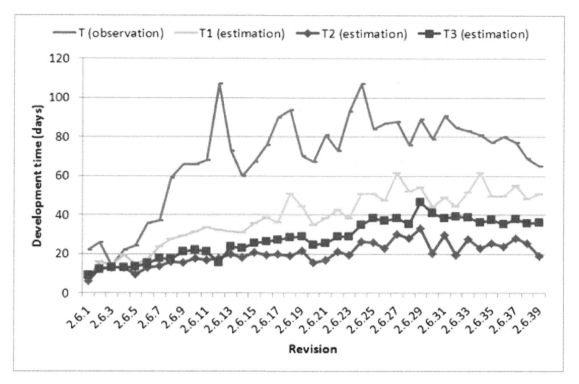

Figure 13. Estimation of the number of committers in the revisions of Linux kernel branch 2.6 based on cross-branch single-variable models

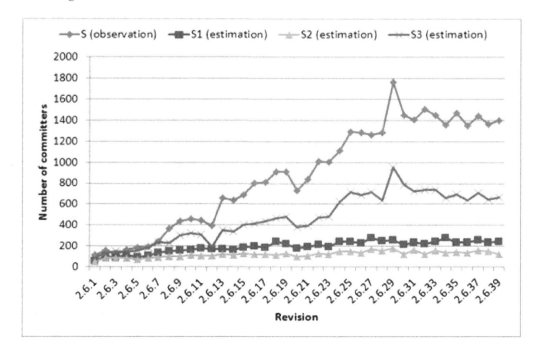

Figure 14. Estimation of the development time of the revisions of Linux kernel branch 2.6 based on the cross-branch multiple-variable model (model 5.4.7)

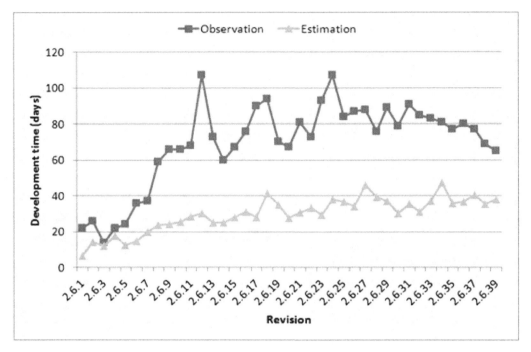

Figure 15. Estimation of the number of committers in the revisions of Linux kernel branch 2.6 based on the cross-branch multiple-variable model (model 5.4.8)

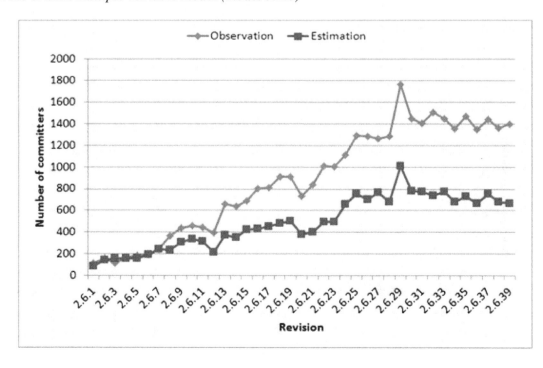

Table 17. Comparisons of the average cross-branch prediction accuracies of single-variable models (5.4.1–5.4.6) and multi-variable models (5.4.7–5.4.8)

	Single-Variable Model			Multi-Variable Model
Independent variable	E_1	E_2	E_3	E_1, E_2, E_3
Dependent variable: development time (T)	57%	32%	42%	45%
Dependent variable: number of committers (S)	30%	21%	60%	61%

Detailed analysis of their cross-branch prediction accuracies is summarized in Table 17.

Let us compare Table 13 and Table 17. Table 13 shows the prediction accuracies of inner-branch models in estimating the development time and the number of committers in the revisions of 2.6.21 through 2.6.39. Table 17 shows the prediction accuracies of cross-branch models in estimating the development time and the number of committers in the revisions of 2.6.1 through 2.6.39. We can see that inner-branch models can produce more accurate predictions than cross-branch models.

Our study found that in Linux Branch 2.5 and Branch 2.6, we can use the power-law models built from part of the revisions in one branch to predict the development time and the number of developers of other revisions within the same branch. However, using power-law models built from revisions of one branch to estimate the development time and the number of committers of revisions in a different branch cannot provide high accuracy predictions. These differences could be due to the configuration management differences between these two branches or due to the working style differences of the developers in these two branches.

5.5. Comparison of Closed-Source Development Time Models and Linux Development Time Models

Using linear regression analysis, we can model the following relations between the development time, measured in months, and code measurement effort E_2, measured in KLOC (thousands of lines of code) for Linux Branch 2.5 (Equation 5.5.1) and Linux Branch 2.6 (Equation 5.5.2). We note here that in these two models, symbol E_2 is replaced with $KLOC$ for the purpose of easy comparisons with closed-source models.

$$T = 0.028 \times KLOC^{0.508} \qquad (5.5.1)$$

$$T = 0.061 \times KLOC^{0.574} \qquad (5.5.2)$$

In COCOMO II 2000 model, development effort E (person-months) has approximately the following relations with development effort $KLOC$ [4].

$$E \approx 2.94 * KLOC^{1.26} \qquad (5.5.3)$$

Replacing KLOC in Equations 5.5.1 and 5.5.2 with effort E (person-month) in Equation 5.5.3, we can obtain two new models for Linux kernel project, Equations 5.5.4 and 5.5.5, where Equation 5.5.4 is for Branch 2.5 and Equation 5.5.5 is for Branch 2.6. These two equations model the relations between development time measured in months and development effort measured in person-months in Linux kernel project.

$$T \approx 0.018 \times E^{0.40} \qquad (5.5.4)$$

$$T \approx 0.037 \times E^{0.46} \qquad (5.5.5)$$

Comparing Equations 5.5.4 and 5.5.5 with the closed-source formulas listed in Table 1, we can see that the power parts of independent variable E have no big differences: in closed-source projects, the power part of variable E is about 0.35 and in Linux project, the power part of variable E is about 0.43. However, the coefficients of variable E differ dramatically between closed-source models (Table 1) and Linux models (Equations 5.5.4 and 5.5.5): in closed-source models, the coefficient is about 2.5 while in Linux models, the coefficient is on average about 0.028.

Summarizing the comparisons, we can see that in Linux kernel project, the development time follow similar power-law relations with development effort as observed in closed-source projects. However, Linux projects have much shorter development time than closed-source projects, which means Linux kernel is delivered much faster than the nominal schedule of closed-source projects, given the same amount of effort that is needed to develop/maintain the product. These observations match the general difference between open-source projects and closed-source projects: open-source projects are released more frequently than closed-source projects.

6. CONCLUSION

In this chapter, we studied the power-law relations between development time and development effort, number of staff and development effort in two branches of the Linux kernel project. Linear regression is used to model specific relations between development time, number of committers and three measurements of development effort. The study showed that in general (1) models built from multiple effort measurements outperform models built from a single effort measurement; (2) models built from revision data of the same branch outperform models built from revision data of a different branch.

Our study also compared the time schedule models of Linux project with the time schedule models of closed-source projects and found Linux project has a much shorter development time than the closed-source projects given the same amount of required effort to complete the project.

As with any empirical studies, there are some threats to the validity of our research. The internal threat to validity is the significance of the results. Although some prediction models can generate high accuracy of predictions, some prediction models do not have high R square values. This means not all the models are guaranteed to provide accurate predictions. The external threat to the validity is that the results found in the Linux kernel project might not be applicable to other open-source projects. To generalize our studies, more work is needed on other open-source projects.

It is our hope that the empirical knowledge of software development effort obtained in this study could help project management and cost control in both open-source communities and closed-source industries.

REFERENCES

Abrahamsson, P., Moser, R., Pedrycz, W., Sillitti, A., & Succi, G. (2007). Effort prediction in iterative software development processes -- Incremental versus global prediction models. In *Proceedings of the 1st International Symposium on Empirical Software Engineering and Measurement* (pp. 344–353). Madrid, Spain. IEEE.

Albrecht, A. J., & Gaffney, J. E. (1983). Software function, source lines of code, and development effort prediction: A software science validation. *IEEE Transactions on Software Engineering*, 9(6), 639–648. doi:10.1109/TSE.1983.235271.

Boehm, B. W. (1981). *Software engineering economics*. Englewood Cliffs, NJ: Prentice-Hall.

Boehm, B. W., Abts, C., Brown, A. W., Chulani, S., Clark, B. K., & Horowitz, E. ... Steece, B. (2000). Software cost estimation with COCOMO II. Englewood Cliffs, NJ: Prentice-Hall.

Caivano, D., Lanubile, F., & Visaggio, G. (2001). Software renewal process comprehension using dynamic effort estimation. In *Proceedings of International Conference on Software Maintenance* (pp. 209–218). Florence, Italy: IEEE.

Chulani, S., Boehm, B. W., & Steece, B. (1999). Bayesian analysis of empirical software engineering cost models. *IEEE Transactions on Software Engineering*, *25*(4), 573–583. doi:10.1109/32.799958.

De Lucia, A., Pompella, E., & Stefanucci, S. (2005). Assessing effort estimation models for corrective maintenance through empirical studies. *Information and Software Technology*, *47*(1), 3–15. doi:10.1016/j.infsof.2004.05.002.

Donelson, W. S. (1976, June). Project planning and control. *Datamation*, 73–80.

Fioravanti, F., & Nesi, P. (2001). Estimation and prediction metrics for adaptive maintenance effort of object-oriented systems. *IEEE Transactions on Software Engineering*, *27*(12), 1062–1084. doi:10.1109/32.988708.

Huang, X., Ho, D., Ren, J., & Capretz, L. F. (2007). Improving the COCOMO model using a neuro-fuzzy approach. *Applied Soft Computing*, *7*(1), 29–40. doi:10.1016/j.asoc.2005.06.007.

Idri, A., Kjiri, L., & Abran, A. (2000). COCOMO cost model using fuzzy logic. In *Proceedings of the 7th International Conference on Fuzzy Theory and Technology* (pp. 219–223). Atlantic City, NJ: IEEE.

Jeffery, D. R., & Low, G. (1990). Calibrating estimation tools for software development. *Software Engineering Journal*, *5*(4), 215–222. doi:10.1049/sej.1990.0024.

Jeffery, D. R., Ruhe, M., & Wieczorek, I. (2000). A comparative study of cost modeling techniques using public domain multi-organizational and company-specific data. *Information and Software Technology*, *42*(14), 1009–1016. doi:10.1016/S0950-5849(00)00153-1.

Jorgensen, M. (1995). Experience with the accuracy of software maintenance task effort prediction models. *IEEE Transactions on Software Engineering*, *21*(8), 674–681. doi:10.1109/32.403791.

Kitchenham, B. A., & Mendes, E. (2009). Why comparative effort prediction studies may be invalid. In *Proceedings of the 5th International Conference on Predictor Models in Software Engineering* (pp. 4:1–4:5). Vancouver, Canada: IEEE.

Koch, S. (2008). Effort modeling and programmer participation in open source software projects. *Information Economics and Policy*, *20*(4), 345–355. doi:10.1016/j.infoecopol.2008.06.004.

Koch, S., & Schneider, G. (2002). Effort, co-operation and co-ordination in an open source software project: GNOME. *Information Systems Journal*, *12*(1), 27–42. doi:10.1046/j.1365-2575.2002.00110.x.

Maxwell, K., Wassenhove, L. V., & Dutta, S. (1999). Performance evaluation of general and company specific models in software development effort estimation. *Management Science*, *45*(6), 77–83. doi:10.1287/mnsc.45.6.787.

Menzies, T., Chen, Z., Hihn, J., & Lum, K. (2006). Selecting best practices for effort estimation. *IEEE Transactions on Software Engineering*, *32*(11), 883–895. doi:10.1109/TSE.2006.114.

Menzies, T., Port, D., Chen, Z., Hihn, J., & Sherry, S. (2005). Validation methods for calibrating software effort models. In *Proceedings of the 27th International Conference on Software Engineering* (pp. 15–21). St. Louis, MO: IEEE.

Nguyen, V. (2010a). Improved size and effort estimation models for software maintenance. In *Proceedings of 26ᵗʰ International Conference on Software Maintenance*. Timisoara, Romania: IEEE.

Nguyen, V. (2010b). *Improved size and effort estimation models for software maintenance.* (Unpublished PhD Dissertation). University of South California, Columbia, SC.

Parkinson, G. N. (1957). *Parkinson's law and other studies in administration.* Boston, MA: Houghton-Mifflin.

Putnam, L. H. (1978). A general empirical solution to the macro software sizing and estimating problem. *IEEE Transactions on Software Engineering, 4*(4), 345–361. doi:10.1109/TSE.1978.231521.

Ramil, J. F. (2000). Algorithmic cost estimation software evolution. In *Proceedings of the 22ⁿᵈ International Conference on Software Engineering* (pp. 701–703). Limerick, Ireland: IEEE.

Reddy, C. S., & Raju, K. (2009). An improved fuzzy approach for COCOMO's effort estimation using Gaussian membership function. *Journal of Software, 4*(5), 452–459. doi:10.4304/jsw.4.5.452-459.

Sneed, H. M. (2004). A cost model for software maintenance and evolution. In *Proceedings of the IEEE International Conference on Software Maintenance* (pp. 264–273). Chicago, IL: IEEE.

Sneed, H. M. (2005). Estimating the cost of a reengineering project. In *Proceedings of the 12ᵗʰ Working Conference on Reverse Engineering* (pp. 111–119). Pittsburgh, PA: IEEE.

Trendowicz, A., Heidrich, J., Münch, J., Ishigai, Y., Yokoyama, K., & Kikuchi, N. (2006). Development of a hybrid cost estimation model in an iterative manner. In *Proceedings of the 28ᵗʰ International Conference on Software Engineering* (pp. 331–340). Shanghai, China: IEEE.

Van Vliet, H. (2008). *Software engineering: Principles and practice.* Chichester, UK: John Wiley & Sons.

Walston, C. E., & Felix, C. P. (1997). A method of programming measurement and estimation. *IBM Systems Journal, 16*, 54–73. doi:10.1147/sj.161.0054.

Yu, L. (2006). Indirectly predicting the maintenance effort of open-source software. *Journal of Software Maintenance and Evolution: Research and Practice, 18*(5), 311–332. doi:10.1002/smr.335.

ENDNOTES

1.   http://www.kernel.org/
2.   http://git.kernel.org
3.   http://git-scm.com/
4.   http://csse.usc.edu/csse/research/COCOMOII/cocomo2000.0/CII_modelman2000.0.pdf

Chapter 7

Understanding Requirement Engineering Practices:
An Empirical Study of the Pakistani Software Industry

Saqib Saeed
Bahria University, Pakistan

Ashi Iram
Bahria University, Pakistan

Kiran Nazeer
Bahria University, Pakistan

Tayyaba Ayub
Bahria University, Pakistan

ABSTRACT

Requirement engineering is a main task in software process. In Software Engineering literature, many best practices and guidelines are present to construct quality software. However, adoption of such uniform guidelines is not in practice across the globe. In this chapter, the authors discuss requirement engineering practices followed in Pakistani small- and medium-scale enterprises. In order to understand work practices the authors conducted a survey and analyzed the responses. They found that cost and budgeting is one of the major issues of Pakistani industry: higher management is not willing to invest to adopt state-of-the-art standardized practices. This situation can be improved by enhancing public private partnerships to get desired quality software in the local IT industry.

DOI: 10.4018/978-1-4666-4229-4.ch007

1. INTRODUCTION

Requirements Engineering (RE) can be defined as the study concerned with examining and documenting requirements for a software application (cf. Thayer & Dorfman, 1997). In this phase requirements of a software system are described, controlled, tested and documented. An effective requirement engineering process ensures that software satisfies customer and user requirements (cf. Kauppinen & Kujala, 2001; Kauppinen et al., 2002; Kauppinen et al., 2004). Davis (1993) highlighted that it may be up to 200 times costly to discover and fix faults in the maintenance phase, compared to discovering and fixing them in requirement engineering phase. Sommerville and Kotonya (1998) described RE process as a planned set of activities followed to obtain, authenticate, and preserve system requirements. Transforming RE research results into work practices are complex tasks and it depends on successful collaboration between researchers and practitioners (Kaindl et al., 2002).

There is a lot of literature in software engineering domain regarding requirement engineering approaches but transferring this knowledge into practice is a complex activity (cf. Siddiqi & Shekaran, 1996; Saeed et al., 2012). Davis and Hsia (1994) described that researchers and practitioner have gap in their practices and it need to be filled to get quality software. Nikula et al., (2000) reported that most companies know the requirements engineering problems but are unable to find the solutions for achieving quality products.

A study on software engineers' practices at Jet Propulsion Laboratory highlighted that requirements were not properly documented and their rationale were also not listed (cf. Kandt et al., 2002; Kandt, 2003). Belgraver (2007) reported that larger IT organizations are using workshops as default techniques for requirement engineering process. Gunda (2008) conducted a survey on requirement elicitation techniques practiced in multinational companies of India and found that a variety of tools (such as interviewing, brainstorming, questionnaire etc) are used but organizations prefer time efficient tool in their organizations. Keeping this in view we carried out a survey to understand the requirement engineering practices followed in Pakistani local organizations. The objective of the investigation was to get knowledge about current practices and to suggest improvements.

Remaining of chapter is structured as follows. Section 2 highlights problem and methodology adopted to answer these problems. Section 3 discusses main findings and is followed by discussion in section 4. Section 5 presents conclusion of our contribution.

2. PROBLEM STATEMENT AND METHODOLOGY

The requirement engineering is a challenging and demanding phase in software development process. Many software development organizations do not follow standardized practices due to many issues such as cost, time, nature of project and geographical diversity of client/development team. Our focus in this chapter is to highlight major challenges that may encounter during requirement engineering process by Small and Medium Scale Enterprises (SMEs) in Pakistan. Software industry in Pakistan is young and mainly comprised of SMEs (cf. Mahmood & Saeed, 2008). Our main focus was to assess and analyze different practices of requirement engineering process in Pakistan.

In order to answer the questions we adopted a quantitative approach and a detailed questionnaire was developed, aimed at determining the different practices of requirement engineering process. There were total 17 questions. The questions addressed the knowledge on RE literature and Requirements Management (RM) tools as well as the current RE practices. Every question can be answered either a strongly agreed, agreed, uncertain, disagreed and strongly disagreed. Thirty questionnaires were sent to different organizations through emails and in person, out of which 19 questionnaire were received back. We analyzed the data and created bar charts against every question to examine the tending behavior of the industry towards every process of the requirement engineering process.

3. SURVEY RESULTS

Communication among customers and development team is very important in an effective requirement engineering process. We wanted to know whether Pakistani SMEs regard this important or not. In response to our question regarding communication between the customer focal person and technical persons, 4 respondents strongly

agreed with this practice, 14 agreed and 1 was uncertain, as shown in Figure 1. Similarly, use of a standardized document template is important for consistency and better knowledge sharing. Organizations use standard document structure across the projects. In our survey we found that 1 respondent strongly agreed with this practice, 12 agreed, 2 were uncertain, 2 disagreed and 2 strongly disagreed (shown in Figure 2).

Validation checklist is an important tool for requirement analysis. As a result of analysis one can find that requirements are complete, feasible and prioritized. In our survey we found that 2 respondents strongly agreed with this practice, 11 agreed, 2 were uncertain, 3 disagreed, and 1 strongly disagreed as shown in Figure 3. Use cases and scenarios are effective tools to capture

Figure 1. Communication between customer and technical person

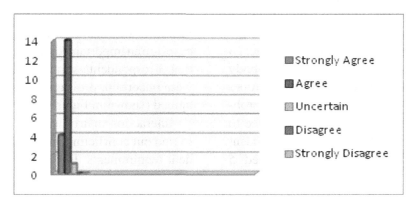

Figure 2. Standardized document structure

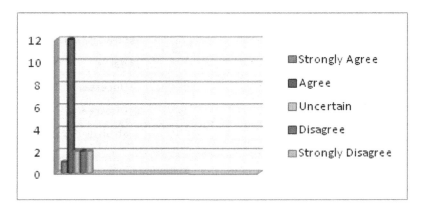

Figure 3. Use of validation checklists

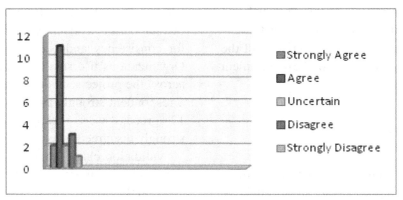

software requirement in an effective manner. In our survey we found that 2 respondents strongly agreed with this practice, 6 agreed, 5 were uncertain, 2 disagreed, and 4 strongly disagreed (shown in Figure 4).

In order to design an effective software application, understanding domain requirements is quite important. In our survey, we found that 6 respondents strongly agreed with this practice, 8 agreed, 4 were uncertain, 1 disagreed and nobody strongly disagreed as shown in Figure 5. Proper examination of requirements helps to detect problems earlier and thus is an essential practice to realize quality software. In our survey 1 respondent strongly agreed with the practice, 10 agreed, 5

were uncertain, 1 disagreed, and 2 strongly disagreed (shown in Figure 6).

Requirement engineering process should ensure that customer satisfaction and objectives are met. In our survey 5 persons strongly agreed, 10 agreed, 2 were uncertain, 1 disagreed and 1 strongly disagreed with this practice as shown in Figure 7. In order to validate requirements test cases are an important tool. In our survey we found that 3 respondents strongly agreed, 8 agreed, 2 were uncertain, 3 disagreed and 3 strongly disagreed (shown in Figure 8).

Interaction matrix is an important technique to find out conflicting, overlapping and independent requirements. In our survey, we found that

Figure 4. Use of use cases and scenarios

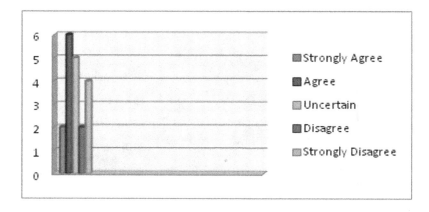

Figure 5. Understanding domain requirements

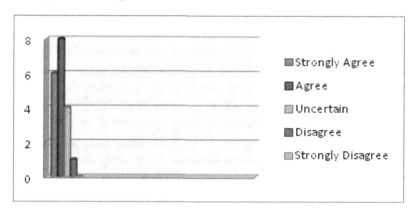

Figure 6. Examination of requirements

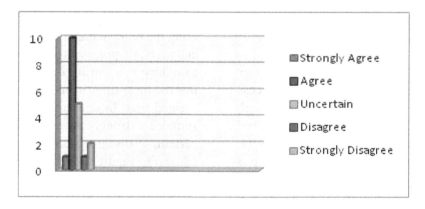

Figure 7. Customer satisfaction and meeting objectives

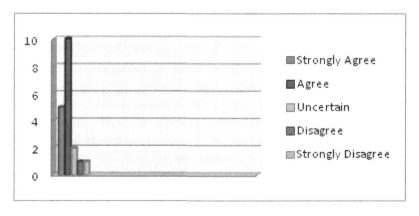

Figure 8. Use of test cases for requirement validation

1 respondent strongly agreed with this practice, 2 agreed, 8 were uncertain, 5 disagreed and 3 strongly disagreed as shown in Figure 9.

Observation is an important tool to extract requirements. In our survey we found that 5 respondents strongly agreed with this practice, 13 agreed, 1 was uncertain, nobody disagreed or strongly disagreed as shown in Figure 10. External reviewers are involved to validate the process. In our survey we found that 1 person strongly agreed, 9 agreed, 2 were uncertain, 6 disagreed, and 1 strongly disagreed as shown in Figure 11.

In an effective requirements engineering process, rejected requirements are used to be recorded along with the reasons to be avoided. In our survey we found that 5 persons strongly agreed with this practice, 3 agreed, 6 were uncertain, 3 disagreed, and 2 strongly disagreed as shown in Figure 12.

Requirement prioritization is used for considering the relative importance of requirements for end users. Requirement prioritization is also used to reduce risk during implementation phase so that the most significant requirements are implemented first. In our survey we found that 2 respondents strongly agreed, 13 agreed, 1 was uncertain, 2 disagreed and 1 strongly disagreed (shown in Figure 13). Requirement engineering process helps in analyzing that given requirements can be implemented in available budget and tech-

Figure 9. Use of interaction matrix in requirement analysis

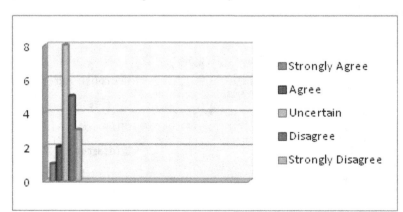

Figure 10. Use of observation in requirement elicitation

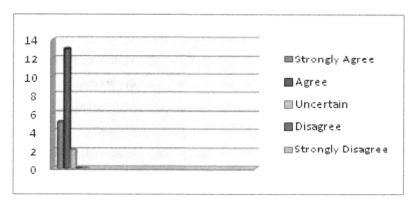

Figure 11. Use of external reviewers in requirement engineering process

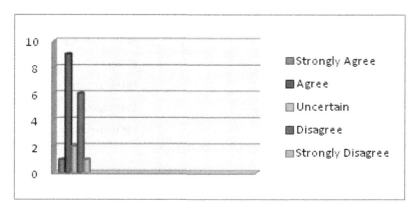

Figure 12. Documenting rejected requirements

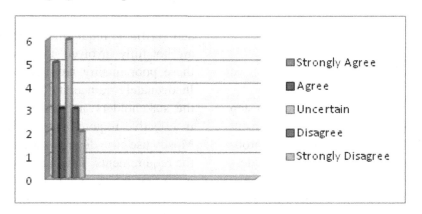

Figure 13. Use of requirement prioritization

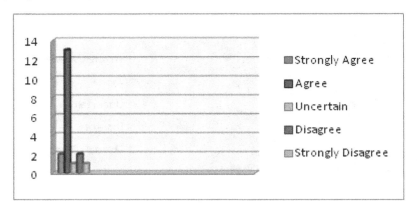

Figure 14. Realistic realization of requirements

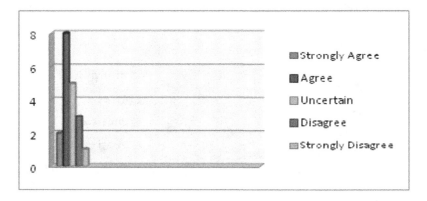

nology. In our survey we found 2 respondents strongly agreed, 8 agreed, 5 were uncertain, 3 disagreed, and 1 strongly disagreed as shown in Figure 14.

4. DISCUSSION

Requirements engineering is very important step in software development process. In requirement elicitation stakeholders play a vital role, but problems start at this stage because all stakeholders are not fully available to discuss the requirements. Use of multiple techniques in requirement elicitation helps to get balanced requirements but we observed that in Pakistani SMEs not all elicitation techniques are used. Furthermore, extensive involvement of stakeholders in requirement elicitation process helps in getting consistent and verifiable requirements. If the stakeholders are not fully involved in elicitation phase then these poor quality requirements are expected. Inadequately trained staff, inadequate access to the stakeholders and limited resources hinder in effective requirements engineering process. Mostly use case diagrams are used for modeling the requirements. Tracing of requirements is an important issue; requirement tracing should be ensured both at early in the project as well as in later design development and maintenance levels.

Otherwise, in many organizations this practice is not followed due to which changes at architectural, design, implementation becomes more difficult and expensive.

Missing requirements is one of the major issues found in practice. Some of the requirements are overlooked by the engineer. Requirement team should collaborate with the representatives from all groups of stakeholders and use mature elicitation techniques like state modeling diagrams. Especially architecturally significant requirements should not be overlooked, because there impact can lead to an undesirable system. Nonfunctional requirements should be handled with care. Many organizations in Pakistan overlook nonfunctional requirements especially who use case modeling. Interactions matrices are used in many organizations to resolve the conflicts in requirements. Mostly these practices are used in organizations of higher level; small organizations are not frequently using requirements matrix.

Evaluation of requirements by stakeholders, architects, designers and testers should be conducted to avoid poor requirements. Sometimes requirements validation is not carried out due to stakeholder's time and project schedule. This results in incomplete requirements that lead to the failure of needs of the stakeholders. Finding these problems in later stages can cause increase in cost and disturbing the schedule and lack of some system properties. In Pakistani organizations only few organizations use this practice. Requirements management process is not well maintained in Pakistani organizations. Some of the practices are very expensive and time consuming.

5. CONCLUSION

In this survey, different practices were discussed in detail in the light of feedback from different Pakistani small and medium scale organizations. As Pakistani IT market is suffering a lot of problems for last ten years due to uncertain political and economic situa-tions. Many practices followed in organizations are based on the product being developed. New and small organizations are using older methods of require-ments elicitation, whereas mature organizations are choosing good practices in order to maintain their repute. To improve the practices in local organiza-tions above-mentioned problems should be solved; training sessions and seminars should be conducted at organizational level.

REFERENCES

Belgraver, A. B. (2007). *The use of workshops for requirements engineering*. (Master Thesis). Universiteit van Amsterdam, Amsterdam, The Netherlands.

Davis, A. M., & Hsia, P. (1994). Giving voice to requirements engineering. *IEEE Software*, *11*(2), 12–16. doi:10.1109/52.268949.

M. Dorfman (Ed.), *(n.d.)*. *Software requirements engineering* (2nd ed.). Los Alamitos, CA: Wiley-IEEE Press.

Gunda, S. G. (2008). *Requirements engineering: Elicitation techniques*. (Doctoral dissertation). University West.

Kaindl, H., Brinkkemper, S., Bubenko, J. A. Jr, Farbey, B., Greenspan, S. J., & Heitmeyer, C. L. et al. (2002). Requirements engineering and technology transfer: Obstacles, incentives and improvement agenda. *Requirements Engineering*, *7*(3), 113–123. doi:10.1007/s007660200008.

Kandt, R. K. (2003). *Software requirements engineering: Practices and techniques (Tech. Report document D-24994)*. Jet Propulsion Laboratory.

Kandt, R. K., Kay-Im, E., Lavin, M. L., & Wax, A. (2002). *A survey of software tools and practices in use at jet propulsion laboratory (Internal Document D-24868)*. Jet Propulsion Laboratory.

Kauppinen, M., & Kujala, S. (2001). Starting improvement of requirements engineering processes: An experience report. *Product Focused Software Process Improvement*, 196-209.

Kauppinen, M., Kujala, S., Aaltio, T., & Lehtola, L. (2002). Introducing requirements engineering: How to make a cultural change happen in practice. In *Proceedings. IEEE Joint International Conference on Requirements Engineering,* (pp. 43-51). IEEE.

Kauppinen, M., Vartiainen, M., Kontio, J., Kujala, S., & Sulonen, R. (2004). Implementing requirements engineering processes throughout organizations: Success factors and challenges. *Information and Software Technology, 46*(14), 937–953. doi:10.1016/j.infsof.2004.04.002.

Mahmood, Z., & Saeed, S. (2008). Software industry in Pakistan: An investigation into the CMMI practice of project planning, monitoring and control. In *Proceedings of the 9th International Conference IBIMA*. Morocco, Tunisia: IBIMA.

Nikula, U., Sajaniemi, J., & Kälviäinen, H. (2000). *A state-of-the-practice survey on requirements engineering in small-and medium-sized enterprises.* Lappeenranta University of Technology.

Saeed, S., Khawaja, F. M., & Mahmood, Z. (2012). A review of software quality methodologies. *Advanced Automated Software Testing: Frameworks for Refined Practice, 129.*

Siddiqi, J., & Shekaran, M. C. (1996). Requirements engineering: The emerging wisdom. *IEEE Software, 13*(2), 15–19. doi:10.1109/MS.1996.506458.

Sommerville, I., & Kotonya, G. (1998). *Requirements engineering: Processes and techniques.* New York: John Wiley & Sons, Inc..

Thayer, R., & Dorfman, M. (1997). Software requirements engineering glossary. In Thayer & Davis (Eds.), Software requirements: Objects, functions, and states. Englewood Cliffs, NJ: Prentice-Hall, Inc.

Chapter 8
The Distribution of Testing Activities in Web Services and SOA Environment

Izzat Alsmadi
Prince Sultan University, Saudi Arabia

Sascha Alda
Bonn-Rhein-Sieg University, Germany

ABSTRACT

Testing in Web services and SOA environment can be far more distributed in comparison with testing stand-alone or traditional applications. This is because such systems are composed of several hybrid components. These include Web servers and their related components, server side applications, communication services, and client side Web services. In this chapter, the authors focus on challenges and opportunities for software testing in SOA environment. They divide testing activities based on three classifications: testing activities that are going to be similar to those in traditional software development environments, testing activities that will be less usable or popular in SOA, and testing activities that will evolve significantly to adapt to the new environment. The authors believe that most generic testing activities are going to stay in any new software development environment. However, their importance, significance, challenges, and difficulties are going to be dependent on the subject environment. Some tasks will be easier to implement and test and others will either be un-applicable or difficult to test and implement in comparison with testing in traditional software development environments.

DOI: 10.4018/978-1-4666-4229-4.ch008

INTRODUCTION

The recent evolution of the Internet includes continuous expansion of what is called Web services. Traditional software applications are offered to users to download or acquire from storage media such as: CDs, DVDs, etc. On the contrary, Web services are available at their server hosts and can be called by clients or users through the network or the Internet. Users get real time access and connection to those services. This form of distribution system is continuously expanding specially with the continuous growth of the Internet. It is envisioned that in future most of software applications will be delivered to customers through Web services. This is largely dependent on the expansion of the Internet with fast speed, large bandwidth, and disk availability. This means that future computers of users will carry much less amount of software components given that the majority of the components will be on the server side. This is usually referred to as thin clients. Such lightweight or mobility approach helps users to access services from anywhere and using and platform or environment (e.g. desktop, smart phone, Windows, Unix, etc.). To software companies, the major advantage of such software marketing policy is that piracy can be significantly reduced. On the other hand, and since software service will be provided in real time, a continuous challenge, risk, and effort is expected from those companies to be able to provide services with the a high quality standard. Software companies may also need to depend on several third party components, which will complicate both the development and testing processes. One more challenge for testing in such environments which is different from traditional environments is that since services are provided in a very generic reusable format, service providers can expect a wide spectrum of ways on how to use such service from the client side. While such isolation is very good for reusability, however, it may complicate the testing process.

In software testing, test cases are created and executed with the goal of trying to find possible errors in the developed programs. It is hoped to deploy software applications to users with the least possible errors. Testing activities tried to find errors no matter of their cause or origin. In one category, testing can be largely divided into black box and white box testing. In black box testing, the program is tested as a black box based on the requirements or expected services. Assertions are created for each test case and comparison is conducted between expected and actual test case results. In white box testing approach, which is usually conducted by testers not developers, developers can see the internal structure of the code. In another high level testing classification, testing can be divided into functional and non functional testing. Similar to black box testing, functional testing checks to see if the developed software performs all required services, from the users' perspective, correctly (i.e. based on users' or requirements' preferences). On the other hand, non functional testing test the high level quality attributes that are applied to the software in general and not a specific part of component of it. Examples of quality attributes that are tested for non functional testing include: performance, reliability, security, usability, etc.

The general trend in testing is that the main activities and original testing stage occur after the coding stage to test the code whether black or white box testing, functional, or non functional testing. However, there are some other portions or approaches for testing. For example, in Test Driven Development (TDD), test cases are written before the existence of the code (i.e. based on the requirements) and then executed and verified on the code. In some other cases, the software design, before the code, can be tested using some formal method approaches to possibly detect errors before even writing the code.

Service Oriented Architecture (SOA) is a relatively new software architecture that is continuously evolving and expanding with Web services' evolution. While in Object Oriented Architecture (OOA) software design is built based on finding objects or entities from the problem and solution domains for the subject software, the core in SOA is the service. A service is a user visible software functionality. This functionality is built or implemented on the server side and then called or used by users from the client side.

Software testing activities can be classified based into several perspectives. In one perspective, software testing activities can be divided into white and black box testing. In black-box testing, the software is tested based into its provided services and functionalities without looking into the software code. On the contrary, white box testing includes testing the software based on its internal structure. We think that for a large percent in the SOA Web services paradigm, traditional black box testing methods are not going to change. Any Web service should include some user level accessed inputs. Those exist on the client side of the Web services' structure. This may make it independent of the lower level details of the overall structure. On the other hand, for white box testing, many changes are expected to occur in Web services' testing in comparison with testing Web and desktop applications. Web services and SOA architectures depend on several heterogeneous components and technologies. Each one of those components can be developed by a different company using different programming language and environment. In Web services environment there are several major components that the system framework is composed from. Each one of those components needs to be tested alone. In addition, for each component, integration testing is important to make sure that the communication and messaging between the subject component and the rest of the framework is normal. Those components largely include: databases, Web servers and their related components, server side applications, communica-

tion services and client side Web services. In SOA, besides dividing testing activities into black or white box testing, or into the several components that form the architecture, testing each component separately and then testing it in integration with the others, in addition testing framework can be divided based on the SOA major testing concerns that include: testing services, security, governance, etc. In this composition, service testing represents the traditional functional.

In any service, the interface is a major component. To ensure a high level of usability, reusability, visibility and accessibility, the interface design should be thoroughly evaluated and tested to make sure that the interface is designed according to the requirements and also according to the comparable standards. A very good Web service may not be useful if its interface is not well defined, described or published as its users may not be able to see or use it as it should be.

With this new technology, several changes are expected to occur in the information technology fields and systems to adapt to this field or technology. It is expected that such new environment will impact all development stages.

For example, the traditional client server system architecture is expected to be significantly impacted with cloud computing new framework. In this chapter, we will focus on software testing activities and how this stage is going to be different in this new software development environment.

LITERATURE SURVEY

In synchronization with the scope of this book in general (i.e. knowledge management in software engineering environments), we will focus on surveying papers that discussed surveys or high level frameworks for testing architecture in SOA and Web services environment.

A Framework for Web Services' Testing

In any testing framework, several test activities occur as part of testing. Some of those activities are generic. Examples of those major testing activities are: test case generation, execution, and verification. Those three compose the minimum generic testing activities for any testing framework. However, there are several related or supporting activities. For example, test automation is considered important and necessary especially as in most cases, testing activities are repetitive and time consuming. Hence conducting such activities by human testers can be expensive and time consuming. For such test automation, another related activity that usually occurs in coordination to generate a software model from which test cases can be generated. While some test automation tools such as: record/play can do this directly from the application user interface, however in several other cases, this model can be generated from the requirements, design or any software related component. Test regression is another related activities in which the database of test cases is saved and in cases where the software program went in an evolution cycle for update or maintenance purposes, such database (also called test oracle) is executed to make sure that new changes or updates to the software did not cause any problem for the software existed parts.

Test case reduction and prioritization algorithms are also proposed to reduce the large possible number or size of test case database. The goal is to find the least possible set of representatives for the test cases that can achieve a high coverage with minimal number of test cases. In an earlier paper (Alsmadi and Magel 2007), first author proposed a complete generic test automation framework based on the data model.

In the subject of SOA and Web services testing, it seems that the proposal of a framework for testing Web services is a trend as many recent papers in this field discussed this very similar subject.

Examples of those that we listed here include: Mei and Zhang (2005), Bertolino and Polini (2005), Zhu (2006), Karam et al. (2007), Rentea et al. (2009), Ladan (2010), Freitas et al. (2010), Sun et al. (2011), and Prasanth et al. (2012). Perhaps, there are two reasons for this: One is that a trivial research experiment and second is due to nature of this area as it is relatively new or recent. In testing in general, there are several major activities that any testing framework should have. This generic framework includes: test case generation, execution and verification. In addition to other related activities: regression testing, test case prioritization, model based testing, test automation, test coverage, etc. As such, any framework, will consider those generic activities but in the context of SOA and Web services. Some of those SOA testing framework proposals may focus on some testing or SOA aspect such as: unit testing, service composition, etc.

Zhu (2006) included a description for a framework for testing Web services. Author also demonstrated a testing model (Figure 1) based on a banking Website case study to show high level testing activities. The figure points to some of the major components that should be tested as part of the Web service framework. F-service represents the functional service provided by WS while T-service represents its corresponding testing service. This indicates that for the framework of SOA, each component can have its testing component in the testing framework. Integration and system level testing components should be further added as they will either be located independently (e.g. stubs and drivers) or as part of the GUI. The paper discussed also details on how to apply the use of testing as a service (TAS). Unlike traditional testing where testing is usually conducted offline before releasing the software product or statically while the software is not live, Web services can be tested at work and the test activities themselves can be services as well.

Framework proposal includes the description of a particular system and its components from

Figure 1. Banking website framework for testing activities (Zhu, 2006)

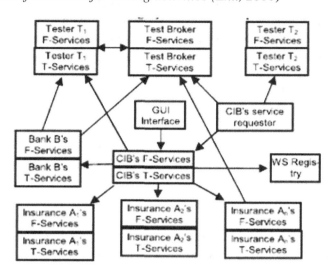

authors' perspectives. In other words, same concepts can be introduced in a different context in each framework. For example, we mentioned the general testing activities that occur in any testing process. For SOA, there are also several generic components that should exist in such architecture. As a result, each SOA testing framework tries to present some model on how to integrate those different components to achieve specific goals. This is why, the goal of the framework and the users' perspectives can judge or decide the overall architecture of such framework. For examples, some frameworks that were proposed in the SOA testing subject, focused on integration testing and how to combine those components to achieve a successful integration testing. Others focused on service composition, load testing, messaging, etc.

Similar to proposing high-level framework for testing in SOA, some papers conducted surveys related to papers published in this field. Those papers tried also to make an ontology or classification for the relevant published papers. In addition, due to the fact that both testing activities and SOA are composed of several components, some papers tried to conduct a survey to classify the types of research papers publish in this field. Examples of such books, book chapters, or papers

include: Baresi and DiNitto (2007), Bozkurt et al. (2009), Canfora and Penta (2009), and Sharma et al. (2012).

BACKGROUND

Initially computers were mainly used for solving mathematical and scientific problems where algorithms were well defined and human involvement was minimal in selecting the workflow of the programs. Programmers employed computers to solve their own problems, writing their instructions in machine readable programs. Later assembly language was used as programming environment followed by structured and object oriented paradigms. Furthermore evolution of mini and personal computers meant that software systems were required in other domains especially for office automation and educational purposes. This resulted in complex software internals, thereby increasing the complexity of its development activity too. As a result now software applications were not only transforming mathematical algorithms into computer instructions but also supporting human practices in carrying their work in efficient manner. There was no standard development methodology employed to carry out software development and as a result most of the software projects turned failure, leading to the software crisis. As a result the concept of software process emerged. Software process simply could be defined as the methodology to realize a software product. Humphrey (1989) described software process as a set of tools, methods and practices used to produce a software product. Pressman (1996) defined software process as a three phase activity i.e. definition, development and maintenance. The definition phase focuses on extending requirements, whereas development phase transforms those requirements into software system and finally maintenance phase aims at corrective actions and enhancements in software system after release.

In typical SOA environment, there are two approaches to implement a Web service: bottom up and top down based on whether the service description or the service itself should be implemented first.

A Web service framework should contain three major components: Web Service Description Language (WSDL), Service Oriented Access Protocol (SOAP), and Universal Data Description Interface (UDDI).

There are several ways and techniques to test Web services. In the following sections, we will discuss testing subjects related to SOA and Web services.

Web Services' Black-Box or Functional Testing

For the users, what matter is to make sure is that the service they requested is working in their scope or environment as they expected. Unlike traditional software developments, Web services are usually designed for a large spectrum of users who may use the same service in a different context. This may in principle be similar to designing bespoke or generic software applications (e.g. operating systems, databases, office applications, etc.). On the other hand, unlike those, largely standalone applications, Web services have a distributed nature and service provider is in a continuous relation with service consumers. Black box or functional testing for Web services then should be ideally conducted by users, service consumers, or third parties. In Web services, public registers can be helpful in this regard as they record history of service invocations.

GUI based Web service testing tools such as SOAPUI exist and available for commercial use. However, such tools can cover one aspect or perspective of testing Web services. As pointed by Martin 2005 that testing through UI is slow, opaque, and dangerous. Nonetheless, in the scope of testing, we define several coverage aspects based on the software artifacts (e.g. requirements, user interface, code, structure, paths, etc.) and research papers in software testing showed that very good coverage in only one aspect can be misleading if we ignore testing the other aspects or artefacts.

Black box testing can be categorized by two major aspects: First, testing based on the user requirements and second testing through the Graphical User Interface (GUI). In reality, both have different perspectives in the SOA environment. For the first one, and since Web services are not developed or meant to be for a specific user or usage, they don't have specific requirements similar to those in traditional Web or desktop applications. Web services are developed to be generic and users can specify their own way of using the service on the client side. As such, if we want to conduct black box testing based on the GUI of the client side applications, some problems may arise due to the client misunderstanding or usage of the service and not due originally to the service itself. The second one is also related to the first one as typical Web services do not have client specific GUIs. They have the generic WSDL XML file that includes the description of the service interface or public methods along with methods' signatures (i.e. their required inputs and produced outputs). The need to understand such difference perspective for black box testing can assist in errors localization through testing in this stage.

Stubs and Drivers for Testing Web Services

Through the development process of a Web service, in some cases, there is a need to test some specific components and their integration with the other components. However, and since the project is not complete, some components that are needed to complete the test may not be ready yet. In traditional software testing approaches, stubs and drivers (also called mock objects) are created to serve in such scenarios. Those are temporary components that are only needed to test for integration aspects and then will be removed once the real or the actual components are ready. The difference between stubs and drivers is based on whether the dummy component is the caller or the callee (aka client or server).

Web services are developed with no specific user or usage in mind. Hence part of Web services testing from the server side, a virtual component that simulates the user should be created to test the service through. Several virtual components that simulate users with different environments, settings, usage level or detail should be all simulated as part of Web service local testing in the server side. For load testing and to evaluate the service ability to handle different volumes of users, tools may used to generate virtual users and test the service ability and performance upon those different scenarios.

In summary, stubs and drivers can be widely used and still applicable in SOA and Web services testing. This is not only for testing through the service development process, but can be used for testing some aspects of Web services after its release or through its usage.

XML Testing

In SOA, XML-based protocols are used to describe Web services (e.g. WSDL). In addition, standardized XML messages (e.g. SOAP) are used by Web services for communication with other services or with the client.

WSDL contains for major components or information: the Website of the service, service interface or public methods that are available to users, and for each public method, WSDL include its interface (i.e. input parameters and return type). In comparison with the traditional software development, WSDL represents the specification artifact. It is the contract that describes what does the Web service offer.

WSDL-based testing has been proposed since few years and implemented in testing tools such as: SOATest (Parasoft), sopaUI (SmartBear), etc.

In XML testing, we mean testing the compliance of the XML document to W3C standards. A WSDL or SOAP XML document that is not in compliance with standard XML specifications may cause indirectly possible problems related to the service.

Messages Testing

As we stated earlier, SOA architecture is distributed. For a test framework to be completed, it should consider testing all architecture components. In this section, we will try to describe the important of messages and SOA architecture and what can go wrong in those messages. Web services send and receive data formatted in XML documents using SOAP over HTTP. The XML document contains elements related to the data carried between the service provider and consumer and other parts related to the message details. The role of messages is very important in SOA in general and in testing SOA services in particular. In this architecture, there are three major classes of messages that SOA components send or receive:

- Service request messages.
- Service response messages.
- Fault messages. In addition to fault messages, messages for testing or quality monitoring can be included.
- Administrative messages (e.g. login, monitoring, etc.)

SOAP messages can be also one way (i.e. either from client to server or from server to client), in addition they can be two ways (i.e. request/response) message.

There are some tools that are used to support Web servers and monitor incoming and outgoing messages. These messages can be then retrieved and debugged in cases of errors or problems. While in most cases SOAP messages are from one sender to one receiver, future extensions of SOAP envision possibly adding messages to intermediaries or broadcast messages (e.g. for alerts, directing messages, etc.).

Integration and Service Composition Testing

Integration testing is very important to make sure that system components work well together and that each component can contribute successfully to the overall system services and functions. For a system with a hybrid structure such that of SOA, integration testing is more important and necessary. For a service request to be fulfilled, end to end system components must be all working correctly and as expected. Deficiency in any part may cause the message to fail or the service provider to fail in fulfilling the service request. Integration testing usually starts after completing unit testing to make sure that each component works correctly as a standalone. Integration testing comes next to make sure that components work together in synchronization to fulfill system high level ser-

vices. In some cases where errors in integration testing are discovered, a debugging process starts to localize the error. Integration testing can be applied also to the software components in either side (i.e. service provider or service user). This is since either side can have a software of several components that needs its own integration testing.

Service composition is combining several services together. The goal can be to respond to a service request. In some cases, mediators exist that can analyse users service requests to see the best service that can assist or fulfill this request. In some cases, one service provider or service may not be able to fulfill this request alone. Algorithms then are proposed first to see what is the best composition or combination of services that can respond to the request. Then, further algorithms are needed to integrate those services together and respond back to the service requestor. Testing is required in all those activities. Some of those activities are implemented automatically while others may need partial or complete human or user intervention.

Business Process Execution Language (BPEL) Testing

BPEL is a Web services' standard executable language that allows performing actions for business processes. Testing business logics is very important and this is why this area is a major focus in Web services' testing. Web services are the interface that BPEL can exchange information through. In BPEL, several services can be possibly composed to fulfil a business request. Testing is then required to orchestrate the integration and evaluation processes. Typical examples of business activities that require several possible Web services is: creating new accounts in banks, ordering or shipping items, financial investments, etc. Each one of those business services needs information from one or more agencies to be able to make a judgement or perform a transaction.

BPEL includes several possible activities: Invoke, receive, reply, and assign. The Web service is invoked in the invoke activity, receive is in charge of receiving outside messages, and reply activity responds back to environment messages. Finally, the assign activity implements the value assignment operation.

QoS Metrics and Quality Assurance (QA) for Web Services

Software testing field of study can be broadly divided into three major sub-fields: testing, metrics and quality assurance. These metrics can be seen as three sides of a triangle where they complement each other. They all have one major goal which is improve the quality of a particular software product. Software metrics include the static analysis of software product, process, etc. to get values and numbers that can be used to compare and assess directly or indirectly the software product. Testing usually comes before that during the software development process to make sure that the software is working according to the requirements and is free or have a minimal amount of bugs. QA sets standards and guidelines on how to evaluate software products and processes and what can be considered as an acceptable level of quality for one or more of the software aspects or artifacts.

In order to reduce the amount of resources required for those activities, automation is usually recommended to do all or most of those activities automatically using software tools with the least amount of human intervention.

In terms of Web services, there are several new issues to discuss and elaborate on that can implement in a different manner in comparison with traditional software products. For example, monitoring is a QA related Web services' activity that includes dynamic or real time observation of a service-in-action. Certain metrics such as those related to performance, can be collected dynamically about the service, through this automatic monitoring process.

QA is usually connected with both software testing and metrics. Software process and product metrics are used to collect quantitative figures on one or more aspects of the software product or process. Software metrics in Web services is a rich research field. For example, for service load testing, several metrics can be collected about the service to assist in its quality for this particular aspect (i.e. performance or load testing). Response time, throughput and availability are examples of load or performance related metrics that can be collected about Web services and that can assist in evaluating its overall quality. Same thing can be applied for all other quality attributes that are related to Web services (e.g. usability, security, reliability, etc.).

Test Driven Development (TDD)

TDD is a software testing methodology that is usually connected with Agile software development methodologies. Unlike the typical or traditional trend, in TDD, test cases are written before producing or developing the software code. This is since those test cases are generated based on the user requirements that are available in the requirement or the design stage. Similar to traditional methods however, test execution and verification activities occur after developing the software or the Web service. The idea of the—driven—concept here is that: test cases are written based on the user requirements and then software code is written to fulfill those test cases. In this case, test cases are guiding the development process and deciding its scope.

In SOA environment, however, this will have a different perspective. As we mentioned earlier, the general trend for developing Web services is that they are developed for generic purposes and not developed for one user or usage in mind. This means that the level of user requirements in Web services is higher than those in traditional methods and hence developing client specific test cases may only be used to simulate one way or aspect of using those Web services without generalizing such usage.

Testing as a Service

This subject can be divided into two parts. The first one discusses a challenge in testing Web services where the client may need to call the service for testing, not for using, purposes. Based on service contract and revenue conditions, and if service provider charges per usage or request, should testing requests be charged also? If yes, then this may impact quality especially if users decided to limit or reduce the level of testing to reduce cost. On the other hand, if the answer is no, how will this be organized between service providers and consumers to discriminate a using or testing request?

The second related issue is whether testing companies can in future offer testing as an external, generic service that can be called from any service provider or service consumer on the fly without the need to build custom testing infrastructure for such purpose. This can be particularly feasible in testing non functional generic quality attributes (e.g. performance, load, security, usability, etc.) that do not depend on the specific functionality of the service or its usage.

Ontology and Model-Based Testing

In traditional testing frameworks, one of the research important tasks is generating the software model. This usually comes first where using the software or one of its related deliverables (e.g. requirement, design, GUI, code, etc.) to generate a formal model. Using a formal method or tool to describe this model, this model then can be used as an input for test case generation, execution and verification. This is usually referred to model-based testing where a particular model drives the testing activities. In the SOA environment,

WSDL description can be a very good starting model. This is since WSDL XML file conveys the most important relevant abstracts of the service interface. As such, using WSDL as an input for a formal method or tool was the subject of several research papers. Test cases can then be generated, manually or automatically, based on this model.

WSDL-Based Test Automation Tool

As mentioned earlier, WSDL XML document for a Web service contains the following information about the Web service: The Website of the service, service interface, or public methods that are available to users, and for each public method, WSDL include its interface (i.e. input parameters and return type). Major interface relevant information are included in the two element types: <portType>, and <message>. Test cases can be automatically generated from WSDL, applied on the Web services, and results can be automatically verified in using data from both WSDL and the actual Web service.

A WSDL definition can host one or more of the following primary constructs: interface (portType), message, service, and binding.

Dynamic Service Composition

In some user scenarios, one atomic Web service may not be able to solve their request. In such cases, it maybe helpful to get a mediator to understand the request and find the best composition of Web services that can fulfill this request. Several algorithms and research papers and algorithms were proposed for either find best ways to search and find bet service or package or services to fulfil a request. On the other hand, in the scope of service composition, algorithms are also proposed to find the best way to integrate several services together and evaluate the outcome and its usability to a particular user request.

A Search Engine for Web Services

Typical search engines search for documents all over the Web. Those search engines do not distinguish or classify the retrieved documents. Special search engines exist to fill this gap. For Web services, some search engines exist to allow users to search specifically for Web services. UDDI is a protocol used to publish Web services and their interface descriptions. UDDIs have their own issues and may need to be tested for correct, accurate and up-to-date information that they publish about Web services specially as those UDDIs do not impose some quality assurance related regulations.

However, Web services' search engines offer far more service related information and assistant. Figure 2 shows a screen shot from Seekda Web services' search engine. Several papers were also published proposing or discussing a search engine dedicated for Web services (e.g. Dong et al 2004). Figures 2 and 3, from testing a service through Seedka search engines, showed that while perhaps correct and error outputs are machine friendly, however, they are not user friendly.

From a testing perspective, those search engines can perform several testing tasks. This is especially relevant where search engines will act as third party external auditors. They have con-

Figure 2. Seedka web service engine output for a service query

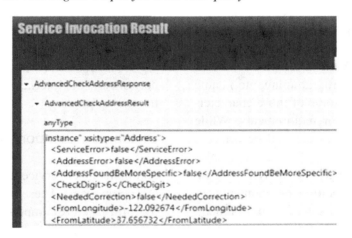

Figure 3. Seedka web service engine bug report

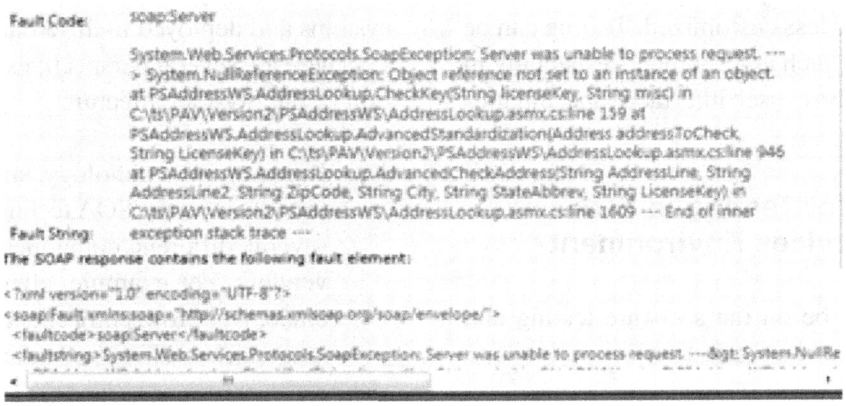

tinuous monitor on those Web services and hence testing some important non functional requirements such as: availability, performance, reliability, security etc. can be more realistic if it is done from their side.

In addition, those search engines provide client side interface that allows user to test and use those Web services.

TESTING IN SOA AND WEB SERVICES ENVIRONMENT

Software engineering field and all its related research and academic subjects continuously evolve. Traditional software development environments assume stable, or somewhat stable, software characteristics upon which project is developed. Examples of such characteristics: team members and roles, scope or requirements, budget, cost and time. More recently, Agile development models (e.g. Scrum, Extreme programming, etc.) came to handle flexibility in some of those characteristics especially scope or requirements. While software development models will be affected by those new models, however, none of the major software engineering stages (i.e. analysis, design, coding, testing and evolution or maintenance) will vanish in any type of software environment. Rather, such stages may have to evolve to fit the new environment.

In terms of Web services, they are usually developed for a wide spectrum of possible users. This makes their less customized. Testing can be also different in such environments especially in terms of black box, user interface, and integration testing.

Challenges for Testing in SOA and Web Services Environment

Focus here will be on the software testing and quality assurance stage or activities.

Scalability and Security

The development and deployment environments of Web services widely vary based on users' preferences. Service providers can hardly predict a service possible load in a specific day or time. Users can vary in usage, size, etc. Achieving through such ambiguous environment a high level of: scalability, performance, security can be challenging.

No Central GUI

Unlike traditional desktop and Web applications, Web services do not have a: one-for-all purposes user interface. Hence manual testing for the user interface in the traditional way is not feasible. WSDL usually contains one or more interfaces that represent the service. For this, the tester needs to have programming skills and knowledge in Web services fundamentals as extra required skills. The network and the Internet will play a major role in the testing process.

Distributed Components

A complete Web service architecture contains several components. These Web services, or some of the infrastructure components, may be developed by the same developers or may be provided by a third party. So thorough black box testing must be performed. These services are distributed over the network and may be hosted on different operating systems and deployed in different environments.

There are several perspectives of the distribution of the SOA architecture.

1. Based on the technology, environment, and the software, the SOA technology may have several different components of different vendors. For example, client side may include, Web browsers or clients, programming languages and IDEs, a database (e.g. Oracle,

MySql, etc.). A Web server (e.g. Apache, IIS, etc.) is also required part of the structure on both service provider and consumer sides. XML and related messaging technologies are required for WDSL, SOAP, etc. From the service provider side several server side components are also required. Those different components usually come from different software providers or vendors.

2. Physical distribution. Similar to any distributed system, the SOA architecture is divided physically into three major sides: client side components, server side components, network or media side components.

3. Based on personal or company roles, SOA architecture can be divided into: service developer: the company or the team who will develop the service, service provider: the company who will offer, host, or sell the service: service integrators, third party certifiers or auditors: those can be different teams for different purposes related to certification, publishing, auditing, testing, QA, etc.

4. Service or end users. In some cases, those can be themselves service providers for end users where they may use or customize the service for a new or different service.

Isolation between service providers and consumers is a core principle in SOA. A service should be developed with no specific user or usage in mind. However, service isolation should be also to the other previously described SOA architectural components. For example, a service should not be platform, database, Web server independent. Even at the server side itself, the service should be layered in a way that isolates business elements of the service from the technical elements so that when one of the two is changing, it will not impact the other.

The distribution of components can cause challenges to control and security measurements. This is since the overall SOA architecture is dis-tributed and it does not have a centralized control for: enforcing, and monitoring of regulatory roles. Building a mutual security and trust between such distributed components is difficult to achieve. Such environment can be challenging for testing, especially if errors or problems occur and it is required to debug the origin of the problem.

Selecting the Best Revenue Model

Companies developing or selling Web services are still trying different alternatives on how or from where to generate revenue. While this challenge may not be directly related to testing, however, several quality attributes such as: security, usability or performance may depend on such model.

In a related subject and if the revenue model used depends on pay-per-usage, will testing service calls be also charged? If this is the case, this may tempt service consumers to reduce the level of testing and hence may impact testing or quality in general.

Future testing perspectives for Web services may also help in allowing testing companies to offer testing dynamically in a generic format regardless of the user or service specific environment.

Service Composition

A major research focus in SOA is the service composition subject. Match algorithms are proposed to either see how to find the best service for a specific user request, or how to compose several services to fulfill a user request. On the other hand, testing or judging such decisions automatically can be complex and may require human interventions in some cases.

The Less Challenging Tasks

On the other hand, some software testing tasks are easier to do or implement in SOA. Generating test cases from the GUI model or the service is now easy and available (WSDL). Test case generation can be easier based on WSDL. Test automation activities can be, relatively, easier and simpler. Test case results verification is also easier in SOA. The last two are true based on two SOA aspects: light user interface and well defined messaging standards.

Non-Functional Testing

In one category, testing can be broadly divided into two major sections: Functional testing that includes testing the services based on their inputs, outputs, preconditions, post conditions, etc. This type of testing validates whether the service performs the intended functions correctly. The second type is called: Non-functional testing. This type of testing is conducted for testing service high level quality attributes in general. Important quality attributes to test in this scope: performance, reliability, load (stress), security, etc.

Load or stress testing is a test of the performance of the Web service when many simultaneous users are accessing the service. The response of the Web service must be consistent and also its performance must not, significantly, degrade with the increase in the number of users. Load testing gives us a feedback on these parameters and due to its very nature automated testing tools must be used. Some of metrics in load testing: response time, throughput, availability, etc.

Functional Testing

Main focus in this testing activity should be to carry out the following procedures:

- Get the WSDL file and test whether it is well-formed and in compliance with the WSDL specifications published by W3C.
- Using this WSDL file, generate test cases based on the service interface that includes all service public methods along with their signatures (i.e. inputs and outputs).

- Test cases should evaluate whether the Web service responds to the requests submitted to it correctly.
- Test cases are then executed by writing and Invoking a sample invoker and for each test case, one aspect of one method of the interface will be assessed.
- For test results verification, check the response of the Web service from a functionality point of view to judge whether the test case passes or fails.

Stubs are virtual components created only for testing purposes. The stub constructs the SOAP message from the parameters passed to it and passes this message to the service. For results automatic evaluation, messages can be monitored by a monitor program.

Web Services Search Engines

Typical search engines search for documents all over the Web. Those search engines do not distinguish or classify the retrieved documents. Special search engines exist to fill this gap. For Web services, some search engines exist to allow users to search specially for Web services. UDDI is a protocol used to publish Web services and their interface descriptions. However, Web services' search engines offer far more service related information and assistant. They can help testing the service on the fly without the need to write a client or an invoker.

From a testing perspective, those search engines can perform several testing tasks. This is especially relevant where search engines will act as third party external auditors. They have a continuous monitor on those Web services and hence can test some important non functional requirements such as: availability, performance, reliability, security etc. It can be more realistic if it is done from their side. In addition, they provide client side interfaces that allow users to test and use those Web services.

Integration and Interoperability Testing

This subject can be addressed from several perspectives. We will focus here on two of them. Those are the interoperability when different programming languages are used to write parts of a complete Web service architecture and the second related to data types defined in service methods (i.e. inputs and outputs). There are some other possible problems related to interoperability from using different standards, encryption methods, etc. Web Services Interoperability (WS-I) is a universally implemented standard that should be observed when developing Web services. Interoperability testing for Web services should test that the Web service is in conformance with WS-I standards. On the other hand, testing activities should try to simulate the different possible environments (e.g. J2EE, .NET, AXIS, etc.). Such types of testing should ensure that the service can respond to a request regardless of the requester platform, operating system, programming language, etc.

CONCLUSION

In this chapter, we described software testing activities in SOA and Web services environment. As relatively, a recent software development environment, it is expected that several testing activities will be impacted by the new model. Nonetheless, regardless of the software environment or type of product, testing activities will always stay necessary and important. While SOA architecture is distributed by nature, testing activities are also distributed with SOA components, with the type of testing or testing activity, with the goals of test-

ing, with the components to test, etc. One of the major new aspects that will be possibly appear and expand widely in and from the SOA environment is using testing as a service. As described in the chapter, this has two meanings: The first meaning indicates that calling the service can be either for using or testing and hence contract between service provider and consumer should identify whether service requests for testing purposes are payable or not. On the other hand, in this environment, software testing companies may in future find ways to provide testing services dynamically in a generic format that does not require significant customization for the service provider or consumer environment. They can act as third party auditors to regulate or control service quality, standards, and regulations.

ACKNOWLEDGMENT

This chapter was conducted as part of a postdoc scholarship for AVEMPACE (Erasmus Mundus [EM] Action 2 Strand 2 Lot 5 AVEMPACE) in 2012.

REFERENCES

Alsmadi, I., & Magel. (2007). An object oriented framework for user interface test automation. In *Proceedings of Midwest Instruction and Computing Symposium (MICS) 2007*. MICS.

Baresi, L., & DiNitto. (2007). *Test and analysis of web services*. Berlin: Springer-Verlag GmbH.

Bertolino, A., & Polini. (2005). The audition framework for testing web services interoperability. In *Proceedings of the 31st EUROMICRO Conference on Software Engineering and Advanced Applications*. EUROMICRO.

Bozkurt, M., Harman, & Hassoun. (2009). Testing & verification in service-oriented architecture: A survey. *Software Testing, Verification and Reliability*, 1–7.

Canfora, G., & Penta. (2009). *Service-oriented architectures testing: A survey*. Berlin: Springer-Verlag.

Dong, X. Halevy, Madhavan, Nemes, & Zhang. (2004). Paper. In *Proceedings of the Thirtieth International Conference on Very Large Databases* (vol. 30, pp. 372 – 383). IEEE.

Freitas, A. L. Parlavantzas, & Pazat. (2010). Survey of quality related aspects relevant for service-based applications. In *Proceedings of the 3rd International Workshop on Monitoring, Adaptation and Beyond (MONA+)*. MONA+.

Karam, M., Safa, H., & Artail, H. (2007). An abstract workflow-based framework for testing composed web services. In *Proceedings of the IEEE/ACS International Conference on Computer Systems and Applications, 2007*. AICCSA.

Ladan, M. (2010). Web services testing approaches: A survey and a classification. In *Proceedings of the International Conference on Networked Digital Technologies*, (pp. 70-79). Beirut, Lebanon: ICNDT.

Martin, R. C. (2005). The test bus imperative: Architectures that support automated acceptance testing. *IEEE Software*, 22(4), 65–67. doi:10.1109/MS.2005.110.

Mei, H., & Zhang. (2005). A framework for testing web services and its supporting tool. In *Proceedings of the IEEE International Workshop on Service-Oriented System Engineering*. IEEE.

Prasanth, Y., Sarika, Santhosh Anuhya, Vineela, & Ajay Babu. (2012). Framework for testing web services through SOA (service oriented architecture). *International Journal of Engineering Trends and Technology*, 3(2).

Rentea, C., Schieferdecker, I., & Cristea, V. (2009). Ensuring quality of web applications by client-side testing using TTCN-3[C/OL]//. In *Proceedings of the 9th International Conference on Web Engineering*. San Sebastian, Spain: IEEE. Retrieved from http://sunsite.informatik.rwth-aachen.de/Publications-/CEUR-WS/Vol-561/paper1.pdf

Sharma, A. Hellmann, & Maurer. (2012). Testing of web services – A systematic mapping. In *Proceedings of the IEEE World Congress on Services (SERVICES 2012)*. Honolulu, HI: IEEE.

Sun, C. Wang, Mu, Liu, Wang, & Chen, T.Y. (2011). Metamorphic testing for web services: Framework and a case study. In *Proceedings of the 2011 IEEE International Conference on Web Services (ICWS)*. ICWS.

Zhu, H. (2006). A framework for service-oriented testing of web services. In *Proceedings of the 30th Annual International Computer Software and Applications Conference*. COMPSAC.

Chapter 9
Managing Knowledge in Open Source Software Test Process

Tamer Abdou
Concordia University, Canada

Peter Grogono
Concordia University, Canada

Pankaj Kamthan
Concordia University, Canada

ABSTRACT

The increasing adoption and use of Open Source Software (OSS) motivates study of its development. This chapter explores the state-of-the art in OSS development processes, in general, and OSS testing processes, in particular. A conceptual model for software Testing Knowledge Management (TKM) that aims to provide an understanding of the testing domain is introduced. The TKM model is informed by earlier studies and guided by international testing standards. Moreover, the TKM model is equipped with different forms of knowledge, reusable across software projects. Using the TKM model as an integrative conceptual model enables understanding of how knowledge life cycle stages are mapped onto the test process of OSS, what type of knowledge is created at each stage, and how knowledge is converted from one stage to another. The chapter is supported by representative examples of OSS that are mature and currently in widespread use.

INTRODUCTION

For the past decade or so, Open Source Software (OSS) has been playing an increasingly significant role in society. OSS has opened new vistas in communication, education, and entertainment.

However, an examination of major, publicly-available, source code foundries reveals that the successes of OSS have come with their share of abandonments. From a software engineering perspective, this brings attention to the quality of OSS, and commitments towards assuring it.

DOI: 10.4018/978-1-4666-4229-4.ch009

The test process aims to improve the quality of software, and is one of the most significant processes in software development (Kaner, Falk, & Nguyen, 1999). This process in the context of OSS can be considered a knowledge-intensive process involving (1) several tasks on different platforms, and (2) several decisions that need to be made to satisfy software requirements. The knowledge required to make proper decisions and to assess them is diverse and broad (such as voting in Apache server and review in Mozilla Firefox browser). This chapter explores Knowledge Management (KM)-related activities in the software test process identified in OSS (Abdou, Grogono, & Kamthan, 2012). Moreover, the chapter reviews various approaches, techniques, and tools that can be used to capture and manage the knowledge that is required or can be produced during the test process.

The rest of the chapter is organized as follows. First, OSS development process and test process in OSS are introduced. Next, an overview of KM is given, including different modes of knowledge conversion from the perspective of software testing. This is followed by a review of different activities of the test process in OSS to illustrate the relation between test process and KM. The chapter ends with directions for future research and concluding remarks.

BACKGROUND

In this section, OSS software development process is discussed, different activities related to the test process in OSS are reviewed and compared with those in conventional software, and basics of knowledge as per OSS are given.

Open Source Software Development Process

The earlier research on OSS focused on the aspects of development, project, virtual community, and the roles of contributors (Raymond, 1999; Zhao & Elbaum, 2003; Lonchamp, 2005). In several initial studies, it was observed that there are stark differences between conventional software engineering and OSS development. In particular, it has been found that, in contrast to conventional software processes, the OSS development process is unstructured (Mockus, Fielding, & Herbsleb, 2002; Zhao & Elbaum, 2003) and lacks formal documentation, including that for testing (Lonchamp, 2005; Wang, Guo, & Shi, 2007).

The OSS development process follows a layered approach with an onion shaped structure (Crowston & Howison, 2005; Showole, Sahibuddin, & Ibrahim, 2011; Crowston & Howison, 2006), as shown in Figure 1. At the center of this structure are the core developers who direct the design, contribute most of the code, and steer the evolution of the software. In the innermost ring are the co-developers who are responsible for submitting patches, which are reviewed and checked-in by core developers. In the intermediate ring are the active users who do not contribute code, but provide use cases and bug reports based on their own test suites. Finally, in the outermost ring are the passive users and observers who are not interested in contributing code, but like to stay informed of the development.

It is only recently that a generic model of OSS development process based on 'mature' OSS projects has been proposed (Lonchamp, 2005). (An OSS project is considered mature if it involves more than ten developers.) The model comprises a set of elements, where each element could represent a process role, tool, activity, or document. In this model, developers work concurrently on either coding or testing. Moreover, this model is consistent with previous OSS development process models (Gillian, 2001; Scacchi, 2003), and enables systematic analysis, reuse, and comparison.

Test Process in Open Source Software Development

There are currently a number of standards for test processes, including ISO/IEC TR 19759,

Figure 1. The layers in the OSS development process

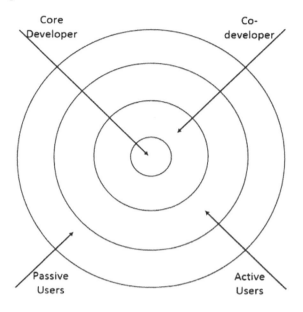

BS 7925-2, and ISO/IEC WD 29119-2 (Reid, 2000; ISO/IEC, 2010). The ISO/IEC 29119 Test Process Standard (or, ISO/IEC Test Process, for short), currently under development, serves as a candidate suitable for defining the test process in OSS projects. The other standards have a number of limitations, including that they do not have support for all the phases of a test process and they do not cover non-functional testing, risk-based testing, and static testing. The ISO/IEC Test Process specifies required operations, as well as their inputs and outputs. Most of the test activities are consistent with the software development activities. Feature sets have to be identified, analyzed, executed, reviewed and accepted.

Figure 2 illustrates how the test activities interact (ISO/IEC, 2010). There are two inputs to the test process, namely test plan and control directives. First, the test plan for the test phase or the test type is created, and forms the basis for the implementation of the test strategy and corresponding test activities. Next, the control directives are obtained from the test management staff, and dictate how testing should be conducted

by the test team. For any particular test, the test activities are executed in a particular order, as shown in Figure 2. These activities are invoked a number of times to complete the testing for a given test phase or a test type.

The outputs of a test activity are test measures, which form an input to the test management processes. These test measures are used to report the status and progress of testing to the test management staff (such as the number of test cases completed by the test team). The Test Design and Implementation activity describes how test cases and test procedures are derived. These are normally documented in a test specification. The Test Environment Set-Up and Maintenance activity describes how the environment, in each test that has been executed, is established and maintained. The maintenance of the test environment involves changes based on the results of earlier tests. The Test Execution activity describes how the test procedures, generated as a result of the Test Design and Implementation activity, are run on the test environment established by the Test Environment Set-Up and Maintenance activity. The Test Execution activity may need to be repeated, as all the available test procedures may not be executed in a single iteration. The purpose of the Test Incident Reporting activity is to report those issues identified by the results of the Test Execution activity that require further action. The aforementioned activities are divided into tasks, as shown in Table 1.

Recently, an Open Source Software Test Process Framework, OSS-TPF, has been proposed (Abdou, Grogono, & Kamthan, 2012). The activities and tasks in OSS-TPF are outlined in Table 1, and are discussed in detail later in this section. There are similarities and differences between the ISO/IEC Test Process and OSS-TPF, per activities and tasks shown in Table 1. In OSS-TPF, there is a lack of Test Environment Set-Up and Maintenance activity due to the informality of the test process and the absence of rigorous test plans. There are also differences in the tasks

Figure 2. ISO/IEC test process activities

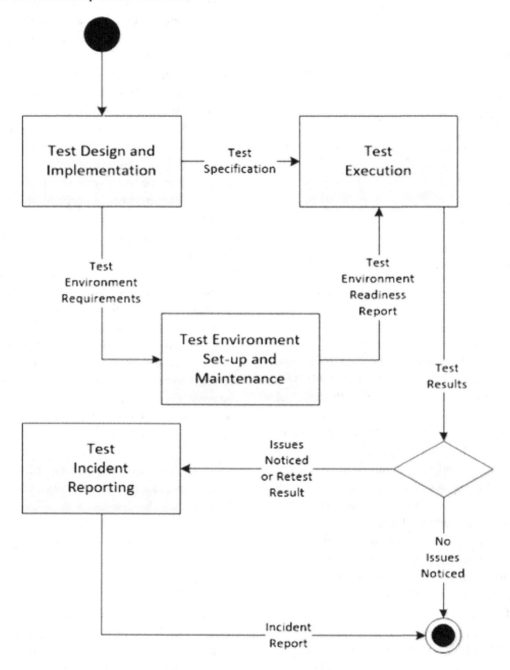

related to each of the assigned activities, as per Table 1. Finally, test procedures in OSS-TPF are accepted only after the Execution activity since the process resources are not allocated effectively.

In the absence of a formal test plan, it is difficult to achieve a test-completion criterion that measures the test coverage of an OSS component. Test cases are derived by determining pre-conditions, selecting input values, and by determining the

Table 1. ISO/IEC test process versus OSS test process

ISO/IEC Test Process	Open Source Test Process
Activities / Tasks	Activities / Tasks
Test Design and Implementation • Identify Feature Sets • Derive Test Conditions • Derive Test Coverage Items • Derive Test Cases • Assemble Test Sets • Derive Test Procedures	Test Design and Implementation • Identify Features Independently • Derive Testable Aspect(s) • Derive Test Cases • Documentation
Test Environment Set-Up and Maintenance • Establish Test Environment • Maintain Test Environment	Test Environment Set-Up and Maintenance
Test Execution • Execute Test Procedure(s) • Compare Test Results • Record Test Execution	Test Execution • Execute • Submit
Test Incident Reporting • Analyze Test Result(s) • Create Incident Report	Test Incident Reporting • Review or Vote • Accept

corresponding expected results. In OSS projects, testers are less concerned about constraints on their execution, and so assembling test sets is not well-appreciated. The contents of the test procedure specification need not be approved by core developers in order to be documented. The testers move directly to test execution activity in order to execute test procedures created in the Test Design and Implementation activity, as there are no specific requirements for test environment in OSS projects (Abdou, Grogono, & Kamthan, 2012).

Knowledge Management in Open Source Software

There are three levels of knowledge:

- **Data:** Content that is directly observable or verifiable. (Dalkir, 2005)
- **Information:** Content that represents analyzed data. (Dalkir, 2005)
- **Knowledge:** A dynamic human process of justifying personal belief toward the truth. (Nonaka, Toyama, & Konno, 2000)

These levels of knowledge are relevant to software testing. For example, a software tester records and submits the bug to a bug tracking system, such as Bugzilla or JIRA. In Bugzilla bug report, a number of fields, such as STATUS, IMPORTANCE, and ASSIGNED TO, are defined. Bugzilla suggests syntactic rules for filling in a bug report. The rules allow UNCONFIRMED, NEW, ASSIGNED, REOPENED, or READY values to STATUS field as an indication of the current state of an opened bug. (However, the rule does not allow REOPENED or READY values to STATUS field in JIRA.) The bug report needs to conform to Bugzilla syntax rules. Therefore, prior to assigning meaning to the values, the report is still data. In particular, someone unfamiliar with Bugzilla will not be able to interpret the bug report.

However, Bugzilla does provide an interpretation of values in the STATUS field. For example, UNCONFIRMED indicates this bug has recently been added to the database and nobody has validated that this bug is true, and READY indicates the bug has enough information so that the developer can start working on a fix. Thus, when data comes with an interpretation, it becomes information.

A developer who sees the bug report perceives it as information. According to the above definition, information turns into knowledge only when programmers understand it and integrate it into their mental models. For example, they may associate the resolution of the bug with a similar fix they already know. As a consequence, they may resolve the problem by using the same technique they used before. A programmer may also remember that there is a tool to help in resolving the bug. Thus, combining the information depicted in the bug report, as well as the knowledge about this tool, increases the support for resolving the problem.

Characteristics of Knowledge

There are certain defining characteristics of any type of knowledge:

- Knowledge is dynamic, as it is created in collaborative media through the interactions between individuals and their environment.
- Knowledge is context-dependent, as it depends on a particular time and space (Hayek, 1945).
- Knowledge is interpreted information, as information becomes knowledge when it is interpreted by individuals and given a context.
- Knowledge is only created by humans, because humans have different views, minds, and hearts.
- Knowledge is mutable for it can take several faces in an organization (Singh & Sharma, 2011).

KM is defined as doing what is needed to get the most out of knowledge resources (Becerra-Fernandez & Sabherwal, 2010). KM starts with information and knowledge as inputs, and results in new knowledge, conversion of knowledge, sharing of knowledge, or application of knowledge.

Dimensions of Knowledge

There are two complementary dimensions of knowledge:

- **Explicit Knowledge:** This is expressed in formal and systematic language, shared in the form of data, and processed and stored relatively. In software testing, explicit knowledge could be a scripted testing or inscription. Scripted testing emphasizes on test planning, design and test execution in sequence (Prakash & Gopalakrishnan, 2011).
- **Tacit Knowledge:** This is expressed in actions and emotions, hard to be shared and formalized as it is an analogue process that requires simultaneous processing (Polanyi, 1967). In software testing, tacit knowledge could be an exploratory testing or interpretation. Exploratory testing emphasizes the personal freedom and responsibility of the tester to optimize the quality of his or her work by treating test planning, design, test execution, test result interpretation, and learning as mutually supporting activities that continue in parallel throughout the project (Prakash & Gopalakrishnan, 2011) (see Table 2).

Benefits of using Knowledge Management in Open Source Software

The apparent benefits of managing knowledge in OSS are due to three different views:

Table 2. Characteristics of knowledge dimensions (Dalkir, 2005)

Properties of Explicit Knowledge	Properties of Tacit Knowledge
Ability to disseminate, to reproduce, access, and to reapply throughout the organization.	Ability to adapt, and to deal with new and exceptional situations.
Ability to teach, and to train.	Expertise, know-how, know-why, and care-why.
Ability to organize, to systematize, and to translate a vision into a mission statement and into operational guidelines.	Ability to collaborate, to share a vision, and to transmit a culture.
Transfer of knowledge via products, services, and documented processes.	Coaching and mentoring to transfer experiential knowledge on a one-to-one, face-to-face basis.

- **Individual View:** In the individual view, there are no differences with respect to age, gender, nationality, culture, or ethnic background. Moreover, as OSS community is based on a voluntary principle, the use of strong hierarchy, position based status and formal power are issues that can be overcome.
- **Organizational View:** In the organizational view, the lack of social networks can be a barrier to knowledge sharing (Riege, 2005). However, these are overcome in OSS development by taking ownership of intellectual property, as implied by the license agreement (such as GPL). These licenses precisely state the rights a user has over the product, according to the Open Source Initiative (OSI). The other barriers in OSS that can be overcome are the fear of misuse knowledge or take unjust credit for it, the lack of trust in colleagues, and the fear of not receiving recognition and accreditation from managers.
- **Technological View:** In the technological view, insufficient communication between project's members is considered to be a barrier to managing knowledge. However, the OSS community provides its participants with adequate tools to communicate and track relevant issues. These tools include those provided by the Social Web (Fancott, Kamthan, & Shahmir, 2012).

Challenges of using KM in OSS

There are certain limitations and shortcomings that OSS process may suffer in capturing, sharing, or applying knowledge:

- **Identification:** It may be difficult to identify the right person to share knowledge with. For example, the test team in Apache HTTP Server rarely meets face-to-face. Moreover, all information on the Apache project is recorded in an explicit form (Mockus, Fielding, & Herbsleb, 2002).
- **Benefits:** The benefits of sharing knowledge with others may be unrealized. One of the risks in knowledge sharing is that individuals are most commonly rewarded for what they know, not what they share (Dalkir, 2005). Restricting the sharing knowledge in OSS results in slower innovation and more abandonment (Raymond, 1999). As OSS is considered to be a utility to empower individuals to manage knowledge, raising the awareness among these individuals allows for developing a society with equal opportunities No initials (Singh, 2007).
- **Elicitation:** The capture, evaluation, and feedback that would improve the individual and community learning effect may be insufficient. In a recent study, the knowledge sharing activities in Debian mailing lists have been investigated (Sowe, Stamelos, &

Angelis, 2008). The study showed a correlation between participants' posting and replying activities in both developer and user's mailing lists; however, the results are based on only two lists and half of the data has been removed due to inconsistency.

- **Experience:** There may be irreconcilable differences in experience levels. It has been noted that, in virtual teams, a transfer of expertise among colleagues requires relatively more time and effort (Cubranic, Holmes, Ying, & Murphy, 2003).

- **Communication:** There may be inadequate verbal and written communication. It has been pointed out that, in any project, verbal and written communication is essential for sharing knowledge effectively (Riege, 2005).

Limitations of Knowledge Management in Testing

In spite of the perceived benefits, there are known problems in software testing from a KM perspective (Desai & Shah, 2011). There is low reuse of software testing knowledge, unsatisfactory distribution of human resources, difficulty in determining whether adequate testing has been carried out, inadequate coverage of test cases, and unclear conclusions about software quality upon completion of testing.

Related Work

There have been relatively few initiatives towards understanding and/or managing the knowledge during software testing, in general, and OSS testing, in particular.

In a proposal of a KM model in the context of software testing process (Liu, Wu, Liu, & Gu, 2009), a knowledge map is used to save time in tracing knowledge source and an ontology is introduced to act as a knowledge database in the knowledge retrieval subsystem. In the knowledge map, the knowledge level is classified according to the SWEBOK Knowledge Areas. The ontology allows for describing the relation restriction between concepts, and helps in finding correlative concepts and relevant attributes when retrieving knowledge. In another proposal, a KM approach is used for industrial model-based testing (Koznov, Malinov, Sokhransky, & Novikova, 2009). In it, the authors use partial specifications (that formalize relevant properties) to identify and classify the knowledge. There has been a study to understand capturing and sharing test knowledge among Motorola's engineers in Malaysia (Desai & Shah, 2011). In it, the authors aim to help testing by integrating and using a KMS. Finally, a model to manage knowledge in software testing environment has been proposed (Abdullah, Eri, & Talib, 2011). The model is based on Community of Practice (CoP) KM approach and aims to verify the usability of the product based on the user specification. The model shows the importance of explicit knowledge over tacit knowledge in KMS of software testing environment. However, it does not show KMS can be accessed and used by CoP members in software testing.

MANAGING TEST PROCESS KNOWLEDGE IN OPEN SOURCE SOFTWARE

There have been several Knowledge Management Life Cycles (KMLCs) that describe different phases of KM (Wiig, 1993; Rollett, 2003). In a recent work, similarities and differences among the popular KMLC approaches are discussed and multiple KMLCs are integrated into a comprehensive approach to manage knowledge effectively (Dalkir, 2005). For its relevance and for its simple high level conceptual representation of KM, it is this approach, termed as Dalkir's Integrated KMLC hereafter, which forms the basis of this chapter.

Dalkir's Integrated KMLC defines three major stages that cover KM main aspects, as shown in Figure 3:

1. Knowledge Capture and/or Creation
2. Knowledge Sharing and Dissemination
3. Knowledge Acquisition and Application

A Conceptual Testing Knowledge Management Model

The proposed software Testing Knowledge Management (TKM) model is based upon the construction of OSS-TPF (Abdou, Grogono, & Kamthan, 2012), the understanding of Dalkir's Integrated KMLC (Dalkir, 2005), and the adaptation of Nonaka-Takeuchi's SECI model (Nonaka & Takeuchi, 1995). This integrative conceptual mapping suggests how KMLC is mapped onto the test process of OSS, what type of knowledge is created at each stage, and how knowledge contents are converted from one stage to another.

To do that, the most appropriate KMLC is selected for this study. Next, each stage in the selected KMLC is mapped to the OSS-TPF by focusing on the main activities of the test process in OSS. Finally, the knowledge conversion between each

stage is described along with the main knowledge outputs, as shown in Figure 4.

Stages of the TKM Model

In this section, each stage in the TKM model is discussed. Moreover, the requirements for these stages to be completed are described based on the relevant test process activities.

Knowledge Capture and/or Creation

In the "Test Design and Implementation" test activity, most OSS projects do not require a test plan prior to the test process taking place (Mockus, Fielding, & Herbsleb, 2002; Zhao & Elbaum, 2003). There is no formal identification of risk. The features to be tested are not prioritized, and selected independently based on developers' interests. The determination of testable aspects of an OSS component is performed by agreeing on attributes of specific interest to volunteers who choose to take over the testing process for that component.

Knowledge capturing assumes the existence of knowledge tacitly. Knowledge needs to be captured, to allow exploratory and scripted tests to be elicited and stored. Knowledge creation assumes the inexistence of knowledge before it is

Figure 3. Dalkir's integrated KMLC (Dalkir, 2005)

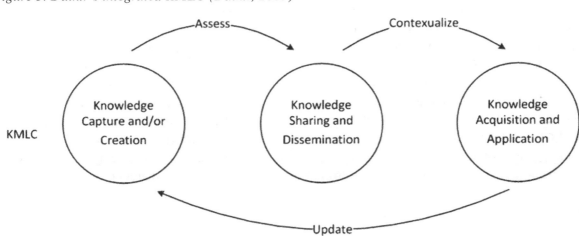

Figure 4. Overview of the TKM model

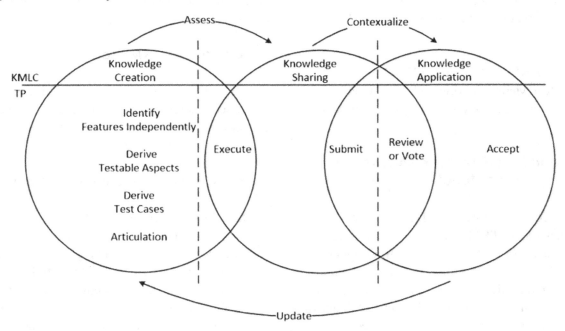

created. Knowledge needs to be created, to allow exploratory and scripted tests to be discovered or synthesized from prior knowledge.

In the Knowledge Capture and/or Creation stage, knowledge is created through the different tasks of the "Test Design and Implementation" test activity, along with individual's shared experiences and ideas. In this stage, OSS contributors identify features, derive testable aspects, articulate them, and begin executing these testable aspects through the derived test cases. There is considerable information and knowledge to be created and captured at this stage, which makes it the most significant stage in the TKM model.

The TKM model needs to be part of an overall organizational KM process. To do that, Nonaka-Takeuchi's SECI model (Nonaka & Takeuchi, 1995; Nonaka & Konno, 1998) could be deployed. The SECI model presents knowledge creation as a spiraling process of interactions between explicit and tacit knowledge. These interactions lead to the creation of new knowledge as knowledge moves through individual, group, and organizational levels. The interaction between these types of knowledge allows for the conceptualization of four conversion modes of knowledge: socialization, externalization, internalization, and combination, as shown in Figure 5. Each arrow in Figure 5 represents either a form of knowledge creation (Socialization and Combination) or a form of knowledge capture (Externalization and Internalization) (Becerra-Fernandez & Sabherwal, 2010).

This process of knowledge creation and transfer in the context of testing in OSS can be described as follows:

- **Socialization (Tacit-to-Tacit Knowledge):** This is the process of sharing knowledge to perform actions and sharing natural interactions. Socialization is to arrive at a mutual understanding of how to share mental models. In software testing (Interpretation-to-Interpretation), this could be the case when a co-developer shares his or her testing plans or applies test levels with a core-developer.

Figure 5. Knowledge conversion and software testing

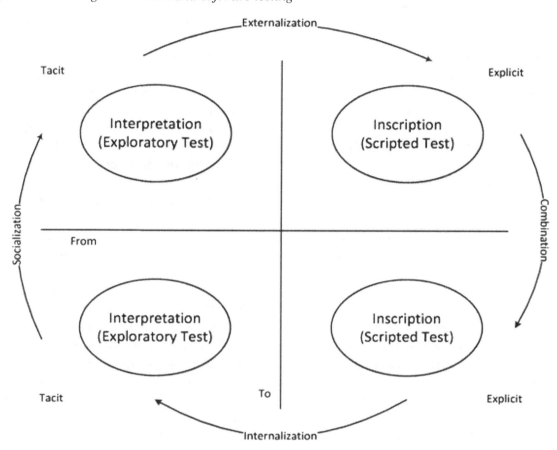

Therefore, knowledge can be organized or can be categorized into different categories.

- **Externalization (Tacit-to-Explicit Knowledge):** This is the process of converting tacit knowledge into explicit knowledge, expressed in some visible form. For example, such conversion can take the form of analogies, concepts, hypotheses, or models. In software testing (Interpretation-to-Inscription), when the testers are uncertain of which level of testing they should perform or how they want to test their components, a scripted approach can be used. The benefits of scripted tests are that they are re-usable and accurate in tracing the test to the corresponding stakeholder.

- **Combination (Explicit-to-Explicit Knowledge):** This is the process of grouping small pieces of explicit knowledge into a new form. For example, such conversion can take the form of review reports, trend analysis, or new data models to organize content. In software testing (Inscription-to-Inscription), scripted tests can be recombined into a form that is manageable. For example, unit test cases could be combined into test suites.

- **Internalization (Explicit-to-Tacit Knowledge):** This is the process of "learning by doing." For example, such conversion can take the form of new behaviors or new mental models. In software testing

(Inscription-to-Interpretation), testers may convert to exploratory mode when new information is revealed by a scripted test. For example, if the tester discovers a new failure that requires him or her to perform further analysis, then he or she might depend on such conversion of knowledge.

Knowledge Sharing and Dissemination

The Test Incident Reporting activity encompasses accepting the test results to be checked-in. In OSS projects, there is no consensus on the means for deciding which of the test results are most appropriate. For example, to decide test results to be checked-in, Test Incident Reporting in Apache depends on discussions on its mailing lists to solicit feedback from interested parties, and uses a system of voting (Fielding, 1999). However, Test Incident Reporting in Mozilla depends on a review by Module Owners instead of a discussion (Mockus, Fielding, & Herbsleb, 2002).

The knowledge, once it has been created and captured, needs to be shared and disseminated throughout the OSS community. In the "Test Execution" activity, the "Execute" task generally starts with a developer testing the local copy of the OSS source code after checking-out. The thoroughness of the test depends on the judgment and skill of the developer. The developer, at the end of test execution, either commits test results directly, or posts them on some collaboration medium, such as mailing lists or Bugzilla, for a review (Mockus, Fielding, & Herbsleb, 2002).

In Knowledge Sharing and Dissemination stage and through the different tasks of the "Test Execution" activity, along with individual's shared experiences and ideas, knowledge is shared. In this stage, contributors execute test procedures and then submit test findings.

The knowledge can be shared and disseminated in many ways. There are knowledge repositories designed to share explicit knowledge of individuals and organizations (Becerra-Fernandez & Sabherwal, 2010). In software testing, knowledge repositories can share inscription knowledge or scripted tests of individuals in organizations. These knowledge repositories can contain knowledge artifacts such as Lesson Learned (learning from success or abandonment activities), Best Practices (describe only success activities), and Incident Reports (Weber, Aha, & Becerra-Fernandez, 2001).

Knowledge Acquisition and Application

The knowledge, once it has been shared and disseminated, needs to be applied throughout the OSS community. In Acquisition and Application stage and through the last task "Accept" of the "Test Incident Reporting" activity knowledge is utilized without actually learning the knowledge. According to Bloom's Taxonomy, Application level is defined as the ability to use learned material in new and concrete situations by using abstraction (theory, principle, idea, or method) suitable to the current situation (Bloom, 1956). In this stage, contributors or core developers accept test results and checked them into their relevant CVSs.

There are several technologies that support knowledge application. These include rule-based systems, Case-Based Reasoning (CBR), constraint-based reasoning, model-based reasoning, and diagrammatic reasoning (Becerra-Fernandez & Sabherwal, 2010). The suitability of a technology is determined by the characteristics of the domain. For example, CBR is more commonly used in the development of systems of weak-theory domains. There are similarities between OSS development and weak-theory domains. The experience base in OSS development is distributed among the entire community, and not a single individual. Moreover, the level of expertise cannot be well-defined in OSS as an expert either does not exist or does not fully understand the system.

Indeed, this similarity has led to studies (Reichle & Hanft, 2006) on the feasibility of implementing CBR system based on KMS in OSS community (specifically, Debian GNU/Linux). The proposed framework consists of CBR module and other machine learning modules to maintain the knowledge base and enhance the CBR module performance.

CONCLUSION

There is production and consumption of knowledge in any process, including testing process. The understanding and management of such knowledge is important for its effective use by stakeholders. This chapter, in general, and the TKM model, in particular, serves as a guide to managing knowledge in OSS through different test process activities. Furthermore, it describes the required knowledge for each test process activity. The novelty of the TKM model lies in its reliance on international standards and established models of knowledge.

The TKM model is prone to evolution. The attention in this chapter is limited to the KM support for four activities of the test process in OSS, namely Test Design and Implementation, Test Environment Set-Up and Maintenance, Test Execution, and Test Incident Reporting. Indeed, one of the possible directions for future research is refining and validating the TKM model empirically.

REFERENCES

Abdou, T., Grogono, P., & Kamthan, P. (2012). A conceptual framework for open source software test process. In *Proceedings of Computer Software and Applications Conference Workshops (COMPSACW),* (pp. 458-463). IEEE.

Abdullah, R., Eri, Z., & Talib, A. (2011). A model of knowledge management system in managing knowledge of software testing environment. In *Proceedings of Software Engineering (MySEC), 2011 5th Malaysian Conference* (pp. 229-233). Piscataway, NJ: IEEE.

Becerra-Fernandez, I., & Sabherwal, R. (2010). *Knowledge management: Systems and processes.* New York: M.E. Sharpe.

Bloom, B. (1956). *Taxonomy of educational objectives: The classification of educational goals.* Ann Arbor, MI: D. McKay Company Inc..

Crowston, K., & Howison, J. (2005). The social structure of free and open source software development. *First Monday, 10*(2). doi:10.5210/fm.v10i2.1207.

Crowston, K., & Howison, J. (2006). Hierarchy and centralization in free and open source software team communications. *Knowledge, Technology & Policy, 18*(4), 65–85. doi:10.1007/s12130-006-1004-8.

Cubranic, D., Holmes, R., Ying, A. T., & Murphy, G. C. (2003). Tool for light-weight knowledge sharing in open-source software development. In *Proceedings of the 3rd ICSE Workshop on Open Source* (pp. 25-29). ICSE.

Dalkir, K. (2005). *Knowledge management in theory and practice.* Oxford, UK: Elsevier Butterworth-Heinemann.

Desai, A., & Shah, S. (2011). Knowledge management and software testing. In *Proceedings on International Conference and Workshop on Emerging Trends in Technology (ICWET).* IJCA.

Fancott, T., Kamthan, P., & Shahmir, N. (2012). Towards next generation requirements engineering. In *Proceedings of the 2012 ASE/IEEE International Conference on Social Informatics (Social Informatics 2012).* Washington, DC: IEEE.

Fielding, R. T. (1999). Shared leadership in the apache project. *Communications of the ACM, 42,* 42–43. doi:10.1145/299157.299167.

Gillian, J. (2001). Improving the open source software model with UML case tools. *Linux Gazette, 67.*

Hayek, F. A. (1945). The use of knowledge in society. *The American Economic Review, 35*(4), 519–530.

ISO/IEC. (2010). *ISO/IEC WD 29119-2, software and systems engineering - Software testing - Part 2: Test process.* ISO.

Kaner, C., Falk, J., & Nguyen, H. (1999). *Testing computer software.* New York: Wiley.

Koznov, D., Malinov, V., Sokhransky, E., & Novikova, M. (2009). *A knowledge management approach for industrial model-based testing.* Setubal, Portugal: Academic Press.

Liu, Y., Wu, J., Liu, X., & Gu, G. (2009). Investigation of knowledge management methods in software testing process. In *Proceedings of the 2009 International Conference on Information Technology and Computer Science* (pp. 90-94). Washington, DC: IEEE Computer Society.

Lonchamp, J. (2005). Open source software development process modeling. In S. Acuna, & N. Juristo (Eds.), *Software Process Modeling* (pp. 29–64). New York: Springer. doi:10.1007/0-387-24262-7_2.

Mockus, A., Fielding, R., & Herbsleb, J. (2002). Two case studies of open source software development: Apache and Mozilla. *ACM Transactions on Software Engineering and Methodology, 11*(3), 309–346. doi:10.1145/567793.567795.

Nonaka, I., & Konno, N. (1998). The Concept of ba: Building a foundation for knowledge creation. *California Management Review, 40*(3), 40–54. doi:10.2307/41165942.

Nonaka, I., & Takeuchi, H. (1995). *The knowledge-creating company: How Japanese companies create the dynamics of innovation.* New York: Oxford University Press.

Nonaka, I., Toyama, R., & Konno, N. (2000). SECI, ba and leadership: A unified model of dynamic knowledge creation. *Long Range Planning, 33*(1), 5–34. doi:10.1016/S0024-6301(99)00115-6.

Polanyi, M. (1967). *The tacit dimension.* Chicago: University of Chicago Press.

Prakash, V., & Gopalakrishnan, S. (2011). Testing efficiency exploited: Scripted versus exploratory testing. In *Proceedings of the International Conference on Electronic Computer Technology.* IEEE.

Raymond, E. S. (1999). The cathedral and the bazaar: Musings on Linux and open source by an accidental revolutionary. Sebastopol, CA: O'Reilly and Accociates Inc.

Reichle, M., & Hanft, A. (2006). The FLOSS-WALD information system on free and open source software. [University of Hildesheim, Institute of Computer Science.]. *Proceedings of, LWA2006,* 229–233.

Reid, S. (2000). BS 7925-2: The software component testing standard. In *Proceedings 1st Asia-Pacific Conference on Quality Software* (pp. 139-148). IEEE.

Riege, A. (2005). Three dozen knowledge sharing barriers managers must consider. *Journal of Knowledge Management, 9*(3), 18–35. doi:10.1108/13673270510602746.

Rollett, H. (2003). *Knowledge management: Processes and technologies.* Dordrecht, The Netherlands: Kluwer Academic Publishers. doi:10.1007/978-1-4615-0345-3.

Scacchi, W. (2003). Issues and experiences in modeling open source software development processes. In *Proceedings of the 3rd ICSE Workshop on Open Source Software Engineering* (pp. 121-125). Portland, OR: ICSE.

Showole, A., Sahibuddin, S., & Ibrahim, S. (2011). Layered approach to open source software development success. In *Proceedings of the Communications of the IBIMA, 2011*. IBIMA.

Singh, A. K., & Sharma, V. (2011). Key attributes of successful knowledge management: An empirical study in telecommunication and software industries. *International Journal of Business Information Systems*, 7(1), 78–92. doi:10.1504/IJBIS.2011.037298.

Singh, J. (2007). Open-source software and knowledge management in digital context: Issues and implications. In *Proceedings of the INFLIBNET's Convention*. INFLIBNET.

Sowe, S., Stamelos, I., & Angelis, L. (2008). Understanding knowledge sharing activities in free/open source software projects: An empirical study. *Journal of Systems and Software*, 81, 431–446. doi:10.1016/j.jss.2007.03.086.

Wang, Y., Guo, D., & Shi, H. (2007). Measuring the evolution of open source software systems with their communities. *SIGSOFT Software Engineering Notes, 32*(6).

Weber, R., Aha, D. W., & Becerra-Fernandez, I. (2001). Intelligent lessons learned systems. *International Journal of Expert Systems Research and Applications*, 20(1), 17–34. doi:10.1016/S0957-4174(00)00046-4.

Wiig, K. (1993). *Knowledge management foundations: Thinking about thinking: How people and organizations create, represent, and use knowledge*. New York: Schema Press.

Zhao, L., & Elbaum, S. G. (2003). Quality assurance under the open source development model. *Journal of Systems and Software*, 66(1), 65–75. doi:10.1016/S0164-1212(02)00064-X.

KEY TERMS AND DEFINITIONS

Community of Practice: A group of people who share a common concern, a set of problems, or interest in a topic and who come together to fulfill both individual and group goals.

Explicit Knowledge: Knowledge that can be expressed in formal and systematic language, shared in the form of data, and processed and stored relatively.

Knowledge Management Life Cycle: The processes of managing the route of information in order to become transformed into a valuable strategic asset for an organization, the earliest definition of KMLC describes it as the process of knowledge production and knowledge integration.

Open Source Software: It refers to software that is developed, tested, or improved through public collaboration and distributed with the idea that it must be shared with others, ensuring an open future collaboration.

Software Engineering: The application of a systematic, disciplined, quantifiable approach to the development, operation, and maintenance of software; that is, the application of engineering to software.

Software Testing: The dynamic verification of the behavior of a software system on a finite set of test cases, suitably selected from the usually infinite executions domain, against the expected behavior.

Tacit Knowledge: Knowledge that can be expressed in actions and emotions, hard to be shared and formalized, as it is an analogue process that requires simultaneous processing.

Testing Knowledge Management (TKM) Model: A conceptual model that serves as a guide to managing testing knowledge in open source software through different test process activities.

Section 3
Applications

Chapter 10
Feature Extraction through Information Sharing in Swarm Intelligence Techniques

Lavika Goel
Delhi Technological University, India

V. K. Panchal
Defence and Research Development Organization, India

ABSTRACT

Swarm Intelligence (SI) refers to a kind of problem-solving ability that emerges by the interaction of simple information-processing units. The overall behaviour of the system results from the interactions of individuals through information sharing with each other and with their environment, i.e., the self-organized group behaviour. The chapter details the theoretical aspects and the mathematical framework of the concept of information sharing in each of the swarm intelligence techniques of Biogeography-Based Optimization (BBO), Ant Colony Optimization (ACO), Particle Swarm Optimization (PSO), and Bee Colony Optimization (BCO), which are the major constituents of the SI techniques that have been used for land cover feature extraction of multi-spectral satellite images. The authors then demonstrate the results of classification after applying each of the above SI techniques presented in the chapter and calculate the classification accuracy for each in terms of the kappa coefficient generated from the error matrix obtained. For verification, they test their results on two datasets and also calculate the producer's and the user's accuracy separately for each land cover feature in order to explore the performance of the technique on different features of the satellite image. From the results, they conclude that the concepts of information sharing can be successfully adapted for the design of efficient algorithms that can be successfully applied for feature extraction of satellite images.

DOI: 10.4018/978-1-4666-4229-4.ch010

1. INTRODUCTION

Swarm intelligence is any attempt to design algorithm or distributed problem-solving devices inspired by collective behavior of social insect colonies or other animal societies (Bonabeau, Dorigo, & Theraulaz, 1999). The social insect colony is a distributed system comprising of direct or indirect interactions through information sharing among relatively simple (social) agents that can solve the problems in a very flexible and robust way: flexibility allow adaptation to changing environment, while robustness endows the colony with the ability to function even though some individuals may fail to perform their tasks (Goel, Gupta, & Panchal, 2011). These swarm intelligence techniques can form the basis of building an optimization algorithm which can adapt itself to suit our purpose of natural terrain feature extraction, and prove to be better by giving more accurate results than the other existing optimization techniques for certain specific applications. The swarm intelligence techniques under this category are listed below.

- Ant Colony Optimization
- Swarm Particle Optimization
- Biogeography Based Optimization
- Bacterial Foraging Optimization

In remote sensing (Lillesand & Kiefer, 2008), the problem of feature extraction has been solved by using the traditional classical approaches of artificial intelligence like Parallel-o-piped Classification (Long & Srihann, 2004), Minimum Distance to Mean Classification (Long & Srihann, 2004), Maximum Likelihood Classification (Long & Srihann, 2004) etc. A major disadvantage of the above traditional AI techniques of natural terrain feature extraction is that these techniques show limited accuracy in information retrieval and high-resolution satellite image is needed. Also these techniques are insensitive to different degrees of variance in the spectral response data. The compu-

tational intelligence techniques like the fuzzy sets based classifier and path planner and the rough set classifier, which have been used recently, are not able to provide good result in case of ambiguity and also result in inaccuracy with low spatial resolution. Also these are not able to handle the continuous and the crisp data separately. Hence we shifted to the fundamentals from Swarm Intelligence, an optimized approach of feature extraction of satellite multi-spectral images. Swarm Intelligence provides a good number of accuracy even with low spatial resolution image. This technique, with lower cost and higher degree of accuracy, will be able to replace high resolution high cost satellite imageries (Lillesand & Kiefer, 2008). Particles involved in these techniques can either interact directly through waggle dancing (BCO), global-best positions (PSO), etc. Or indirectly through the environment via pheromone update (ACO), migration of SIV's between candidate solutions (BBO) etc. *Ant colony optimization* was proposed by Marco Dorigo (Dorigo & Stuetzle, 2004; Dorigo, Maniezzo, & Colorni, 1996) in 1992. ACO has since been applied to many search, optimisation and anticipatory problems (Piatrik & Izquierdo, 2006). Similarly, particle swarm optimization algorithm which simulates the social behaviour of bird flocking or fish schooling was introduced by Eberhart and Kennedy (Bratton & Kennedy, 2007) in 1995. PSO is a population based stochastic optimization technique and is well adapted to the optimization of nonlinear functions in multidimensional space (Kennedy & Eberhart, 1995). PSO has been applied to several real-world problems. Likewise, motivated by the foraging behaviour of honeybees, researchers Riley et al., Karaboga and Basturk (2005), proposed artificial bee colony algorithm for solving various optimization problems (Karaboga, 2005; Karaboga & Basturk, 2007; Karaboga & Akay, 2009). This algorithm is easy to implement and robust. Also a novel approach is added in this category called biogeography-based optimization and was recently proposed by Dan Simon (2008).

The key to maintaining global, self-organized behaviour is social interaction. The fundamental principle of these techniques is cooperation and sharing of knowledge. The basis of the increased intelligence is the shared information discovered individually and communicated to the swarm by different mechanisms of social interaction. In this way, intelligent solutions to problems naturally emerge from the self-organization and communication among simple individuals.

In this paper, the first section is an introduction highlighting why we are studying swarm intelligence and information sharing and the milestones that have been reached in this field. The second section gives details of SI and discusses information sharing in various swarm-based approaches like BBO, ACO, PSO, and BCO. This section is divided into four subsections each of which gives the details of the concept of information sharing and the adaptive framework for natural terrain feature elicitation using the SI technique described. Also, this section presents the feature extraction results on different datasets for each of the above SI techniques. The last section presents concluding remarks and the future scope of the discussion.

2. INFORMATION SHARING IN SI TECHNIQUES FOR LAND COVER FEATURE EXTRACTION

Swarm Intelligence (SI) is artificial intelligence based on the collective behavior of decentralized, self-organized systems. In swarm-based techniques, there is no centralized controller but the groups exhibit complex global behaviour. Individuals follow simple rules to interact with neighbors. The information-processing units that compose a swarm can be animate, mechanical, computational, or mathematical; they can be insects, birds, or human beings; they can be array elements, robots, or standalone workstations; they can be real or imaginary. Examples of systems studied by swarm intelligence are colonies of ants and termites, schools of fish, flocks of birds, herds of land animals. Rules followed by the groups in swarm intelligence are collision avoidance, velocity matching, and Flock Centering.

Swarms have the ability to solve problems and possess a meta-heuristic that can be used to solve hard problems like TSP, Quadratic Assignment Problem (QAP), etc. Some of the real world applications in which swarm intelligence can be successfully applied are:

- In Movies: Graphics in movies.
- Unmanned underwater vehicles(UUV):
  ○ Groups of UUVs used as security units
  ○ Only local maps at each UUV
  ○ Joint detection of and attack over enemy vessels by co-ordinating within the group of UUVs
- Swarm-casting:
  ○ For fast downloads in a peer-to-peer file-sharing network.
  ○ Fragments of a file are downloaded from different hosts in the network, parallelly.
- Routing algorithms modelling the communicative behaviour of social insects / birds / honey bees, etc.
- The European Space Agency is thinking about an orbital swarm for self assembly and interferometry. NASA is investigating the use of swarm technology for planetary mapping.

The particles in a swarm try to solve a problem as a group by using the information contained by their peer mates. This sharing of information enables swarm particles to be more efficient and to achieve goals that they could not achieve individually. Although there is normally no centralized control structure dictating how individual agents should behave; local interactions between such agents often lead to the emergence of global behaviour. The characterizing property of a swarm intelligence system is its ability to act in a coordinated way without the presence of a coordinator or of an external controller. Notwithstanding the lack of individuals in charge of the group, the swarm as a whole can show intelligent behaviour. This section discusses the information sharing in various swarm-based techniques (Goel, Gupta, & Panchal, 2011) and how it can be utilized and adapted for the feature extraction of satellite images.

Figure 1 presents an overview of this section. The figure describes each of the SI techniques, which are based on the information sharing concept along with the heuristic function which forms the base of the mathematical framework for adapting the respective SI technique to suit our purpose of feature extraction (Goel, Gupta, & Panchal, 2011). We also summarize the classification accuracy in terms of the kappa coefficient after adapting each of the above SI techniques for our purpose of land cover feature extraction. Each of these heuristic equations and the corresponding classification accuracy provided by using them for each of the SI techniques has been presented and described in detail in the respective subsections below. We verify the classification (or feature extraction) results on two different datasets as will be detailed in the later sections and hence summarize the complete results in the Figure 1.

2.1. Ant Colony Optimization

This section discusses the concept of information sharing in ACO and its perspective application for the elicitation of natural terrain features.

2.1.1. Information Sharing In ACO

Ants use the environment as a medium of communication. They exchange information indirectly by depositing pheromones, all detailing the status of their work. In ACO algorithms, local pheromone trails (only an ant located where the pheromones were left has a notion of them) are the only communication channels among the ants. This system that occurs in many social animal societies is called stigmergy. ACO is a mechanism of indirect coordination between agents or actions. The principle is that the trace left in the environment by an action stimulates the performance of a next action, by the same or a different agent. In that way, subsequent actions tend to reinforce and build on each other, leading to the spontaneous emergence of coherent, apparently systematic activity. It solves problems too complex to be addressed by single ants without need for any planning, control, or even direct communication between the agents. As such it supports efficient collaboration between extremely simple agents, who lack any memory, intelligence or even awareness of each other.

Using ACO ants is an example of a self-organized system. This system is based on positive (the deposit of pheromone attracts other ants that strengthen it themselves) and negative feedback (dissipation of the route by evaporation prevents the system from thrashing). Theoretically, if the quantity of pheromone remained the same over time on all edges, no route would ever be chosen.

However, because of feedback, a slight variation on an edge will be amplified and thus allow the choice of an edge. Thus, a stable state with a route composed of the strongest edges is constructed. ACO involves the movement of a colony of ants through the different states of the problem influenced by two local decision policies, viz., *trails* and *attractiveness*.

- Whenever an ant finds food, it marks its return journey with pheromones.
- Pheromones evaporate faster on longer paths.
- Shorter paths serve as the way to food for most of the other ants.
- The shorter path is thus further reinforced by the pheromones and the ants arrive at the optimal path.

Figure 1. Feature extraction techniques based on the concepts of information sharing in swarm intelligence

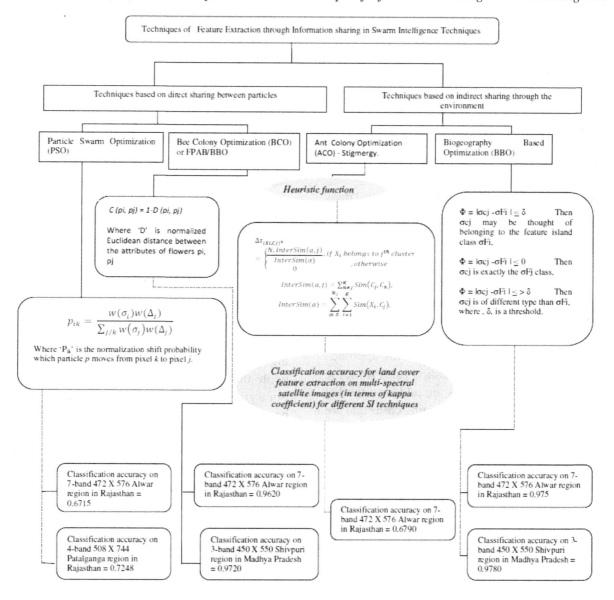

Furthermore, the algorithm includes, *trail evaporation* and *daemon actions*. *Trail evaporation* reduces all trail values over time thereby avoiding any possibilities of getting stuck in local optima. The *daemon actions* are used to bias the search process from a non-local perspective. Information Sharing is a key design component of ACO algorithms. Ants within the population communicate among themselves by means of the information they read/write on the problems states that they visit.

Artificial ants also modify some aspects of their environments, by mimicking the pheromone depositing behavior. This artificial pheromone trail changes some numeric information locally stored in the problem's state they visit. This information takes into account the ant's current history/performance and can be read/written by any ant accessing the state. Artificial ants deposit an amount of pheromone that is a function of the quality of solution found.

In remote sensing κ, the kappa coefficient is very important and prevalent as a measure of accuracy assessment of Land cover classification. κ can be derived from the confusion matrix or error matrix. Hence,

κ ∝ Knowledge

if κ=0 then the classifier is inconsistent and does not represent the requisite knowledge

if κ=1 then the classifier is consistent and represent the requisite knowledge.

The AntMiner algorithm given below (Dorigo & Stuetzle, 2004; Parpinelli, Lopes, & Freitas, 2002; Bansal, Gupta, Panchal, & Kumar, 2009) in Figure 2 follows a sequential covering approach to discover a list of classification rules from the given data set. These rules are added to the list of discovered rules and the training cases that are covered correctly by these rules, are removed from the training set. It covers all or almost all the training cases. Each classification rule has the form

IF <term1 AND term2 AND...> Then <CLASS>.

Ant miner requires the discretization method as a pre-processing method and it is suitable only for the nominal attributes (Parpinelli, Lopes, & Freitas, 2002; Bansal, Gupta, Panchal, & Kumar, 2009).

2.1.2. Elicitation of Land Cover Features through Information Sharing in ACO

Next, we discuss the adaptive strategy we followed to use the concept of information sharing in ACO for elicitation of topographical features. The major steps are image clustering and heuristic method (HSI) implementation, which form the pillars of the concept of adaptive application of information sharing for terrain features elicitation, and are explained next (Piatrik & Izquierdo, 2006).

A widely adopted definition of information sharing through optimal clustering is a partitioning that the intra cluster similarity is minimized while the inter cluster similarity is maximized. For a given problem the pheromone can be set to be proportional to above criteria of the desired. In ACO, we assign each image to a cluster and each ant is giving its own classification solution. The algorithm starts by assigning a pheromone level τ and a heuristic information η to each image.

Figure 2. cAntMiner algorithm (Dorigo & Stuetzle, 2004; Bansal, Gupta, Panchal, & Kumar, 2009)

```
Training set = all training cases;
WHILE (No. of cases in the Training set > max_uncovered_cases)
i=0;
REPEAT
i=i+1;
Ant 'i' incrementally constructs a classification    rule;
Prune the just constructed rule;
Update the pheromone of the trail followed by Ant i;
UNTIL (i ≥ No_of_Ants) or (Anti constructed the same rule as the
previous No_Rules_Converg-1 Ants)
Select the best rule among all constructed rules;
Remove the cases correctly covered by the selected rule from the
training set;
END WHILE
```

The value for the pheromone level τ assigned to each image is initialized to 1 so that it does not have effect on the probability at the beginning. Heuristic information $\eta\ (X\ i\ C\ j)$ is obtained from the following formula:

$$\eta_{(X_i,C_j)} = \frac{B}{Sim(X_i,C_j)}\ ,$$

where X_i represents the feature vector of ith image and C_j is the feature vector representing j^{th} centroid of the cluster. $Sim\ (Xi, Cj)$ is the similarity between an image X_i and Cj. B is a constant where K is the number of clusters. Assume a number m of ants is chosen for clustering based on the K-Means approach. After all ants have done their classification, the assigned pheromone to this solution is incremented. In order to find global minimum, the pheromone value is updated according to quality of the solution. For updating the pheromone to each clustering the following formula is used:

$$\tau_{(X_i,C_j)}\left(t\right) = \rho.\tau_{(X_i,C_j)}\left(t-1\right) + \sum_{a=1}^{m}\Delta\tau_{(X_i,C_j)^a}\left(t\right),$$

where ρ is the pheromone trail evaporation coefficient $(0 <= \rho <= 1)$ which causes vanishing of the pheromones over the iterations. $\tau\ (Xi, Cj)\ (t\text{-}1)$ represents the pheromone value from previous iteration. $\Delta\tau\ (Xi, Cj)\ ^a(t)$ in the equation above is a new amount of pheromones calculated from all m ants that assign image X_i to j^{th} cluster. This approach of marking solutions by pheromone is depicted in Figure 3 and proposed as follows:

$$InterSim(a, j) = \sum_{n \neq j}^{K}Sim\left(C_j,C_n\right),$$

$$InterSim(a) = \sum_{i \in S_j}^{N_j}\sum_{j=1}^{K}Sim\left(X_i,C_j\right),$$

$$\Delta\tau_{(Xi,Cj)^a}$$
$$= \begin{cases} \dfrac{N.InterSim\left(a,j\right)}{InterSim\left(a\right)}, & if\ X_i\ belongs\ to\ j^{th}\ cluster \\ 0 & ,otherwise \end{cases}$$

Classification accuracy of our proposed algorithm is expressed using classification *error matrix* which is constructed in Table 1.

Figure 3. Working of Ant Colony Optimization based on the concept of Information Sharing

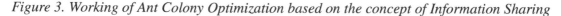

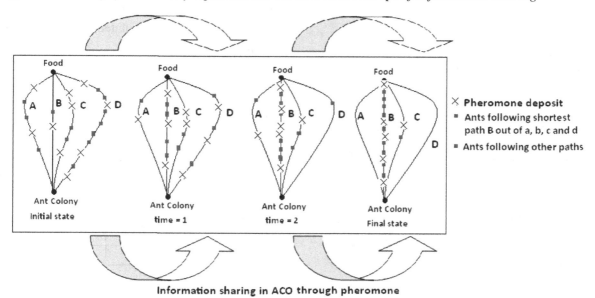

Table 1. Error matrix for ACO based feature elicitator on Alwar region

	Vegetation	**Urban**	**Rocky**	**Water**	**Barren**	**Total**
Vegetation	314	1	0	0	0	315
Urban	6	410	0	0	14	430
Rocky	2	0	276	0	1	279
Water	3	0	2	204	0	209
Barren	2	6	9	2	174	193
Total	327	417	287	206	189	1426

InterSim(a, j) represents the sum of the similarities obtained by ant a, between j^{th} centroid and the rest of centroids. *IntraSim* (a) represents the sum of the similarities obtained by ant a, between each image and its centroid. N is the number of images in the dataset and this variable keeps the values of *InterSim*(a, j) and *IntraSim*(a) in the same order. It becomes clear that the pheromone increases when clusters get more apart and when each cluster has more similar images. Next, the classification performed by each ant is driven by the quality of previous solutions. This is repeated until the best solution for all ants is achieved.

2.1.2.1. 7-Band 472 × 576 Pixels Cartoset Satellite Image of Alwar Region in Rajasthan

After applying the proposed algorithm to the 7-band of Alwar Image, the classified image is

Figure 4. Classification results of ACO on Alwar region (Bansal, Gupta, Panchal, & Kumar, 2009)

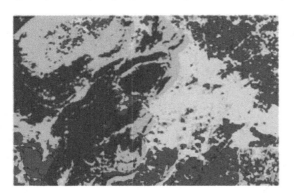

obtained in Figure 4 (Bansal, Gupta, Panchal, & Kumar, 2009).

The Kappa (κ) coefficient of the Alwar image is 0.962 which indicates that an observed classification is 96.2% better than one resulting from chance. Producer's and user's accuracies are calculated in Tables 2 and 3 respectively.

2.1.2.2. 3-Band Cartoset Satellite Image of Size 450 × 550 Pixels of Shivpuri Region in Madhya Pradesh

In this section, we discuss the results we got on the Shivpuri image for demonstrating the concept of information sharing for the elicitation of natural terrain features. The classified image of Shivpuri has been shown in Figure 5 with kappa coefficient .972 (Bansal, Gupta, Panchal, & Kumar, 2009). Error matrix is given in Table 4. Producer's and user's accuracies are calculated in Tables 5 and 6 respectively.

Table 2. Producer's accuracy

Feature	**Accuracy Calculation**	**Producer's Accuracy**
Vegetation	314/327	96%
Urban	410/417	98.3%
Rocky	276/287	96.2%
Water	204/206	99.1%
Barren	174/189	92.1%

Table 3. User's accuracy

Feature	Accuracy Calculation	User's Accuracy
Vegetation	314/315	99.7%
Urban	410/430	95.3%
Rocky	276/279	98.9%
Water	204/209	97.6%
Barren	174/193	90.2%

Figure 5. Classification results of ACO on Shivpuri region (Bansal, Gupta, Panchal, & Kumar, 2009)

2.2. Biogeography-Based Optimization (BBO)

This section discusses the concept of information sharing in BBO and its perspective application for the elicitation of land cover features.

2.2.1. Information Sharing in BBO

Each problem solution can share its features with other solutions. BBO is based on the idea of probabilistically sharing features between solutions based on the solutions' fitness values. The probability that a given solution shares its features is proportional to its fitness, and the probability that a given solution receives features from other solutions is inversely proportional to its fitness. This is shown pictorially in Figure 6. In BBO, mutation is used to increase the diversity of the population to get good solutions.

BBO is an evolutionary process that achieves information sharing by biogeography based migration operators (Ma, 2010). In biogeography, species migrate between islands. In BBO, problem solutions are represented as islands, and the sharing of features (SIVs) between solutions is represented as migration between islands. We use the migration rates of each solution to probabilistically share features between solutions The Mutation operator modifies a habitat's SIV's randomly based on the mutation rate (for the case of $E = I$). Also for each generation, BBO uses the fitness of each solution to determine its emigration and immigration rate (Simon, 2008; Ma, 2010; Ma, Ni, & Sun, 2009). High HSI solutions tend to share their features with low HSI solutions. Low HSI solutions accept a lot of new features from high HSI solutions (Simon, 2008; Ma, 2010; Ma, Ni, & Sun, 2009). The BBO algorithm based on the concept of information sharing as proposed

Table 4. Error matrix for ACO based feature elicitator on Shivpuri region

	Vegetation	Open	Crop	Water	Shallow Water	Total
Vegetation	24	0	0	0	4	28
Open	0	181	0	0	0	181
Crop	0	0	53	0	0	53
Water	0	0	0	33	0	33
Shallow Water	2	1	0	1	29	33
Total	26	182	53	34	33	328

Table 5. Producer's accuracy

Feature	Accuracy Calculation	Producer's Accuracy
Vegetation	24/26	92.3%
Open	181/182	99.4%
Crop	53/53	100%
Water	33/34	97.1%
Shallow Water	29/33	87.8%

Table 6. User's accuracy

Feature	Accuracy Calculation	User's Accuracy
Vegetation	24/28	85.7%
Open	181/181	100%
Crop	53/53	100%
Water	33/33	100%
Shallow Water	29/33	87.8%

by Dan Simon is as given in Figure 7 (Simon, 2008; Ma, 2010; Ma, Ni, & Sun, 2009).

2.2.2. Elicitation of Land Cover Features through Information Sharing in BBO

Next, we discuss the adaptive strategy we followed to use the concept of information sharing in BBO for elicitation of land cover features. The major steps for image clustering and heuristic method (HSI) implementation, which form the pillars of the concept of adaptive application of information sharing for land cover features elicitation, are explained next (Goel, Panchal, & Gupta, 2010; Panchal, Singh, Kaur, & Kundra, 2009). The m-bands image is clustered into *Hi,* using rough set theory. The parameters of clustering are NIR and MIR bands. The resultant clusters or the habitats *Hi,* are species in universal habitat as depicted in Figure 8 (Goel, Panchal, & Gupta, 2010; Panchal, Singh, Kaur, & Kundra, 2009).

These species are migrated to the suitable habitats i.e. feature islands. The heuristic method decides which species are moved to which habitat using a fitness function, which we call as the

Figure 6. Biogeography-based optimization based on the concept of information sharing

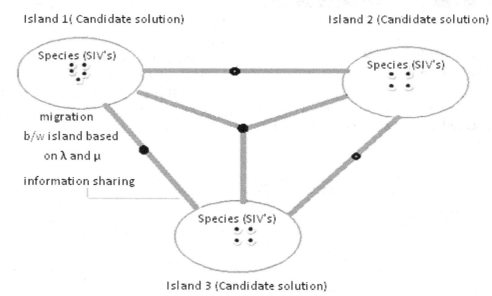

Figure 7. Biogeography based optimization algorithm (Simon, 2008)

Initialize the BBO parameters. This means deriving a method of mapping problem solutions to SIVs and habitats which is problem dependent.

Initialize the maximum species count S_{max} and the maximum migration rates E and I, the maximum mutation rate m_{max}, and an elitism parameter.

The maximum species count and the maximum migration rates are relative quantities. That is, if they all change by the same percentage, then the behavior of BBO will not change. This is because if E, I, and S_{max} change, then the migration rates immigration rate (μ), emigration rate (λ), and the species count S will change by the same relative amount for each solution.

Initialize a random set of habitats, each habitat corresponding to a potential solution to the given problem.

For each habitat

Map the HSI to the number of species S, the immigration rate λ, and the emigration rate μ.

Probabilistically use immigration and emigration to modify each non-elite habitat.

Re-compute each HSI.

Update the probability of its species count using (4). Then mutate each non-elite habitat based on its probability and re-compute each HSI.

End For

This loop can be terminated after a predefined number of generations or after an acceptable problem solution has been found.

Figure 8. Initial state of the ecosystem (Goel, Panchal, & Gupta, 2010; Panchal, Singh, Kaur, & Kundra, 2009)

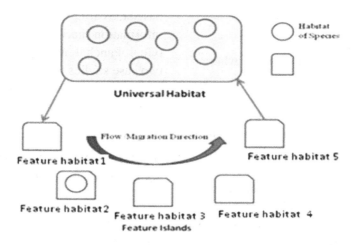

habitat suitability index. Here we have used mean of standard deviation as the HSI function. This function for a specific class takes up the corresponding training sets and then calculates the required function values, which further helps to decide the most suitable habitat. Let σF_i, be the average of the standard deviations of any of the feature islands.

$$\sigma F_i = (\sigma_{1_i} + \sigma_{2_i} + \sigma_{3_i} + \sigma_{4_i} + \ldots\ldots + \sigma_{m_i}) \;/m$$

where $\sigma_{1_i}, \sigma_{2_i}, \sigma_{3_i}, \sigma_{4_i}, \ldots\ldots, \sigma_{m_i}$ are the standard deviations of the DN values of each of the m bands respectively of the ith feature island.

Similarly, let the average of the standard deviation of the species habitat C_j from H_i of the Universal Habitat Π be represented by:

$$\sigma_{c_j} = (\sigma_{1_j} + \sigma_{2_j} + \sigma_{3_j} + \sigma_{4_j} + \ldots\ldots + \sigma_{m_j}) \;/m$$

Then the heuristic function (or the HSI function) Φ be defined as

$$\Phi = |\,\sigma_{c_j} - \sigma_{F_i}\,| \leq \delta$$

Then σc_j may be thought of belonging to the feature island class σF_i,

$$\Phi = |\,\sigma_{c_j} - \sigma_{F_i}\,| \leq 0$$

Then σc_j is exactly the σF_j class,

$$\Phi = |\,\sigma_{c_j} - \sigma_{F_i}\,| \leq> \delta$$

Then σc_j is of different type than σF_i, where, δ, is a threshold.

Also, the HSI function makes use of a specific threshold value. For higher accuracy, the threshold value should be low. But with low threshold value the number of generations rises at a rapid pace. If for a species, no suitable habitat is found in the current generation, it implies that there are a large number of mixed pixels in the given section of the image (defined as a species). This unclassified cluster migrates to the universal habitat. Here it is further partitioned into smaller unsupervised clusters which are again classified using rough set theory. This is termed as second generation. The HSI function decides which value of mean

of standard deviation has minimum difference from the original class. If this value is within the threshold then that equivalence class (species) will migrate to that feature habitat. The recalculated HSI after the migration of species to the feature habitat is compared with the original HSI of the feature habitat (that contained training pixels only). If the compared HSI is within the threshold i.e., it varies from -1 to +1 from the original HSI then it means that the habitat is suitable for that species and hence it can migrate to it. If the recalculated HSI is not within the threshold for any of the original habitat then the particular elementary equivalence class contained a mixture of species and it is again partitioned into smaller equivalence classes. These classes are migrated into the universal habitat and considered as unclassified species. These are further used for the next generation /iteration. The iteration continues until all the equivalence classes (species habitats) have been checked and then we move towards the second generation for further refinement following the similar process. The whole process continues until there are no more unclassified classes (species) that are left in the universal habitat. The mathematical interpretation of the biogeography based classifier which is based on the concept of information sharing as is represented by Figure 9 (Goel, Panchal, & Gupta, 2010). We have taken two case studies, of Alwar area in Rajasthan and Patalganga region in Shivalik mountains, to demonstrate the information sharing concept of BBO for the detection of landscape traits.

2.2.2.1. 7-Band 472 × 576 Pixels Cartoset Satellite Image of Alwar Region in Rajasthan

After applying the proposed algorithm to the 7-band of Alwar Image, the classified image is obtained in Figure 10 (Panchal, Singh, Kaur, & Kundra, 2009). Classification accuracy of our proposed algorithm is expressed using classification error matrix which is constructed in Table

Figure 9. Mechanism of Biogeography based feature elicitator in mathematical notation (Goel, Panchal, & Gupta, 2010)

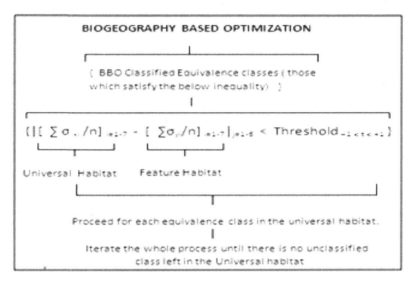

Figure 10. Classification of Alwar image based on BBO (Panchal, Singh, Kaur, & Kundra, 2009)

7. The Kappa coefficient of the Alwar image is calculated using the method described in (Bansal, Gupta, Panchal, & Kumar, 2009).

The Kappa (κ) coefficient of the Alwar image is 0.6715 which indicates that an observed classification is 67.15% better than one resulting from chance. Error Matrix is represented in Table 7.

Several other descriptive measures can be obtained from error matrix. The accuracy of individual category can be calculated by dividing the number of correctly classified pixels in each category by either the total number of pixels in corresponding row or column. Producer's accuracies (as shown in Table 8) result from dividing the number of correctly classified pixels in each category (on the major diagonal) by the number of training set pixels used for that category(the column total). This figure indicates how well the training pixels of a given cover type are classified.

User's Accuracy (as shown in Table 9) is computed by dividing the number of correctly classified pixels in each category by the total number of pixels that were classified in that category (the row total).This figure is a measure of commission error and indicates the probability that a pixel classified into a given category actually represents that category on the ground.

2.2.2.2. 4-Band Landsat-1 Satellite Image of size 508 × 744 pixels of Patalganga Region in Shivalik

In this section, we discuss the results we got on the Patalganga image for demonstrating the concept of information sharing for the elicitation of natural terrain features. The classified image of Patalganga has been shown in Figure 11 with

Table 7. Error matrix for BBO-based feature extractor on Alwar region

	Vegetation	**Urban**	**Rocky**	**Water**	**Barren**	**Total**
Vegetation	127	9	0	0	2	138
Urban	0	88	1	0	32	121
Rocky	6	2	176	1	17	202
Water	0	0	3	69	0	72
Barren	17	91	20	0	119	247
Total	150	190	200	70	170	780

Table 8. Producer's accuracy

Feature	**Accuracy calculation**	**Producer's Accuracy**
Vegetation	127/150	84.6%
Urban	92/189	48.6%
Rocky	175/202	86.6%
Water	70/70	100%
Barren	128/170	75.3%

Table 9. User's accuracy

Feature	**Accuracy Calculation**	**User's Accuracy**
Vegetation	127/129	98.4%
Urban	92/129	71.3%
Rocky	175/194	90.2%
Water	70/70	100%
Barren	128/256	50%

Figure 11. Classification of Patalganga image based on BBO (Panchal, Singh, Kaur, & Kundra, 2009)

kappa coefficient .7248 (Goel, Panchal, & Gupta, 2010; Panchal, Singh, Kaur, & Kundra, 2009). Error matrix is given in Table 10.

Now that we have obtained the classified image from BBO for the Patalganga region, we proceed with the similar procedure for this case too as was done for the Alwar image. We also obtain the accuracy measures from the user's and the producer's perspective and generate the Tables 11 and 12.

In this study, we have attempted to demonstrate the fact that the image classification done by BBO is based on the underlying concept of information sharing. In a very innovative way the uncertainty is resolved by making use of rough sets, in the

Table 10. Error matrix for the satellite image of Patalganga region when BBO is applied

	Vegetation	**Snow**	**Rocky**	**Total**
Vegetation	89	7	7	103
Snow	48	181	4	224
Rocky	24	5	189	227
Total	161	200	200	561

Table 11. Producer's accuracy

Feature	**Accuracy Calculation**	**Producer's Accuracy**
Vegetation	89/161	55.3%
Snow	181/200	90.5%
Rocky	189/200	94.5%

Table 12. User's accuracy

Feature	Accuracy Calculation	User's Accuracy
Vegetation	89/103	86.4%
Snow	181/224	80.8%
Rocky	189/227	83.3%

form of unsupervised clusters i.e. the habitat H_i. Then, its distance is measured from the feature island class. More the distance, more distinct is the H_i. The distinct class is granularized again into new set of habitats in the universal habitat. The iterations keep refining the results.

2.3. Bee Colony Optimization (BCO)

This section discusses the concept of information sharing in BCO and its perspective application for the elicitation of natural terrain features.

2.3.1. Information Sharing In BCO

BCO Algorithm is an optimization algorithm based on the intelligent behaviour of honey bee swarm (Karaboga, 2005). In Bee Colony Optimisation algorithm, artificial bees fly around in a multidimensional search space and some (employed and onlooker bees) choose food sources depending on their own and their nest mates' experience; they then adjust their positions accordingly. Some (scouts) fly and choose the food sources randomly without using experience. If the nectar amount of a new source is higher than that of the previous one in their memory, they memorize the new position and forget the previous one. Thus, the BCO algorithm combines local search methods, carried out by employed and onlooker bees, with global search methods, managed by onlookers and scouts, attempting to balance exploration and exploitation process.

In Bee Colony Optimisation, each cycle of search consists of three steps shown in Figure

12-sending the employed bees onto the food sources and then measuring their nectar amounts; selection of food sources by the onlookers after sharing the information of employed bees and determining the nectar amount of the food; determining the scout bees and then sending them onto possible food sources. At the initialization stage, a set of food source positions are randomly selected by the bees and their nectar amounts are determined. Then, these bees come into the hive and share the nectar information of the sources with the bees waiting on the dance area within the hive. At the second stage, after sharing the information, every employed bee goes to the food source visited by itself in the previous cycle since that food source exists in her memory, and then chooses a new food source by means of visual information, in the neighbourhood of the present one. Visual information is based on the comparison of food source positions. At the third stage, an onlooker prefers a food source area depending on the nectar information distributed by the employed bees on the dance area. As the nectar amount of a food source increases, the probability with which that food source is chosen by an onlooker increases, too. After all employed bees complete the search process; they share the nectar information of the food sources (solutions) and their position information with the onlooker bees on the dance area. An onlooker bee evaluates the nectar information taken from all employed bees and chooses a food source with a probability related to its nectar amount (Karaboga, 2005).

Bee Colony Optimisation in fact employs four different selection processes (Das, Biswas, Dasgupta, & Abraha, 2009; Karaboga, 2005):

1. A global selection process used by the artificial onlooker bees for discovering promising regions.
2. A local selection process carried out in a region by the artificial employed bees and the onlookers depending on local information (in case of real bees, this information

Figure 12. Working of bee colony optimization based on the concept of information sharing

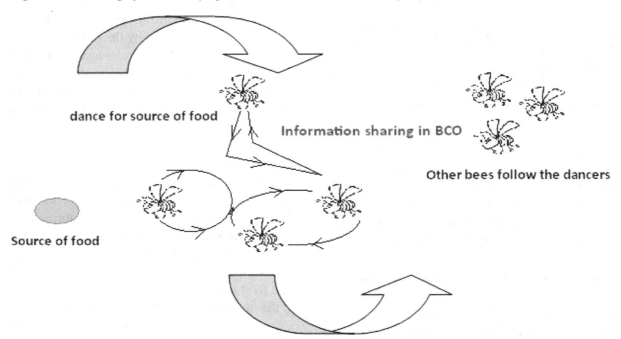

includes the colour, shape and fragrance of the flowers) for determining a neighbour food source around the source in the memory.

3. A local selection process called greedy selection process is carried out by all bees is that if the nectar amount of the candidate source is better than that of the present one, the bee forgets the present one and memorizes the candidate source. Otherwise, the bee keeps the present one in the memory.

4. A random selection process is carried out by scouts.

The exchange of information among bees contributes to the formation of collective knowledge (Karaboga, 2005; Karaboga & Basturk, 2007; Karaboga & Akay, 2009). The most important part of the hive with respect to exchanging information is the dancing area-where communication related to the quality of food sources takes place. Since information about all the current rich sources is available to an onlooker on the dance floor,

probably she could watch numerous dances and choose to employ herself at the most profitable source. Figure 12 illustrates this. There is a greater probability of onlookers choosing more profitable sources since more information is circulating about the more profitable sources. Employed foragers share their information with a probability which is proportional to the profitability of the food source, and the sharing of this information through waggle dancing is longer in duration (Teodorovici & Dell'Orco, 2000). Hence, the recruitment is proportional to profitability of a food source. The BCO algorithm is described in Figure 13.

2.3.2. Elicitation of Land Cover Features through a Combined Application of Information Sharing in BCO and BBO, i.e. FPAB

Next, we discuss the adaptive strategy we followed to use the concept of information sharing in BCO through FPAB/BBO algorithm for elicitation of

Figure 13. BCO algorithm

Determine the number of bees B, and the number of iterations I. Select the set of stages ST={ st_1, st_2,...., st_n}. Find any feasible solution x of the problem. This solution is the initial best solution.

Set i=1. Until i=I, repeat the following steps:

Set j=1. Until j=m, repeat the following steps:

Forward Pass: Allow bees to fly from the hive and to choose B partial solutions from the set of partial solutions S_j at stage st_j.

Backward Pass: Send all bees back to the hive. Allow bees to exchange information about the quality of the partial solutions and become again uncommitted follower. Continue to expand some partial solution without recruiting the nestmates, or dance and thus recruit the nestmates before returning to the created partial solution. Set j=j+1.

If the best solution xi obtained during the ith iteration is better than the best known solution, update the best known solution (x=x_i).

Set i=i+1.

---

topographical features. The major steps are image clustering and heuristic method (HSI) implementation, which form the pillars of the concept of adaptive application of information sharing for land cover features extraction, are explained next.

Initially, flowers scattered randomly on 2D discrete grid, which is named as jungle. This jungle can be considered as a matrix of M × M cells. The matrix is toroidal which allows the bees to fly from one end to another easily and there is no initially more than one flower in each cell of jungle. The size of the jungle depends on the number of flowers. We have used a jungle of M × M such $m^2 = 4n$ that where n is the total number of flowers (objects) to be clustered.

Initially, the bees are randomly scattered throughout the jungle. We use n/3 bees, where n is the total number of flowers to be clustered. Each garden defined as a collection of 2 or more flowers (or pollens) and for simplicity of algorithm each garden spatially located in a single cell. Consider a garden G with n_g flowers. We define the following parameters:

The compatibility between two flowers in the garden

$$C\left(p_i, p_j\right) = 1 - D(p_i, p_j)$$

where 'D' is normalized Euclidean distance between the attributes of flowers p_i, p_j.

The center of garden G

$$O_{center}\left(G\right) = \frac{1}{n_g} \sum_{O_i \in G}^{n} O_i$$

The growth of the pollen in a garden

$$G\left(p_i\right) = C(p_i, O_{center})$$

The flower with minimum growth in a garden G

$$p_{min} = \arg\min G(p_i)$$

where $p_i \in G$.

The main FPAB algorithm (Johal, Singh, & Kundra, 2010; Passino, 2002) is written below:

1.   Randomly scatter bees and flowers into the jungle (atmost one flower per cell)

2. Set the initial growth of all flowers to zero
3. Repeat 4, 5, 6 until stopping criteria
4. For each bee do
    a. Fly the bee in jungle
    b. If the bee does not carry any pollen then it possibly picks up a pollen else the bee possibly pollinates.
5. Next bee
6. Natural Selection

Initially, the bees are randomly scattered into the jungle and also randomly pick up or pollinate when they reach a new garden in the jungle. Here, the stopping criterion for the bees is the number of times through the repeat loop.

For elicitation of terrain features, we proceed as explained next. Initially homogeneous clusters of image pixels are obtained using FPAB algorithm discussed above. Clusters obtained by honey bees are treated as species in BBO and are put to universal habitats. There are other feature habitats containing the training pixels of the corresponding feature produced by experts. For example, water habitat initially contains pixels of water and standard deviation of all the training pixels of water is calculated in each of seven bands. The HSI is calculated on these training pixels. Each species is taken from the universal habitat and is migrated to each feature habitat one at a time. The HSI of the habitat is recalculated after migrating the species to it. The difference between the original HSI and recalculated HSI is calculated. And if the difference is minimum in some particular feature habitat, species is migrated to that habitat.

2.3.2.1. 7-Band 472 × 576 Pixels Cartoset Satellite Image of Alwar Region in Rajasthan

After applying the proposed algorithm to the 7-band of Alwar Image, the classified image is obtained in Figure 14 (Johal, Singh, & Kundra, 2010).

Figure 14. Classification results of BCO on Alwar (Johal, Singh, & Kundra, 2010)

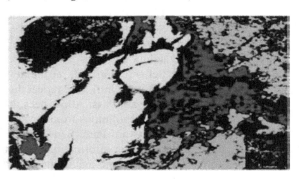

The Kappa (κ) coefficient of the Alwar image is 0.679 which indicates that an observed classification is 67.9% better than one resulting from chance. Error Matrix is represented in Table 13. The producer's and the user's accuracy are calculated in Tables 14 and 15 respectively.

2.4. Particle Swarm Optimization (PSO)

This section discusses the concept of information sharing in PSO and its perspective application for the elicitation of natural terrain features.

2.4.1. Information Sharing In PSO

Particle Swarm Optimisation algorithm imitates human (or insects) social behaviour. Individuals interact with one another while learning from their own experience, and gradually the population members move into better regions of the problem space. PSO uses the fitness concept, but, less-fit particles do not die. No "survival of the fittest."

Each particle keeps track of its coordinates in the problem space, which were associated with the best solution (fitness) that it has achieved so far. This value is called 'pbest'. Another best value that is tracked by PSO is the best value obtained so far by any particle in the neighborhood of the

Table 13. Error matrix of FPAB algorithm on Alwar region

	Vegetation	Urban	Rocky	Water	Barren	Total
Vegetation	138	11	0	0	1	150
Urban	0	90	2	0	36	128
Rocky	10	0	181	0	28	219
Water	0	0	0	70	0	70
Barren	2	89	17	0	105	213
Total	150	190	200	70	170	780

Table 14. Producer's accuracy

Feature	Accuracy Calculation	Producer's Accuracy
Vegetation	138/150	92%
Urban	90/190	47.3%
Rocky	181/200	90.5%
Water	70/70	100%
Barren	105/170	61.8%

Table 15. User's accuracy

Feature	Accuracy Calculation	User's Accuracy
Vegetation	138/150	92%
Urban	90/128	70.3%
Rocky	181/219	82.6%
Water	70/70	100%
Barren	105/213	49.3%

particle. This value is called 'gbest'.The PSO concept consists of changing the velocity of each particle toward its 'pbest' and the 'gbest' position at each time step. Each particle tries to modify its current position and velocity according to the distance between its current position and 'pbest', and the distance between its current position and 'gbest' (Kennedy & Eberhart, 1995).

Each particle in the search space evolves its candidate solution over time, making use of its individual memory and knowledge gained by the swarm as a whole. Information Sharing in PSO includes the global best particle found in

the swarm and direct communication between particles (candidate solutions). This is shown in Figure 16. The PSO algorithm (Bratton & Kennedy, 2007; Kennedy & Eberhart, 1995) is outlined in Figure 15.

2.4.2. Elicitation of Land Cover Features through Information Sharing in PSO

Next, we discuss the adaptive strategy we followed to use the concept of information sharing in PSO for elicitation of topographical features. The major steps are image clustering and heuristic method (HSI) implementation, which form the pillars of the concept of adaptive application of information sharing for land cover features extraction, are explained next (Dong & Xiang-Bin, 2008).

Particle swarm classification model can be adapted for feature extraction of remote sensing images by treating two dimensional remote sensing images as a gravitational field. Each of the pixels in the image is considered having different gravitation to particles locating in neighboring of the pixel. By gravitation, we mean searching similarity information in the above-mentioned process, but it is updated continually by those particles which have reached the pixel according to classification rules. If the pixel belongs to the type to which the particle belongs, the gravitation of the pixel to the particles located in 8- neighborhood around the pixel will be increased by a certain number, otherwise the gravitation will be

Figure 15. PSO algorithm

```
Main Program
    Iteration=100
    Particle=10
    While Fitness value= Threshold value
    For each iteration
    For each particle in the swarm
    Initialize each particle randomly respective regions
    If particle finds best local best value (best object)
    Then update particle position and velocity
    Else
    Not updated
    End For
    Find best global best particle (Fitness function)
    End For
    End While
    End Program loop.
```

Figure 16. Working of particle swarm optimization based on the concept of information sharing

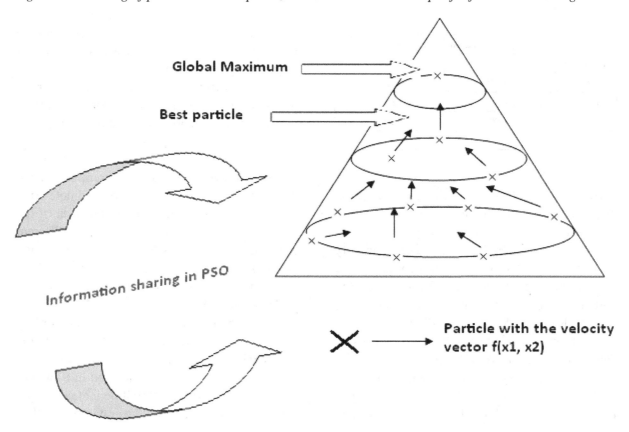

decreased gradually until to 0. The gravitation can be described using quantitative indicators, and is real number in [0, 1]. A higher value of gravitation indicates a stronger gravitation and a lower value of gravitation which indicates a weak gravitation.

Particles explore next pixels with certain probability in each time-step, but weight value W of next pixels along with searching path are different. At the same time, there is only one particle in each of pixels because operation environment of particles is two-dimensional images. In order to keep consistency as far as possible with natural behavior of bird swarms, time will be dispersed. Each of particles is permitted to move one and only one step in a time-step. In other words, particles must select one pixel to reach from 8 neighboring pixels. At certain time-step t, if the pixel in which the particle locates belongs to congener through distinguished by the particle, the particle will adjusts gravitation of the pixel. Adjustment range is η. In the meanwhile, all of pixels' gravitations will be weakened along with the process of time. The weaken range is κ. According to above conditions, definition of normalization shift probability which particle p moves from pixel k to pixel j:

$$p_{ik} = \frac{y(\sigma_i)\,y(\Delta_i)}{\sum_{j/k} y(\sigma_j)\,y(\Delta_j)}$$

In above formula, denominator is a summation formula which represents a weighted sum of gravitations belonging to all of pixels j from 8 neighboring pixels of pixel k. Δj represents direction change quantity of particle p at t-1 time. Its value is one of five discrete Y values. Each of particles will move stochastically with probability *pik* after establishing these parameter values. By this time, each of particles will explore next pixels according to above-mentioned mechanism.

2.4.2.1. 7-Band 472 × 576 Pixels Cartoset Satellite Image of Alwar Region in Rajasthan

After applying the proposed algorithm to the 7-band of Alwar Image, the classified image is obtained in Figure 17 (Bansal, Gupta, Panchal, & Kumary, 2009; Dong & Xiang-Bin, 2008).

The Kappa (κ) coefficient of the Alwar image is 0.975 which indicates that an observed classification is 97.5% better than one resulting from chance. Error Matrix is represented in Table 16.

Figure 17. Classification results of PSO on Alwar (Bansal, Gupta, Panchal, & Kumary, 2009; Dong & Xiang-Bin, 2008)

Table 16. Error matrix for PSO based elicitator on Alwar region

	Vegetation	Urban	Rocky	Water	Barren	Total
Vegetation	79	0	0	47	0	126
Urban	4	22	0	0	7	33
Rocky	18	3	286	0	0	307
Water	28	0	0	59	0	87
Barren	1	7	0	0	24	32
Total	130	32	286	106	31	585

The producer's and the user's accuracy are calculated in Tables 17 and 18 respectively.

2.4.2.2. 3-Band Cartoset Satellite Image of Size 450 × 550 Pixels of Shivpuri Region in Madhya Pradesh

In this section, we discuss the results we got on the Shivpuri image for demonstrating the concept of

Table 17. Producer's accuracy

Feature	Accuracy Calculation	Producer's Accuracy
Vegetation	79/130	60%
Urban	22/32	68%
Rocky	286/286	100%
Water	59/106	55%
Barren	24/31	77%

Table 18. User's accuracy

Feature	Accuracy Calculation	User's Accuracy
Vegetation	79/126	62.6%
Urban	22/33	66%
Rocky	286/307	93%
Water	59/87	67.8%
Barren	24/32	75%

information sharing for the elicitation of natural terrain features. The classified image of Shivpuri has been shown in Figure 18 with kappa coefficient .978 (Bansal, Gupta, Panchal, & Kumary, 2009; Dong & Xiang-Bin, 2008). Error matrix is given in Table 19. The producer's and the user's accuracy are calculated in Tables 20 and 21 respectively.

Figure 18. Classification results of PSO on Shivpuri region (Bansal, Gupta, Panchal, & Kumary, 2009; Dong & Xiang-Bin, 2008)

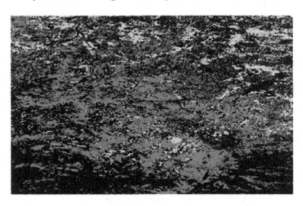

3. CONCLUSION AND FUTURE WORK

In this chapter, we have tried to present the working framework of the recent swarm intelligence algorithms. We have tried to explore how the concept of information sharing is exploited by these techniques to adapt them to various real life applications. From the discussion in the paper, we can conclude that information sharing is the basic pillar for the success of the recent swarm intelligence techniques and provides the reason as to why the swarm intelligence techniques possess very strong optimization capabilities and have emerged as the most popular optimization techniques that can be adapted for a wide variety of applications. Ant Colony Optimization, Particle Swarm Optimization, Biogeography based Optimization and Bee Colony Optimization are the four major constituents of the swarm intelligence techniques and hence these are the techniques that we chose for our demonstration. The application that we choose for our demonstration is the land cover feature extraction of multi-spectral multi-resolution satellite images.

Table 19. Error matrix for PSO based feature elicitator on Shivpuri region

	Vegetation	Open	Crop	Water	Shallow Water	Total
Vegetation	24	0	0	1	2	27
Open	0	182	0	0	0	182
Crop	0	0	53	0	0	53
Water	0	0	0	33	0	33
Shallow Water	2	0	0	0	31	33
Total	26	182	53	34	33	328

Table 20. Producer's accuracy

Feature	Accuracy Calculation	Producer's Accuracy
Vegetation	24/26	92.3%
Open	182/182	100%
Crop	53/53	100%
Water	33/34	97.1%
Shallow Water	31/33	93.9%

Table 21. User's accuracy

Feature	Accuracy Calculation	User's Accuracy
Vegetation	24/27	88.8%
Open	182/182	100%
Crop	53/53	100%
Water	33/33	100%
Shallow Water	31/33	93.9%

We first describe the theoretical aspects of how each of the techniques can be adapted to suit the feature extraction application and then demonstrate the results of classification after applying each of the SI techniques and calculate the classification accuracy for each in terms of the kappa coefficient generated from the error matrix. For verification, we also tested our results on a second satellite image dataset and also calculated the producer's and the user's accuracy separately for each land cover feature in order to explore the performance of the technique on different features of the satellite image. From the results, we conclude that the concepts of information sharing can be successfully adapted for the design of efficient algorithms, which can be successfully applied for feature extraction of satellite images. In future, we can also adapt the concepts of information sharing to suit more applications such as in situation awareness (Goel, Gupta, & Panchal, 2010), cross country path planning, robotics, face recognition, etc. In fact, the information sharing concept is flexible enough and can be suited to a variety of military, scientific and commercial applications as well.

REFERENCES

Bansal, Gupta, & Panchal, & Kumar. (2009). Remote sensing image classification by improved swarm inspired techniques. In *Proceedings of the International Conference on Artificial Intelligence and Pattern Recognition (AIPR-09)*. AIPR.

Bonabeau, E., Dorigo, M., & Theraulaz, G. (1999). *Swarm intelligence from natural to artificial system*. Oxford, UK: Oxford University Press.

Bratton & Kennedy. (2007). Defining a standard for particle swarm optimization. In *Proceedings of the 2007 IEEE Swarm Intelligence Symposium*. Honolulu, HI: IEEE.

Das, Biswas, Dasgupta, & Abraham. (2009). Bacterial foraging optimization algorithm: Theoritical foundations, analysis and applications. *Foundations of Computational Intelligence, 3*, 23–55.

Dong, & Xiang-Bin. (2008). Particle swarm intelligence classification algorithm for remote sensing images. In *Proceedings of the IEEE Pacific-Asia Workshop on Computational Intelligence and Industrial Application*. IEEE.

Dorigo, Maniezzo, & Colorni. (1996). Ant system: Optimization by a colony of cooperating agents. *IEEE Transactions on Systems, Man, and Cybernetics–Part B, 26*(1), 29–41.

Dorigo & Stuetzle. (2004). *Ant colony optimization*. Cambridge, MA: MIT Press.

Goel, Gupta, & Panchal. (2011). Information sharing in swarm intelligence techniques: A perspective application for natural terrain feature elicitation in remote sensing images. *International Journal of Computers and Applications, 32*(2).

Goel, Panchal, & Gupta. (2010). Embedding expert knowledge to hybrid bio-inspired techniques- An adaptive strategy towards focused land cover feature extraction. *International Journal of Computer Science & Information Security, 8*(2), 244–253.

Johal, Singh, & Kundra. (2010). A hybrid FPAB/BBO algorithm for satellite image classification. *International Journal of Computers and Applications, 6*(5).

Karaboga & Akay. (2009). A comparative study of artificial bee colony algorithm. *Applied Mathematics and Computation, 214*, 108–132. doi:10.1016/j.amc.2009.03.090.

Karaboga & Basturk. (2007). A powerful and efficient algorithm for numerical function optimization: Artificial bee colony algorithm. Berlin: Springer Science+Business Media B.V.

Karaboga. (2005). *An idea based on honey bee swarm for numerical optimization*. Technical Report-TR06.

Lillesand, & Kiefer. (2008). *Remote sensing and image interpretation* (6th Ed.). New York: Wiley.

Long, III., & Srihann. (2004). Geoscience and remote sensing symposium. In Proceedings of Unsupervised and Supervised Classifications: Land Cover Classification using ERDAS Imagine, (vol. 4, pp. 20-24). IEEE.

Ma, Ni, & Sun. (2009). *Equilibrium species counts and migration model tradeoffs for biogeography based based optimization*. Paper presented at the Joint 48th IEEE Conference on Decision and Control and 28th Chinese Control Conference. Shanghai, China. Kennedy, J., & Eberhart, R. (1995). Particle swarm optimization. In *Proceedings of IEEE International Conference on Neural Networks*, (vol. 4, pp. 1942–1948). IEEE. Goel, Gupta, & Panchal. (2010). Hybrid ACO-BBO approach for predicting the deployment strategies of enemy troops in a military terrain application. In *Proceedings of the Second International Conference on Intelligent Systems and Nanotechnology*. IEEE.

Ma. (2010). An analysis of the equilibrium of migration models for biogeography-based optimization. *Information Sciences, 180*, 3444–3464.

Panchal, V., Singh, P., Kaur, N., & Kundra, H. (2009). Biogeography based satellite image classification. *International Journal of Computer Science and Information Security, 6*(2), 269–274.

Parpinelli, Lopes, & Freitas. (2002). Data mining with an ant colony optimization algorithm. *IEEE Transactions on Evolutionary Computation, 6*(4), 321–332. doi:10.1109/TEVC.2002.802452.

Passino, K. M. (2002). Biomimicry of bacterial foraging for distributed optimization and control. *IEEE Control Systems Magazine, 22*(3), 52–67. doi:10.1109/MCS.2002.1004010.

Piatrik & Izquierdo. (2006). Image classification using an ant colony optimization approach. *Lecture Notes in Computer Science, 4306*, 159–168. doi:10.1007/11930334_13.

Simon, D. (2008). Biogeography based optimization. *IEEE Transactions on Evolutionary Computation, 12*(6). doi:10.1109/TEVC.2008.919004.

Teodorović, & Dell'Orco. (2000). Bee colony optimization – A cooperative learning approach to complex transportation problems. *Advanced OR and AI Methods in Transportation.*

Chapter 11
A Software System for Grading Diabetic Retinopathy by Analyzing Retinal Images

M. Usman Akram
Bahria University, Pakistan

Shehzad Khalid
Bahria University, Pakistan

ABSTRACT

Medical imaging is very popular and is vital in designing Computer-Aided Diagnosis (CAD) for various diseases such as tumor detection using MRI. Diabetic retinopathy is an eye disease that is caused by the increase of insulin in blood in diabetic patients. It can cause total blindness if not detected and treated in time. The disease affects human retina and shows different signs on retinal surface as time passes. In this chapter, the authors present a software based on novel algorithms for early detection of diabetic retinopathy. It detects dark (Microaneurysms, Haemorrhages) and bright (hard exudates, cotton wool spots) lesions from retinal image. The algorithms consist of retinal image preprocessing, main component extraction, detection of candidate lesions, feature extraction, and finally classification using modified m-mediods based classifier. The proposed system is evaluated using publicly available retinal image databases, and results demonstrate the validity of proposed system.

1. INTRODUCTION

Diabetes is a disease that occurs when the pancreas does not secrete enough insulin or the body is unable to process it properly (Amos, McCarty, & Zimmet, 1997). Insulin is the hormone that regulates the level of sugar (glucose) in the blood. Diabetes can affect children and adults. Patients with diabetes are more likely to develop eye problems such as cataracts and glaucoma, but the disease's affect on the retina is the main threat to vision (Kohner, et al., 1998). Most patients develop diabetic changes in the retina after approximately 20 years. The effect of diabetes on the eye is called Diabetic Retinopathy (DR). DR

DOI: 10.4018/978-1-4666-4229-4.ch011

is the newly emerging research area in medical image processing and has real time application in assisting the ophthalmologists for improved and efficient diagnosis of retinopathy (Amos, McCarty, & Zimmet, 1997). Figure 1 shows the difference in vision from a healthy and an affected retina.

Human retina has mainly two parts i.e. macula and peripheral retina. Macula is the main central part of retina which is used in order to see fine details whereas peripheral part is responsible for side vision which is also known as peripheral vision. Macula is very small part of retina as compared to peripheral but still it is too more sensitive to give details than peripheral. Other than these, a healthy retina consists of blood vessels, Optic Disc (OD) and fovea as well. Fovea is the central part of macula and it is responsible for sharp vision. Blood vessels are used to provide blood, oxygen and nutrition to retina and they originate from OD which is the brightest circular region of retina (Molven, et al., 2008). Figure 2 shows main components of retina.

Diabetes affects the blood vessels of the retina as time pases which causes DR. Early stages of DR are known as Non-Proliferative Diabetic Retinopathy (NPDR) (Lee, Lee, Kingsley, Wang, Russell, Klein, & Wanr, 2001). In DR the blood vessels of the retina become weak and develop

tiny leaks. These leaks cause fluid or blood to seep into the retina. The retina then becomes wet and swollen and cannot work properly. NPDR contains the earliest changes in retina due to diabetes and is important to detection in its early stages. Different lesions (abnormalities) which may occur in NPDR are Microaneurysms (MAs), Haemorrhages (HM), Hard Exudates (HE), and Cotton Wool Spots (CWS) (Lee, Lee, Kingsley, Wang, Russell, Klein, & Wanr, 2001).

MAs are basically red dots that appear in retinal capillaries and are usually 10 to 100 microns in diameter. They are usually seen at the posterior pole especially temporal to the fovea. MAs are the first detectable change in retina due DR. Retinal HM is formed when the wall of a capillary or MA becomes weak and gets ruptured. The deep HM is usually round or oval and it is also called blot or dot HM. Dot HMs appear as bright red dots and are of same size as that of large MAs. Blot haemorrhages are larger lesions and they are located within the mid retina and often within or surrounding areas of ischemia. HE are the yellow deposits of lipid and protein present in the retina represent hard exudates. These deposits of lipid and proteins leak from surrounding capillaries and MAs and form circular patterns in the retina. In addition to this, small and thin blood vessel may

Figure 1. Visions from a normal and an affected retina

 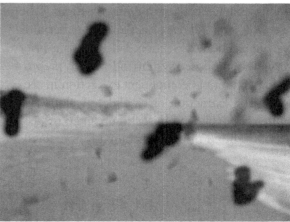

Figure 2. Digital human retina with its main components

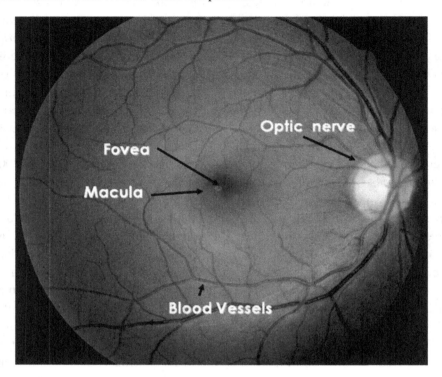

close off causing some patches of retina deprived of blood supply. These small fluffy white patches in retina and known as CWS. They are also called soft exudates which are white, fluffy lesions in the nerve fibre layer. MAs and HMs as a combined known as dark lesions and HE and CWS are known as bright lesions (Usher, Dumskyj, Himaga, Williamson, Nussey, & Boyce, 2003). Figure 3 shows all lesions which may appear in NPDR.

This chapter consists of nine sections. The review of some relevant background material is given in Section 2. Section 3 describes a brief overview of proposed system followed by preprocessing and retinal component extraction in section 4. The extraction of candidate lesions and features are explained in section 5 and 6 respectively. Modified m-mediods based lesion classi-

Figure 3. NPDR lesions: a) dark lesions (MAs, HMs), b) bright lesions (HE, CWS)

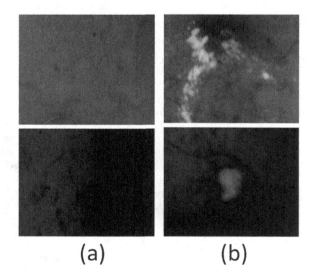

(a)   (b)

fication is given in section 7. Section 8 describes testing and evaluation of proposed system. It explains datasets which we have used for testing, performance matrices and results. Last section contains conclusion.

2. RELATED WORK

A number of methods for DR lesions detection have been proposed by different authors. A Recursive region growing segmentation combined with Moat Operator, is used in (Sinthanayothin, et al., 2002) to detect features of NPDR. The method is tested on local retinal images. Hatanaka et al. (Hatanaka, Nakagawa, Hayashi, Kakogawa, Sawada, Kawase, Hara, & Fujita, 2008) proposed a novel method for detection of hemorrhage based on density analysis. Lesions are detected by performing finite difference calculations along with smoothing and segmented by the thresholding technique. The method is evaluated on local images. A Hybrid technique for an automated detection of dark lesions is proposed in (Niemeijer, van Ginneken, Staal, Suttorp-Schulten, & Abramoff, 2005). Pixels are identified using new red lesion candidate detection system. The features are classified using k-nearest neighbor classifier. Akram et al. (Akram, Khalid, & Khan, 2013) has proposed a method for early detection of diabetic retinopathy. They detected MAs using a new hybrid classifier and a detailed feature set. Antal et al. (Antel & Hajdu, 2012) presented a method based on combinations of several preprocessing and candidate extractors. They used an ensemble learning based criteria for classification. A multi-scale correlation coefficients based method was proposed by Zhang et al. (Zhang, Wu, Yo, Li, & Karray, 2010). They used dynamic thresholding for accurate detection of MAs. A morphological operations based technique for detecting candidate MAs was proposed by Walter et al. (Walter, Massin, Erginay, Ordonez, Jeulin, & Klein, 2007). They used just 20 images with total 297 manu-

ally detected MAs. A supervised density-based classifier was used for MA classification. An online competition for MAs detection with the name of Retinopathy Online Challenge (ROC) is introduced by the University of Iowa and ROC organizers(University of Iowa, n.d.). The purpose is to improve the quality of computer aided and automated diagnosis of DR. The results of first international competition were reported in (Niemeijer, et al., 2010). A decision support system for dark lesion detection is proposed by (Kahai, Namuduri, & Thompson, 2006).

Fleming et. al proposed an automated microaneurysm detection using local contrast normalization and local vessel detection technique (Fleming, Philip, Goatman, Olson, & Sharp, 2006). In (Quellec, Lamard, Josselin, Cazuguel, Cochener, & Roux, 2008), optimal wavelet transform based method is proposed for the detection of microaneurysms. They proposed to detect MAs by locally matching a lesion template by best adapted wavelet in subbands of wavelet transformed images. The optimization process is based on a genetic algorithm followed by Powell's direction set descent. Acharya et al. (Acharya, Chua, Ng, Wei, & Chee, 2008) presented a higher order spectra and SVM based system for NPDR and PDR detection. They classified all three stages of NPDR with accuracies of 90%, 85%, and 70% for mild, moderate and severe NPDR respectively. A computer aided system for classification of MAs, H, HE and CWS was proposed in (Lee, Lee, Wang, Klein, Kingsley, & Warn, 2005). They were able to identify HMA, HE and CWS with an accuracy of 82.6%, 82.6%, and 88.3%, respectively.

A.W. Reza et. al proposed an automatic tracing of exudates from retinal images using fixed and variable thresholds. The technique for exudates detection consists of morphological opening, extended maxima operator, minima imposition, and watershed transformation. The method is evaluated on DRIVE and STARE databases and achieved sensitivity value of 96.7% (Reza, Eswaran, & Hati, 2009). A neuro fuzzy based classifier is used by

Akram et al. (Akram & Khan, 2011) for detection of dark and bright lesions. A limited number of features are used to support classification. In [HYazid], automated identification of exudates using inverse surface thresholding is proposed. This method includes fuzzy c-means (fcm) clustering, edge detection and otsu thresholding also. The technique is tested on two databases i.e. STARE and a database provided by a local hospital. The sensitivity and specificity for STARE is 97.8% and 99% respectively while for a custom database 90.7% and 99.4% respectively.

This chapter describes a system for detection and classification of different types of NPDR lesions. The proposed technique extracts potential candidates for all four signs of NPDR i.e. MAs, H, HE and CWS then it generates a features set for each lesion depending upon their shape, gray level, color and statistical properties. The true lesions are selected and classified using a multivariate m-mediods based classifier.

3. SYSTEM OVERVIEW

In this chapter, we describe a software-based system suitable for medical diagnosis. We have to identify different levels of decomposition of the task of automated detection of diabetic retinopathy. We continually make choices regarding the granularity level of each sub-task that we have identified during the decomposition process. When a given sub-task is complex itself and requires various algorithms, these are then further decomposed so that their details could be elaborated. The modularity of this approach facilitates the development of the proposed software using an iterative/incremental approach. Various tasks that are hierarchically identified to be implemented using iterative approach is shown in Figure 4.

The development methodology used for the proposed medical system development is the combination of iterative and incremental approach. In the first iteration, we build a basic prototype

Figure 4. Development methodology of proposed system

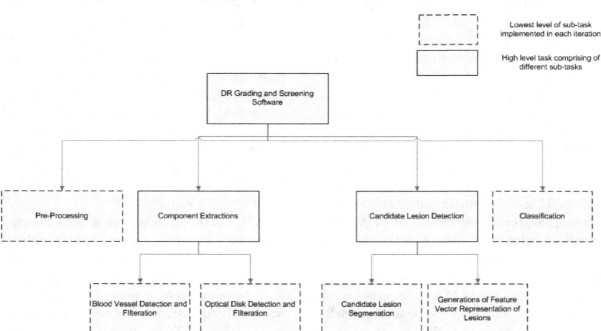

of a diabetic retinopathy system using general and easily implemented approaches, as proposed in literature, for each task as highlighted in Figure 4. This helps in providing a playing ground to evaluate various components of proposed approach independently. The remaining iterations basically act as increment to the software as we design and implement a sophisticated algorithm for each sub-task in the coming iterations. This helps us in and analyzing the impact on the proposed algorithm for a given sub-task in the overall performance of the complete system. In second iteration, we increment the system by designing and developing a pre-processing technique to enhance the fundus image for effective segmentation and detection of candidate lesions. Third iteration in the development of DR diagnostic system is associated with the actual segmentation and extraction of all possible candidate regions representing different lesions. In the fourth iteration, we increment our system by incorporating a feature extraction mechanism that generates feature vector representation of lesions containing features modeling shape, color, gray and statistical properties of the lesions. The final iteration involves the development of a classifier to classify the candidate lesions to identify different stages in diabetic retinopathy. At the end of each iteration, the improvement in the software due to the incorporation of proposed algorithms for a given sub-task is tested using variety of annotated diabetic retinopathy datasets. The quality metrics used for the evaluation of proposed algorithms include sensitivity, specificity and accuracy. These metrics are explained in testing section.

4. PREPROCESSING AND RETINAL COMPONENT EXTRACTION

4.1. Preprocessing

Preprocessing is done to extract fundus area from background and to enhance its quality by removing noisy areas. In automatic diagnosis of diabetic retinopathy, the processing of the surrounding background and noisy areas in retinal image is not necessary and consumes more processing time at all stages. Cutting or cropping out the region that contains the retinal image feature minimizes the number of operations on the retinal image. Noise in color retinal image is normally due to noise pixels and pixels whose color is distorted. Both seem to exist in regions where illumination has been inadequate. Since illumination is usually adequate in the center of the image, poor image quality regions are located near the edge of the retinal image. Regions with poor image quality may cause errors in abnormality detection. That is why they should be detected and removed before detection of abnormalities. In proposed system, the preprocessing is done to create background and noise removal masks using rate of change in image gradient and Hue, Saturation and Intensity (HSI) channels respectively (Tariq & Akram, 2010). The algorithm applies adaptive thresholding technique for creating binary background and noise masks. Figure 5 shows the original images and preprocessing masks for these images.

4.2. Vessel Enhancement and Segmentation

Blood vessels present in retina are important as they provide blood and oxygen to retina for its nourishment. Insulin in blood due to diabetes weakens the walls of vessels and blood starts leaking out of the vessels to surface of retina which eventually leads to blindness. In DR self diagnostic systems, vascular pattern helps a lot in detection of different vascular abnormalities and also in extraction of dark lesions such as MAs and HM. The literature review about DR highlights the importance of blood vessel extraction and a lot of research in field of DR is carried out on reliable extraction of vascular pattern. The open challenge in vessel segmentation was the reliable extraction of blood vessels including large

Figure 5. Original retinal image and its preprocessing mask

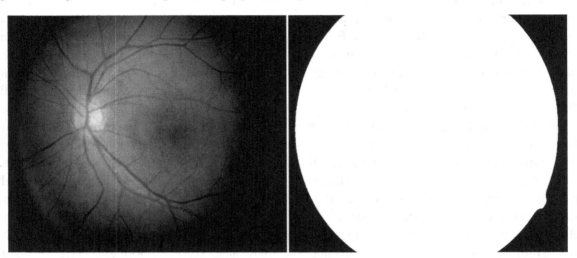

as well as small blood vessels. The detection of small vessels (capillaries) helps in detection of Neovascularization. We have solved this problem by using 2-D Gabor wavelets and a novel multi-layered thresholding based segmentation method (Akram & Khan, 2012). The 2-D Gabor wavelet which we have used is defined as

$$\psi_G(\mathbf{x}) = \exp(j\mathbf{k}_0\mathbf{x}) \exp(-\frac{1}{2} \mid \mathbf{Ax} \mid^2)$$

$$\hat{\psi}_G(\mathbf{x}) = (detB)^{1/2} \exp(-\frac{1}{2}(B(\mathbf{k} - \mathbf{k}_0)^2))$$

where $\mathbf{k}_0 \in \mathcal{R}^2$ is a vector that defines the frequency of the complex exponential, $B = A^{-1}$ and

$$A = \begin{bmatrix} \epsilon^{-1/2} & 0 \\ 0 & 1 \end{bmatrix}$$

with elongation $\epsilon \geq 1$ is a 2×2 positive definite diagonal matrix which defines the wavelet anisotropy and elongation of filter in any desired direction. For each pixel position and considered scale value, the Gabor wavelet transform $M_\psi(\mathbf{b}, a)$ is computed for θ spanning from 0° up to 165° at steps of 15° and the maximum is taken (see Figure 6).

Figure 6. Blood vessel segmentation: a) original retinal image from DRIVE database, b) segmented blood vessels, c) original retinal image from STARE database, d) segmented blood vessels

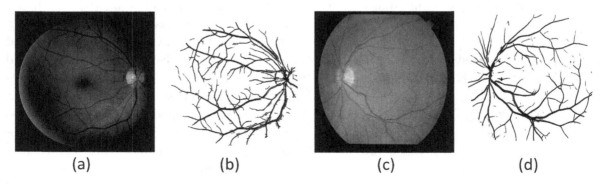

(a)   (b)   (c)   (d)

4.3. Optic Disc(OD) Localization and Detection

The OD generally appears as a bright circular or elliptic region on fundus image. The OD acts as a landmark and reference for extraction of other features, such as fovea. Its location helps to locate the fovea and its exclusion is essential in achieving robust bright lesion detection. We present a method for OD localization and segmentation using averaging filter and hough transform (Akram, Khan, Iqbal, & Butt, 2010). In OD localization, first original retinal image is preprocessed by averaging mask of size 31x31 (equation 3) in order to remove the background and lesions artifacts which can cause false localization and then maximum gray values from image histogram is detected because the gray values of OD are higher than the background values.

$$Z = \frac{1}{961} \sum_{i=1}^{961} F_i$$

where F's are values of image gray levels and Z is the averaged image. Figure 7 shows the result of OD localization.

5. CANDIDATE LESION DETECTION

MAs and HM are the dark lesions and HE and CWS are bright lesions. The presence of blood vessels and Optic Disc (OD) make it difficult for automated system to detect dark and bright lesions with high specificity due to occupance of false positives. In proposed system we extract blood vessels and OD prior to lesions detection so that pixels containing vessels and OD can be removed to reduce spurious regions. Followings steps are used for candidate lesion detection:

- Take retinal image as an input and apply morphological closing and opening operations separately to remove the effect of blood vessels and OD respectively.
- Apply adaptive contrast enhancement technique to improve the contrast of lesions on retinal surface.
- Create filter bank given in equation 4 based on Gabor kernel and convolve it with contrast enhanced image to further enhance the bright lesions (Akram, Tariq, Anjum, & Javed, 2012).

Figure 7. OD localization: a) original retinal image, b) green channel, c) average filtered image, d) localized OD

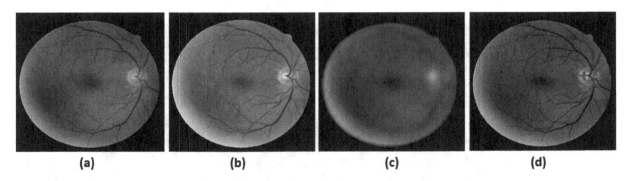

(a)   (b)   (c)   (d)

$$G_{FB} = \frac{1}{\sqrt{\pi r \sigma}} e^{-\frac{1}{2}[(\frac{d_1}{\sigma})^2 + (\frac{d_2}{\sigma})^2]} (d_1 (cos\Omega + \iota sin\Omega))$$

where σ, Ω and r are the standard deviations of Gaussian, spatial frequency and aspect ratio respectively θ is the orientation of filter and

$$d_1 = xcos\theta + ysin\theta$$

and

$$d_2 = -xsin\theta + ycos\theta$$

(Akram, Tariq, Anjum, & Javed, 2012).

- Create binary map containing candidate lesion regions by applying adaptive threshold value T which is calculated using OTSU algorithm (Gonzalez & Woods, 2002).
- Remove blood vessel and OD pixels to form final candidate lesion binary map.

Figure 8 shows the outputs of candidate lesion detection steps.

6. FEATURE EXTRACTION

NPDR lesions appear with distinguishable properties such as color, size and shape etc. Microaneurysms (MA) are small in size and they appear in dark red color circles shape, Haemorrhages (H) are medium size dark red color dots. Exudates (HE) and Cotton Wool Spots (CWS) are of yellow and whitish colors respectively. In this chapter, we made a feature vector

$$V = \{f_1, f_2, f_3, \cdots, f_m\}$$

for candidate lesions. The description of features which we use in proposed systems are as following:

1. Area (f_1), is the count of number of pixels in candidate exudate region and defined as $A = \sum_{v_i} 1$ sum of all pixels in candidate region v_i.

2. Compactness (f_2) is measure of shape defined as $C = p^2 / (4\pi A)$ where p and A are the perimeter length and area of candidate region respectively.

Figure 8. Candidate lesion detection: a) original retinal image; b) morphological closing; c) filter bank applied on (b); d) binary map for dark lesions; e) morphological opening; f) filter bank applied on (e); g) binary map for bright lesions; h) combined binary map for NPDR lesions.

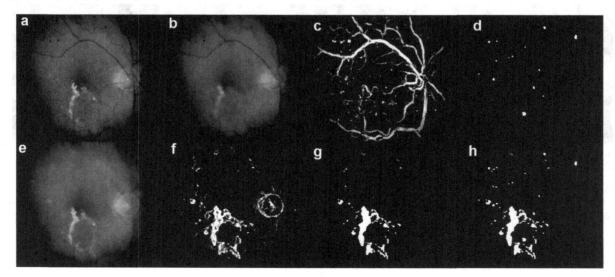

3. Mean Intensity (f_3) is the mean intensity value of contrast enhanced green channel for all pixels within the candidate region.

4. Mean Hue (f_4), mean Saturation (f_5) and mean Value (f_6) for each candidate region are calculated in order to differentiate exudate and non exudate regions on basis of their color properties.

5. Mean gradient magnitude (f_7) for edge pixels is computed to differentiate between strong and blur edges.

6. Entropy (f_8) value of all pixels in square region including candidate region pixels and its neighboring pixels.

7. Energy (f_9) is calculated by summing the intensity values of all pixels within the candidate region and dividing it by total number of candidate region pixels.

8. Third Moment (f_{10}) value of all pixels in square region including candidate region pixels and its neighboring pixels. It is the measure of skewness.

7. CLASSIFICATION

A lesion pattern within the training dataset is modeled by a set of cluster centers of mutually disjunctive sub-classes (referred to as mediods) within the pattern. Our modeling approach, referred to as *m*-Mediods modeling, models the class containing n members with m mediods known *a-priori* (Khalid, 2010). The generated models of known lesion patterns can then be used to classify new unseen lesion data to one of the modeled classes. We take a neural network approach for the identification of mediods. Let $DB^{(i)}$ be the classified training samples associated to lesion class i and W the weight vector associated to each output neuron.

The modeling algorithm comprises the following steps:

Initialize the learning vector quantization LVQ network with a greater number of output neurons than the desired number of mediods m that we wish to produce. Empirically, it has been observed that a good approximate on the number of output neurons for initialization of self organizing map SOM network can be obtained as:

$$\#_{output} = \begin{cases} \xi & if\ \xi < 150 \wedge \xi > (m \times 2) \\ m \times 2 & if\ \xi < (m \times 2) \\ 150 & if\ \xi > 150 \end{cases}$$

where $\xi = size(DB^{(i)})$.

2. Initialize W_i (where $1 \le i \le \#_{output}$) from the PDF $N(\mu, \Sigma)$ estimated from training samples in $DB^{(i)}$.

Sequentially input feature vectors from DB^i and identify the winning output neuron k (indexed by c) as:

$$c = \arg\min_k \quad F, W_k(t) \quad \forall k$$

Train LVQ network by adjusting the weight vector of winning output node c using

$$W_c(t+1) = W_c(t) + \alpha(t)(F - W_c(t))$$

where $\alpha(t)$ is the learning rate of LVQ and t is the training cycle index.

Decrease the learning rate $\alpha(t)$ exponentially over time using:

$$\alpha(t) = 1 - e^{\frac{2(t - t_{max})}{t_{max}}}$$

where t_{max} is the maximum number of training iterations. t_{max} is lower bounded by the number of samples in training dataset.

6. Repeat steps 3-5 for all the training iterations.
7. Ignore output neurons with no training data associated to them.

Select the closest pair of weight vectors (i, j) (indexed by (a, b)) given by the condition

$$(a, b) = \arg\min_{(i,j)}$$
$$\sqrt{(W_i - W_j)^T (W_i - W_j)} \times \sqrt{|W_i| + |W_j|}$$
$$\forall i, j \wedge i \neq j$$

where |.| is the membership count function. Scaling the distance between two weight vectors by their membership counts discourages the merging of weight vectors that are modeling a dense distribution of samples. This in turn will have more mediods presence with high density of training samples belonging to a particular class and vice versa. This is critical to the modeling of multimodal distribution of samples with a class.

9. Merge the selected pair of weight vectors using

$$W_{ab} = \frac{|W_a| \times W_a + |W_b| \times W_b}{|W_a| + |W_b|}$$

10. Repeat steps 8-9 till the number of weight vectors gets equivalent to $\#_{mediods}$. Append weight vector W_k to the list of mediods $\mathbf{M}^{(i)}$ modeling the pattern i.
11. Compute the distance of each mediod from its k nearest mediods and calculate the mean to approximate the local density of the distribution. Append the mean distance to $\mathbf{D}^{(i)}$ in correspondence to a given mediod in the mediods list $\mathbf{M}^{(i)}$.

Once the multivariate m-Mediods based model for all the classes have been learnt, the classification of unseen samples to known classes is performed by computing the relative closeness of test sample w.r.t. local densities of differ-ent class distributions. The proposed multimodel m-Mediods based classification comprises the following steps:

Identify k nearest mediods, from each m-Mediod model $\mathbf{M}^{(i)}$, to unseen sample Q as:

$$k - NM\{i\}(Q, \mathbf{M}, k)$$
$$= \{\mathbf{C} \in \mathbf{M}^{(i)} \mid \forall R \in \mathbf{C}, S \in \mathbf{M}^{(i)} - \mathbf{C},$$
$$Q, R \leq (Q, S \wedge |\mathbf{C}| = k\}\forall i$$

where $\mathbf{M}^{(i)}$ is the set of mediods from modeling class i. and $\mathbf{C}$ is the ordered set of k closest mediods starting from the nearest mediod.

Compute the fuzzy (probabilistic) membership $\Im\{i\}$ of test sample from class i as:

$$\Im\{i\} = 1 - \frac{\sum_{j=1}^{k} Q, k - NM\{i\}_j}{\frac{k}{\mathbf{D}^{(i)}}}$$

where $\overline{\mathbf{D}^{(i)}}$ is the average of mean distances corresponding to mediods in $\mathbf{C}$ as identified in equation 11. The mean distance corresponding to a given mediod is precomputed and stored in $D^{(i)}$ as specified in step 11 of modeling algorithm.

3. Classify sample to the lesion class with highest probability ($\Im$).

Figure 9 shows the flow diagram for m-mediod based classification.

8. TESTING AND EVALUATION

8.1. Data Sets

Medical diagnostic systems are very critical and their proper testing and evaluation are very important. A number of retinal image databases

Figure 9. Flow diagram for m-mediod based classifier

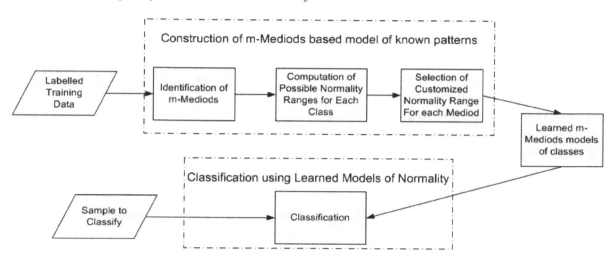

are available for algorithm testing and research purposes. We have used four main retinal image databases for thorough testing. Their description is given below.

One of the oldest and mostly used retinal image databases is the STARE dataset which was designed for structured analysis of retina (Hoover, n.d.). There are total 81 retinal images which are acquired using TopCon TRV-50 retinal camera with 35° Field Of View (FOV) out of which 30 are from healthy retinal and remaining 50 contain different lesions related to DR.

The DRIVE is another database which has been designed in Netherlands to evaluate and compare different algorithms on vessel segmentation (Staal, Abramoff, Neimeijer, Viergever, & van Ginneken, 2004). The images were captured by screening of 400 diabetic patients between 25-90 years of age and forty of them have been selected randomly. Thirty-three out of forty do not show any signs of DR while remaining seven has mild DR.

STARE and DRIVE databases are formed to facilitate vessel segmentation but they don't contain any ground truth or marking for lesions detection. DIARTDB is a database which is designed to evaluate automated lesion detection algorithms (Kauppi, et al., 2006). It contains 89 retinal images with different retinal abnormali-

ties and provides a best mean to check accuracy of lesions detection. Eighty four images out of eighty nine contain different signs of DR and five represent healthy retina.

The MESSIDOR is another database which has been established to facilitate computer aided DR lesions detection (MESSIDOR, n.d.). The database is collected using TopCon TRC NW6 Non-Mydriatic fundus camera with 45° FOV and resolutions of 1440×960, 2240×1488 or 2304×1536 with 8 bits per color plane. It contains total 1200 images which are divided into three sets of 400 images and each set is further divided into 4 parts to facilitate thorough testing.

8.2. Performance Matrices

We have used different performance matrices for proper statistical evaluation of proposed system. Sensitivity, specificity, accuracy and area under the receiver operating characteristics curves are used as performance measures. These matrices are computed using following parameters:

- T_p **(True Positive):** Regions that are graded as lesion and they also belong to lesion in ground truth.

- F_P **(False Positive):** Regions that are computed as lesion but they are non lesion in ground truth.
- T_N **(True Negative):** Regions that are computed as non lesion and they are also non lesion in ground truth.
- F_N **(False Negative):** Regions that are computed as non lesion but they belong to lesion in ground truth.

The statistical analysis of proposed system is done with the help of Receiver Operating Characteristics (ROC) curves which are plots of true positive rate (sensitivity) versus false positive rate (1-specificity). Other matrices are defined in equations 13, 14, and 15.

$$Sensitivity = \frac{T_P}{(T_P + F_N)}$$

$$Specificity = \frac{T_N}{(T_N + F_P)}$$

$$Accuracy = \frac{(T_P + T_N)}{(T_P + T_N + F_P + F_N)}$$

8.3. Results

The detailed quantitative and comparative analysis of proposed system is performed in this section. Detailed feature vectors for lesions present in ground truth are used to generate models for m-mediods. Patterns for m-mediods are modeled using 100 mediods per pattern. Figure 10 shows examples of dark and bright lesions detection. It shows the marked outputs of classification stage by eliminating the blood vessels, OD and spurious lesion pixels and by dividing the lesions into different classes.

Figure 10. Dark and bright lesions detection. MAs and HMs are highlighted with blue boundary and EXs are highlighted with green boundary

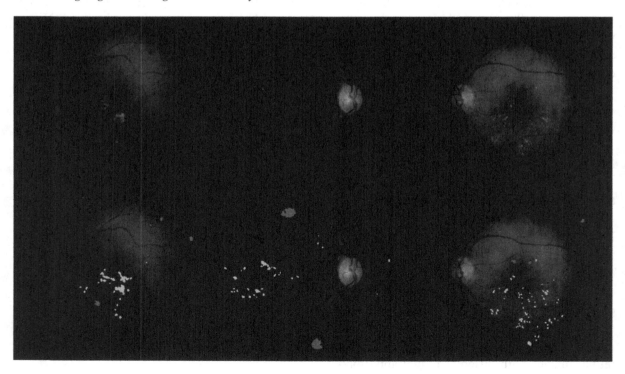

A total of 20 images are selected from all four databases at random and for those images, a comparison between proposed method and ground truth for lesion detection is given in Table 1. Table 1 shows that 3 out of 20 retinal images are wrongly classified (shown in bold font) and it is because of confusion between MA and thinnest vessels or capillaries.

Figure 11 shows the ROC curves using for dark and bright lesions using proposed system. The system achieves sensitivity values of 96.27% and 95.12% against specificity of 90% for dark and bright lesions respectively.

To further evaluate the performance of proposed method, we divide the lesions into two groups i.e red or dark lesions and bright lesions and compare the results with previously proposed techniques. Table 2 and Table 3 show the comparison of different methods with Proposed Method (PM) for red and bright lesions respectively but the issue is that everyone has used their own local datasets and not all the databases are publicly available for benchmarking. We have used the databases that are publicly available for benchmarking and comparison.

9. CONCLUSION

In this chapter, we proposed a digital diabetic retinopathy system for early detection of diabetic retinopathy. NPDR consists of dark and bright lesions but it is difficult to classify them in the presence of blood vessels and optic disc. So it is good to segment them out prior to lesion detection. First step of proposed system is preprocessing. The objective of preprocessing is to separate the background and noisy area from the overall image to enhance the quality of acquired retinal image and to lower the processing time. After preprocessing, blood vessels are enhanced and segmented

Table 1. Performance comparison of lesion detection with ground truth

Images	Detected Lesion	Detected Lesions
	(Ground truth)	(Proposed DDRS)
im0001	H, HE	H, HE
im0009	MA, H, HE, CWS	MA, H, HE, CWS
im0013	MA, H, HE, CWS	H, HE, CWS
im0022	-	-
im0031	CWS	CWS
im0139	MA, H, HE, CWS	MA, H, HE, CWS
03_test	MA, HE	MA, HE
06_test	-	-
14_test	MA, H	MA, H
17_test	HE	HE
image003	MA, H, HE, CWS	MA, H, HE
image009	MA, H, HE, CWS	MA, H, HE, CWS
image012	MA, HE	MA, HE
image025	MA, H, HE	MA, H, HE
image064	MA	MA
image074	MA, HE, CWS	MA, HE
20051020_53178_0100_PP	MA, H, HE	MA, H, HE
20051020_43808_0100_PP	-	-
20051020_45068_0100_PP	MA, H, HE, CWS	MA, H, HE, CWS
20051020_43832_0100_PP	MA	MA

Figure 11. ROC curves: Lesion level performance of proposed HC for two classes (i.e. dark and bright lesions)

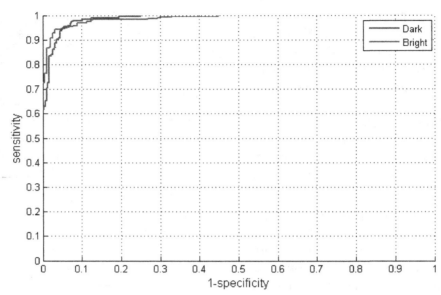

Table 2. Comparison of proposed method against previous techniques for dark lesions (MAs and H)

Methods	Sen	Spec	Acc
Niemeijer et al. (Niemeijer, et al., 2010)	100	87	-
Fleming et al. (Fleming, Philip, Goatman, Olson, & Sharp, 2006)	85.4	83.1	-
Kahai et al. (Kahai, Namuduri, & Thompson, 2006)	100	67	-
Quellec et al.(Quellec, Russell, & Abramoff, 2011)	-	-	0.927
Larsen et al. (Larsen, et al., 2003)	71.4	96.7	82.6
Sinthanayothin et al. (Sinthanayothin, et al., 2002)	77.5	88.7	-
PM	96.21	91.93	94.86

Table 3. Comparison of proposed method against previous techniques for bright lesions (HE and CWS)

Methods	Sen	Spec	Acc
Sinthanayothin et al. (Sinthanayothin, et al., 2002)	88.5	99.7	-
Clara et al. (Sancheza, Garciaa, Mayoc, Lopezb, & Horneroa, 2009)	90.2	90	-
Niemeijer et al. (Niemeijer, van Ginneken, Russell, Suttorp-Schulten, & Abra'moff, 2007)	95.0	86.0	-
Larsen et al. (Larsen, et al., 2003)	-	-	82.6
Osareh et al. (Osareh, Mirmehdi, Thomas, & Markham, 2002)	93	94.1	93.4
Ahmed et al. (Reza, Eswaran, & Hati, 2009)	94.90	100	97
walter et al. (Walter, Klein, Massin, & Erginay, 2002)	92.74	100	96.7
PM	94.75	97.12	96.59

by using Gabor wavelet and multilayered thresholding respectively. Then we localized optic disk using average filter and thresholding and detected the optic disk boundary using Hough transform and edge detection. Once blood vessels and OD are segmented out, dark and bright lesions are detected using filter bank and m-mediods based classifier. Methods are tested using four retinal image databases and results show that proposed system gives comparable results and can be used in a computer aided system for accurate and early detection of diabetic retinopathy.

REFERENCES

Acharya, Chua, Ng, E. Y. K., Wei, W., & Chee. (2008). Application of higher order spectra for the identification of diabetes retinopathy stages. *Journal of Medical Systems*, *32*(6), 431–488. doi:10.1007/s10916-008-9154-8 PMID:19058652.

Akram, K. Iqbal, & Butt. (2010). Retinal image: Optic disk localization and detection. In Proceedings of Image Analysis and Recognition (LNCS), (vol. 6112, pp. 40-49). Berlin: Springer.

Akram, Khalid, & Khan. (2013). Identification and classification of microaneurysms for early detection of diabetic retinopathy. *Pattern Recognition*, *46*(1), 107–116. doi:10.1016/j.patcog.2012.07.002.

Akram, M. U., & Khan, S. A. (2011). Automated detection of dark and bright lesions in retinal images for early detection of diabetic retinopathy. *Journal of Medical Systems*. doi: doi:10.1007/s10916-011-9802-2 PMID:22090037.

Akram, Tariq, Anjum, & Javed. (2012). Automated detection of exudates in colored retinal images for diagnosis of diabetic retinopathy. *OSA Journal of Applied Optics, 51*(20), 4858-4866.

Akram & Khan. (2012). Multilayered thresholding-based blood vessel segmentation for screening of diabetic retinopathy. [EWCO]. *Engineering with Computers*. doi: doi:10.1007/s00366-011-0253-7.

Amos, A.F., McCarty, D.J., & Zimmet, P. (1997). The rising global burden of diabetes and its complications: Estimates and projections to the year 2010. *Diabetic Medicine*.

Antel & Hajdu. (2012). Improving microaneurysm detection using an optimally selected subset of candidate extractors and preprocessing methods. *Pattern Recognition*, *45*(1), 264–270. doi:10.1016/j.patcog.2011.06.010.

Fleming, Philip, & Goatman, Olson, & Sharp. (2006). Automated microaneurysm detection using local contrast normalization and local vessel detection. *IEEE Transactions on Medical Imaging*, *25*(9), 1223–1232. doi:10.1109/TMI.2006.879953 PMID:16967807.

Gonzalez & Woods. (2002). *Digital image processing* (2nd ed.). Upper Saddle River, NJ: Prentice Hall.

Hatanaka, N., Hayashi, K., & Sawada, K. Hara, & Fujita. (2008). Improvement of automatic hemorrhages detection methods using brightness correction on fundus images. In Proceedings of SPIE, (Vol. 6915). SPIE. doi: doi:10.1117/12.771051.

Hoover. (n.d.). *STARE database*. Retrieved from http://www.ces.clemson.edu/ahoover/stare

Kahai, Namuduri, & Thompson. (2006). A decision support framework for automated screening of diabetic retinopathy. *International Journal of Biomedical Imaging*, 1–8. doi:10.1155/IJBI/2006/45806 PMID:23165030.

Kauppi, T., Kalesnykiene, V., Kamarainen, J.-K., Lensu, L., Sorri, I., Raninen A., ... Pietilä, J. (2006). *DIARETDB1 diabetic retinopathy database and evaluation protocol* (Technical report).

Khalid. (2010). Activity classification and anomaly detection using m-mediods based modeling of motion patterns. *Pattern Recognition, 43*(10), 3636-3647.

Kohner, E. M., Aldington, S. J., Stratton, I. M., Manley, S. E., Holman, R. R., & Matthews, D. R. et al. (1998). United Kingdom prospective diabetes study, 30: Diabetic retinopathy at diagnosis of noninsulin-dependent diabetes mellitus and associated risk factors. *Archives of Ophthalmology, 116*(3), 297–303. doi:10.1001/archopht.116.3.297 PMID:9514482.

Larsen, M., Godt, J., Larsen, N., Lund-Andersen, H., Sjolie, A. K., & Agardh, E. et al. (2003). Automated detection of fundus photographic red lesions in diabetic retinopathy. *Investigative Ophthalmology & Visual Science, 44*(2), 761–766. doi:10.1167/iovs.02-0418 PMID:12556411.

Lee, Lee, Kingsley, Wang, & Russell, Klein, & Wanr. (2001). Comparison of diagnosis of early retinal lesions of diabetic retinopathy between a computer system and human experts. *Graefes Archive for Clinical and Experimental Ophthalmology, 119*(4), 509–515. doi:10.1007/s004170100310 PMID:11296016.

Lee, Lee, & Wang, Klein, Kingsley, & Warn. (2005). Computer classification of nonproliferative diabetic retinopathy. *Archives of Ophthalmology, 123*(6), 759–764. doi:10.1001/archopht.123.6.759 PMID:15955976.

MESSIDOR. (n.d.). Retrieved from http://messidor.crihan.fr/index-en.php

Molven, A., Ringdal, M., Nordbo, A. M., Raeder, H., Stoy, J., & Lipkind, G. M. et al. (2008). Mutations in the insulin gene can cause MODY and autoantibody-negative type 1 diabetes. *Diabetes, 57*(4), 1131–1135. doi:10.2337/db07-1467 PMID:18192540.

Niemeijer, Ginneken, Cree, Mizutani, & Quellec, Sanchez, … Abramoff. (2010). Retinopathy online challenge: Automatic detection of microaneurysms in digital color fundus photographs. *IEEE Transactions on Medical Imaging, 1*(29), 185–195. doi:10.1109/TMI.2009.2033909 PMID:19822469.

Niemeijer, van Ginneken, Russell, Suttorp-Schulten, & Abra'moff. (2007). Automated detection and differentiation of drusen, exudates, and cotton-wool spots in digital color fundus photographs for diabetic retinopathy diagnosis. *Investigative Ophthalmology & Visual Science, 48*(5), 2260-2267.

Niemeijer, van Ginneken, Staal, Suttorp-Schulten, & Abràmoff. (2005). Automatic detection of red lesions in digital color fundus photographs. *IEEE Transactions on Medical Imaging, 24*(5), 584-592.

Osareh, A., Mirmehdi, M., Thomas, B., & Markham, R. (2002). Comparative exudate classification using support vector machines and neural networks. In *Proceedings of the 5th International Conference on Medical Image Computing and Computer-Assisted Intervention*, (pp. 413-420). IEEE.

Quellec, Lamard, & Josselin, Cazuguel, Cochener, & Roux. (2008). Optimal wavelet transform for the detection of microaneurysms in retina photographs. *IEEE Transactions on Medical Imaging, 27*(9), 1230–1241. doi:10.1109/TMI.2008.920619 PMID:18779064.

Quellec, Russell, & Abràmoff. (2011). Optimal filter framework for automated, instantaneous detection of lesions in retinal images. *IEEE Transactions on Medical Imaging, 30*(2), 523–533. doi:10.1109/TMI.2010.2089383 PMID:21292586.

Reza, Eswaran, & Hati. (2009). Automatic tracing of optic disc and exudates from color fundus images using fixed and variable thresholds. *Journal of Medical Systems*, *33*, 73–80. doi:10.1007/s10916-008-9166-4 PMID:19238899.

Sáncheza, Garcíaa, & Mayoc, Lópezb, & Horneroa. (2009). Retinal image analysis based on mixture models to detect hard exudates. *Medical Image Analysis*, *13*(4), 650–658. doi:10.1016/j.media.2009.05.005 PMID:19539518.

Sinthanayothin, Boyce, Williamson, Cook, & Mensah, Lal, & Usher. (2002). Automated detection of diabetic retinopathy on digital fundus images. *Journal of Diabetic Medicine*, *19*, 105–112. doi:10.1046/j.1464-5491.2002.00613.x PMID:11874425.

Staal, Abramoff, & Niemeijer, Viergever, & van Ginneken. (2004). Ridge-based vessel segmentation in color images of the retina. *IEEE Transactions on Medical Imaging*, *23*(4), 501–509. doi:10.1109/TMI.2004.825627 PMID:15084075.

Tariq & Akram. (2010). An automated system for colored retinal image background and noise segmentation. In *Proceedings of the IEEE Symposium on Industrial Electronics and Applications (ISIEA 2010)*, (pp. 405-409). IEEE.

University of Iowa. (n.d.). *Retinopathy online challenge website*. Retrieved from http://roc.healthcare.uiowa.edu/results.php

Usher, Dumskyj, & Himaga, Williamson, Nussey, & Boyce. (2003). Automated detection of diabetic retinopathy in digital retinal images: A tool for diabetic retinopathy screening. *Diabetic Medicine*, *21*(1), 84–90. doi:10.1046/j.1464-5491.2003.01085.x PMID:14706060.

Walter, Klein, Massin, & Erginay. (2002). A contribution of image processing to the diagnosis of diabetic retinopathy—Detection of exudates in color fundus images of the human. *IEEE Transactions on Medical Imaging*, *21*(10), 1236–1243. doi:10.1109/TMI.2002.806290 PMID:12585705.

Walter, Massin, & Erginay, Ordonez, Jeulin, & Klein. (2007). Automatic detection of microaneurysms in color fundus images. *Medical Image Analysis*, *11*(6), 555–566. doi:10.1016/j.media.2007.05.001 PMID:17950655.

Yazid, Arof, & Isa. (2011). Automated identification of exudates and optic disc based on inverse surface thresholding. *Journal of Medical Systems*. doi: doi:10.1007/s10916-011-9659-4 PMID:21318328.

Zhang, Wu, & Yo, Li, & Karray. (2010). Detection of microaneurysms using multi-scale correlation coefficients. *Pattern Recognition*, *43*(6), 2237–2248. doi:10.1016/j.patcog.2009.12.017.

Chapter 12
Demonic Fuzzy Relational Calculus

Fairouz Tchier
King Saud University, Saudi Arabia

Huda Alrashidi
King Saud University, Saudi Arabia

ABSTRACT

In this chapter, the authors categorize methods that are used to formally specify and verify software requirements. They discuss several formal method-related subjects such as calculus fuzzy and relational calculus.

MOTIVATION

The importance of relations is almost self-evident. Science is, in a sense, the discovery of relations between observables. Zadeh has shown the study of relations to be equivalent to the general study of systems (a system is a relation between an input space and an output space.) (Goguen, 2009).

The calculus of relations has been an important component of the development of logic and algebra since the middle of the nineteenth century. George Boole, in his "Mathematical Analysis of Logic" (Boole, 1847), initiated the treatment of

DOI: 10.4018/978-1-4666-4229-4.ch012

logic as part of mathematics, specifically as part of algebra. Quite the opposite conviction was put forward early this century by Bertrand Russell and Alfred North Whitehead in their *Principia Mathematica* (Whitehead & Russell, 1910): that mathematics was essentially grounded in logic. The logic is developed in two streams. On the one hand algebraic logic, in which the calculus of relations played a particularly prominent part, was taken up from Boole by Charles Sanders Peirce, who wished to do for the *"calculus of relatives"* what Boole had done for the calculus of sets, Peirce's work was in turn taken up by Schröder in "Algebra und Logik der Relative." Schröder's work, however, lay dormant for more than 40 years, until revived by Alfred Tarski in his seminal paper

"On the Calculus of Binary Relations" (Tarski, 1941). Tarski's paper is still often referred to as the best introduction to the calculus of relations. It gave rise to a whole field of study, that of relation algebras, and more generally Boolean algebras with operators. This important work defined much of the subsequent development of logic in the 20th century, completely eclipsing for some time the development of algebraic logic. In this stream of development, relational calculus and relational methods appear with the development of universal algebra in the 1930's, and again with model theory from the 1950s onwards. In so far as these disciplines in turn overlapped with the development of category theory, relational methods sometimes appear in this context as well. It is fair to say that the role of the calculus of relations in the interaction between algebra and logic is by now well understood and appreciated, and that relational methods are part of the toolbox of the mathematician and the logician.

The main advantages of the relational formalization are uniformity and modularity. Actually, once problems in these fields are formalized in terms of relational calculus, these problems can be considered by using formulae of relations, that is, we need only calculus of relations in order to solve the problems. This makes investigation on these fields easier.

Over the past twenty years relational methods have however also become of fundamental importance in computer science. For example, much of the theory of nonclassical logics is used (though sometimes re-invented) in the new so-called program logics. These arose from the realization that a program may be thought as an input-output relation over some state space: an accessibility relation. This point of view, that the calculus of relations is fundamental to programs, was clearly enunciated by the Oxford group of Tony Hoare in an influential paper on "Laws of Programming" (Hoare, et al., 1987). Also during the 1980s, much of the equational theory of relation algebras were

already being applied to program semantics and program development. For example, the book Relations and Graphs by Schmidt and Strohlein (in German, 1989 [Schmidt & Ströhlein, 1989]; in English, 1993 [Schmidt & Ströhlein, 1993]) started from the basis of programs as graphs with Boolean matrices. Thus computer science, as the new application field for relational methods, has both drawn from and contributed to previous logic/mathematical work; this is a sign of healthy development.

Demonic Relational Calculus

In the context of software development, one important approach is that of developing programs from specifications by stepwise refinement (e.g. Back, 1981; Fchier, 2002a, 2003; Wirth, 1971). One point of view is that a specification is a relation constraining the input-output (respectively, argument-result) behaviour of programs. Inspired by interpretation of relations as non-deterministic programs, demonic, angelic and erratic variants of relational operations have been studied. The demonic interpretation of non-deterministic turns out to closely correspond to the concept of under-specification, and therefore the demonic operations are used in most refinement calculus (Wolfram, 2001).

The demonic calculus of relations (Boudriga, Elloumi, & Mili, 1992; Desharnais, Mili, & Nguyen, 1997) views any relation R from a set A to another set B as specifying those programs that terminate for all $a \in A$ wherever R associates any values from B with a, and then the program may only return values b for which $(a, b) \in R$. Consequently, a relation R refines another relation S if R specifies a larger domain of termination and fewer possibilities for return values. The demonic calculus of relations has the advantage that the demonic operations are defined on top of the conventional relation algebraic operations, and can easily and usefully be mixed with the latter, allowing the application of numerous algebraic properties.

Boudriga *et al.* (1992) give a refinement order introduced initially in Mili (1987). The set of relations with this order is a semilattice. Similar notions have been defined in Back (Back & von Wright, 1992; Back, 1981), Morgan and Robinson (1987), and Morris (1987). In the following, we will give the rationale behind the definition of refinement called the refinement ordering. If we consider a relation R as a specification of the input-output behavior of a program p, then p *refines* R (or that p is correct with respect to R) if:

- For any input i in the domain of R, i' is a possible output of p only if $(i, i') \in R$,
- p always terminates for any input belonging to the domain of R (Mili, 1983). For an input that does not belong to the domain of specification R, program p may return any result or return no result; that is, the specifier does not care what happens following the submission of such an input.

Fuzzy Calculus

As the complexity of a system increases, our ability to make precise and yet significant statements about its behavior diminishes until a threshold is reached beyond which precision and significance (or relevance) become almost mutually exclusive characteristics. (Zadeh, 1973).

Let us consider characteristic features of real-world systems again: real situations are very often uncertain or vague in a number of ways. Due to lack of information the future state of the system might not be known completely. This type of uncertainty has long been handled appropriately by probability theory and statistics. This Kolmogoroff-type probability is essentially frequentistic and bases on set-theoretic consider-

ations. Koopman's probability refers to the truth of statement and therefore bases on logic. On both types of probabilistic approaches it is assumed, however, that the events (elements of sets) or the statements, respectively, are well defined. We shall call this type of uncertainty or vagueness stochastic uncertainty by contrast to the vagueness concerning the description of the semantic meaning of the events, phenomena or statements themselves, which we shall call fuzziness. Fuzziness can be found in many areas of daily life, such as in engineering (Blockley, 1980), in medicine (Vila & Delgado, 1983), in meteorology (Cao & Chen, 1983), in manufacturing (Mamdani, 1981); and others.

It is important to realize what fuzzy logic actually is. Fuzzy logic is a superset of conventional logic that has been extended to handle the concept of partial truth-truth values between "completely true" and "completely false." As its name suggests, it is the logic underlying modes of reasoning which are approximate rather than exact. The importance of fuzzy theory derives from the fact that most modes of human reasoning and especially common sense reasoning are approximate in nature.

The first publications in fuzzy set theory by Zadeh (1965) and Goguen (2009, n.d.) show the intention of the authors to generalize the classical notion of a set. Zadeh (1965) writes:"The notion of a fuzzy set provides a convenient point of departure for the construction of a conceptual framework which parallels in many respects the framework used in the case of ordinary sets, but is more general than the latter and, potentially, may prove to have a much wider scope of applicability, particularly in the fields of mathematics and computer science (pattern classification and information processing).

Fuzzy set theory provides a strict mathematical framework (there is nothing fuzzy about fuzzy set theory) in which vague conceptual phenomena can be precisely and rigorously studied. It can also be considered as a modeling language well suited for situations in which fuzzy relations, criteria, and phenomena exist. It will mean different things, depending on the application area and the way it is measured. In the meantime, numerous authors have contributed to this theory. In 1984 as many as 4000 publications may already exist. The specialization of those publications conceivably increases, making it more and more difficult for new comers to this area. Roughly speaking, fuzzy set theory in the last two decades has developed a long two lines:

1. As a formal theory which, when maturing, became more sophisticated and specified and was enlarged by original ideas and concepts as well as by "embracing" classical mathematical areas such as algebra, graph theory, topology, and so on by generalizing (fuzzifying) them.
2. As a very powerful modeling language, that can cope with a large fraction of uncertainties of real-life situations.

Because of its generality it can be well adapted to different circumstances and contexts. In many cases this will mean, however, the context dependent modification and specification of the original concepts of the formal fuzzy set theory.

There are countless applications for fuzzy logic. In fact, some claim that fuzzy logic is the encompassing theory over all types of logic. The items in this list are more common applications that one may encounter in everyday life.

1. Temperature Control (Heating/Cooling)

I don't think the university has figured this one out yet.

The trick in temperature control is to keep the room at the same temperature consistently. Well, that seems pretty easy, right? But how much does a room have to cool off before the heat kicks in again? There must be some standard, so the heat (or air conditioning) isn't in a constant state of turning on and off. Therein lies the fuzzy logic. The set is determined by what the temperature is actually set to. Membership in that set weakens as the room temperature varies from the set temperature. Once membership weakens to a certain point, temperature control kicks in to get the room back to the temperature it should be.

2. Medical Diagnoses

How many of what kinds of symptoms will yield a diagnosis?

How often are doctors in error? Surely everyone has seen those lists of symptoms for a horrible disease that say "if you have at least 5 of these symptoms, you are at risk." It is a hypochondriac's haven. The question is, how do doctors go from that list of symptoms to a diagnosis? Fuzzy logic. There is no guaranteed system to reach a diagnosis. If there were, we wouldn't hear about cases of medical misdiagnosis. The diagnosis can only be some degree within the fuzzy set.

3. Predicting Travel Time

This is especially difficult for driving, since there are plenty of traffic situations that can occur to slow down travel.

As with bus timetabling, predicting ETA's is a great exercise in fuzzy logic. That's why it is called an estimated time of arrival. A major player in predicting travel time is previous experience. It took me six hours to drive to Philadelphia last time, so it should take me about that amount of time when I make the trip again. Unfortunately, other factors are not typically considered. Weather, traffic, construction, accidents should all be added into the fuzzy equation to deliver a true estimate.

4. Antilock Braking System

It's probably something you hardly think about when you're slamming on the brakes in your car.

The point of an ABS is to monitor the braking system on the vehicle and release the brakes just before the wheels lock. A computer is involved in determining when the best time to do this is. Two main factors that go into determining this are the speed of the car when the brakes are applied, and how fast the brakes are depressed. Usually, the times you want the ABS to really work are when you're driving fast and slam on the brakes. There is, of course, a margin for error. It is the job of the ABS to be "smart" enough to never allow the error go past the point when the wheels will lock. (In other words, it doesn't allow the membership in the set to become too weak.)

5. Auto-Focus on a Camera

How does the camera even know what to focus on?

Auto-focus cameras are a great revolution for those who spent years struggling with "old-fashioned" cameras. These cameras somehow figure out, based on multitudes of inputs, what is meant to be the main object of the photo. It takes fuzzy logic to make these assumptions. Perhaps the standard is to focus on the object closest to the center of the viewer. Maybe it focuses on the object closest to the camera. It is not a precise science, and cameras err periodically. This margin of error is acceptable for the average camera owner, whose main usage is for snapshots. However, the "old-fashioned" manual focus cameras are preferred by most professional photographers. For any errors in those photos cannot be attributed to a mechanical glitch. The decision making in focusing a manual camera is fuzzy as well, but it is not controlled by a machine.

6. Predicting Genetic Traits

Does everyone remember Punnet Squares?

Genetic traits are a fuzzy situation for more than one reason. There is the fact that many traits can't be linked to a single gene. So only specific combinations of genes will create a given trait. Secondly, the dominant and recessive genes that are frequently illustrated with Punnet squares, are sets in fuzzy logic. The degree of membership in those sets is measured by the occurrence of a genetic trait. In clear cases of dominant and recessive genes, the possible degrees in the sets are pretty strict. Take, for instance, eye color. Two brown-eyed parents produce three blue-eyed children. Sounds impossible, right? Brown is dominant, so each parent must have the recessive gene within them. Their membership in the blue eye set must be small, but it is still there. So their children have the potential for high membership in the blue eye set, so that trait actually comes through. According to the Punnet square, 25% of their children should have blue eyes, with the other 75% having brown. But in this situation, 100% of their children have the recessive color. Was the wife being unfaithful with that nice, blue-eyed salesman? Probably not. It's just fuzzy logic at work.

7. Bus Time Tables

How accurately do the schedules predict the actual travel time on the bus?

Bus schedules are formulated on information that does not remain constant. They use fuzzy logic because it is impossible to give an exact answer to when the bus will be at a certain stop. Many unforeseen incidents can occur. There can be accidents, abnormal traffic backups, or the bus could break down. An observant scheduler would take all these possibilities into account, and include them in a formula for figuring out the approximate schedule. It is that formula which imposes the fuzziness.

In this section, we will present useful mathematics concepts. First, we will give certain notions about elementary theory on relations and ordered structures. Finally, relational calculus and some relational notions needed in the following of our chapter.

ELEMENTARY THEORY ON RELATIONS

Using Alfred Tarski (1941) approach, we distinguish two levels of abstraction in the study of binary relations: *the elementary theory of relations* and *relational calculus*. First level define the relations as sets of (pairs) and second level defines the relations as elementary objects on which the operations are defined and studied in an algebraic point of view.

In this chapter, we need both levels of abstraction. The first one will give us our examples and the second one is useful for our proofs and formulas. So, in this section we will present both levels.

1. **Definition:** A relation R from a set X to a set Y is a subset of pairs (x, y) where $x \in X$ and $y \in Y$. Formally,

$$R \subseteq X \times Y = \{(x, y) \mid x \in X \ and \ y \in Y\}.$$

If $X = Y$, then R is *homogeneous* on X.

2. **Remark:** The relations on finite sets can be represented by matrices. For example, the relation:

$$R = \{(a, b), (a, c), (b, d), (c, d), (d, e)\}$$

can be represented by:

$$R = c \begin{array}{c} \\ a \\ b \\ c \\ d \\ e \end{array} \begin{array}{ccccc} a & b & c & d & e \\ \left(\begin{array}{ccccc} 0 & 1 & 1 & 0 & 0 \\ 0 & 0 & 0 & 1 & 0 \\ 0 & 0 & 0 & 1 & 0 \\ 0 & 0 & 0 & 0 & 1 \\ 0 & 0 & 0 & 0 & 0 \end{array}\right) \end{array}$$

The graphs and relations are closely linked. We will give the definition of a graph.

3. **Definition:** A graph $G = (X, R)$ consists of a finite set of vertices X and of a relation $R \subseteq X \times X$.

Every finite relation can be interpreted as a representation graph and vice versa. In matrix

Figure 1. The graph associated to relation R

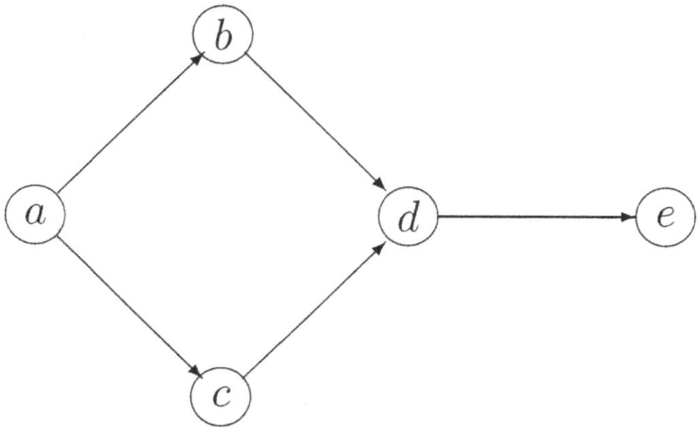

notation, an entry 0 corresponds to the absence of an edge between two vertices of the graph (the absence of the pair in the relation) and an entry 1 means the opposite.

As relations are sets, they are ordered by inclusion. The least relation between sets X and Y is the *empty* (also called zero), noted $\emptyset_{XY}$, and the greatest one, called *universal* relation, and noted L_{XY}. A particular relation defined for every set X is the *identity* relation, noted $I_X \overset{\text{def}}{=} \{(x,x) \mid x \in X\}$. The set of elements of X whose images by R is called *domain* of R, noted $\mathrm{dom}(R)$, and the set of images is noted $\mathrm{img}(R)$. Formally,

$$\mathrm{dom}(R) \overset{\text{def}}{=} \{x \mid (\exists y : (x,y) \in R)\},$$

$$\mathrm{img}(R) \overset{\text{def}}{=} \{y \mid (\exists x : (x,y) \in R)\}.$$

Operations on Relations

As relations are particular sets, we can apply the usual sets operations, which are union $(\cup)$, intersection $(\cap)$ and complementation $(\overline{})$. Relations are ordered by inclusion. More, their structure helps us to define other operations which are:

- Inverse of a relation R, denoted $R^\smile$:

$$R^\smile = \{(x,y) \mid (y,x) \in R\}.$$

- For $R \subseteq X \times Z$ and $S \subseteq Z \times Y$, we define the composition of R and S, noted $R \circ S$, as:

$$R \circ S = \{(x,y) \mid (\exists z : z \in Z : (x,z) \in R \\ \text{and } (z,y) \in S)\}.$$

We remark that $R \circ S \subseteq X \times Y$.

4. **Remark**: The composition operator symbol $(\circ)$ will be omitted (that is, we write (RS) for $(R \circ S)$.

Properties of Relations

In the following, we will give definitions and properties of relations.

5. **Definition:** A relation $R \subseteq X \times X$ is:
   a. Reflexive iff $I \subseteq R$, *i.e.*

$$(\forall x : (x,x) \in R),$$

   b. Transitive iff $RR \subseteq R$, *i.e*

$$(\forall x,y,z : (x,z) \in R \text{ and} \\ (z,y) \in R \Rightarrow (x,y) \in R),$$

   c. Symmetric iff $R \subseteq R^\smile$, *i.e.*

$$(\forall x,y : (x,y) \in R \Leftrightarrow (y,x) \in R),$$

   d. Antisymmetric iff $R \cap R^\smile \subseteq I$, *i.e*

$$(\forall x,y : (x,y) \in R \text{ and} \\ (x,y) \in R^\smile \Rightarrow x = y),$$

   e. Equivalence iff R verifies properties (a), (b) and (c),
   f. Order iff R verifies properties (a), (b) and (d),
   g. Pre-ordre iff R verifies properties (a) and (b).

We can now define the abstract algebraic structures having many properties of the relations. They are based on boolean algebras and other operators which are the composition ($\circ$) and the inverse ($\smile$) and also a particular element I (identity relation).

RELATIONAL CALCULUS

The origin of relational calculus back to century last with the work of De Morgan (1864, 1856), Dedekind and Schröder (1895), also in the be that beginning of present century with those of Peirce (1885, 1880). Their study has been revived by the work of Chin and Tarski (Chin & Tarski, 1951; Tarski, 1941). For more details on the algebra of relations see Chin and Tarski (1951), Jonsson (1991, 1982), Jonsson and Tarski (1952, 1948), and Maddux (1991a, 1991b). In what follows, we will give a definition of the algebra of relations and some important models of axioms characterizing this algebra. Most of our definitions are from (Schmidt & Ströhlein, 1993).

6. **Definition:** An abstract heterogeneous relational algebra is an algebraic structure ($\mathcal{R}$, $\cup$, $\cap$, $^-$, $\smile$, $\circ$, $\varnothing$, L, I) on a nonempty set $\mathcal{R}$ of elements called *relations*, such that the next conditions are satisfied.

   a. Every relation R in $\mathcal{R}$ belongs to a subset $\mathcal{B}_R$ of the set $\mathcal{R}$ such that the structure ($\mathcal{B}_R$, $\cup$, $\cap$, $^-$, $\varnothing$, L) is a complete atomic boolean algebra.

   b. Every relation R has an inverse $R^\smile$.

   c. Given two relations Q and R from boolean algebras $\mathcal{B}_Q$ and $\mathcal{B}_R$ respectively, a *composition* associative $Q \circ R$ is defined. It exists the identities a right and left (note I) for each together $\mathcal{B}_R$ of relations. The existence of a composition $Q \circ R$ implies that $P \circ R$ is defined for all relations P in $\mathcal{B}_Q$. The compositions $R^\smile \circ R$ and $R \circ R^\smile$ are always defined.

   d. Schröder rule
   $$P \circ Q \subseteq R \Leftrightarrow P^\smile \circ \overline{R} \subseteq \overline{Q} \Leftrightarrow \overline{R} \circ Q^\smile \subseteq \overline{P}$$
   is valid if one expression is defined.

   e. Tarski rule is valid: $L \circ R \circ L = L$ iff $R \neq \varnothing$.

If $R^\smile \in \mathcal{B}_R$, then R is called *homogeneous*.

For simplicity, the universal, zero, and identity elements are all denoted by L, $\varnothing$ and I respectively. One can use subscripts to make the typing explicit, but this will not be necessary here. The precedence of the relational operators, from highest to lowest, is the following: $^-$, $\smile$, bind equally, followed by ($\circ$) followed by $\cap$ and finally by $\cup$. The scope of $\bigcup_i$ and $\bigcap_i$ goes to the right as far as possible. The relation $R^\smile$ is called the *converse* of R. The partial operations involved in relational expressions are assumed to be defined, even when it is not explicitly mentioned. From Definition (4), the usual rules of the calculus of relations can be derived (see, e.g., Berghammer & Zierer, 1986; Chin & Tarski, 1951; Schmidt & Ströhlein, 1993; Tchier, 2002b). We assume these rules to be known and simply recall a few of them. We will present certain examples of models satisfying these axioms.

7. **Example:**

The algebra of binary relations on different sets is an important relation algebra, because it is very useful. Let $S_1, ..., S_n$ be sets.

$$\mathcal{R} \overset{\text{def}}{=} \{R \mid R \subseteq S_i \times S_j, 1 \leq i, j \leq n\},$$

with relation operators, is a relation algebra. The operations $\cup$ and $\cap$ between relations Q and

R are defined iff Q and R have the same type. A relation is homogeneous iff $R : S_i \leftrightarrow S_i$ for a certain i. The composition $Q \circ R$ is defined iff $Q : S_i \leftrightarrow S_j$ and $R : S_j \leftrightarrow S_k$ for certain i, j, k.

The set of all homogeneous binary relations on a set X, denoted:

$$\text{Rel}(X) \overset{\text{def}}{=} (\mathcal{P}(X \times X),$$
$$\cup, \cap, \check{\ }, \bar{\ }, \circ, \varnothing, X \times X, I_X$$

is a relation algebra.

The algebra of boolean matrices is another important relation algebra.

We recall by the next examples how some of the operators are applied to boolean matrices. To respect the usual convention, we will use the boolean values $\{0, 1\}$ instead of the values $\{\varnothing, L\}$.

$$I_{2 \times 2} = \begin{pmatrix} 1 & 0 \\ 0 & 1 \end{pmatrix},$$

$$\varnothing_{1 \times 2} = \begin{pmatrix} 0 & 0 \end{pmatrix},$$

$$L_{2 \times 3} = \begin{pmatrix} 1 & 1 & 1 \\ 1 & 1 & 1 \end{pmatrix},$$

$$\begin{pmatrix} 1 & 0 \\ 0 & 1 \\ 1 & 0 \end{pmatrix}^{\smile} = \begin{pmatrix} 1 & 0 & 1 \\ 0 & 1 & 0 \end{pmatrix},$$

$$\begin{pmatrix} 1 & 0 & 1 \\ 0 & 1 & 0 \end{pmatrix} \begin{pmatrix} 1 & 0 \\ 0 & 1 \\ 0 & 1 \end{pmatrix} = \begin{pmatrix} 1 & 1 \\ 0 & 1 \end{pmatrix}.$$

We will give another example. The set of matrices whose entries are relations constitutes a relation algebra (Schmidt & Ströhlein, 1993), with the operators defined as follows.

$$
\begin{aligned}
(R \cup S)_{ij} &= R_{ij} \cup S_{ij}, \\
(\overline{R})_{ij} &= \overline{R_{ij}}, \\
(RS)_{ij} &= \bigcup_k R_{ik} S_{kj}, \qquad\qquad (1) \\
(R \cap S)_{ij} &= R_{ij} \cap S_{ij}, \\
(R^{\smile})_{ij} &= (R_{ji})^{\smile}.
\end{aligned}
$$

The constant relations are defined as follows:

$$
\begin{aligned}
L_{ij} &= L, \\
\varnothing_{ij} &= \varnothing, \\
I_{ij} &= \begin{cases} I & \text{if } i = j \\ \varnothing & \text{otherwise.} \end{cases}
\end{aligned}
$$

where $R_{i,j}$ denotes entry i, j of matrix R. Of course, $R \cup S$ and $R \cap S$ exist only if matrices R and S have the same dimension; the composition RS exists only if the number of columns of R is the same as the number of rows of S. The entries of the identity matrix (which is square) are 0, except those of the diagonal, which are 1. The entries of the zero matrix are $\varnothing$ and those of the universal matrix are L.

From definition (4), the usual rules of the calculus of relations can be derived (see, e.g., Berghammer & Zierer, 1986; Chin & Tarski, 1951; Schmidt & Ströhlein, 1993, 1985; Tchier, 2002b). We assume these rules to be known and simply recall a few of them.

9. **Theorem:** *Let P, Q, R be relations and X be an arbitrary index set.*

$$\overline{\bigcup_{i \in X} R_i} = \bigcap_{i \in X} \overline{R_i},$$

$$\overline{Q \cup R} = \overline{Q} \cap \overline{R},$$

$$\overline{\bigcap_{i \in X} R_i} = \bigcup_{i \in X} \overline{R_i},$$

$$\overline{Q \cap R} = \overline{Q} \cup \overline{R},$$

$$(Q \cap R) \cup \overline{R} = Q \cup \overline{R},$$

$$P \cap Q \subseteq R \Leftrightarrow P \subseteq \overline{Q} \cup R,$$

$$Q \subseteq R \Leftrightarrow \overline{R} \subseteq \overline{Q},$$

$$Q \left(\bigcup_{i \in X} R_i \right) = \bigcup_{i \in X} Q R_i,$$

$$P \left(Q \cup R \right) = PQ \cup PR,$$

$$\left(\bigcup_{i \in X} Q_i \right) R = \bigcup_{i \in X} Q_i R,$$

$$(P \cup Q) R = PR \cup QR,$$

$$Q \left(\bigcap_{i \in X} R_i \right) \subseteq \bigcap_{i \in X} Q R_i,$$

$$P \left(Q \cap R \right) \subseteq PQ \cap PR,$$

$$\left(\bigcap_{i \in X} Q_i \right) R \subseteq \bigcap_{i \in X} Q_i R,$$

$$(P \cap Q) R \subseteq PR \cap QR,$$

$$Q \subseteq R \Rightarrow PQ \subseteq PR,$$

$$P \subseteq Q \Rightarrow PR \subseteq QR,$$

$$R \emptyset = \emptyset R = \emptyset,$$

$$RI = IR = R,$$

$$Q \subseteq R \Leftrightarrow Q^{\smile} \subseteq R^{\smile},$$

$$\left(\bigcup_{i \in X} R_i \right)^{\smile} = \bigcup_{i \in X} R_i^{\smile},$$

$$(Q \cup R)^{\smile} = Q^{\smile} \cup R^{\smile},$$

$$\left(\bigcap_{i \in X} R_i \right)^{\smile} = \bigcap_{i \in X} R_i^{\smile},$$

$$(Q \cap R)^{\smile} = Q^{\smile} \cap R^{\smile},$$

$$(QR)^{\smile} = R^{\smile} Q^{\smile},$$

$$R^{\smile\smile} = R,$$

$$I^{\smile} = I,$$

$$\overline{R}^{\smile} = \overline{R^{\smile}},$$

$$PQ \cap R \subseteq \left(P \cap RQ^{\smile} \right) \left(Q \cap P^{\smile} R \right),$$

$$PQ \cap R \subseteq P \left(Q \cap P^{\smile} R \right),$$

$$PQ \cap R \subseteq \left(P \cap RQ^{\smile} \right) Q,$$

$$LL = L,$$

$$\left(\bigcap_{i \in X} R_i L \right) L = \bigcap_{i \in X} R_i L,$$

$$(QL \cap RL) L = QL \cap RL,$$

$$\left(\bigcap_{i \in X} R_i L \right) L = \bigcap_{i \in X} R_i L,$$

$$(QL \cup RL) L = QL \cup RL,$$

$$(P \cap QL) R = PR \cap QL,$$

$$\left(P \cap LQ^{\smile} \right) R = P \left(R \cap QL \right),$$

$$QLR = QL \cap LR,$$

$$\overline{RLL} = \overline{RL},$$

$$R = \left(I \cap RR^\smile \right) R.$$

10. **Remark:** Sometimes, instead to refer to laws 8, 9, 10 and 11, we refer as the operation $\left(\circ \right)$ is distributive.

Then, we have $\left(\circ \right)$ is monotonic instead to refer to laws 16 and 17.

In the following, we will give the definitions of certain properties.

11. **Definition:** A relation R is:
    a. *Deterministic* iff $R^\smile R \subseteq I$,
    b. *Total* iff $L = RL$ (equivalent to $I \subseteq RR^\smile$),
    c. An *application* iff it is total and deterministic,
    d. *Injective* iff $R^\smile$ is deterministic (*i.e.* $RR^\smile \subseteq I$),
    e. *Surjective* iff $R^\smile$ is total (*i.e.* $LR = L$, or also $I \subseteq R^\smile R$),
    f. A *partial identity* iff $R \subseteq I$ (sub-identity),
    g. A *vector* iff $R = RL$ (the vectors are usually denoted by the letter v),
    h. A *point* iff $R \neq \emptyset$, $R = RL$ and $RR^\smile \subseteq I$.

12. **Remark:** A function is a deterministic relation.

The vectors RL and $R^\smile L$ are particular vectors characterizing respectively the domain and codomain of R. The set of vectors of a certain type is a complete boolean algebra (Schmidt & Ströhlein, 1993; Tchier, 2002b).

In an algebra of boolean matrices, a vector is a matrix in which the rows are constant and a point is a vector with a nonzero row.

13. **Example:** Let $X = \{0,1,2\}$ and $V = \{0,1\}$. Then

$$v \overset{\text{def}}{=} V \times X = \{(0,0),(0,1),(0,2),(1,0),(1,1),(1,2)\}$$

is a vector that corresponds to a set of points V. The partial identity corresponds to v is $a = \{(0,0),(1,1)\}$.

Let $R \overset{\text{def}}{=} \{(0,1),(0,2),(2,1)\}$, v and a be the vector and the partial identity given before.

Prerestriction of R to v (or to a) is:

$$v \cap R = aR = \{(0,1),(0,2)\}.$$

Postrestriction of R to v (or to a) is:

$$v^\smile \cap R = Ra = \{(0,1),(2,1)\}.$$

Domain of R is:

$$RL = \{(0,0),(0,1),(0,2),$$
$$(2,0),(2,1),(2,2)\}.$$

The vector represents the subset $\{0,2\}$.
The relation:

$$R^\smile L = \{(1,0),(1,1),(1,2),$$
$$(2,0),(2,1),(2,2)\}$$

is the vector characterizing the subset $\{1,2\}$, which is the codomain of R.

FUZZY RELATIONAL CALCULUS

Fuzzy set theory has been studied extensively over the past 30 years. Most of the early interest in fuzzy set theory pertained to representing uncertainty in human cognitive processes (Zadeh, 1965). Fuzzy set theory is now applied to problems in engineering, business, medical and related health sciences, and the natural sciences. Fuzzy relations play an important role in fuzzy modeling, fuzzy diagnosis, and fuzzy control. They also have applications in fields such as psychology, medicine, economics, and sociology. In this section, we define and discuss fuzzy sets and fuzzy relations. Beginning with a definition of fuzzy sets, we then talk about expressing fuzzy relations in terms of matrices and graphical visualizations. Later, we discuss the various properties of fuzzy relations and operations that can be performed with fuzzy relations. We illustrate the basic properties of fuzzy relations using the graphical functions of Fuzzy Logic.

FUZZY RELATIONS

The concept of a fuzzy relation on a set was defined by Zadeh (1965, 1971) and other authors like Rosenfeld (1975), Tamura et. al. (1971), and Yeh and Bang (1975) considered it further. Fuzzy relations are of fundamental importance in fuzzy logic and fuzzy set theory, including particularly fuzzy preference modeling, fuzzy mathematics, fuzzy inference, and many more.

14. **Definition:** Let $A, B \subseteq U$ be two sets, a *fuzzy relation* on $A \times B$ is defined by:

$$\tilde{R} = \{((x,y), \mu_{\tilde{R}}(x,y) \mid (x,y) \in A \times B, \mu_{\tilde{R}}(x,y) \in [0,1]\}.$$

As fuzzy relations are sets, they are ordered by inclusion. The least fuzzy relation between sets A and B is the *empty* (also called zero), noted $\emptyset_{AB}$, and the greatest one, called *universal* fuzzy relation, and noted $\tilde{L}_{AB}$. A particular fuzzy relation defined for every set A is the *identity* fuzzy relation, noted:

$$\tilde{I}_A \overset{\text{def}}{=} \{((x,y), \mu_{\tilde{I}}(x,y)) \mid x \in A\},$$

where $\mu_{\tilde{I}}(x,y) = 1$ if $x = y$ and 0 otherwise. The domain of $\tilde{R}$, denoted by dom$(\tilde{R})$, is defined as:

15. $$dom(\tilde{R}) \overset{\text{def}}{=} \sup_{y \in B}$$
$$\{((x,y), \mu_{\tilde{R}}(x,y)) \mid \forall x \in A\},$$

and the codomain of $\tilde{R}$, denoted by codom $(\tilde{R})$, is expressed by finding the maximal value of $\tilde{R}$ a long A :

16. $$codom(\tilde{R}) \overset{\text{def}}{=} \sup_{x \in A}$$
$$\{((x,y), \mu_{\tilde{R}}(x,y)) \mid \forall y \in B\}.$$

The domain and codomain are regarded as the height of row and columns of the fuzzy relation (Pedrycz & Gomides, 1998).

Operations on Fuzzy Relations

As fuzzy relations are particular fuzzy sets, we can apply the usual fuzzy sets operations, which are union $(\cup)$, intersection $(\cap)$ and complementation $(\bar{})$, given in Tchier (1996). More, their structure helps us to define other operations which are:

17. **Definition:** Let A, B and C are sets,

$$\tilde{R} = \{[(x,y), \mu_{\tilde{R}}(x,y)] \mid (x,y) \in A \times B\},$$

$$\tilde{S} = \{((y,z), \mu_{\tilde{S}}(y,z)) \mid (y,z) \in B \times C\},$$

Inverse of a fuzzy relation $\tilde{R}$, denoted $\tilde{R}^{\smile}$:

$$\tilde{R}^{\smile} = \{[(x,y), \mu_{\tilde{R}}(x,y)] \mid ((y,x), \mu_{\tilde{R}}(y,x)) \in \tilde{R}\}.$$

The max-min composition $\tilde{R} \circ \tilde{S}$ is the fuzzy relation

$$\tilde{R} \circ \tilde{S} = \{[(x,z), \vee_{y \in B}\{\mu_{\tilde{R}}(x,y) \wedge \mu_{\tilde{S}}(y,z)\}] \mid x \in A, y \in B, z \in C\}$$

From now on, the composition operator symbol $(\circ)$ will be omitted (that is, we write $(\tilde{R}\tilde{S})$ for $(\tilde{R} \circ \tilde{S})$).

The semi-scalars multiplication $k\tilde{R}$ of a fuzzy relation $\tilde{R}$ by a scalar $k(\in [0,1])$ is a fuzzy relation such that:

$$k\tilde{R} = \{[(x,y), k\mu_{\tilde{R}}(x,y)] \mid (x,y) \in A \times B\}$$

18. **Example:** Let $\tilde{R}$ and $\tilde{S}$ be two fuzzy relations given as follows and $k = 0.3$,

Let

$A = \{x_1, x_2, x_3\}$,

$B = \{y_1, y_2, y_3, y_4\}$,

$\tilde{R} = $ "x considerably larger than y",

and

$\tilde{S} = $ "y very close to x",

then:

$$\tilde{R} = \begin{array}{c} x_1 \\ x_2 \\ x_3 \end{array} \begin{pmatrix} 0.8 & 1 & 0.1 & 0.7 \\ 0 & 0.8 & 0 & 0 \\ 0.9 & 1 & 0.7 & 0.8 \end{pmatrix}$$

and

$$\tilde{S} = \begin{array}{c} x_1 \\ x_2 \\ x_3 \end{array} \begin{pmatrix} 0.4 & 0 & 0.9 & 0.6 \\ 0.9 & 0.4 & 0.5 & 0.7 \\ 0.3 & 0 & 0.8 & 0.5 \end{pmatrix}$$

we have,

$$\tilde{R} \cup \tilde{S} = \begin{array}{c} x_1 \\ x_2 \\ x_3 \end{array} \begin{pmatrix} 0.8 & 1 & 0.9 & 0.7 \\ 0.9 & 0.8 & 0.5 & 0.7 \\ 0.9 & 1 & 0.8 & 0.8 \end{pmatrix}$$

$$\tilde{R}^{\smile} = \begin{array}{c} y_1 \\ y_2 \\ y_3 \\ y_4 \end{array} \begin{pmatrix} 0.8 & 0 & 0.9 \\ 1 & 0.8 & 1 \\ 0.1 & 0 & 0.7 \\ 0.7 & 0 & 0.8 \end{pmatrix}$$

$$\tilde{R} \cap \tilde{S} = \begin{array}{c} x_1 \\ x_2 \\ x_3 \end{array} \begin{pmatrix} 0.4 & 0 & 0.1 & 0.6 \\ 0 & 0.4 & 0 & 0 \\ 0.3 & 0 & 0.7 & 0.5 \end{pmatrix}$$

$$k\tilde{S} = \begin{array}{c} x_1 \\ x_2 \\ x_3 \end{array} \begin{pmatrix} 0.12 & 0 & 0.27 & 0.18 \\ 0.27 & 0.12 & 0.15 & 0.21 \\ 0.9 & 0 & 0.24 & 0.15 \end{pmatrix}$$

These operations are illustrated respectively by the next figures.

19. **Remark:** Different versions of "composition" have been suggested which differ in their results and also with respect to their mathematical properties. The max-min composition has become the best known and the most frequently used. However, often the so-called *max-product* or *max-average*

compositions lead to results that are more appealing, see Rosenfeld (1975).

a. The max-prod composition $(\tilde{R} \circ \tilde{S})$ defined as:

$$\tilde{R} \circ \tilde{S} = \{[(x,z), \vee_y \{\mu_{\tilde{R}_1}(x,y) \cdot \mu_{\tilde{R}_2}(y,z)\}] \mid$$
$$x \in A, y \in B, z \in C\}.$$

b. The max-av composition $(\tilde{R} \circ_{av} \tilde{S})$ defined as:

$$\tilde{R} \circ_{av} \tilde{S} = \{[(x,z), \frac{1}{2} \vee_y \{\mu_{\tilde{R}}(x,y) + \mu_{\tilde{S}}(y,z)\}] \mid$$
$$x \in A, y \in B, z \in C\}.$$

20. **Example:** Let $\tilde{R}$ and $\tilde{S}$ be defined by the following matrices (Kaufmann, 1975):

$$\tilde{R} = \begin{array}{c} \\ x_1 \\ x_2 \\ x_3 \end{array} \begin{array}{ccccc} y_1 & y_2 & y_3 & y_4 & y_5 \\ \begin{pmatrix} 0.1 & 0.2 & 0 & 1 & 0.7 \\ 0.3 & 0.5 & 0 & 0.2 & 1 \\ 0.8 & 0 & 1 & 0.4 & 0.3 \end{pmatrix} \end{array},$$

$$\tilde{S} = \begin{array}{c} \\ y_1 \\ y_2 \\ y_3 \\ y_4 \\ y_5 \end{array} \begin{array}{cccc} z_1 & z_2 & z_3 & z_4 \\ \begin{pmatrix} 0.9 & 0 & 0.3 & 0.4 \\ 0.2 & 1 & 0.8 & 0 \\ 0.8 & 0 & 0.7 & 1 \\ 0.4 & 0.2 & 0.3 & 0 \\ 0 & 1 & 0 & 0.8 \end{pmatrix} \end{array}$$

We shall first compute the max-min composition $\tilde{R}\tilde{S}$. We shall show in details the determination for $x = x_1$, $z = z_1$; Let $x = x_1$, $z = z_1$ and $y = y_i$, $1 \le i \le 5$:

$$\wedge \{\mu_{\tilde{R}}(x_1, y_1), \mu_{\tilde{S}}(y_1, z_1)\}$$
$$= \wedge \{0.1, 0.9\} = 0.1$$

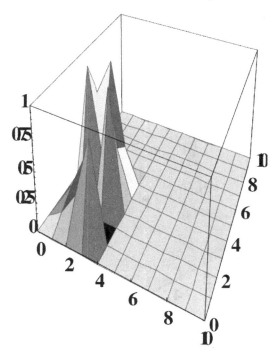

Figure 2. Fuzzy relation $\tilde{R}$ in example

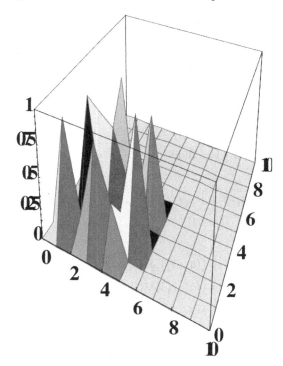

Figure 3. Fuzzy relation $\tilde{S}$ in example

Figure 4. The max-min composition of Fuzzy relation $\tilde{R}$ and $\tilde{S}$

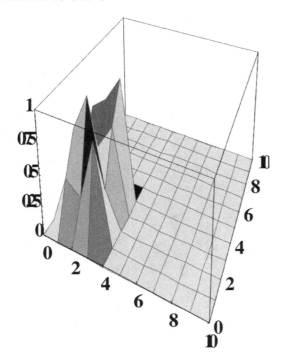

$$\tilde{R}\tilde{S} = \begin{array}{c} \\ x_1 \\ x_2 \\ x_3 \end{array} \begin{array}{cccc} z_1 & z_2 & z_3 & z_4 \\ \left[\begin{array}{cccc} 0.4 & 0.7 & 0.3 & 0.7 \\ 0.3 & 1 & 0.5 & 0.8 \\ 0.8 & 0.3 & 0.7 & 1 \end{array} \right] \end{array}$$

For the max-prod we obtain,

$$x = x_1,\ z = z_1\ y = y_i,\ 1 \leq i \leq 5:$$

$$\mu_{\tilde{R}}(x_1, y_1) \cdot \mu_{\tilde{S}}(y_1, z_1) = 0.1 \cdot 0.9 = 0.09$$

$$\mu_{\tilde{R}}(x_1, y_2) \cdot \mu_{\tilde{S}}(y_2, z_1) = 0.2 \cdot 0.2 = 0.04$$

$$\mu_{\tilde{R}}(x_1, y_3) \cdot \mu_{\tilde{S}}(y_3, z_1) = 0 \cdot 0.8 = 0$$

$$\mu_{\tilde{R}}(x_1, y_4) \cdot \mu_{\tilde{S}}(y_4, z_1) = 1 \cdot 0.4 = 0.4$$

$$\mu_{\tilde{R}}(x_1, y_5) \cdot \mu_{\tilde{S}}(y_5, z_1) = 0.7 \cdot 0 = 0$$

$$\wedge\{\mu_{\tilde{R}}(x_1, y_2), \mu_{\tilde{S}}(y_2, z_1)\}$$
$$= \wedge\{0.2, 0.2\} = 0.2$$

$$\wedge\{\mu_{\tilde{R}}(x_1, y_3), \mu_{\tilde{S}}(y_3, z_1)\}$$
$$= \wedge\{0, 0.8\} = 0$$

$$\wedge\{\mu_{\tilde{R}}(x_1, y_4), \mu_{\tilde{S}}(y_4, z_1)\}$$
$$= \wedge\{1, 0.4\} = 0.4$$

$$\wedge\{\mu_{\tilde{R}}(x_1, y_5), \mu_{\tilde{S}}(y_5, z_1)\}$$
$$= \wedge\{0.7, 0\} = 0$$

$$\tilde{R}\tilde{S}(x_1, z_1) = ((x_1, z_1), \mu_{\tilde{R}\tilde{S}}(x_1, z_1))$$
$$= ((x_1, z_1), \vee\{0.1, 0.2, 0, 0.4, 0\})$$
$$= ((x_1, z_1), 0.4)$$

In analogy to the above computation we now determine the grades of membership for all pairs (x_i, z_i), $1 \leq i \leq 3, 1 \leq j \leq 4$ and finally we have:

Then:

$$\tilde{R}\tilde{S}(x_1, z_1) = ((x_1, z_1), \mu_{\tilde{R}\tilde{S}}(x_1, z_1))$$
$$= ((x_1, z_1), \{0.09 \vee 0.04$$
$$\vee 0 \vee 0.4 \vee 0\})$$
$$= ((x_1, z_1), 0.4)$$

After performing the remaining computations we obtain,

$$\tilde{R} \circ \tilde{S} = \begin{array}{c} \\ x_1 \\ x_2 \\ x_3 \end{array} \begin{array}{cccc} z_1 & z_2 & z_3 & z_4 \\ \left[\begin{array}{cccc} 0.4 & 0.7 & 0.3 & 0.56 \\ 0.27 & 1 & 0.4 & 0.8 \\ 0.8 & 0.3 & 0.7 & 1 \end{array} \right] \end{array}$$

The max-av composition finally yields Table 1.then:

$$\frac{1}{2} \cdot \vee_y \{\mu_{\tilde{R}}(x_1, y_i) + \mu_{\tilde{S}}(y_i, z_1)\} = \frac{1}{2} \cdot (1.4) = 0.7$$

Figure 5. The max-product composition of Fuzzy relation $\tilde{R}$ and $\tilde{S}$

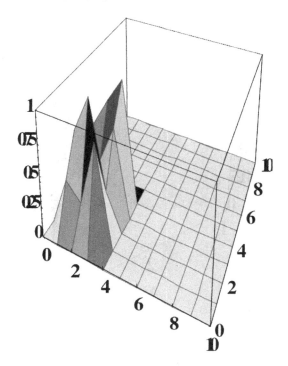

Figure 6. The max-av composition of Fuzzy relation $\tilde{R}$ and $\tilde{S}$

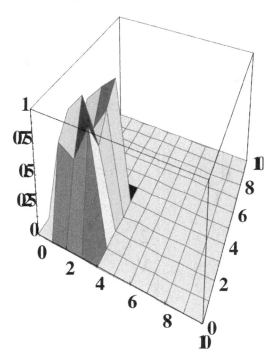

Table 1. Yield of max-av composition

i	$\mu(x_1, y_i) + \mu(y_i, z_1)$
	1
	0.4
	0.8
	1.4
	0.7

$$\tilde{R} \circ_{av} \tilde{S} = \begin{matrix} & z_1 & z_2 & z_3 & z_4 \\ x_1 \\ x_2 \\ x_3 \end{matrix} \begin{pmatrix} 0.7 & 0.85 & 0.65 & 0.75 \\ 0.6 & 1 & 0.65 & 0.9 \\ 0.9 & 0.65 & 0.85 & 1 \end{pmatrix}$$

These operations are respectively illustrated by the next figures.

21. **Remark:** The vectors $\tilde{R}\tilde{L}$ and $\tilde{R}^{\smile}\tilde{L}$ are particular vectors characterizing respectively the domain and codomain of $\tilde{R}$, which are defined in Equations (2) and (3).

Properties of Fuzzy Relations

Just as for relations, the properties of commutativity, associativity, distributivity, involution, and idempotency all hold for fuzzy relations. Moreover, De Morgan's principles hold for fuzzy relations just as they do for relations, and the empty relation $\tilde{\varnothing}$, and the universal relation $\tilde{L}$ are analogous to the empty set and the whole set in set-theoretic form, respectively. Fuzzy relations are not constrained, as is the case for fuzzy sets in general, by the excluded middle axioms. Since a fuzzy relation $\tilde{R}$ is also a fuzzy set, there is overlap between a relation and its complement [56]; hence,

$$\tilde{R} \cup \overline{\tilde{R}} \neq \tilde{L} \ \tilde{R} \cap \overline{\tilde{R}} \neq \tilde{\varnothing}.$$

22. **Example:** Let

$$\tilde{R} = \begin{array}{c} \\ x_1 \\ x_2 \\ x_3 \end{array} \begin{array}{ccccc} y_1 & y_2 & y_3 & y_4 & y_5 \\ \begin{pmatrix} 0.1 & 0.2 & 0 & 1 & 0.7 \\ 0.3 & 0.5 & 0 & 0.2 & 1 \\ 0.8 & 0 & 1 & 0.4 & 0.3 \end{pmatrix} \end{array}.$$

Figure 7. The fuzzy relation $\tilde{R}$

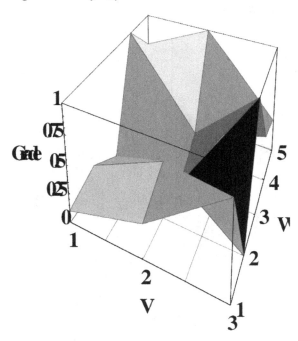

Then:

$$\overline{\tilde{R}} = \begin{array}{c} \\ x_1 \\ x_2 \\ x_3 \end{array} \begin{array}{ccccc} y_1 & y_2 & y_3 & y_4 & y_5 \\ \begin{pmatrix} 0.9 & 0.8 & 1 & 0 & 0.3 \\ 0.7 & 0.5 & 1 & 0.8 & 0 \\ 0.2 & 1 & 0 & 0.6 & 0.7 \end{pmatrix} \end{array},$$

$$\tilde{R} \cap \overline{\tilde{R}} = \begin{array}{c} \\ x_1 \\ x_2 \\ x_3 \end{array} \begin{array}{ccccc} y_1 & y_2 & y_3 & y_4 & y_5 \\ \begin{pmatrix} 0.1 & 0.2 & 0 & 0 & 0.3 \\ 0.3 & 0.5 & 0 & 0.2 & 0 \\ 0.2 & 0 & 0 & 0.4 & 0.3 \end{pmatrix} \end{array} \neq \tilde{\varnothing},$$

Figure 8. The complement of fuzzy relation $\tilde{R}$

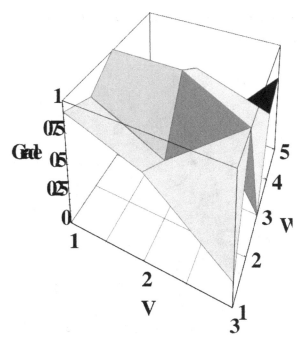

$$\tilde{R} \cup \overline{\tilde{R}} = \begin{array}{c} \\ x_1 \\ x_2 \\ x_3 \end{array} \begin{array}{ccccc} y_1 & y_2 & y_3 & y_4 & y_5 \\ \begin{pmatrix} 0.9 & 0.8 & 1 & 1 & 0.7 \\ 0.7 & 0.5 & 1 & 0.8 & 1 \\ 0.8 & 1 & 1 & 0.6 & 0.7 \end{pmatrix} \end{array} \neq \tilde{L}.$$

In the following, we will give some properties of fuzzy relations.

23. **Definition:** Let $\tilde{R}_1$ and $\tilde{R}_2$ be fuzzy relations on $A \times B$, we have;

$$\tilde{R}_1 = \{((x,y), \mu_{\tilde{R}_1}(x,y))\},$$

$$\tilde{R}_2 = \{((x,y), \mu_{\tilde{R}_2}(x,y))\}.$$

Figure 9. The fuzzy relation $\tilde{R} \cup \overline{\tilde{R}} \neq \tilde{L}$

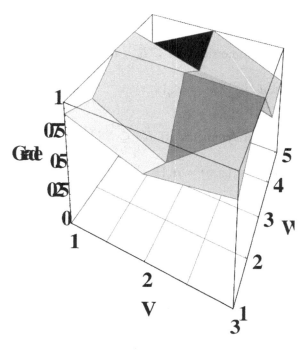

Then:

- Equality
  - $\tilde{R}_1 = \tilde{R}_2$ if and only if $\mu_{\tilde{R}_1}(x, y) = \mu_{\tilde{R}_2}(x, y)$.
- Inclusion
  - If $\mu_{\tilde{R}_1}(x, y) \leq \mu_{\tilde{R}_2}(x, y)$, the relation $\tilde{R}_1$ is included in $\tilde{R}_2$ or $\tilde{R}_2$ is larger $\tilde{R}_1$, denoted by $\tilde{R}_1 \subseteq \tilde{R}_2$.
  - If $\tilde{R}_1 \subseteq \tilde{R}_2$ and in addition if for at least one pair (x, y),
  - $\mu_{\tilde{R}_1}(x, y) < \mu_{\tilde{R}_2}(x, y)$.

Then we have the proper inclusion $\tilde{R}_1 \subseteq \tilde{R}_2$.

The following properties have been proved to hold for fuzzy relations (see Kaufmann, 1977; Kawahara & Furusawa, 1995);

24. **Theorem:** Let $\tilde{R}$, $\tilde{S}$ and $\tilde{T}$ be fuzzy relations. Then:

    a. **Associativity of Composition:**

$$\tilde{R}(\tilde{S}\tilde{T}) = (\tilde{R}\tilde{S})\tilde{T}$$

    b   **Distributivity over Union:**

$$\tilde{R}(\tilde{S} \cup \tilde{T}) = (\tilde{R}\tilde{S}) \cup (\tilde{R}\tilde{T})$$

    c. **Weak Distributivity over Intersection:**

$$\tilde{R}(\tilde{S} \cap \tilde{T}) \subseteq (\tilde{R}\tilde{S}) \cap (\tilde{R}\tilde{T})$$

    d. **Commutativity:**

$$\tilde{R} \cap \tilde{S} = \tilde{S} \cap \tilde{R}, \quad \tilde{R} \cup \tilde{S} = \tilde{S} \cup \tilde{R},$$

    e. **Associativity:**

Figure 10. The fuzzy relation $\tilde{R} \cap \overline{\tilde{R}} \neq \tilde{\emptyset}$

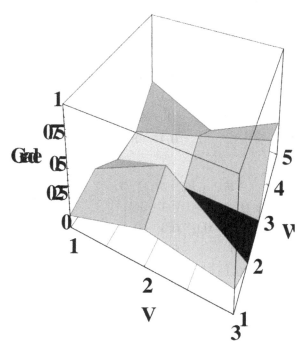

$$\tilde{R} \cap (\tilde{S} \cap \tilde{T}) = (\tilde{R} \cap \tilde{S}) \cap \tilde{T},$$
$$\tilde{R} \cup (\tilde{S} \cup \tilde{T}) = (\tilde{R} \cup \tilde{S}) \cup \tilde{T},$$

   f.   **Distributivity:**

$$\tilde{R} \cap (\tilde{S} \cup \tilde{T}) =$$

$$(\tilde{R} \cap \tilde{S}) \cup (\tilde{R} \cap \tilde{T}),$$

$$\tilde{R} \cup (\tilde{S} \cap \tilde{T}) =$$

$$(\tilde{R} \cup \tilde{S}) \cap (\tilde{R} \cup \tilde{T}),$$

   g .   **Idempotency:**

$$\tilde{R} \cup \tilde{R} = \tilde{R}, \, \tilde{R} \cap \tilde{R} = \tilde{R}$$

   h.   **Identity:**

$$\tilde{R} \cap \tilde{\phi} = \tilde{\phi}, \, \tilde{R} \cup \tilde{\phi} = \tilde{R},$$

$$\tilde{R} \cap \tilde{L} = \tilde{R}, \, \, \tilde{R} \cup \tilde{L} = \tilde{L}$$

   i.   **Involution:** $\overline{\overline{\tilde{R}}} = \tilde{R}$
   j.   **De Morgans Law:**

$$\overline{\tilde{R} \cup \tilde{S}} = \overline{\tilde{R}} \cap \overline{\tilde{S}}, \, \overline{\tilde{R} \cap \tilde{S}} = \overline{\tilde{R}} \cup \overline{\tilde{S}}$$

25.   **Proposition:** A fuzzy relation $\tilde{R} \subseteq A \times A$ is:
Reflexive iff $\tilde{I} \subseteq \tilde{R}$, *i.e.*

$$(\forall x : \mu_{\tilde{R}}(x,x) = 1)$$

Transitive iff $\tilde{R}\tilde{R} \subseteq \tilde{R}$, *i.e*

$$(\forall x,y,z : \mu_{\tilde{R}}(x,z) \geq$$
$$\wedge\{\mu_{\tilde{R}}(x,y), \mu_{\tilde{R}}(y,z)\})$$

Symmetric iff $\tilde{R} \subseteq \tilde{R}^{\smile}$, *i.e.*

$$(\forall x,y : \mu_{\tilde{R}}(x,y) = \mu_{\tilde{R}}(y,x)$$

Antisymmetric iff $\tilde{R}^{\smile} \subseteq \overline{\tilde{R}} \cup \tilde{I}$, *i.e.*

$$(\forall x,y : \mu_{\tilde{R}}(x,y) \neq \mu_{\tilde{R}}(y,x)$$

or

$$\mu_{\tilde{R}}(x,y) = \mu_{\tilde{R}}(y,x) = 0$$

   a.   Equivalence iff $\tilde{R}$ verifies properties (a), (b) and (c)
   b.   Order iff $\tilde{R}$ verifies properties (a), (b) and (d)
   c.   Pre-order iff $\tilde{R}$ verifies properties (a) and (b)

26.   **Example:** Let $\tilde{R}$, $\tilde{S}$, $\tilde{Q}$, $\tilde{T}$ and $\tilde{P}$ be fuzzy relations:

$$\tilde{R} = \begin{array}{c} \\ x_1 \\ x_2 \\ x_3 \\ x_4 \end{array} \begin{array}{cccc} y_1 & y_2 & y_3 & y_4 \\ \begin{pmatrix} 1 & 0 & 0.2 & 0.3 \\ 0 & 1 & 0.1 & 1 \\ 0.2 & 0.7 & 1 & 0.4 \\ 0 & 1 & 0.4 & 1 \end{pmatrix} \end{array}$$

$$\tilde{S} = \begin{array}{c} \\ x_1 \\ x_2 \\ x_3 \\ x_4 \end{array} \begin{array}{cccc} y_1 & y_2 & y_3 & y_4 \\ \begin{pmatrix} 0.2 & 1 & 0.4 & 0.4 \\ 0 & 0.6 & 0.3 & 0 \\ 0 & 1 & 0.3 & 0 \\ 0.1 & 1 & 1 & 0.1 \end{pmatrix} \end{array}$$

$$\tilde{P} = \begin{array}{c} \\ x_1 \\ x_2 \\ x_3 \\ x_4 \\ x_5 \\ x_6 \end{array} \begin{array}{cccccc} y_1 & y_2 & y_3 & y_4 & y_5 & y_6 \\ \begin{pmatrix} 1 & 0.2 & 1 & 0.6 & 0.2 & 0.6 \\ 0.2 & 1 & 0.2 & 0.2 & 0.8 & 0.2 \\ 1 & 0.2 & 1 & 0.6 & 0.2 & 0.6 \\ 0.6 & 0.2 & 0.6 & 1 & 0.2 & 0.8 \\ 0.2 & 0.8 & 0.2 & 0.2 & 1 & 0.2 \\ 0.6 & 0.2 & 0.6 & 0.8 & 0.2 & 1 \end{pmatrix} \end{array}$$

$$\tilde{T} = \begin{array}{c} \\ x_1 \\ x_2 \\ x_3 \\ x_4 \end{array} \begin{array}{cccc} y_1 & y_2 & y_3 & y_4 \\ \begin{pmatrix} 0.4 & 0 & 0.7 & 0 \\ 0 & 1 & 0.9 & 0.6 \\ 0.8 & 0.4 & 0.7 & 0.4 \\ 0 & 0.1 & 0 & 0 \end{pmatrix} \end{array}$$

$$\tilde{Q} = \begin{array}{c} \\ x_1 \\ x_2 \\ x_3 \\ x_4 \end{array} \begin{array}{cccc} y_1 & y_2 & y_3 & y_4 \\ \begin{pmatrix} 0 & 0.1 & 0 & 0.1 \\ 0.1 & 1 & 0.2 & 0.3 \\ 0 & 0.2 & 0.8 & 0.8 \\ 0.1 & 0.3 & 0.8 & 1 \end{pmatrix} \end{array}$$

$\tilde{R}$ is a reflexive fuzzy relation, $\tilde{S}$ is a transitive fuzzy relation, $\tilde{Q}$ is a symmetric fuzzy relation, $\tilde{T}$ is an antisymmetric fuzzy relation and $\tilde{P}$ is an equivalence fuzzy relation.

DEMONIC FUZZY ORDER AND FUZZY DEMONIC OPERATORS

In this section, we will define the refinement fuzzy ordering (*demonic fuzzy inclusion*). The associated fuzzy operator are fuzzy demonic join ($\tilde{\sqcup}$), fuzzy demonic meet ($\tilde{\sqcap}$) and fuzzy demonic composition ($\mathring{\Box}$). We will give the definitions and needed properties of these operators. We will illustrate them with simple examples using mathematica (*fuzzy logic*).

A Demonic Fuzzy Order Refinement

27. **Definition**: We say that a fuzzy relation $\tilde{Q}$ *fuzzy refines* a fuzzy relation $\tilde{R}$, denoted by $\tilde{Q} \tilde{\sqsubseteq} \tilde{R}$, iff

$$\vee_{y \in B}\{\mu_{\tilde{R}}(x,y)\} \subseteq \vee_{y \in B}\{\mu_{\tilde{Q}}(x,y)\}$$

and

$$\wedge\{\mu_{\tilde{Q}}(x,y), \vee_{y \in B}\{\mu_{\tilde{R}}(x,y)\}\} \subseteq \mu_{\tilde{R}}(x,y)$$

where $\mu_{\tilde{R}}$ and $\mu_{\tilde{Q}}$ are respectively the membership functions of $\tilde{R}$ and $\tilde{Q}$.

In other words, $\tilde{Q}$ fuzzy refines $\tilde{R}$ if and only if the prerestriction of $\tilde{Q}$ to the domain of $\tilde{R}$ is included in $\tilde{R}$: this means that $\tilde{Q}$ must not produce results not allowed by $\tilde{R}$ for those states that are in the domain of $\tilde{R}$.

It is easy to show that this definition is equivalent to definition(given [57]) ajout . In other words,

$$\tilde{Q}\tilde{L} \subseteq \tilde{R}\tilde{L} \ \wedge \ \tilde{Q} \cap \tilde{R}\tilde{L} \subseteq \tilde{R}$$

if and only if

$$\vee_{y \in B}\{\mu_{\tilde{R}}(x,y)\} \subseteq \vee_{y \in B}\{\mu_{\tilde{Q}}(x,y)\}$$

and

$$\wedge\{\mu_{\tilde{Q}}(x,y), \vee_{y \in B}\{\mu_{\tilde{R}}(x,y)\}\} \subseteq \mu_{\tilde{R}}(x,y)$$

28. **Example:**

Let,

$$\tilde{Q} = \begin{pmatrix} 0.1 & 0 \\ 1 & 0.2 \end{pmatrix}$$

213

and

$$\tilde{R} = \begin{pmatrix} 0.1 & 0.1 \\ 0.4 & 0.4 \end{pmatrix}$$

We have:

$$\vee_{y \in B} \mu_{\tilde{R}} = \begin{pmatrix} 0.1 \\ 0.4 \end{pmatrix} \subseteq \begin{pmatrix} 0.1 \\ 1 \end{pmatrix} = \vee_{y \in B} \mu_{\tilde{Q}}$$

and

$$\wedge \{\mu_{\tilde{Q}}(x,y), \vee_{y \in B}\{\mu_{\tilde{R}}(x,y)\}\} =$$
$$\begin{pmatrix} 0.1 & 0 \\ 0.4 & 0.2 \end{pmatrix} \subseteq \begin{pmatrix} 0.1 & 0.1 \\ 0.4 & 0.4 \end{pmatrix} = \mu_{\tilde{R}}$$

Then:

$$\tilde{Q} \;\underset{\sim}{\sqsubseteq}\; \tilde{R}$$

Let

$$\tilde{P} = \begin{pmatrix} 0.3 & 0.2 & 0.5 \\ 0.4 & 0.5 & 0.9 \\ 0.1 & 0.2 & 0.7 \end{pmatrix}$$

and

$$\tilde{S} = \begin{pmatrix} 0.3 & 0.2 & 0.4 \\ 0.7 & 0.8 & 0.8 \\ 0.3 & 0.5 & 0.6 \end{pmatrix}$$

We have:

$$\vee_{y \in B} \mu_{\tilde{S}} = \begin{pmatrix} 0.4 \\ 0.8 \\ 0.6 \end{pmatrix} \subseteq \begin{pmatrix} 0.5 \\ 0.9 \\ 0.7 \end{pmatrix} = \vee_{y \in B} \mu_{\tilde{P}}$$

and

$$\wedge \{\mu_{\tilde{P}}(x,y), \vee_{y \in B}\{\mu_{\tilde{S}}(x,y)\}\} =$$
$$\begin{pmatrix} 0.3 & 0.2 & 0.4 \\ 0.4 & 0.5 & 0.8 \\ 0.1 & 0.2 & 0.6 \end{pmatrix} \subseteq \begin{pmatrix} 0.3 & 0.2 & 0.4 \\ 0.7 & 0.8 & 0.8 \\ 0.3 & 0.5 & 0.6 \end{pmatrix} = \mu_{\tilde{S}}$$

Then:

$$\tilde{P} \;\underset{\sim}{\sqsubseteq}\; \tilde{S}$$

Let

$$\tilde{Q} = \begin{pmatrix} 0.1 & 0.2 & 0.4 \\ 0.5 & 0.7 & 0.9 \end{pmatrix}$$

and

$$\tilde{R} = \begin{pmatrix} 0.2 & 0.2 & 0.3 \\ 0.4 & 0.5 & 0.8 \end{pmatrix}$$

$$\tilde{Q} \;\underset{\sim}{\sqsubseteq}\; \tilde{R}$$

$$\wedge \{\mu_{\tilde{Q}}(x,y), \vee_{y \in B}\{\mu_{\tilde{R}}(x,y)\}\} =$$
$$\begin{pmatrix} 0.1 & 0.2 & 0.3 \\ 0.5 & 0.7 & 0.8 \end{pmatrix} \subseteq \begin{pmatrix} 0.2 & 0.2 & 0.3 \\ 0.4 & 0.5 & 0.8 \end{pmatrix} = \mu_{\tilde{R}}$$

Let

$$\tilde{P} = \begin{pmatrix} 0.5 & 0.2 & 0.7 \\ 0.7 & 0 & 0.3 \end{pmatrix}$$

and

$$\tilde{S} = \begin{pmatrix} 0.1 & 0.3 & 0.4 \\ 0.9 & 1 & 0.5 \end{pmatrix}$$

$$\tilde{P} \quad \tilde{\not\sqsubseteq} \quad \tilde{S}$$

$$\vee_{y \in B} \mu_{\tilde{S}} = \begin{pmatrix} 0.4 \\ 1 \end{pmatrix} \not\subseteq \begin{pmatrix} 0.7 \\ 0.7 \end{pmatrix} = \vee_{y \in B} \not\subseteq \mu_{\tilde{P}}$$

29. **Theorem:** The fuzzy relation $\tilde{\sqsubseteq}$ is a partial order.

Fuzzy Demonic Operators and Illustration with Mathematica

In this subsection, we will present fuzzy demonic operators and some of their properties.

30. **Definition.** Let $\tilde{Q}$ and $\tilde{R}$ be fuzzy relations:

Their supremum is $\tilde{Q} \ \tilde{\sqcup} \ \tilde{R}$ and their membership is:

$$\mu_{(\tilde{Q} \tilde{\sqcup} \tilde{R})}(x,y) = [\mu_{\tilde{Q}}(x,y) \vee \mu_{\tilde{R}}(x,y)]$$
$$\wedge [\vee_{y \in B}(\mu_{\tilde{Q}}(x,y))]$$
$$\wedge [\vee_{y \in B}(\mu_{\tilde{R}}(x,y))]$$

and satisfies

$$\vee_{y \in B}\{\mu_{(\tilde{Q} \tilde{\sqcup} \tilde{R})}(x,y)\} = [\vee_{y \in B}(\mu_{\tilde{Q}}(x,y))]$$
$$\wedge [\vee_{y \in B}(\mu_{\tilde{R}}(x,y))].$$

The operator $(\tilde{\sqcup})$ is called *fuzzy demonic union*. This definition is equivalent to the definition ([57]). In other words,

$$Q \sqcup R = (Q \cup R) \cap QL \cap RL$$

if and only if

$$\mu_{(\tilde{Q} \tilde{\sqcup} \tilde{R})}(x,y) = [\mu_{\tilde{Q}}(x,y) \vee \mu_{\tilde{R}}(x,y)]$$
$$\wedge [\vee_{y \in B}(\mu_{\tilde{Q}}(x,y))] \wedge [\vee_{y \in B}(\mu_{\tilde{R}}(x,y))]$$

Their infimum, if it exists, is $\tilde{Q} \ \tilde{\sqcap} \ \tilde{R}$ and their membership is:

$$\mu_{(\tilde{Q} \tilde{\sqcap} \tilde{R})}(x,y) = [\mu_{\tilde{Q}}(x,y) \wedge \mu_{\tilde{R}}(x,y)]$$
$$\vee [\mu_{\tilde{Q}}(x,y) \wedge (1 - \vee_{y \in B}(\mu_{\tilde{R}}(x,y)))]$$

$$\vee [\mu_{\tilde{R}}(x,y) \wedge (1 - \vee_{y \in B}(\mu_{\tilde{Q}}(x,y)))]$$

and it satisfies

$$\vee_{y \in B}\{\mu_{(\tilde{Q} \tilde{\sqcap} \tilde{R})}(x,y)\} = [\vee_{y \in B}(\mu_{\tilde{Q}}(x,y))]$$
$$\vee [\vee_{y \in B}(\mu_{\tilde{R}}(x,y))].$$

The operator $(\tilde{\sqcap})$ is called *fuzzy demonic intersection*. This definition is equivalent to the definition given in ([12, 14, 15, 57, 58, 59, 60]). In other words,

$$Q \sqcap R = Q \cap R \cup Q \cap \overline{RL} \cup R \cap \overline{QL}$$

if and only if

$$\mu_{(\tilde{Q} \tilde{\sqcap} \tilde{R})}(x,y) = [\mu_{\tilde{Q}}(x,y) \wedge \mu_{\tilde{R}}(x,y)]$$
$$\vee [\mu_{\tilde{Q}}(x,y) \wedge (1 - \vee_{y \in B}(\mu_{\tilde{R}}(x,y)))]$$

$$\vee [\mu_{\tilde{R}}(x,y) \wedge (1 - \vee_{y \in B}(\mu_{\tilde{Q}}(x,y)))]$$

For $\tilde{Q} \ \tilde{\sqcap} \ \tilde{R}$ to exist, we have to verify:

$$\mu_{\tilde{L}}(x,y) \subseteq \vee_{y \in B}[(\mu_{\tilde{Q}}(x,y) \vee$$
$$(1 - \vee_{y \in B}\mu_{\tilde{Q}}(x,y)))$$
$$\wedge (\mu_{\tilde{R}}(x,y) \vee (1 - \vee_{y \in B}\mu_{\tilde{R}}(x,y)))].$$

This condition is equivalent to:

$$(\vee_{y \in B}\mu_{\tilde{Q}}(x,y)) \wedge (\vee_{y \in B}\mu_{\tilde{R}}(x,y)) \subseteq$$
$$\vee_{y \in B}(\mu_{\tilde{Q}}(x,y) \wedge \mu_{\tilde{R}}(x,y)),$$

Figure 11. The demonic fuzzy relation $\tilde{Q}$

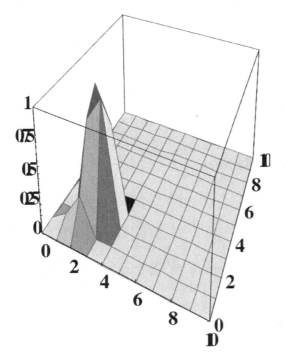

Figure 13. Demonic union of fuzzy relations $\tilde{Q}$ and $\tilde{R}$.

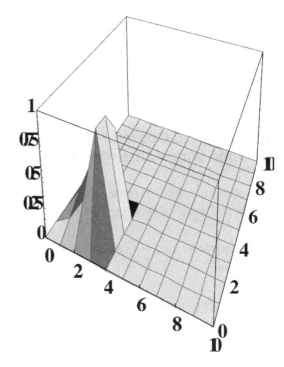

Figure 12. The demonic fuzzy relation $\tilde{R}$

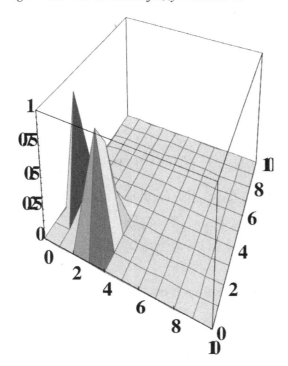

Figure 14. Angelic union of fuzzy relations $\tilde{Q}$ and $\tilde{R}$.

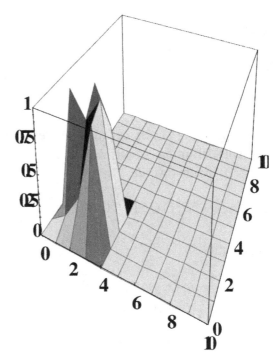

which can be interpreted as follows: the existence condition simply means that on the intersection of their domains, $\tilde{Q}$ and $\tilde{R}$ have to agree for at least one value.

31. Example:

We know that:

$$\tilde{Q} \ \tilde{\sqcup} \ \tilde{R} \neq \tilde{Q} \cup \tilde{R}$$

and

$$\tilde{Q} \ \tilde{\sqcap} \ \tilde{R} \neq \tilde{Q} \cap \tilde{R}$$

Let

$$\tilde{Q} = \begin{pmatrix} 0.1 & 0 & 0.2 \\ 0.3 & 0.8 & 1 \\ 0 & 1 & 0.7 \end{pmatrix},$$

$$\tilde{R} = \begin{pmatrix} 0 & 1 & 0 \\ 0.3 & 0.5 & 0.4 \\ 0.9 & 0.7 & 0.2 \end{pmatrix}$$

$$\tilde{Q} \ \tilde{\sqcup} \ \tilde{R} = \begin{pmatrix} 0.1 & 0.2 & 0.2 \\ 0.3 & 0.5 & 0.5 \\ 0.9 & 0.9 & 0.7 \end{pmatrix}$$

but

$$\tilde{Q} \cup \tilde{R} = \begin{pmatrix} 0.1 & 1 & 0.2 \\ 0.3 & 0.8 & 1 \\ 0.9 & 1 & 0.7 \end{pmatrix}$$

$$\tilde{Q} \ \tilde{\sqcap} \ \tilde{R} = \begin{pmatrix} 0 & 0.8 & 0 \\ 0.3 & 0.5 & 0.5 \\ 0 & 0.7 & 0.2 \end{pmatrix}$$

but

$$\tilde{Q} \cap \tilde{R} = \begin{pmatrix} 0 & 0 & 0 \\ 0.3 & 0.5 & 0.4 \\ 0 & 0.7 & 0.2 \end{pmatrix}$$

Let

$$\tilde{Q} = \begin{pmatrix} 0.3 & 0.1 \\ 0.2 & 0.5 \end{pmatrix}, \ \tilde{R} = \begin{pmatrix} 0.1 & 0 \\ 1 & 0.7 \end{pmatrix}$$

$$\tilde{Q} \ \tilde{\sqcup} \ \tilde{R} = \begin{pmatrix} 0.1 & 0.1 \\ 0.5 & 0.5 \end{pmatrix}$$

but

$$\tilde{Q} \cup \tilde{R} = \begin{pmatrix} 0.3 & 0.1 \\ 1 & 0.7 \end{pmatrix}.$$

$$\tilde{Q} \ \tilde{\sqcap} \ \tilde{R} = \begin{pmatrix} 0.3 & 0.1 \\ 0.5 & 0.5 \end{pmatrix}$$

but

$$\tilde{Q} \cap \tilde{R} = \begin{pmatrix} 0.1 & 0 \\ 0.2 & 0.5 \end{pmatrix}$$

These demonic operations are illustrated respectively by the next figures.

Now we need to define the relative fuzzy implication.

Figure 15. Demonic intersection of fuzzy relations $\tilde{Q}$ and $\tilde{R}$

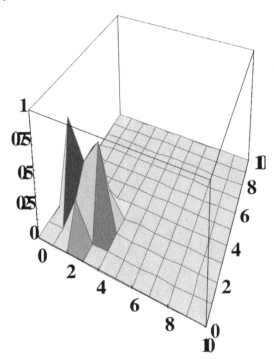

Figure 17. The demonic fuzzy relation $\tilde{Q}$

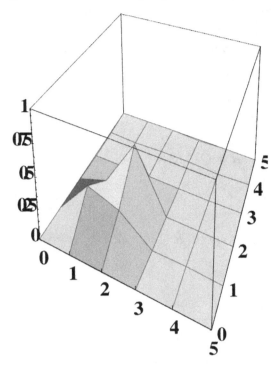

Figure 16. Angelic intersection of fuzzy relations $\tilde{Q}$ and $\tilde{R}$

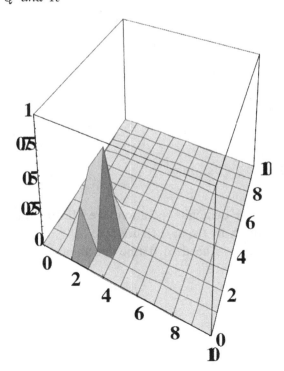

Figure 18. The demonic fuzzy relation $\tilde{R}$

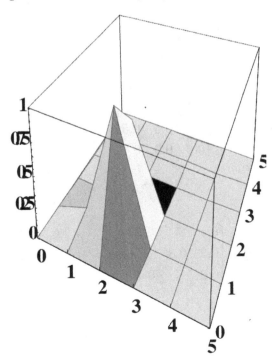

Figure 19. Demonic union of fuzzy relations $\tilde{Q}$ and $\tilde{R}$

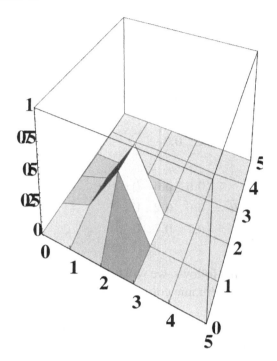

Figure 20. Angelic union of fuzzy relations $\tilde{Q}$ and $\tilde{R}$

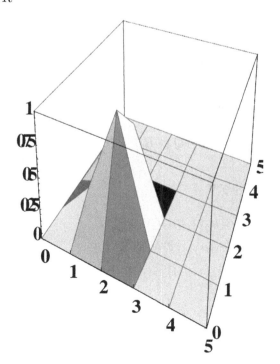

Figure 21. Demonic intersection of fuzzy relations $\tilde{Q}$ and $\tilde{R}$

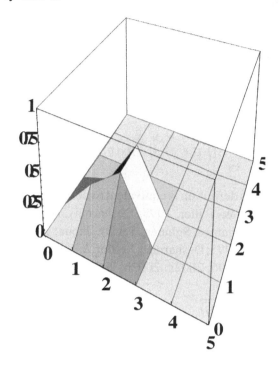

Figure 22. Angelic intersection of fuzzy relations $\tilde{Q}$ and $\tilde{R}$

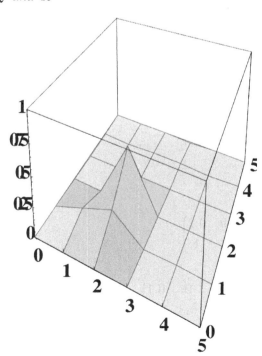

In what follows, we will give our definition of the relative fuzzy implication and some examples.

32. **Definition:** The binary operator $(\tilde{\rhd})$, is called *relative fuzzy implication*, and its a membership function is defined as follows:

$$\mu_{\tilde{Q}\tilde{\rhd}\tilde{R}}(x,z) = 1 - \vee_{y \in B}\{\wedge\{\mu_{\tilde{Q}}(x,y), 1 - \mu_{\tilde{R}}(y,z)\}\}$$

This definition is equivalent to definition (Desharnais & Tchier, 1995; Desharnais, Belkhiter, Ben Mohamed Sghaier, Tchier, Jaoua, Mili, & Zaguia, 1995; Desharnais, Moller, & Tchier, 2000; Tchier, 1996, 2002a, 2002b, 2003). Which is,

$$Q \rhd R \overset{\text{def}}{=} \overline{Q\overline{R}}$$

if and only if

$$\mu_{\tilde{Q}\tilde{\rhd}\tilde{R}}(x,z) = 1 - \vee_{y \in B}\{\wedge\{\mu_{\tilde{Q}}(x,y), 1 - \mu_{\tilde{R}}(y,z)\}\}$$

33. **Example:**

Let

$$\tilde{Q} = \begin{pmatrix} 0 & 0.1 \\ 0.3 & 0.5 \end{pmatrix}$$

and

$$\tilde{R} = \begin{pmatrix} 0.9 & 0.2 \\ 0.7 & 1 \end{pmatrix}.$$

$$\tilde{Q} \ \tilde{\rhd} \ \tilde{R} = \begin{pmatrix} 0 & 0.1 \\ 0.3 & 0.5 \end{pmatrix}$$

Let

$$\tilde{Q} = \begin{pmatrix} 0.1 & 0.2 & 0.4 \\ 0.5 & 0.5 & 1 \\ 0 & 0 & 0.3 \end{pmatrix}$$

and

$$\tilde{R} = \begin{pmatrix} 0.7 & 0.8 & 0.9 \\ 1 & 0 & 0.1 \\ 0.6 & 0.2 & 0.3 \end{pmatrix}$$

$$\tilde{Q} \ \tilde{\rhd} \ \tilde{R} = \begin{pmatrix} 0.6 & 0.6 & 0.6 \\ 0.6 & 0.2 & 0.3 \\ 0.7 & 0.7 & 0.7 \end{pmatrix}$$

In what follows, we will give the definition of the fuzzy demonic composition.

34. **Definition:** The *fuzzy demonic composition* of relations $\tilde{Q}$ and $\tilde{R}$ is $(\tilde{Q} \ \tilde{\square} \ \tilde{R})$, and its membership function is given by:

$$\mu_{\tilde{Q}\tilde{\square}\tilde{R}}(x,y) = \wedge[\vee_{y \in B}\{\wedge\{\mu_{\tilde{Q}}(x,y), \mu_{\tilde{R}}(y,z)\}\}, 1 - \vee_{y \in B}\{\wedge\{\mu_{\tilde{Q}}(x,y), 1 - \vee_{y \in B}(\mu_{\tilde{R}}(x,y))\}\}].$$

This definition is equivalent to:

$$Q \ \square \ R = QR \cap Q \rhd RL$$

if and only if

$$\wedge[\vee_{y \in B}\{\wedge\{\mu_{\tilde{Q}}(x,y), \mu_{\tilde{R}}(y,z)\}\}, 1 - \vee_{y \in B}\{\wedge\{\mu_{\tilde{Q}}(x,y), 1 - \vee_{y \in B}(\mu_{\tilde{R}}(x,y))\}\}]$$

35. **Example.**

a. $\begin{pmatrix} 0.3 & 0.1 \\ 0.2 & 0.5 \end{pmatrix} \tilde{\odot} \begin{pmatrix} 0.1 & 0 \\ 1 & 0.7 \end{pmatrix} = \begin{pmatrix} 0.1 & 0.1 \\ 0.5 & 0.5 \end{pmatrix}$

b. $\begin{pmatrix} 0.1 & 0 & 0.2 \\ 0.3 & 0.8 & 1 \\ 0 & 1 & 0.7 \end{pmatrix} \tilde{\odot} \begin{pmatrix} 0 & 1 & 0 \\ 0.3 & 0.5 & 0.4 \\ 0.9 & 0.7 & 0.2 \end{pmatrix}$

$= \begin{pmatrix} 0.2 & 0.2 & 0.2 \\ 0.5 & 0.5 & 0.4 \\ 0.5 & 0.5 & 0.4 \end{pmatrix}$

Figures 23 and 24 represent the fuzzy demonic composition of two relations.

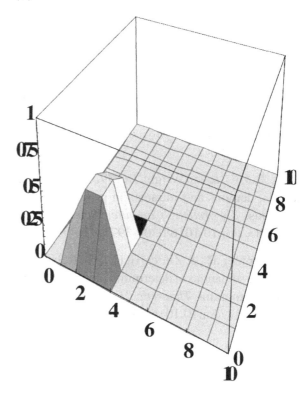

Figure 24. Demonic composition in example(35) (b)

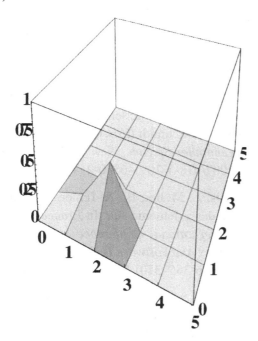

Figure 23. Demonic composition in example(35) (a)

CONCLUSION

In this chapter, we have presented the notion of relational fuzzy calculus specially a fuzzy refinement order ($\tilde{\sqsubseteq}$) also the definitions of the operators associated to this order which are ($\tilde{\rhd}$), fuzzy demonic operators ($\tilde{\sqcap}, \tilde{\sqcup}$) and fuzzy composition ($\tilde{\odot}$) and give some of their properties. These operators have been illustrated by mathematica (*fuzzy logic*).

ACKNOWLEDGMENT

This research project was supported by a grant from the "Research Center of the Center for Female Scientific and Medical Colleges," Deanship of Scientific Research, King Saud University.

REFERENCES

Back, R. J. R. (1981a). Proving total correctness of nondeterministic programs in infinty logic. *Acta Informatica*, *15*(3), 233–249. doi:10.1007/BF00289263.

Back, R. J. R. (1981b). On correct refinement of programs. *Journal of Computer and System Sciences*, *23*(1), 49–68. doi:10.1016/0022-0000(81)90005-2.

Back, R. J. R., & von Wright, J. (1992). Combining angels, demons and miracles in program specifications. *Theoretical Computer Science*, *100*, 365–383. doi:10.1016/0304-3975(92)90309-4.

Berghammer, R., & Zierer, H. (1986). Relational algebraic semantics of deterministic and nondeterministic programs. *Theoretical Computer Science*, *43*, 123–147. doi:10.1016/0304-3975(86)90172-6.

Blockley, D. I. (1981). *The nature of structural design and safety*. Chichester, UK: Academic Press.

Boole, G. (1847). *The mathematical analysis of logic, being an essay toward a calculus of deductive reasoning*. Cambridge, UK: Macmillan.

Boudriga, N., Elloumi, F., & Mili, A. (1992). On the lattice of specifications: Applications to a specification methodology. *Formal Aspects of Computing*, *4*, 544–571. doi:10.1007/BF01211474.

Cao, H., & Chen, G. (1983). Some applications of fuzzy sets of meteorological forecasting. *FSS*, *9*, 1–12. doi:10.1016/S0165-0114(83)80001-3.

Chin, L. H., & Tarski, A. (1951). Distributive and modular laws in the arithmetic of relation algebras. *University of California Publications*, *1*, 341–384.

De Morgan, A. (1856). On the symbols of logic, the theory of the syllogism, and in particular of the copula, and the application of the theory of probabilities to some questions in the theory of evidence. *Trans. of the Cambridge Philosophical Society*, *9*, 79–127.

De Morgan, A. (1864). On the syllogism and on logic in general. *Trans. of the Cambridge Philosophical Society*, *10*, 173–230.

Desharnais, J. (1989). *Abstract relational semantics*. (Thesis). School of Computer Science, Univ. McGill, Montreal, Canada.

Desharnais, J., Baltagi, S., & Chaib-Draa, B. (1994). *Simple weak sufficient conditions for sharpness. Rapport de recherche DIUL-RR-9405*. Universite Laval, Quebec, Canada: Departement d'Informatique.

Desharnais, J., Belkhiter, N., Ben Mohamed Sghaier, S., Tchier, F., Jaoua, A., Mili, A., & Zaguia, N. (1995). Embedding a demonic semilattice in a relation algebra. *Theoretical Computer Science*, *149*(2), 333–360. doi:10.1016/0304-3975(94)00271-J.

Desharnais, J., Mili, A., & Nguyen, T. T. (1997). Refinement and demonic semantics. In C. Brink, W. Khal, & G. Schmidt (Eds.), *Relational methods in Computer Science*. New York: Springer. doi:10.1007/978-3-7091-6510-2_11.

Desharnais, J., Möller, B., & Tchier, F. (2000). Kleene under a demonic star. In *Proceedings of the 8th International Conference on Algebraic Methodology And Software Technology* (LNCS), (Vol. 1816, pp. 355–370). Berlin: Springer-Verlag.

Desharnais, J., & Tchier, F. (1995). *Demonic relational semantics of sequential programs. Rapport de recherche DIUL-RR-9406*. Universite Laval, Quebec, Canada: Departement d'Informatique.

Dijkstra, E. W., & Feijn, W. (1988). *Predicate calculus and program semantics*. Reading, MA: Addison-Wesley.

Dubois, D., & Prade, H. (1982a). A class of fuzzy measures based on triangular norms. *International Journal of General Systems, 8*, 43–61. doi:10.1080/03081078208934833.

Feijen, W. H. (1988). *A bagatelle (for files)*. Austin, TX: University of Texas at Austin.

Freyd, P., & Scedrov, A. (1990). *Categories, allegories*. Amsterdam: North-Holland.

Furusawa, H. (1998). *Algebraic formalisations of fuzzy relations and their representation theorems*. Department of Informatics Kyushu University Fukuoka.

Goguen, J. A. (2009). L-fuzzy sets. *JMAA, 18*, 145–174.

Goguen, J. A. (n.d.). The logic of inexact concepts. *Synthese, 19*, 325-373.

Gunther, S., & Thomas, S. (1992). *Relations and graphs: Discrete mathematics for computer scientists*. Berlin: Springer-Verlag.

Hoare, C. A. R. et al. (1987). Laws of programming. *Communications of the ACM, 30*, 672–686. doi:10.1145/27651.27653.

Jonsson, B. (1982). Varieties of relation algebras. *Algebra Universalis, 15*, 273–298. doi:10.1007/BF02483728.

Jonsson, B. (1991). The theory of binary relations. *Algebairc Logic, Colloq. Math. Soc.*, 245–292.

Jonsson, B., & Tarski, A. (1948). Representation problems for relation algebra. *Bulletin of the American Mathematical Society*, 80.

Jonsson, B., & Tarski, A. (1951). Boolean algebras with operators, part I. *American Journal of Mathematics, 73*, 891–939. doi:10.2307/2372123.

Jonsson, B., & Tarski, A. (1952). Boolean algebras with operators, part II. *American Journal of Mathematics, 74*, 127–162. doi:10.2307/2372074.

Kahl, W. (2001). Parallel composition and decomposition of specifications. *Information Sciences, 139*, 197–220. doi:10.1016/S0020-0255(01)00165-7.

Kaufmann, A. (1975). *Introduction to the theory of fuzzy subsets*. New York: Academic Press.

Kaufmann, A. (1977). *Theorie des sous-ensembles flous (fuzzy set theory)*. Paris: Masson.

Kawahara, Y. (1990). Pushout-complements and basic concepts of grammars in topoi. *Theoretical Computer Science, 77*, 267–289. doi:10.1016/0304-3975(90)90171-D.

Kawahara, Y. (1995). Relational set theory. *Lecture Notes in Computer Science, 953*, 44–58. doi:10.1007/3-540-60164-3_19.

Kawahara, Y., & Furusawa, H. (1995). *An algebraic formatisation of fuzzy relations*. Paper presented at second International Seminar on Relational Methods in Computer Science. Rio de Janeiro, Brazil.

Kawahara, Y., & Mizoguchi, Y. (1992). Categorical assertion semantics in topoi. *Adv. in Software Sci. and Technol., 4*, 137–150.

Kawahara, Y., & Mizoguchi, Y. (1994). Relational structures and their partial morphisms in the view of single pushout rewriting. *Lecture Notes in Computer Science, 776*, 218–233. doi:10.1007/3-540-57787-4_14.

Maddux, R. D. (1991a). Introductory course on relations algebras, finite-dimensional cylindric algebras, and their interconnections. *Colloq. Math. Soc., 54*, 361–392.

Maddux, R. D. (1991b). The origin of relation algebras in the developement and axiomatization of the calculus of relations. *Studia Logica, 50*, 421–455. doi:10.1007/BF00370681.

Mamdani, E. H. (1981). *Advances in the linguistic syntesis of fuzzy controllers in fuzzy reasoning and its applications*. London: Academic Press.

Mili, A. (1983). A relational approach to the design of deterministic programs. *Acta Inf.*, 315-328.

Mili, A., Desharnais, J., & Mili, F. (1987). Relational heuristics for the design of deterministic programs. *Acta Informatica, 24*(3), 239–276. doi:10.1007/BF00265990.

Morgan, C. C., & Robinson. (1987). Specification statements and refinement. *IBM Journal of Research and Development, 32*(5), 546–555. doi:10.1147/rd.315.0546.

Morris, J. M. (1987). A theoretical basis for stepwise refinement and the programming calculus. *Theoretical Computer Science, 9*, 287–306.

Pedrycz, W., & Gomides, F. (1998). *An Introduction to fuzzy sets: Analysis and design*. Academic Press.

Peirce, C. S. (1880). On the algebra of logic. *American Journal of Mathematics, 3*, 15–57. doi:10.2307/2369442.

Peirce, C. S. (1885). On the algebra of logic: A contribution to the philosophy of notation. *American Journal of Mathematics, 7*, 180–202. doi:10.2307/2369451.

Ross, T. J. (2004). *Fuzzy logic with engineering applications*. Albuquerque, NM: University of New Mexico.

Schmidt, G., Kahl, W., & Brink, C. (1997). *Relational methods in computer science*. Berlin: Springer.

Schmidt, G., & Ströhlein, T. (1985). Relations algebras: Concept of points and representability. *Disc. Math., 54*, 83–92. doi:10.1016/0012-365X(85)90064-0.

Schmidt, G., & Ströhlein, T. (1989). *Relationen und graphen*. Berlin: Springer-Verlag. doi:10.1007/978-3-642-83608-4.

Schmidt, G., & Ströhlein, T. (1993). *Relations and graphs*. Berlin: Springer-Verlag. doi:10.1007/978-3-642-77968-8.

Ströhlein, E. (1895). *Vorlesungen über die algebra der logik(exacte logik)*. Leipzig, Germany: Teubner.

Tamura, S., Higuchi, S., & Tanaka, K. (1971). Pattern classification based on fuzzy relations. *IEEE Transactions on Systems, Man, and Cybernetics, 1*, 61–66. doi:10.1109/TSMC.1971.5408605.

Tarski, A. (1941). On the calculus of relations. *J. Symb. Log., 6*(3), 73–89. doi:10.2307/2268577.

Tchier, F. (1996). *Sémantiques relationnelles démoniaques et vérification de boucles non déterministes. (Theses of doctorat)*. Département de Mathématiques et de statistique. Canada: Université Laval.

Tchier, F. (2002a). Demonic semantics by monotypes. In *Proceedings of the International Arab Conference on Information Technology (Acit2002)*. University of Qatar.

Tchier, F. (2002b). Demonic relational semantics of compound diagrams. In J. Desharnais, M. Frappier, & W. MacCaull (Eds.), Relational Methods in computer Science: The Québec Seminar, (pp. 117-140). Methods Publishers.

Tchier, F. (2003). While loop demonic relational semantics monotype/residual style. In *Proceedings of the 2003 International Conference on Software Engineering Research and Practice (SERP'03)*. Las Vegas, NV: SERP.

Tchier, F. (2004). Demonic semantics: Using monotypes and residuals. *International Journal of Mathematics and Mathematical Sciences, 3*, 135–160. doi:10.1155/S016117120420415X.

Vila, M. A., & Delgado, M. (1983). On medical diagnosis using possibility measures. *FSS, 10*, 211–222. doi:10.1016/S0165-0114(83)80116-X.

Whitehead, A. N., & Russell, B. (1910). *Principia mathematica* (Vol. I). Cambridge, UK: Cambridge Univ. Press.

Wirth, N. (1971). Program development by stepwise refinement. *Communications of the ACM, 14*(4), 221–227. doi:10.1145/362575.362577.

Zadeh, L. A. (1965). Fuzzy sets. *Information and Control, 8*, 338–353. doi:10.1016/S0019-9958(65)90241-X.

Zadeh, L. A. (1971). Similarity relations and fuzzy orderings. *Information Sciences, 3*, 177–206. doi:10.1016/S0020-0255(71)80005-1.

Zadeh, L. A. (1973). *The concept of a linguistic variable and its application to approximate reasoning*. Memorandum ERL-M 411 Berkeley.

Zadeh, L. A. (1975). Calculus of fuzzy restrictions. In Zadeh et al. (Eds.), *Fuzzy Sets and Their Applications to Cognitive and Decision Processes*. New York: Academic Press.

Zimmermann, H. J. (1990). *Fuzzy set theory and its applications* (2nd ed.). Boston: Kluwer Academic Publishers.

Chapter 13
ONTO–KMS–TEC:
An Ontology–Based Knowledge Management Framework to Teach Engineering Courses

C. R. Rene Robin
Jerusalem College of Engineering, India

D. Doreen Hepzibah Miriam
Loyola-ICAM College of Engineering and Technology, India

G. V. Uma
Madras Institute of Technology, India

ABSTRACT

Knowledge management tools have been used in higher educational institutions for years to improve the effectiveness of teaching methodologies. Knowledge management in pedagogical includes processes of knowledge discovery, capture, storage, retrieval, sharing, and understanding. According to Pundt and Bishr, knowledge management aims at facilitating knowledge flow and utilization across every beneficeiary, such as faculty members and students. An ontology can be used to support knowledge retrieval, store, and sharing domain knowledge. The framework and the case studies described in this chapter detail how the knowledge of an engineering subject can be effectively retrieved, stored, and shared among the teachers and the students.

INTRODUCTION

In general, the knowledge management system addresses knowledge gathering, knowledge organization, knowledge refinement, and knowledge distribution. The knowledge gathering deals with

DOI: 10.4018/978-1-4666-4229-4.ch013

acquisition and collection of knowledge to be managed. The knowledge organization imposing a structure on the knowledge acquired in order to manage it effectively. The knowledge refinement will also be called as knowledge maintaining includes correcting, updating, adding, and deleting knowledge. Finally, the knowledge distribution is nothing but bringing the knowledge to the professionals who need it. This chapter deals with how the knowledge of engineering subjects is gathered, organized, refined and distributed. The framework described in this chapter uses a hybrid technique encompasses various mechanism for gathering, organizing, refining and distributing knowledge

The artificial intelligence area has developed techniques for representing knowledge in forms that can be exploited by computational procedures and heuristics. The knowledge of a domain is normally available in any one of the forms such as structured, semi-structured or unstructured. In order to make such knowledge portable and sharable, it is necessary to have an effective elicitation method, a useful representation scheme, and an e-learning system to demonstrate and share such knowledge. In order to capture, represent, and organize this knowledge, we need to find a way to group, index, or categorize it in some way. When the question for classifying and representing the knowledge arose, it was natural to think about building of an ontology. Ontology has been developed to offer a commonly agreed understanding of a domain that is required for knowledge representation, knowledge exchange and reuse across domains. Ontology organizes information into taxonomies of terms and shows the relationships between them.

Emphasizing on the profound importance of risk management in the IT industry, the need of the hour is to educate potential software engineers. Hence a framework for ontology based knowledge management system is proposed and implemented, that uses an underlying ontology to organize course content based on semantics. It aims to periodically update the knowledge presented by the system to keep track of current trends in the learning domain. The system is not only used to educate the students but also focuses on providing an innovative tool to budding engineers in order to equip them for the IT industry and also intends to serve as a reference for professionals working on software projects. Figure 1 shows the architectural diagram for ONTO-KMS-TEC.

LITERATURE REVIEW

Knowledge Management

It is known that "knowledge management is an approach to discovering, capturing, and reusing both tacit (in people's heads) and explicit (digital- or paper-based) knowledge as well as the cultural and technological means of enabling the knowledge management process to be successful

Figure 1. Architectural diagram of ONTO-KMS-TEC

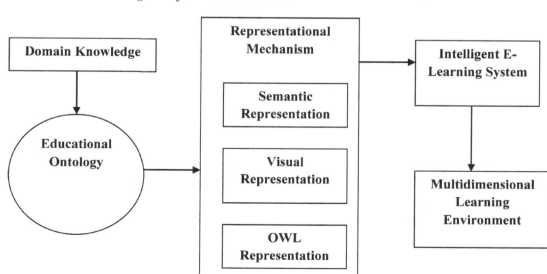

(Russell Records, 2005)". Recently, ontologies have become a popular research topic in many areas, including electronic learning, knowledge management, knowledge engineering, and natural language processing. This chapter focuses on the ontology based knowledge management framework to teach engineering courses. For knowledge management system, ontology can be regarded as the classification of knowledge. Ontologies are different from traditional search engines that directly search for the contents of data. Ontologies are metadata that provide the search engine with the functionality of a semantic match (Youn et al., n.d.). Typically, an ontology consists of hierarchical description of important concepts in domain and the descriptions of the properties of each concept.

ONTOLOGY

Knowledge is central in learning; learners consume content to acquire knowledge. Knowledge is also important for the content developer, as content can be an elaboration of explicitly represented knowledge, and therefore a central ingredient for the development of content. Knowledge engineering addresses the structuring and representation of knowledge (Sowa, 2000). Ontologies have emerged as a central technique (Daconta et al., 2003) for knowledge integration, sharing and reuse. Ontology is a formal representation of knowledge as a set of concepts within a domain, and the relationships between those concepts, in terms of computer science and information science. It is used to reason about the entities within that domain, and may be used to describe the domain. From the artificial intelligence point of view, ontology is a formal, explicit specification of a shared conceptualization (Gruber, 1993). Ontologies help us to make the knowledge that is represented in learning content explicit. Ontologies can fill the gap between authors and content, and

instruction representations in authoring systems (Mizoguchi & Bourdeau, 2000). Ontology (Wang, et al., 2010) is not just a hierarchical collection of concepts with parent-child relation. In recent years Ontologies (Brewster et al. 2007) have become the knowledge representation media of choice for a range of computer science specialities, including the Semantic Web, Agents, and Bio-informatics. Ontologies can be used to represent knowledge about content, supporting instructors in creating content, or learners in accessing content in a knowledge-guided way.

In computer and information science, ontology (Gruber et al., n.d.) is defined as a shared explicit specification of conceptualization and relationship in certain domain knowledge. Ontologies are formalized vocabularies of terms, often covering a specific domain and shared by a community of users. They include machine-interpretable definitions of basic concepts in the domain, and the relations between them.

An ontology may contain classes, properties, axioms and relationships between concepts in domain knowledge (Noy et al., n.d.). Developing an ontology involves the following steps:

1. Acquiring domain knowledge.
2. Designing its conceptual structure.
3. Ontology implementation and formalization.
4. Evaluation (verification and validation) and documentation.

The design architecture for the required ontology can also be sketched out manually with the identified concepts and properties. In order to reduce implementation efforts, the Protégé platform, a scalable and integrated framework for ontological engineering, has been used to construct the ontology. The constructed ontology has been represented in owl format, which makes it more machine understandable. Then the semantic representation of the knowledge has been made using the OWL document generator, which automatically generates a set of documents from the ontology. In order to understand the knowledge in more detailed way again the ontology has been visualized using ontoviz tool.

EDUCATIONAL ONTOLOGY

While ontologies exist for many subject domains, their quality and suitability for the educational context might be unclear. For numerous subjects, ontologies do not exist. The following paragraphs explain a few exiting educational ontologies.

An Ontology for C Programming (Sosnovsky et al., 2005) was developed for the purpose of education. The authors proposed a stepwise algorithm for ontology development, and implemented this algorithm for the creation of the educational ontology for C programming. A created ontology does not simply replicate the hierarchical structure of the C language standard, but reflects the authors' vision on what is important in studying C, and accumulates their experience of teaching C-related programming courses.

Cryptography Ontology (Takahashi, 2005) defines various concepts in the cryptographic domain and the relations between them. In this ontology, the relation between words (concepts) important in the cryptographic domain is organized. The related two words are connected by an arrow and the name of the relation is attached to the arrow. There exist relations such as subClassof, has, type, equivalentClass, etc. This ontology can be used during the learning process, to provide the learner with intelligible learning information for cryptography. In practice, this ontology is applicable to cases where a search for (the meaning of) a word is performed, a review of the portion mistaken in an assessment (test) is performed, etc.

Software Testing Ontology (Zhu et al, 2004), is designed based on the domain knowledge of software testing to mediate the communications between the agents. It was represented in XML to codify the knowledge of software testing for the agents' processing of messages. The representation in XML for run-time communications between agents achieved a flexibility of modification and extendibility very well. However, during the testing and validation of the prototype system, it is realised that XML representation is at a rather low level of abstraction. It is not very readable for domain experts to validate the ontology.

E-R Model Ontology (Boyce, 2007), an interesting feature in the ER-diagram ontology is the use of reification. While reification is used in Semantic Web languages such as RDF (W3C, 2004) to enable statements to be made about statements, it is used slightly differently when structuring an ontology. The ER-diagram ontology, shows that it is permissible for the representation of some of the concepts in a graph, instead of a tree structure.

An ontology-based course enables the e-learning to do efficient semantic querying and navigation through the learning content, and it is easily reusable, shareable and interchangeable (Jiang, 2008). This paper gives an idea to explore and to create an ontology-oriented course of Computer Networks (CN) based on topic maps, it is for the organization and retrieval of online information in the CN Web based course. It introduced the designing of the educational ontology of CN and the development of the ontology--based course of CN.

An Upper Level Ontology for Chemistry (Batchelor, 2008) was developed by taking the ChEBI (Chemical Entities of Biological Interest) as a starting point. The author has presented an upper-level ontology for chemistry based on an analysis of the foundational and disguised foundational relations in ChEBI. The case for an upper-level ontology for chemistry is therefore twofold; first, defining what the objects referred to in an ontology actually are, allows the curators to set its scope and determine the genera for high-level genus–differential definitions; second, it allows the types in the ontology to be reused safely by other ontologys, with scope for overlapping.

Finally, an ontology model of software engineering (Wongthongtham, et al., 2008, 2009; Dillon et al., 2008) representing the software engineering knowledge is reviewed. The Software Engineering Ontology (SEONTO) is constructed, based on the fundamental knowledge related to software engineering described in the textbook entitled Software Engineering by Sommerville (2004) and the white paper, Software Engineering Body of Knowledge (SWEBOK), by the IEEE (Bourque, 2003). The definition of SEONTO, its components and its characteristics are clearly presented in this paper. Its users are software engineers sharing domain knowledge as well as the instance knowledge of software engineering.

Marko Grobelnik, et al. (2008) demonstrated one possible scenario about exploiting contextual information during a semi-automatic ontology construction from text corpora. Boyce and Pahl (2007) presented a method for domain experts rather than ontology engineers to develop ontologies for use in the delivery of courseware content.

Building Domain Ontologies from a Text for Educational Purposes (Zouaq et al., 2008) presents a semiautomatic framework, that aims to produce domain concept maps from a text, and then to derive domain ontologies from these concept maps. This methodology particularly targets the e-learning and Artificial Intelligence in Education (AIED) communities, as they need such structures to sustain the production of e-learning resources tailored to learners' needs. It details the steps to transform textual resources, particularly textual Learning Objects (LOs), into domain concept maps, and it explains the transformation of abstract structure into a formal domain ontology. The paper bridges the gap between e-learning and Intelligent Tutoring Systems, by providing a common domain model.

ONTOLOGY CONSTRUCTION METHOD

This sub topic describes the processes of conceptualization and specification, or the building of the educational ontology named Software Risk Management Ontology (SRMONTO). Figure 2 shows the design architecture used for the construction of the SRMONTO.

The process of constructing SRMONTO has the following five stages

Figure 2. Design architecture of the ontology construction process

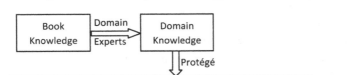

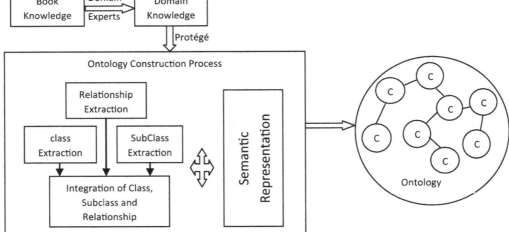

- Studying domain-related issues.
- Building a methodology for developing an ontology.
- Developing sub ontologies for the target ontology.
- Merging of sub ontologies yields the target ontology.
- Implementing the environment and investigating the applicability of the environment.

The required concepts, the semantic description of the concepts and the interrelationship among the concepts along with all other ontological components has to be collected from various literatures subject experts. From which, a taxonomy has to be constructed by using the property 'isA'. Taxonomy is a way of classifying or categorizing a set of things using a hierarchical structure, which is a tree like structure, with the most general category as the root of the tree. Each node, including the root note, is information entity that represents some object in the real world that is being modeled. The hierarchical structure i.e. the taxonomical arrangement of concepts has been structured by considering the following rules

Rule 1: Concepts of one level should be linked to their parent concept by the relationships "is-a". This means that concepts of one layer should have similar nature and level of granularity.

Rule 2: Cross-links should be avoided as much as possible.

The taxonomical arrangement of identified concepts of software risk identification is presented in Figure 3.

The corresponding design architectures for the ontology can also be sketched out manually with identified concepts and different types of properties. Figure 4 shows the overview of a portion of the design architecture of the Software Risk Iden-

tification Ontology (SRIONTO), sketched out manually, with 86 concepts and four different properties.

When a new ontology is going to be built, the following questions arise related to the methodologies.

- Which tools and languages to be used in its development process.
- Which language should I use to implement my ontology?

Seongwook Youn et al have made a survey about Ontology Development Tools and the results are given in the Table 1 and Table 2. It gives basic idea about the tools.

In order to reduce the implementation efforts, the authors suggest the Protégé platform, a scalable and integrated framework for ontological engineering, can be used to construct the ontology.

Figure 5 shows the snapshot of the construction of the Software Risk Analysis ontology, an educational ontology developed by the authors using protégé tool. As part of this construction a total of 13 risk analysis techniques were reviewed, and a full fledged ontology for software risk analysis has been developed with more than fifty concepts. There were seven object properties such as *"KindOf", "IsA", "BasedOn", "HasA", "DependsOn", "isPartOf"* and *"MayBe",* used to relate the identified concepts. The "RiskAnalysis" concept is at the highest level of this ontology. At the next level there are three concepts, namely, "Composition_exit_int" "Proposed_Methodologies" and "Factors". At the next level, there are three concepts, which form the sub-class of "Proposed_Methodologies". These are the *"Qualitative_Methodologies", "Tree_Based_Techniques",* and *"Techniques_For_Dynamic_System."*

The constructed ontology has been represented in the OWL format, which makes it more

Figure 3. Portion of the taxonomy of software risk identification concepts

1. Product Engineering
   1.1. Requirements
      1.1.1. Stability
      1.1.2. Completeness
      1.1.3. Clarity
      1.1.4. Validity
      1.1.5. Feasibility
      1.1.6. Precedent
      1.1.7. Scale
   1.2. Design
      1.2.1. Functionality
      1.2.2. Difficulty
      1.2.3. Interfaces
      1.2.4. Performance
      1.2.5. Testability
      1.2.6. H/W Constraints
      1.2.7. Non-Developmental S/w
   1.3. Engg. Specialties
      1.3.1. Maintainability
      1.3.2. Reliability
      1.3.3. Safety
      1.3.4. Security
      1.3.5. Human Factors
      1.3.6. Specifications

2. Development Environment
   2.1. Development Process
      2.1.1. Formality
      2.1.2. Suitability
      2.1.3. Process Control
      2.1.4. Familiarity
   2.2. Management Methods
      2.2.1. Monitoring
      2.2.2. Personnel
      2.2.3. Quality Assurance
   2.3. Work Environment
      2.3.1. Quality Attitude
      2.3.2. Cooperation
      2.3.3. Communication
      2.3.4. Morale
3. Program Constraints
   3.1. Resources
      3.1.1. Schedule
      3.1.2. Staff
      3.1.3. Budget
      3.1.4. Facilities
   3.2. Contract
      3.1.1. Type of Contract
      3.1.2. Restrictions
      3.1.3. Dependencies

machine understandable. Web Ontology Language (OWL) (Grigoris, et al., 2003; McGuinness, et. al., 2004; Dean, et al., 2003; Patel-Schneider, et al., 2004), which is a language for processing Web information and provides a richer integration and interoperability of data among communities and domains.

All classes in software risk identification ontology are subclasses of class 'Thing'. Its notation description is the same with an ontology class notation. OWL documents are usually called OWL Ontologies, and the elements of which are Namespaces, Housekeeping, Classes, Properties, Property restrictions, Enumerations and Instances. Because OWL is written in RDF, and RDF is written in XML, so OWL documents start with several namespace declarations using RDF, XML Namespace, and URIs. rdf:RDF is the root element of a OWL Ontology, and also specifies a number of namespaces. Figure 6 shows the Namespace declaration of the developed ontology.

After rdf:RDF, some declarations to identify namespaces associated with this Ontology could be added. The effect of all of these namespaces

Figure 4. Portion of the design architecture of the SRIONTO

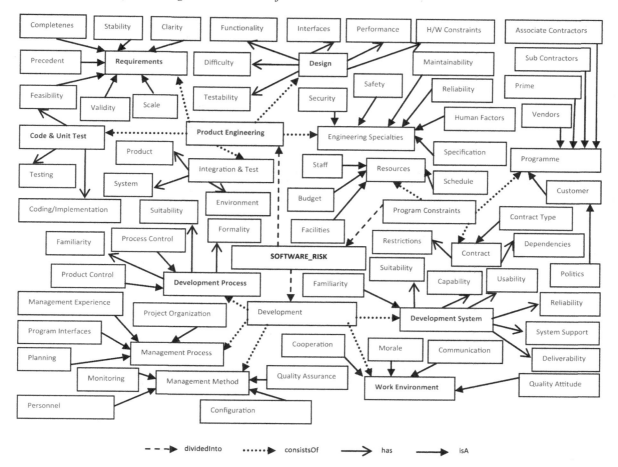

is that such prefixes as owl and rdf should be understood as referring to things drawn from following namespaces, as for example http://www.w3.org/2002/07/owl#.

In OWL, classes are defined by using an owl:Class element that is a subclass of rdfs:Class.

Figure 7 shows the owl representation of Super Class and Sub Class relationship. The concept "Design" which is the subclass of the concept "Product_Engineering" and its data type, i.e. string are represented.

One of the power elements of OWL is a "owl:disjointWith", which is missing from RDFS, and is used to disjoint one class from others. "owl:equivalentClass" is another element that could be used to establish equivalence between classes. Along with the elements discussed above, there are two more predefined classes, such as owl:Thing (which defines everything) and owl:Nothing, which is empty set. A fragment of OWL representation of SRMONTO is shown in Figure 8.

In OWL it is possible to talk about Boolean combinations such as union, intersection, or complement of classes. For example it can be said that "Stability", "Completeness", and "Validity" are collection of "Risk_Factors".

Then the semantic representation of the knowledge has been made, using the OWL document generator, which automatically generates a set of documents from the ontology. Since ontologies provide semantic Web agents with the background

Table 1. Comparison of various ontology editors

Tool	Import Format	Export Format	Graph View	Consistency Check	Multi-User	Web Support	Merging
Protégé 2000	XML, RDF(S), XML Schema	XML, RDF(S), XML Schema, FLogic, CLIPS, Java html	Via plug-ins like Graph-Viz and Jambalaya	Via plug-ins like PAL and FaCT	Limited (Multi-user capability added to it in 2.0 version)	Via Protégé-OWL plug-in	Via Anchor-PROMPT plug-in
OilEd	RDF(S), OIL, DAML+OIL	RDF(S), OIL, DAML+OIL, SHIQ, dotty, html	No	Via FaCT	No	Very limited namespaces	No
Apollo	OCML, CLOS	OCML, CLOS	No	Yes	No	No	No
RDFedt	RDF(S), OIL, DAML, SHOE	RDF(S), OIL, DAML, SHOE	No	Only checks writing mistakes	No	Via RSS (RDF Site Summary)	?
OntoLingua	IDL, KIF	KIF, CLIPS, IDL, OKBC syntax, Prolog syntax	No	Via Chimaera	Via write-only locking, user access levels	Yes	?
OntoEdit (Free version)	XML, RDF(S), FLogic and DAML+OIL	XML, RDF(S), FLogic and DAML+OIL	Yes	Yes	No	Yes	?
WebODE	RDF(S), UML, DAML+OIL and OWL	RDF(S), UML, DAML+OIL, OWL, PROLOG, X-CARIN, Java/Jess	Form based graphical user interface	Yes	By synchronization, authentication and access restriction	Yes	Via ODE-merge
KAON	RDF(S)	RDF(S)	No	Yes	By concurrent access control	Via KAON portal	No
ICOM	XML, UML	XML, UML	Yes	Via FaCT	No	No	With inter-ontology mapping
DOE	XSLT, RDF(S), OIL, DAML+OIL, OWL and CGXML	XSLT, RDF(S), OIL, DAML+OIL, OWL and CGXML	No	Via type inheritance and detection of cycles in hierarchies	No	Load ontology via URL	No
WebOnto	OCML	OCML, GXL, RDF(S) and OIL	Yes	Yes	With global write-only locking	Web based	?
Medius VOM	XML Schema, RDF and DAML+OIL	XML Schema, RDF and DAML+OIL	UML diagrams via Rose	With a set of ontology authoring wizards	Network based	Via read-only browser support from Rose	Limited (only native Rose model)
LinKFactory	XML, RDF(S), DAML+OIL and OWL	XML, RDF(S), DAML+OIL, OWL and html	No	Yes	Yes	Yes	Yes
K-Infinity	RDF	RDF	With Graph editor	Yes	Network based	No	?

Table 2. Comparison of various ontology editors

	Collaborative Working	Ontology Library	Inference Engine	Exception Handling	Ontology Storage	Extensibility	Availability
Protégé 2000	No	Yes	With PAL	No	File & DBMS (JDBC)	Via plug-ins	Free
OilEd	No	Yes	With FaCT	No	File	No	Free
Apollo	No	Yes	No	No	Files	Via plug-ins	Free
RDFedt	No	No	No	Yes	Files	No	Free
OntoLingua	Yes	Yes	No	No	Files	No	Free
OntoEdit	No	No	No	No	File	Via plug-ins	Free
WebODE	Yes	No	Prolog	No	DBMS (JDBC)	Via plug-ins	Free
KAON	?	Yes	Yes	No	?	No	Free
ICOM	No	?	Yes	No	DBMS	Yes	Free
DOE	No	No	Yes	No	File	No	Free
WebOnto	Yes	Yes	Yes	No	File	No	Free Web access
Medius VOM	Yes	Yes (IEEE SUO)	Yes	?	?	Yes	Commercial
LinKFactory	Yes	Yes	Yes	No	DBMS	Yes	Commercial
K-Infinity	Yes	Yes	Yes	?	DBMS	No	Commercial

Figure 5. Development of the SRAONTO with the Protégé editor

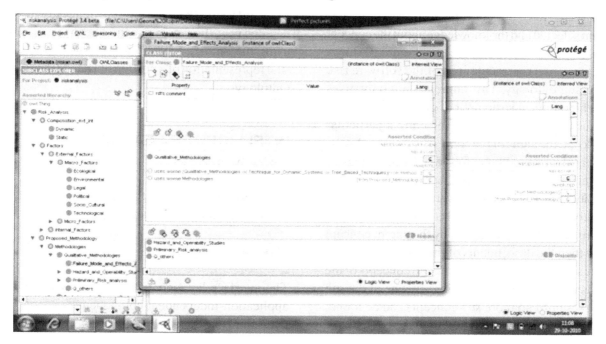

Figure 6. Representation of namespace declaration

```
<rdf:RDF
    xmlns:rdf="http://www.w3.org/1999/02/22-rdf-syntax-ns#"
    xmlns:xsd="http://www.w3.org/2001/XMLSchema#"
    xmlns:rdfs="http://www.w3.org/2000/01/rdf-schema#"
    xmlns:owl="http://www.w3.org/2002/07/owl#"
```

Figure 7. Sample representation for SuperClass-SubClass relationship

```
<owl:Class rdf:about="#Design">
<rdfs:subClassOf rdf:resource="#Product_Engineering"/> <rdfs:comment
rdf:datatype="http://www.w3.org/2001/XMLSchema#string"   >The translation of requirements into an
effective design within project and operational constraints</rdfs:comment>   </owl:Class>
```

knowledge about domain concepts and their relationships, using it in knowledge representation will become more effective. Figure 9 shows the snapshot of the main page used for the semantic representation of the software risk management knowledge. On the left side, all the major areas of software risk management are displayed. The desired knowledge can be obtained by selecting the area. Here, the concept 'Risk Analysis' has been selected and the knowledge about the concept has been effectively represented. Figure 10 shows the semantic representations of the software risk tracking ontology. This approach not only gives the hierarchical structure but gives four different types of knowledge. After selecting a particular concept, the name of the concept is displayed at the top as the 'class' name, followed by the semantic description of the concept. Then, the taxonomical arrangement of the domain starting from the top level concept to the selected concept, is displayed from the ontology followed by the parent concept and then the descendents of the selected concept. The system will find out all the sub concepts of the selected concepts by selecting any one of the sub classes until no more sub concepts can be found.

In Figure 11, the semantic representation of stack, a concept of data structures onltology has been developed by the authors is listed. It contains the links to its superclass 'Abstract data type', its relations like 'hasimplementation', 'has operations', 'has states', 'has terminology' etc. It also contains the list of disjoint/sibling classes and its domains.

In order to understand the knowledge in a more detailed way, the ontology can be been visualized using the ontoviz tool. Figure 12 shows the visual representation of a portion of Data Structures Ontology.

INTELLIGENT E-LEARNING ENVIRONMENT

The overall architecture of an intelligent ontology-based E-learning tool is shown in Figure 13.

Interface Layer

The interface layer contains the following three application-independent components:

Figure 8. Portion of SRMONTO represented in OWL format

```
<?xml version="1.0"?>
<rdf:RDF
   xmlns:rdf="http://www.w3.org/1999/02/22-rdf-syntax-ns#"
   xmlns:xsd="http://www.w3.org/2001/XMLSchema#"
   xmlns:rdfs="http://www.w3.org/2000/01/rdf-schema#"
   xmlns:owl="http://www.w3.org/2002/07/owl#"
   xmlns="http://www.owl-ontologies.com/unnamed.owl#"
  xml:base="http://www.owl-ontologies.com/unnamed.owl">
  <owl:Ontology rdf:about=""/>
  <owl:Class rdf:ID="Dependencies">
   <rdfs:subClassOf>
     <owl:Class rdf:ID="Contract"/>
   </rdfs:subClassOf>
   <rdfs:comment rdf:datatype="http://www.w3.org/2001/XMLSchema#string"
   >This attribute refers to the possible contractual dependencies on outside contractors or vendors,
customer-furnished equipment or software, or other outside products and services.</rdfs:comment>
  </owl:Class>

                                             ...
<owl:FunctionalProperty rdf:about="#Risk_Factors">
   <rdfs:label rdf:datatype="http://www.w3.org/2001/XMLSchema#string"
   >Risk Factors</rdfs:label>
   <rdfs:comment rdf:datatype="http://www.w3.org/2001/XMLSchema#string"
   >a. Stability, Quality, Functionality, Schedule, Integration, Design, Testing </rdfs:comment>
   <rdf:type rdf:resource="http://www.w3.org/2002/07/owl#DatatypeProperty"/>
   <rdfs:domain>
    <owl:Class>
     <owl:unionOf rdf:parseType="Collection">
      <owl:Class rdf:about="#Stability"/>
      <owl:Class rdf:about="#Completeness"/>
      <owl:Class rdf:about="#Validity"/>
     </owl:unionOf>
    </owl:Class>
   </rdfs:domain>
   <rdfs:range rdf:resource="http://www.w3.org/2001/XMLSchema#string"/>
</owl:FunctionalProperty>
</rdf:RDF>
<!-- Created with Protege (with OWL Plugin 3.4, Build 125) http://protege.stanford.edu -->
```

Figure 9. Main page contains five major categories of the domain

SOFTWARE RISK MANAGEMENT
Class: Risk_Analysis
Super Classes
Usage
Class Description/Definition (Necessary Conditions)

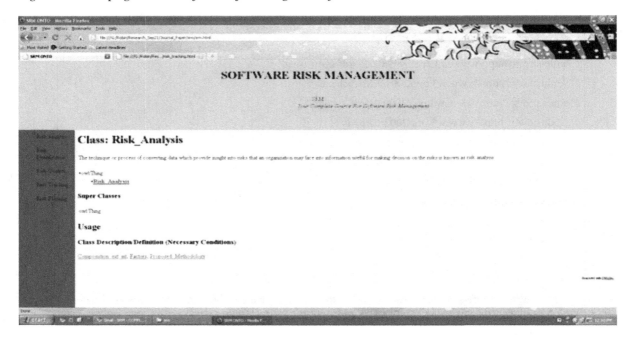

Figure 10. Representation of the SRTONTO

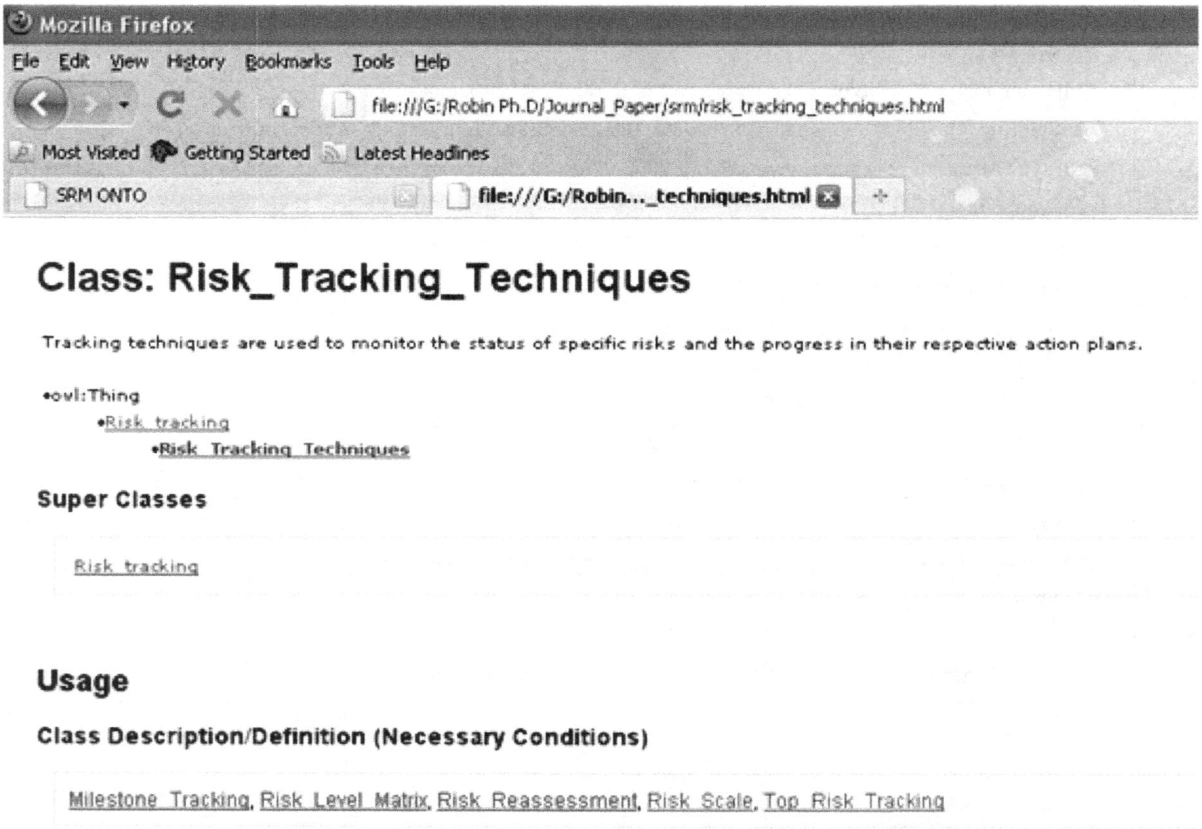

Mozilla Firefox
File Edit View History Bookmarks Tools Help
file:///G:/Robin Ph.D/Journal_Paper/srm/risk_tracking_techniques.html
Most Visited Getting Started Latest Headlines
SRM ONTO
file:///G:/Robin..._techniques.html
Class: Risk_Tracking_Techniques
Tracking techniques are used to monitor the status of specific risks and the progress in their respective action plans.
•owl:Thing
•Risk_tracking
•Risk_Tracking_Techniques
Super Classes
Risk_tracking
Usage
Class Description/Definition (Necessary Conditions)
Milestone_Tracking, Risk_Level_Matrix, Risk_Reassessment, Risk_Scale, Top_Risk_Tracking

Figure 11. Representation of stack concept

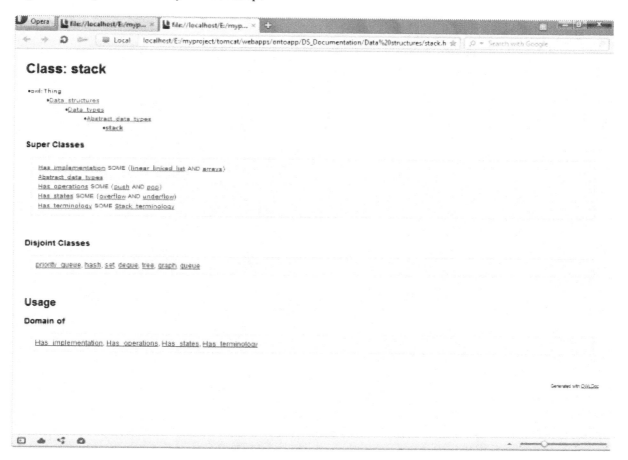

Knowledge Diagnosis Tools

Knowledge diagnosis is performed on the newly registered learner to determine his/her knowledge level. The system presents the learner with a set of predetermined questions from each topic of Software Risk Management, which forms a node in the Bayesian network. The knowledge level of the learner in related topics is predicted, using the network model and presented to the learner as inferences.

Representation of Educational Resources

Java Server Pages are used to represent the educational resources in a learner-friendly manner. Each phase of the Software Risk Management is associated with an ontology whose visualization diagram is displayed, from which each topic may be selected for study.

Learner Profile Manager

The learner profile contains the personal information of the learner which is displayed on successful login. The scores secured by the learner on completion of the diagnosis test and computer-adaptive test at the end of the course, are updated in the profile and displayed to the learner.

Intelligent Layer

The intelligent layer consists of the intelligent components in the e-learning system.

Figure 12. A portion of the visual representation of data structures ontology

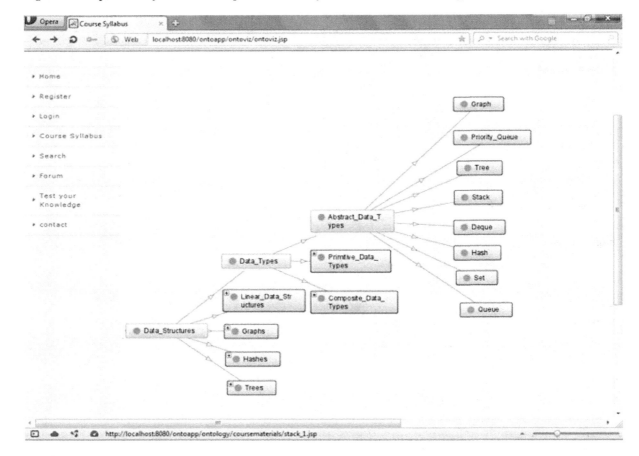

Support for the Study Process

The subsystem for supporting the study process is the Bayesian network engine that produces inferences for the learner. Once the newly-registered learner logs in to the system, his knowledge level in different topics of Software Risk Management is assessed using a diagnosis test. The results of this test are used to predict the knowledge level of the learner in related topics, and this indication is useful to the learner during the study process.

Search Logistics

The learner can search for a particular topic which may or may not be present in the local ontology. The subsystem of the search logistics initially searches for the requested topic in the local ontology. In case the information about the keyword requested by the learner is unavailable in the local ontology, the subsystem transfers the control to the module for accessing remote knowledge bases and updating the system knowledge accordingly. The system keeps track of all the topics searched by various learners. The ontology manager is informed of the list of topics that are not present in the local ontology to enable updating.

Subsystem of Intelligent Testing

The system is capable of testing the learner intelligently and generates questions dynamically on the basis of the performance of the learner in the previous question. Such computer-adaptive testing

Figure 13. System architecture for intelligent e-learning environment

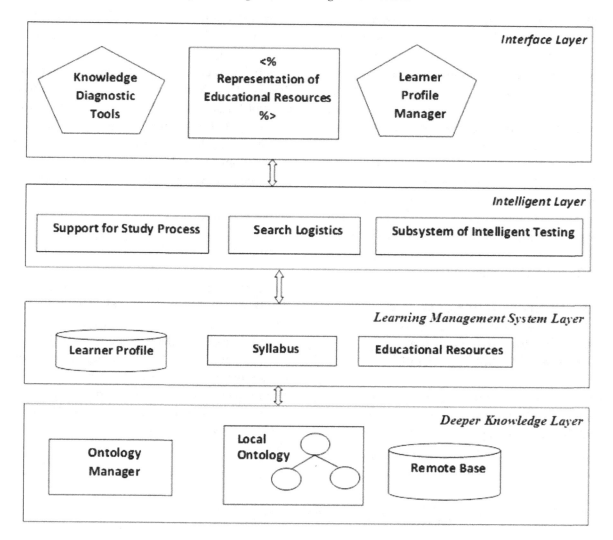

techniques are used widely in globally standardized tests such as GRE, TOEFL etc.

The computer-adaptive testing technique involves the following process. The learner is initially presented with a question of medium-level difficulty. If the question is answered right, then the learner is presented with a question of high-level difficulty. If not, the learner is presented with a question of low-level difficulty. Thus the testing subsystem adapts to the knowledge level of the learner. At the end of the test, the results are displayed and updated in the learner's profile.

Essential Components

The branches of Artificial Intelligence such as Bayesian Network and Decision Tree can also be used in this environment. The following sub topics describe how and where these techniques are effectively used.

Role of Bayesian Network

Bayesian networks have been successfully used to model knowledge under conditions of uncertainty within expert systems (Colace et al 2010). In the context of e-learning, Bayesian networks can be used to assess the learner's capabilities and interests (Kao et al 2009). The newly-registered learner may present himself for assessment by the system, to predict his aptitude and obtain personalized suggestions. Bayesian networks provide two major advantages. Firstly, it is easy to encode expert knowledge and such knowledge can be used to improve learning accuracy and efficiency. Secondly, the nodes and arcs of the learned Bayesian network indicate causal relationships. Therefore, users can understand and more easily exploit the knowledge encoded in the representation. The authors share their experience (19-26) in the following case study.

Case Study 1: Diagnosis Test of "An Intelligent Ontology-Based E-Learning Tool for Software Risk Management"

After the new learner registers into the system, the diagnosis test is displayed. A total of 20 have been identified from the key areas of software risk man-

agement such as Risk Factors, Categories of Risk, Implementation Factors, Risk Assessment, Planning Process, Control Process, Risk Identification Techniques, Qualitative Risk Analysis Techniques, Tree based Techniques, Techniques for Dynamic System, Risk Management Strategies and Risk Control Strategies. A Bayesian Network Model is constructed to predict the knowledge level of the newly-registered learner. The joint probability distributions of the above identified related topics are calculated based on the similarity of topics.

Rule Syntax

If <topic1> = high Then <topic2> = high

Rules of the above form are identified to form the Bayesian Network Model. The rule may be interpreted as "if the knowledge level of the learner in topic1 is determined to be high, then, based on the model, the knowledge level of the learner in topic2 may also be predicted as high." The following rules have been identified for the domain Software Risk Management. The rules are visualized by the Figure 14.

Figure 14. Bayesian network model for software risk management

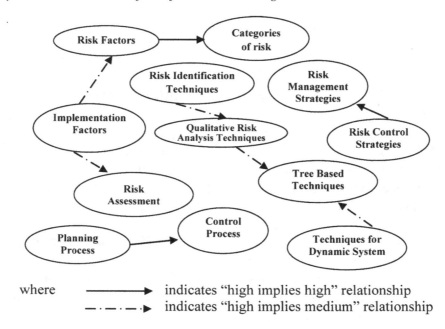

where ———▶ indicates "high implies high" relationship
– · – · –▶ indicates "high implies medium" relationship

Rule 1: If risk_factors = high Then categories_ of_risk = high

Rule 1 states that if the knowledge level of the learner in the topic "Risk Factors" is determined to be high, then it may be predicted that the knowledge level of the learner in the topic "Categories of Risk" is also high.

Rule 2: If risk_identification_techniques = high Then qualitative_risk_ analysis_techniques = medium

Rule 2 states that if the knowledge level of the learner in the topic "Risk Identification Techniques" is determined to be high, then it may be predicted that the knowledge level of the learner in the topic "Qualitative Risk Analysis Techniques" is medium.

Rule 3: If implementation_factors = high Then risk_assessment = medium

Rule 3 states that if the knowledge level of the learner in the topic "Implementation Factors" is determined to be high, then it may be predicted that the knowledge level of the learner in the topic "Risk Assessment" is medium.

Rule 4: If risk_control_strategies = high Then risk_management_ strategies = high

Rule 4 states that if the knowledge level of the learner in the topic "Risk Control Strategies" is determined to be high, then it may be predicted that the knowledge level of the learner in the topic "Risk Management Strategies" is also high.

Rule 5: If qualitative_risk_analysis_techniques = high Then tree_ based_techniques = medium

Rule 5 states that if the knowledge level of the learner in the topic "Qualitative Risk Analysis Techniques" is determined to be high, then it may be predicted that the knowledge level of the learner in the topic "Tree-Based Techniques" is medium.

Rule 6: If planning_process = high Then control_process = high

Rule 6 states that if the knowledge level of the learner in the topic "Planning Process" is determined to be high, then it may be predicted that the knowledge level of the learner in the topic "Control Process" is also high.

Rule 7: If techniques_for_dynamic_systems = high Then tree_based_techniques = medium

Rule 7 states that if the knowledge level of the learner in the topic "Techniques for Dynamic Systems" is determined to be high, then it may be predicted that the knowledge level of the learner in the topic "Tree Based Techniques" is medium.

Rule 8: If implementation_factors = high Then risk_factors = medium

Rule 8 states that if the knowledge level of the learner in the topic "Implementation Factors" is determined to be high, then it may be predicted that the knowledge level of the learner in the topic "Risk Factors" is medium.

Complex Rule 1: If Qualitative Risk Analysis Techniques = high and Techniques for Dynamic System = high Then Tree Based Technique = Medium

It states that if the knowledge level of the learner in the topics "Qualitative Risk Analysis

Techniques and "Techniques for Dynamic Systems" are determined to be high, then it may be predicted that the knowledge level of the learner in the topic "Tree Based Techniques" is medium.

Complex Rule 2: If Risk_Factors = Medium or Risk_Assessment = Medium Then Implementation_Factor = High.

It states that if the knowledge level of the learner in the topics "Risk Factor" or "Risk Assessment" is determined to be medium, then it may be predicted that the knowledge level of the learner in the topic "Implementation Factor" is High.

Questions for the Diagnosis Test have been selected from topics that form the "If" clause of each rule in the Bayesian Network. The knowledge level of the learner in that particular topic is determined based on the number of questions that are answered rightly for that topic. This determined knowledge level is then applied to the model, and inferences about the knowledge level of the learner in the "Then" clause of each rule are made. These inferences are presented to the learner to indicate in the topics which they are deficient.

ROLE OF DECISION TREE

Decision tree is a classifier in the form of a tree structure, where each node is either:

- **A Leaf Node:** Indicates the value of the target attribute (class) of examples, or
- **A Decision Node:** Specifies some test to be carried out on a single attribute-value, with one branch and sub-tree for each possible outcome of the test.

A decision tree can be used to classify an example by starting at the root of the tree and moving through it until a leaf node, which provides the classification of the instance. Decision tree induction is a typical inductive approach to learn

knowledge on classification. The key requirements to do mining with decision trees are:

- **Attribute-Value Description:** Object or case must be expressible in terms of a fixed collection of properties or attributes. This means that we need to discretize continuous attributes, or this must have been provided in the algorithm.
- **Predefined Classes (Target Attribute Values):** The categories to which examples are to be assigned must have been established beforehand (supervised data).
- **Discrete Classes:** A case does or does not belong to a particular class, and there must be more cases than classes.
- **Sufficient Data:** Usually hundreds or even thousands of training cases

Case Study 2: Decision Tree Construction for Pre-Diagnosis Test

Initially a set of fifteen questions are selected from the database and displayed to the user. The question pattern is of multiple choice type. Once the user completes the test and presses submit the learner answers are retrieved and by comparing with the answers in the database the score is calculated based on which the knowledge level of the learner is determined. The inferences are predicted based on Decision Tree model. These inferences are presented to the learner to indicate in which topics they lack.

Here leaf nodes represent the classification of the learner's knowledge and the interior nodes denote the condition (see Table 3).

The following diagram shows the Decision tree constructed for prediagnosis test (see Figure 15).

Additional Features

The following features can also be added in the e-learning tool.

Table 3. Score of users X1 to X6

Example	Attributes			Goal
	Easy	Medium	Hard	Classification
X1	8	7	6	Expert
X2	8	9	4	Intermediate
X3	8	7	5	Intermediate
X4	8	5	3	Intermediate
X5	6	3	1	Beginner
X6	8	9	5	Expert

Content Manager

- Manages the course material contents.
- Users can upload materials which can be verified by the admin.

Forum

- If the learner has any doubts about the subject, then he/she can post the question in the forum.

- Other users can reply to the question or comments within the feeds.
- The users can also view the most recent topics which are under discussion.

Video

- Each course material is provided with the video for better understanding about the topic.
- The videos contain clear explanations about the topic along with examples.
- The videos were downloaded from NPTEL Website.

Working Demos

- Each topic in data structure is provided with a working demo.
- After the learner completes a topic he/she can practice working on the demo provided.

Figure 15. Decision tree constructed for prediagnosis test

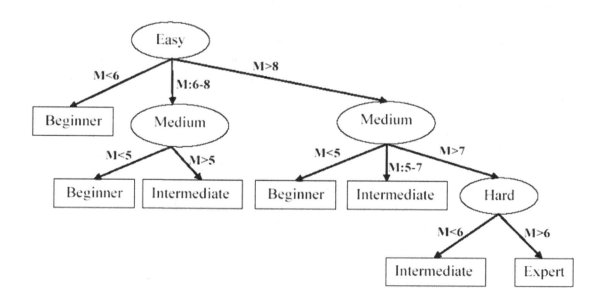

Evaluation Parameters

The tool can be evaluated using the following questionnaires

1. The e-Learning system provides content that exactly fits your needs.
2. The e-Learning system provides up-to-date content.
3. The e-Learning system makes it easy for you to find the content you need.
4. The e-Learning system is user-friendly.
5. The e-Learning system allows you to evaluate your learning performance.
6. The testing methods provided by the e-Learning system are fair.
7. The e-Learning system enables you to choose what you want to learn.
8. The e-Learning system records your learning progress and performance.
9. The systems can upgrade your information literacy.
10. You can use the learning management tools smoothly.
11. You can study by yourself and take notes.
12. You can choose various Web resources to study effectively .
13. The e-Learning system evaluates your subject knowledge effectively.
14. The e-Learning system provides secure testing environments.
15. The e-Learning system provides sufficient and useful content.
16. The e-Learning system can be made available for everyone easily.
17. The learning content has a proper syllabus.
18. The e-Learning system has a very effective user interface.
19. The e-Learning system allows you to apply the learnt knowledge to solve problems.
20. The course content meets your preferred learning style.

MULTIDIMENSIONAL LEARNING ENVIRONMENT

The dimensions of learning are a comprehensive model used to define the learning process. The five dimensions of learning are

- Attitude and Perception.
- Acquire and Integrate Knowledge.
- Extend and Refine Knowledge.
- Use Knowledge Meaningfully.
- Habits of Mind.

The diagrammatic representation of various dimensions of learning is given in Figure 16. Among these five dimensions, this work mainly concentrates on 'Use Knowledge Meaningfully' dimensions, as the system has been developed with a specific objective of training the users and making the user more familiarize in the subjects. The system has to be developed with an optimistic view of the learner successfully attempting to answer all levels of difficulty and use this knowledge effectively. The circle representing 'Use Knowledge Meaningful' subsumes the other two, and the circle representing 'Extending and Refining Knowledge' subsumes the circle representing 'Acquiring and Integrating Knowledge'. Hence it is inferred that these two dimensions 'Extending & Refining Knowledge' and 'Acquiring and Integrating Knowledge' are implicitly presented in the learner if 'Use Knowledge Meaningful' is observed in a learner. The I and V dimensions namely 'Attitude and Perception' and 'Habits of Mind' are not considered in this framework.

CONCLUSION

The primary aim of this chapter has been to provide an ontology based knowledge management system to reach engineering subjects. To achieve

Figure 16. Dimensions of learning

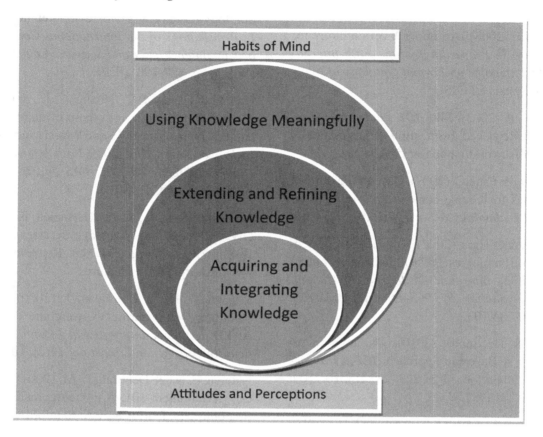

this (1) an educational ontology for the subject has to be designed and developed. (2) The developed ontology has to be effectively represented, using powerful ontology representation mechanisms such as the OWL, semantic and visual. (3) A 4-tier architecture for an intelligent ontology-based e-learning system has to be designed and implemented. The ontology has to be constructed, based on the information available in the literature and the experience of the course instructors. The main objective of any educational ontology is to use it as a content ontology, to express the formal domain model in e-learning to teach the subject. The educational ontology explained in this chapter named software risk management ontology has been constructed by the authors. It is represented

in the OWL to codify the knowledge of the domain for the agents to process messages. The representation in the OWL for run-time communications between agents achieved a flexibility of modification and extendibility very well. However, it is realized that the OWL representation is at a rather low level of abstraction. It is not very readable for domain experts to validate the ontology. So the developed ontology has been processed again, and semantically represented using the OWL document generator, and visualized using the OntoViz. The role of Bayesian network and decision tree in knowledge management system are clearly explained with case studies. Finally various dimensions of learning environment are discussed.

REFERENCES

Batchelor. (2008). An upper level ontology for chemistry. In *Proceedings of the Fifth International Conference on Formal Ontology in Information Systems*. FOIS.

Bourque, P. (2003). *SWEBOK guide call for reviewers*. Retrieved from http://serl.cs.colorado.edu/~serl/seworld/database/3552.html

Boyce, S., & Pahl, C. (2007). Developing domain ontologies for course content. *Journal of Educational Technology & Society*, *10*(3), 275–288.

Brewster & O'Hara. (2007). Knowledge representation with ontologies: Present challenges – Future possibilities. *International Journal of Human-Computer Studies*, *65*, 563–568. doi:10.1016/j.ijhcs.2007.04.003.

Colace & De Santo. (2010). Ontology for e-learning: A Bayesian approach. *IEEE Transactions on Education*, *53*(2), 223–233. doi:10.1109/TE.2009.2012537.

Daconta, M. C., Obrst, L. J., & Smith, K. T. (2003). The semantic web – A guide to the future of XML. In *Web Services and Knowledge Management*. Indianapolis, IN: Wiley & Sons.

Grobelnik, Brank, Fortuna, & Mozetič. (2008). Contextualizing ontologies with OntoLight: A pragmatic approach. *Informatica*, *32*, 79–84.

Gruber, T. R. (1993). Towards principles for the design of ontologies used for knowledge sharing. In *Proceedings of the International Workshop on Formal Ontology*. Retrieved from ftp.ksl.ftanford.edu/pub/ KSL_Reports/KSL-983-04.ps

Jiang, Zhao, & Wei. (2008). The development of ontology-based course for computer networks. In *Proceedings of the International Conference on Computer Science and Software Engineering*, (Vol. 5, pp. 487-490). IEEE.

Kao, H. Y., Liu, M. C., Huang, C. L., & Chang, Y. C. (2009). E-learning systems evaluation with data envelopment analysis and Bayesian networks. In *Proceedings of the 2009 Fifth International Joint Conference on INC, IMS and IDC*, (pp. 1207-1210). INC/IMS/IDC.

McGuinness, D. L., & Van Harmelen, F. (2004). OWL web ontology language overview. *World Wide Web Consortium (W3C)*. Retrieved from www.w3.org/TR/owl-features

Mizoguchi, R., & Bourdeau, J. (2000). Using ontological engineering to overcome common AI-ED problems. *International Journal of Artificial Intelligence in Education*, *11*(2), 107–121.

Natalya, F. N., & Deborah, L. M. (2001). Ontology development 101: A guide to creating your first ontology. Palo Alto, CA: Stanford.

Patel-Schneider, P. F., Hayes, P., & Horrocks, I. (2004). OWL web ontology language: Semantics and abstract syntax. *W3C Recommendation*. Retrieved from http://www.w3.org/TR/owl-semantics/

Pundt, H., & Bishr. (1999). Domain ontologies for data sharing-An example from environmental monitoring using field GIS. *Computers & Geosciences*, *28*, 98–102.

Robin, Hepzibah Miriam, & Uma. (2012). Design and development of an ontology for data structure. *Archives des Sciences*, *65*(4), 74–85.

Robin & Uma. (2010). Ontology based semantic knowledge representation for software risk management. *International Journal of Engineering Science and Technology*, 2(10), 5611–5617.

Robin & Uma. (2011a). An intelligent ontology-based e-learning tool for software risk management. *International Journal of Education Economics and Development*, 2(4), 320–346. doi:10.1504/IJEED.2011.043830.

Robin & Uma. (2011e). Development of educational ontology for software risk ananlysis. In *Proceedings of the International Conference on Communication, Computing & Security-ICCCS2011*. ACM.

Robin & Uma. (2011f). An ontology based linguistic infrastructure to represent software risk identification knowledge. In *Proceedings of the International Conference & Workshop on Emerging Trends in Technology (ICWET '11)*. ACM.

Robin, & Uma. (2011b). Design and development of ontology suite for software risk planning, software risk tracking and software risk control. *Journal of Computer Science, 7*(3), 320-327.

Robin, & Uma. (2011c). An ontology driven elearning agent for software risk management. *International Journal of Academic Research, 3*(2), 30-36.

Robin, & Uma. (2011d). Design and development of SRI ONTO: An educational ontology representing software risk identification knowledge. *International Journal of Computer Applications, 15*, 5-13.

Russell Records, L. (2005). The fusion of process and knowledge management. *BPTrends*. Retrieved from www.bptrends.com

Sommerville, I. (2004). *Software engineering* (8th ed.). Englewood Cliffs, NJ: Pearson Education.

Sosnovsky & Gavrilova. (2005). Development of educational ontology for c-programming. In *Proceeding of XI International Conference on Knowledge - Dialogue - Solution*, (Vol. 1, pp. 127-131). IEEE.

Sowa, J. F. (2000). *Knowledge representation – Logical, philosophical, and computational foundations*. Pacific Grove, CA: Brooks/Cole.

Takahashi, Abiko, Negishi, Itabashi, Kato, Takahashi, & Shiratori. (2005). An ontology-based e-learning system for network security. In *Proceedings of the 19th International Conference on Advanced Information Networking and Applications*, (Vol. 1, pp. 197-202). IEEE.

Wang, Jiang, Chia, & Tan. (2010). Wikipedia-2Onto – Building concept ontology automatically, experimenting with web image retrieval. *Informatica, 34*, 297–306.

Wongthongtham, P., Kasisopha, N., Chang, E., & Dillon, T. A. (2008). Software engineering ontology as software engineering knowledge representation. In *Proceedings of the Third International Conference on Convergence and Hybrid Information Technology*, (pp. 668-675). IEEE.

Zhu & Huo. Q. (2005). Developing a software testing ontology in UML for a software growth environment of web-based applications. In Software Evolution with UML and XML, (pp. 263-295). Hershey, PA: IDEA Group Inc.

Zouaq & Nkambou. (2008). Building domain ontologies from text for educational purposes. *IEEE Transactions on Learning Technologies, 1*(1), 49–62. doi:10.1109/TLT.2008.12.

Compilation of References

Abdou, T., Grogono, P., & Kamthan, P. (2012). A conceptual framework for open source software test process. In *Proceedings of Computer Software and Applications Conference Workshops (COMPSACW)*, (pp. 458-463). IEEE.

Abdullah, R., Eri, Z., & Talib, A. (2011). A model of knowledge management system in managing knowledge of software testing environment. In *Proceedings of Software Engineering (MySEC), 2011 5th Malaysian Conference* (pp. 229-233). Piscataway, NJ: IEEE.

Abrahamsson, P., Moser, R., Pedrycz, W., Sillitti, A., & Succi, G. (2007). Effort prediction in iterative software development processes -- Incremental versus global prediction models. In *Proceedings of the 1st International Symposium on Empirical Software Engineering and Measurement* (pp. 344–353). Madrid, Spain. IEEE.

Abufardeh, S. (2009). *A framework for the integration of I18N & L10N activities in the software development process*. (Unpublished doctoral dissertation). North Dakota State University, Fargo, ND.

Abufardeh, S., & Magel, K. (2008). Culturalization of software architecture: Issues and challenges. In *Proceedings of the International Conference on Computer Science and Software Engineering (CSSE 2008)*. Wuhan, China: IEEE.

Abufardeh, S., & Magel, K. (2010). The impact of global software cultural and linguistic aspects on global software development process (GSD), issues and challenges. In *Proceedings of the 4th International Conference on New Trends in Information Science and Service Science*, (pp. 133–138). IEEE.

Acharya, Chua, Ng, E. Y. K., Wei, W., & Chee. (2008). Application of higher order spectra for the identification of diabetes retinopathy stages. *Journal of Medical Systems, 32*(6), 431–488. doi:10.1007/s10916-008-9154-8 PMID:19058652.

Adamopoulou, P., Sakkopoulos, Tsakalidis, & Lytras. (2007). Web service selection based on QoS knowledge management. *Journal of UCS, 13*(9), 1138-1156.

Akram & Khan. (2012). Multilayered thresholding-based blood vessel segmentation for screening of diabetic retinopathy.[EWCO]. *Engineering with Computers*. doi: doi:10.1007/s00366-011-0253-7.

Akram, K. Iqbal, & Butt. (2010). Retinal image: Optic disk localization and detection. In Proceedings of Image Analysis and Recognition (LNCS), (vol. 6112, pp. 40-49). Berlin: Springer.

Akram, Tariq, Anjum, & Javed. (2012). Automated detection of exudates in colored retinal images for diagnosis of diabetic retinopathy. *OSA Journal of Applied Optics, 51*(20), 4858-4866.

Akram, Khalid, & Khan. (2013). Identification and classification of microaneurysms for early detection of diabetic retinopathy. *Pattern Recognition, 46*(1), 107–116. doi:10.1016/j.patcog.2012.07.002.

Akram, M. U., & Khan, S. A. (2011). Automated detection of dark and bright lesions in retinal images for early detection of diabetic retinopathy. *Journal of Medical Systems*. doi: doi:10.1007/s10916-011-9802-2 PMID:22090037.

Alavi, M., & Leidner, D. (2001). Knowledge management and knowledge management systems: Conceptual foundations and research issues. *Management Information Systems Quarterly*, *25*(1), 107–136. doi:10.2307/3250961.

Albrecht, A. J., & Gaffney, J. E. (1983). Software function, source lines of code, and development effort prediction: A software science validation. *IEEE Transactions on Software Engineering*, *9*(6), 639–648. doi:10.1109/TSE.1983.235271.

Alesso, P. (2012). *Preparing for semantic web services*. Retrieved from www.sitepoint.com/article/semantic-web-services

C. Alexander (Ed.). (1979). *The timeless way of building*. New York: Oxford University Press.

Alostath, J. M., & Wright, P. (2004). Pattern languages towards a tool for cross-cultural user interface design development. In H. M. Khalid (Ed.), *Proceedings of 7th International Conference on Work With Computing Systems*. Kuala Lumpur, Malaysia: Damai Sciences.

Alrawi, K., & Alrawi, W. (2011). Managers' perception of potential impact of knowledge management in the workplace: Case study. *American Journal of Social and Management Sciences*, *2*(1), 188–195. doi:10.5251/ajsms.2011.2.1.188.195.

Alsmadi, I., & Magel. (2007). An object oriented framework for user interface test automation. In *Proceedings of Midwest Instruction and Computing Symposium (MICS) 2007*. MICS.

Amine, M., & Ahmed-Nacer, M. (2011). An agile methodology for implementing knowledge management systems: A case study in component-based software engineering. *International Journal of Software Engineering and Its Applications*, *5*(4), 159–170.

Ammerman, M. (1998). *The root cause analysis handbook: A simplified approach to identifying, correcting, and reporting workplace errors*. Academic Press.

Amos, A.F., McCarty, D.J., & Zimmet, P. (1997). The rising global burden of diabetes and its complications: Estimates and projections to the year 2010. *Diabetic Medicine*.

Anand, A., & Singh, M. (2011). Understanding knowledge management: A literature review. *International Journal of Engineering Science and Technology*, *3*(2), 926–939.

Anisseh, M., & Yusuff, R. (2011). A fuzzy group decision making model for multiple criteria based on Borda count. *International Journal of the Physical Sciences*, *6*(3), 425–433.

Ankolekar, A. Burstein, Hobbs, Lassila, Martin, McDermott, … Sycara. (2002). DAML-S: Web service description for the semantic web. In *Proceedings International Semantic Web Conference (ISWC)* (LNCS), (vol. 2342). Berlin: Springer.

Antel & Hajdu. (2012). Improving microaneurysm detection using an optimally selected subset of candidate extractors and preprocessing methods. *Pattern Recognition*, *45*(1), 264–270. doi:10.1016/j.patcog.2011.06.010.

Appelt, K., Milch, K., Handgraaf, M., & Weber, E. (2011). The decision making individual differences inventory and guidelines for the study of individual differences in judgment and decision-making research. *Judgment and Decision Making*, *6*(3), 252–262.

Arora, E. (2011). Knowledge management in public sector. *International Refereed Research Journal*, *2*(1), 165–171.

Aurum, A., Daneshgar, F., & Ward, J. (2008). Investigating knowledge management practices in software development organizations: An Australian experience. *Information and Software Technology*, *50*(6), 511–533. doi:10.1016/j.infsof.2007.05.005.

Ausubel, D. P. (1968). *Educational psychology: A cognitive view*. New York: Holt, Rinehart and Winston.

Azhar, D., Mendes, E., & Riddle, P. (2012). A systematic review of web resource estimation.[Promise.]. *Proceedings of Promise*, *12*, 49–58.

Back, R. J. R. (1981a). Proving total correctness of nondeterministic programs in infinty logic. *Acta Informatica*, *15*(3), 233–249. doi:10.1007/BF00289263.

Back, R. J. R. (1981b). On correct refinement of programs. *Journal of Computer and System Sciences*, *23*(1), 49–68. doi:10.1016/0022-0000(81)90005-2.

Back, R. J. R., & von Wright, J. (1992). Combining angels, demons and miracles in program specifications. *Theoretical Computer Science*, *100*, 365–383. doi:10.1016/0304-3975(92)90309-4.

Baker, S. (2009). *Towards the construction of large Bayesian networks for web cost estimation*. (Unpublished Master's Thesis). University of Auckland, Auckland, New Zealand.

Bal, M., Bal, Y., & Demirhan, A. (2011). Creating competitive advantage by using data mining technique as an innovative method for decision making process in business. In *Proceeding of Annual Conference on Innovations in Business & Management*. London, UK: CIBM.

Bansal, Gupta, & Panchal, & Kumar. (2009). Remote sensing image classification by improved swarm inspired techniques. In *Proceedings of the International Conference on Artificial Intelligence and Pattern Recognition (AIPR-09)*. AIPR.

Baresi, L., & DiNitto. (2007). *Test and analysis of web services*. Berlin: Springer-Verlag GmbH.

Baresi, L., Morasca, S., & Paolini, P. (2002). An empirical study on the design effort for web applications.[WISE.]. *Proceedings of WISE*, *2002*, 345–354.

Batchelor. (2008). An upper level ontology for chemistry. In *Proceedings of the Fifth International Conference on Formal Ontology in Information Systems*. FOIS.

Becerra-Fernandez, I., & Sabherwal, R. (2010). *Knowledge management: Systems and processes*. New York: M.E. Sharpe.

Belgraver, A. B. (2007). *The use of workshops for requirements engineering*. (Master Thesis). Universiteit van Amsterdam, Amsterdam, The Netherlands.

Berghammer, R., & Zierer, H. (1986). Relational algebraic semantics of deterministic and nondeterministic programs. *Theoretical Computer Science*, *43*, 123–147. doi:10.1016/0304-3975(86)90172-6.

Bertolino, A., & Polini. (2005). The audition framework for testing web services interoperability. In *Proceedings of the 31st EUROMICRO Conference on Software Engineering and Advanced Applications*. EUROMICRO.

Bianchini, D. De Antonellis, & Melchiori. (2009). Service-based semantic search in P2P systems. In *Proceedings of the 2009 Seventh IEEE European Conference on Web Services*. IEEE.

Bibi, S., & Stamelos, I. (2004). Software process modelling with Bayesian belief networks.[IEEE.]. *Proceedings of IEEE Software Metrics*, *2004*, 1–10.

Bjornson, F. (2007). *Knowledge management in software process improvement*. Retrieved from idi.ntnu.no/grupper/su/publ/phd/bjornson-thesis-final-26sep07.pdf

Bjornson, F., & Dingsoyr, T. (2008). Knowledge management in software engineering: A systematic review of studied concepts, fiKnowle and research methods used. *Information and Software Technology*, *50*(11), 1055–1068. doi:10.1016/j.infsof.2008.03.006.

Blockley, D. I. (1981). *The nature of structural design and safety*. Chichester, UK: Academic Press.

Bloom, B. (1956). *Taxonomy of educational objectives: The classification of educational goals*. Ann Arbor, MI: D. McKay Company Inc..

Boehm, B. W., Abts, C., Brown, A. W., Chulani, S., Clark, B. K., & Horowitz, E. … Steece, B. (2000). Software cost estimation with COCOMO II. Englewood Cliffs, NJ: Prentice-Hall.

Boehm, B. W. (1981). *Software engineering economics*. Englewood Cliffs, NJ: Prentice-Hall.

Bohanec, M. (2009). Decision making: A computer-science and information-technology viewpoint. *Interdisciplinary Description of Complex Systems*, *7*(2), 22–37.

Bonabeau, E., Dorigo, M., & Theraulaz, G. (1999). *Swarm intelligence from natural to artificial system*. Oxford, UK: Oxford University Press.

Boole, G. (1847). *The mathematical analysis of logic, being an essay toward a calculus of deductive reasoning*. Cambridge, UK: Macmillan.

Boudriga, N., Elloumi, F., & Mili, A. (1992). On the lattice of specifications: Applications to a specification methodology. *Formal Aspects of Computing*, *4*, 544–571. doi:10.1007/BF01211474.

Bourque, P. (2003). *SWEBOK guide call for reviewers.* Retrieved from http://serl.cs.colorado.edu/~serl/seworld/database/3552.html

Boyce, S., & Pahl, C. (2007). Developing domain ontologies for course content. *Journal of Educational Technology & Society, 10*(3), 275–288.

Bozkurt, M., Harman, & Hassoun. (2009). Testing & verification in service-oriented architecture: A survey. *Software Testing, Verification and Reliability*, 1–7.

Bratton & Kennedy. (2007). Defining a standard for particle swarm optimization. In *Proceedings of the 2007 IEEE Swarm Intelligence Symposium.* Honolulu, HI: IEEE.

Brewster & O'Hara. (2007). Knowledge representation with ontologies: Present challenges – Future possibilities. *International Journal of Human-Computer Studies, 65*, 563–568. doi:10.1016/j.ijhcs.2007.04.003.

Brown, J. S., Collins, A., & Duguid, P. (1989). Situated cognition and the culture of learning. *Educational Researcher, 18*(1), 32–41. doi:10.3102/0013189X018001032.

Caivano, D., Lanubile, F., & Visaggio, G. (2001). Software renewal process comprehension using dynamic effort estimation. In *Proceedings of International Conference on Software Maintenance* (pp. 209–218). Florence, Italy: IEEE.

Canfora, G., & Penta. (2009). *Service-oriented architectures testing: A survey.* Berlin: Springer-Verlag.

Cao, H., & Chen, G. (1983). Some applications of fuzzy sets of meteorological forecasting. *FSS, 9*, 1–12. doi:10.1016/S0165-0114(83)80001-3.

Carmel. (1999). *Global software teams collaborating across borders and time zones.* New York: Prentice Hall.

Carmel, E. (2003). The new software exporting nations: Success factors. *Electronic Journal of Information Systems in Developing Countries, 13*(4), 1–12.

Chin, L. H., & Tarski, A. (1951). Distributive and modular laws in the arithmetic of relation algebras. *University of California Publications, 1*, 341–384.

Chou, S. (2011). Management of system development knowledge: A cognitive approach. *Behaviour & Information Technology, 30*(3), 389–401. doi:10.1080/0144929X.2010.528451.

Chulani, S., Boehm, B. W., & Steece, B. (1999). Bayesian analysis of empirical software engineering cost models. *IEEE Transactions on Software Engineering, 25*(4), 573–583. doi:10.1109/32.799958.

Cob, Z. C., & Abdullah. (2008). Ontology-based semantic web services framework for knowledge management system. In *Proceedings of the International Symposium on Information Technology, 2008.* ITSim.

Colace & De Santo. (2010). Ontology for e-learning: A Bayesian approach. *IEEE Transactions on Education, 53*(2), 223–233. doi:10.1109/TE.2009.2012537.

Conchuir, H. Agerfalk, & Fitzgerald. (2006). Exploring the assumed benefits of global software development. In *Proceedings of the IEEE International Conference on Global Software Engineering (ICGSE'06)*, (pp. 159-168). IEEE.

Cost, R. Finin, Joshi, Peng, Nicholas, Soboroff, … Tolia. (2001). *ITTalks: A case study in the semantic web and DAML.* Retrieved from http://www.semanticWeb.org/SWWS/program/full/paper41.pdf

Costagliola, G., di Martino, S., Ferrucci, F., Gravino, C., Tortora, G., & Vitiello, G. (2006). Effort estimation modeling techniques: a case study for web applications. In *Proceedings of the International Conference on Web Engineering (ICWE'06)*, (pp. 9-16). ICWE.

Crowston, K., & Howison, J. (2005). The social structure of free and open source software development. *First Monday, 10*(2). doi:10.5210/fm.v10i2.1207.

Crowston, K., & Howison, J. (2006). Hierarchy and centralization in free and open source software team communications. *Knowledge, Technology & Policy, 18*(4), 65–85. doi:10.1007/s12130-006-1004-8.

Cubranic, D., Holmes, R., Ying, A. T., & Murphy, G. C. (2003). Tool for light-weight knowledge sharing in open-source software development. In *Proceedings of the 3rd ICSE Workshop on Open Source* (pp. 25-29). ICSE.

Cusick & Prasad. (2006). A practical management and engineering approach to offshore collaboration. *IEEE Software, 23*(5), 20–29. doi:10.1109/MS.2006.118.

Daconta, M. C., Obrst, L. J., & Smith, K. T. (2003). The semantic web – A guide to the future of XML. In *Web Services and Knowledge Management*. Indianapolis, IN: Wiley & Sons.

Dalkir, K. (2005). *Knowledge management in theory and practice*. Oxford, UK: Elsevier Butterworth-Heinemann.

Damian, & Zowghi. (2003). Challenges in multi-site software development organizations. *Requirements Engineering, 8*(3), 149–160.

Darr, T. Benjamin, Mayer, Fernandes, & Jain. (2010). *Semantic services for intelligence preparation of the battlefield (IPB) composition*. Paper presented at the 2010 International Symposium on Collaborative Technologies and Systems. New York, NY.

Das, Biswas, Dasgupta, & Abraham. (2009). Bacterial foraging optimization algorithm: Theoritical foundations, analysis and applications. *Foundations of Computational Intelligence, 3*, 23–55.

Davis, A. M., & Hsia, P. (1994). Giving voice to requirements engineering. *IEEE Software, 11*(2), 12–16. doi:10.1109/52.268949.

De Lucia, A., Pompella, E., & Stefanucci, S. (2005). Assessing effort estimation models for corrective maintenance through empirical studies. *Information and Software Technology, 47*(1), 3–15. doi:10.1016/j.infsof.2004.05.002.

De Morgan, A. (1856). On the symbols of logic, the theory of the syllogism, and in particular of the copula, and the application of the theory of probabilities to some questions in the theory of evidence. *Trans. of the Cambridge Philosophical Society, 9*, 79–127.

De Morgan, A. (1864). On the syllogism and on logic in general. *Trans. of the Cambridge Philosophical Society, 10*, 173–230.

Del Galdo, E. M. (1996). Culture and design. In E. M. Del Galdo, & J. Neilsen (Eds.), *International UI*. New York: John Wiley & Sons.

Desai, A., & Shah, S. (2011). Knowledge management and software testing. In *Proceedings on International Conference and Workshop on Emerging Trends in Technology (ICWET)*. IJCA.

Desharnais, J. (1989). *Abstract relational semantics*. (Thesis). School of Computer Science, Univ. McGill, Montreal, Canada.

Desharnais, J., Möller, B., & Tchier, F. (2000). Kleene under a demonic star. In *Proceedings of the 8th International Conference on Algebraic Methodology And Software Technology* (LNCS), (Vol. 1816, pp. 355–370). Berlin: Springer-Verlag.

Desharnais, J., Baltagi, S., & Chaib-Draa, B. (1994). *Simple weak sufficient conditions for sharpness. Rapport de recherche DIUL-RR-9405*. Universite Laval, Quebec, Canada: Departement d'Informatique.

Desharnais, J., Belkhiter, N., Ben Mohamed Sghaier, S., Tchier, F., Jaoua, A., Mili, A., & Zaguia, N. (1995). Embedding a demonic semilattice in a relation algebra. *Theoretical Computer Science, 149*(2), 333–360. doi:10.1016/0304-3975(94)00271-J.

Desharnais, J., Mili, A., & Nguyen, T. T. (1997). Refinement and demonic semantics. In C. Brink, W. Khal, & G. Schmidt (Eds.), *Relational methods in Computer Science*. New York: Springer. doi:10.1007/978-3-7091-6510-2_11.

Desharnais, J., & Tchier, F. (1995). *Demonic relational semantics of sequential programs. Rapport de recherche DIUL-RR-9406*. Universite Laval, Quebec, Canada: Departement d'Informatique.

Desouza, K. C., Awazu, & Baloh. (2006). Managing knowledge in global software development efforts: Issues and practices. *IEEE Software, 3*(5), 30–37. doi:10.1109/MS.2006.135.

Dietze, S. Gugliotta, & Domingue. (2008). *Situation-driven processes for semantic web services*. Paper presented at the 5th International Conference on Service Systems and Service Management (ICSSSM'08). Melbourne, Australia.

Dijkstra, E. W., & Feijn, W. (1988). *Predicate calculus and program semantics*. Reading, MA: Addison-Wesley.

Diosteanu, A., & Cotfas. (2009). Agent based knowledge management solution using ontology, semantic web services and GIS. *Informatica Economică, 13*(4).

Domingue, J. Galizia, & Cabral. (2006). The choreography model for IRS-III. In *Proceedings of the 39th Hawaii International Conference on System Sciences*. IEEE.

Donelson, W. S. (1976, June). Project planning and control. *Datamation*, 73–80.

Dong, & Xiang-Bin. (2008). Particle swarm intelligence classification algorithm for remote sensing images. In *Proceedings of the IEEE Pacific-Asia Workshop on Computational Intelligence and Industrial Application*. IEEE.

Dong, X. Halevy, Madhavan, Nemes, & Zhang. (2004). Paper. In *Proceedings of the Thirtieth International Conference on Very Large Databases* (vol. 30, pp. 372 – 383). IEEE.

M. Dorfman (Ed.), *(n.d.). Software requirements engineering* (2nd ed.). Los Alamitos, CA: Wiley-IEEE Press.

Dorigo & Stuetzle. (2004). *Ant colony optimization.* Cambridge, MA: MIT Press.

Dorigo, Maniezzo, & Colorni. (1996). Ant system: Optimization by a colony of cooperating agents. *IEEE Transactions on Systems, Man, and Cybernetics–Part B, 26*(1), 29–41.

Dubois, D., & Prade, H. (1982a). A class of fuzzy measures based on triangular norms. *International Journal of General Systems, 8*, 43–61. doi:10.1080/03081078208934833.

Erickson, T. (2000). Lingua francas for design: Sacred places and pattern languages. In D. Boyarski & W. A. Kellogg (Eds.), *Proceedings of the 3rd Conference on Designing Interactive Systems* (pp. 357-368). New York: ACM Press.

Faiz, R., & Edirisinghe, E. (2009). Decision making for predictive maintenance in asset information management. *Interdisciplinary Journal of Information, Knowledge, and Management, 4*(1), 23–36.

Fancott, T., Kamthan, P., & Shahmir, N. (2012). Towards next generation requirements engineering. In *Proceedings of the 2012 ASE/IEEE International Conference on Social Informatics (Social Informatics 2012)*. Washington, DC: IEEE.

Feijen, W. H. (1988). *A bagatelle (for files)*. Austin, TX: University of Texas at Austin.

Ferrucci, F., Gravino, C., & Di Martino, S. (2008). A case study using web objects and COSMIC for effort estimation of web applications. In Proceedings of EUROMICRO-SEAA, (pp. 441-448). SEAA.

Fielding, R. T. (1999). Shared leadership in the apache project. *Communications of the ACM, 42*, 42–43. doi:10.1145/299157.299167.

Fioravanti, F., & Nesi, P. (2001). Estimation and prediction metrics for adaptative maintenance effort of object-oriented systems. *IEEE Transactions on Software Engineering, 27*(12), 1062–1084. doi:10.1109/32.988708.

Fleming, Philip, & Goatman, Olson, & Sharp. (2006). Automated microaneurysm detection using local contrast normalization and local vessel detection. *IEEE Transactions on Medical Imaging, 25*(9), 1223–1232. doi:10.1109/TMI.2006.879953 PMID:16967807.

Forrester. (2010). Making collaboration work for the 21st century's distributed workforce (White paper). *Forrester Research Inc.* Retrieved Aug. 25, 2012 from http://www.idgconnect.com/view_abstract/6086/making-collaboration-work-21st-century-s-distributed-workforce

Freitas, A. L. Parlavantzas, & Pazat. (2010). Survey of quality related aspects relevant for service-based applications. In *Proceedings of the 3rd International Workshop on Monitoring, Adaptation and Beyond (MONA+)*. MONA+.

Freyd, P., & Scedrov, A. (1990). *Categories, allegories.* Amsterdam: North-Holland.

Fu, X. Li, Guo, & He. (2003). Distributed configuration knowledge model. In *Proceedings of the 8th International Conference on Computer Supported Cooperative Work in Design*. IEEE.

Furusawa, H. (1998). *Algebraic formalisations of fuzzy relations and their representation theorems*. Department of Informatics Kyushu University Fukuoka.

Gallagher, K., & Binkley, D. (2008), Program slicing. In Proceedings of Frontier of Software Maintenance, (pp. 58-67). Frontier of Software Maintenance.

Gamma, E. Helm, Johnson, & Vlissides. (1995). Design patterns: Elements of reusable object-oriented software. Reading, MA: Addison-Wesley.

Ghose, D., & Choudhury, D. (2010). Information system evaluation and information system development process. *The IUP Journal of Systems Management, 8*(4), 19–32.

Gillian, J. (2001). Improving the open source software model with UML case tools. *Linux Gazette, 67.*

Goel, Gupta, & Panchal. (2011). Information sharing in swarm intelligence techniques: A perspective application for natural terrain feature elicitation in remote sensing images. *International Journal of Computers and Applications, 32*(2).

Goel, Panchal, & Gupta. (2010). Embedding expert knowledge to hybrid bio-inspired techniques- An adaptive strategy towards focused land cover feature extraction. *International Journal of Computer Science & Information Security, 8*(2), 244–253.

Goguen, J. A. (n.d.). The logic of inexact concepts. *Synthese, 19*, 325-373.

Goguen, J. A. (2009). L-fuzzy sets. *JMAA, 18*, 145–174.

Gonzalez & Woods. (2002). *Digital image processing* (2nd ed.). Upper Saddle River, NJ: Prentice Hall.

Goswami, C. (2008). Knowledge management in India: A case study of an Indian bank. *The Journal of Nepalese Business Studies, 5*(1), 37–49.

Grobelnik, Brank, Fortuna, & Mozetič. (2008). Contextualizing ontologies with OntoLight: A pragmatic approach. *Informatica, 32*, 79–84.

Gruber, T. R. (1993). Towards principles for the design of ontologies used for knowledge sharing. In *Proceedings of the International Workshop on Formal Ontology.* Retrieved from ftp.ksl.ftanford.edu/pub/ KSL_Reports/KSL-983-04.ps

Gulser, G., & Badur, B. (2011). Developing a framework for integrating knowledge management and decision support systems: Application to time series forecasting. *Communications of the IBIMA, 1*(1), 1–15. doi:10.5171/2011.137658.

Gunda, S. G. (2008). *Requirements engineering: Elicitation techniques.* (Doctoral dissertation). University West.

Gunther, S., & Thomas, S. (1992). *Relations and graphs: Discrete mathematics for computer scientists.* Berlin: Springer-Verlag.

Hall, P. (2001). The cross-cultural web: Designing for global markets. In *Proceedings of the 3rd International Workshop on Internationalizations of Products and Systems*, (pp. 109–113). IEEE.

Hashim, F., Alam, G., & Siraj, S. (2010). Information and communication technology for participatory based decision-making-e-management for administrative efficiency in higher education. *International Journal of Physical Sciences, 5*(4), 383–392.

Hatanaka, N., Hayashi, K., & Sawada, K. Hara, & Fujita. (2008). Improvement of automatic hemorrhages detection methods using brightness correction on fundus images. In Proceedings of SPIE, (Vol. 6915). SPIE. doi: doi:10.1117/12.771051.

Hayek, F. A. (1945). The use of knowledge in society. *The American Economic Review, 35*(4), 519–530.

Heath, W. S. (1991). *Real-time software techniques.* New York: Van Nostrand Reinhold.

Heeks, R., & Nicholson, B. (2004). Software export success factors and strategies in follower nations. *Competition and Change, 8*(3), 267–302. doi:10.1080/1024 529042000301962.

Hennell, M. A., Hedley, D., & Riddell, I. J. (1987). Automated testing techniques for real-time embedded software. In *Proceedings of the European Software Engineering Conference ESEC '87.* Strasbourg, France: ESEC.

Hepp, M. Leymann, Domingue, Wahler, & Fensel. (2005). Semantic business process management: A vision towards using semantic web services for business process management. In *Proceedings of the 2005 IEEE International Conference on e-Business Engineering (ICEBE'05).* IEEE.

Herbsleb. (2007). Global software engineering: The future of socio-technical coordination. In *Proceedings of the 2007 Future of Software Engineering (FOSE'07),* (pp. 188-198). FOSE.

Hislop. (2005). Knowledge management in organizations: A critical introduction. Oxford, UK: Oxford University Press.

Hoare, C. A. R. et al. (1987). Laws of programming. *Communications of the ACM, 30*, 672–686. doi:10.1145/27651.27653.

Hofstede, G. (n.d.). *Cultural dimensions*. Retrieved Sep. 2012 from http://www.geert-hofstede.com/index.shtml

G. Hofstede (Ed.). (2001). *Culture's consequences: Comparing values, behaviors, institutions, and organizations across nations* (2nd ed.). London: Sage Publications.

Hoover. (n.d.). *STARE database*. Retrieved from http://www.ces.clemson.edu/ahoover/stare

Howard, R., & Kerschberg. (2004). A knowledge-based framework for dynamic semantic web services brokering and management. In *Proceedings of the 15th International Workshop on Database and Expert Systems Applications (DEXA'04)*. DEXA.

Hu, X.-X., Wang, H., & Wang, S. (2007). Using expert's knowledge to build Bayesian networks. In *Proceedings of the 2007 International Conference on Computational Intelligence and Security Workshops*, (pp. 220-223). IEEE.

Huang & Trauth. (2007). Cultural influences and globally distributed information systems development: Experiences from Chinese IT professionals.[CPR.]. *Proceedings of CPR, 2007*, 36–45.

Huang, H., & Trauth, E. M. (2006). Cultural diversity challenges: Issues for managing globally distributed knowledge workers in software development. P. Yoong & S. Huff (Eds.), Managing IT Professionals in the Internet Age, (pp. 253-275). Hershey, PA: Idea Group Inc.

Huang, X., Ho, D., Ren, J., & Capretz, L. F. (2007). Improving the COCOMO model using a neuro-fuzzy approach. *Applied Soft Computing, 7*(1), 29–40. doi:10.1016/j.asoc.2005.06.007.

Idri, A., Kjiri, L., & Abran, A. (2000). COCOMO cost model using fuzzy logic. In *Proceedings of the 7th International Conference on Fuzzy Theory and Technology* (pp. 219–223). Atlantic City, NJ: IEEE.

Ismail, S. (2011). The role of marketing information system on decision making: An applied study on royal Jordanian air lines (RJA). *International Journal of Business and Social Science, 2*(3), 175–185.

ISO/IEC. (2010). *ISO/IEC WD 29119-2, software and systems engineering - Software testing - Part 2: Test process*. ISO.

Jeffery, D. R., & Low, G. (1990). Calibrating estimation tools for software development. *Software Engineering Journal, 5*(4), 215–222. doi:10.1049/sej.1990.0024.

Jeffery, D. R., Ruhe, M., & Wieczorek, I. (2000). A comparative study of cost modeling techniques using public domain multi-organizational and company-specific data. *Information and Software Technology, 42*(14), 1009–1016. doi:10.1016/S0950-5849(00)00153-1.

Jensen, R., Smullin, F., Peters, J., Thompson, K., & Gordon, D. (2011, May/June). Improving software engineering through holistic project coaching. *Cross Talk Magazine*, 9-15.

Jensen, F. V. (1996). *An introduction to Bayesian networks*. London: UCL Press.

Jiang, Zhao, & Wei. (2008). The development of ontology-based course for computer networks. In *Proceedings of the International Conference on Computer Science and Software Engineering*, (Vol. 5, pp. 487-490). IEEE.

Jinbo, W., Xuefeng, L., & Ming, D. (2011). A framework of knowledge management system for support decision making on web-enabled environment. *Journal of Convergence Information Technology, 6*(7), 133–139. doi:10.4156/jcit.vol6.issue7.17.

Johal, Singh, & Kundra. (2010). A hybrid FPAB/BBO algorithm for satellite image classification. *International Journal of Computers and Applications, 6*(5).

Jones, K. (2006). Knowledge management as a foundation for decision support systems. *Journal of Computer Information Systems, 46*(4), 116–124.

Jonsson, B. (1991). The theory of binary relations. *Algebairc Logic, Colloq. Math. Soc.*, 245–292.

Jonsson, B. (1982). Varieties of relation algebras. *Algebra Universalis, 15*, 273–298. doi:10.1007/BF02483728.

Jonsson, B., & Tarski, A. (1948). Representation problems for relation algebra. *Bulletin of the American Mathematical Society*, 80.

Jonsson, B., & Tarski, A. (1951). Boolean algebras with operators, part I. *American Journal of Mathematics*, *73*, 891–939. doi:10.2307/2372123.

Jonsson, B., & Tarski, A. (1952). Boolean algebras with operators, part II. *American Journal of Mathematics*, *74*, 127–162. doi:10.2307/2372074.

Jorgensen, M. (1995). Experience with the accuracy of software maintenance task effort prediction models. *IEEE Transactions on Software Engineering*, *21*(8), 674–681. doi:10.1109/32.403791.

Jørgensen, M., & Grimstad, S. (2009). Software development effort estimation: Demystifying and improving expert estimation. In A. Tveito, A. M. Bruaset, & O. Lysne (Eds.), *Simula Research Laboratory - By Thinking Constantly About It* (pp. 381–404). Heidelberg, Germany: Springer. doi:10.1007/978-3-642-01156-6_26.

Kahai, Namuduri, & Thompson. (2006). A decision support framework for automated screening of diabetic retinopathy. *International Journal of Biomedical Imaging*, 1–8. doi:10.1155/IJBI/2006/45806 PMID:23165030.

Kahl, W. (2001). Parallel composition and decomposition of specifications. *Information Sciences*, *139*, 197–220. doi:10.1016/S0020-0255(01)00165-7.

Kaindl, H., Brinkkemper, S., Bubenko, J. A. Jr, Farbey, B., Greenspan, S. J., & Heitmeyer, C. L. et al. (2002). Requirements engineering and technology transfer: Obstacles, incentives and improvement agenda. *Requirements Engineering*, *7*(3), 113–123. doi:10.1007/s007660200008.

Kandt, R. K. (2003). *Software requirements engineering: Practices and techniques (Tech. Report document D-24994)*. Jet Propulsion Laboratory.

Kandt, R. K., Kay-Im, E., Lavin, M. L., & Wax, A. (2002). *A survey of software tools and practices in use at jet propulsion laboratory (Internal Document D-24868)*. Jet Propulsion Laboratory.

Kaner, C., Falk, J., & Nguyen, H. (1999). *Testing computer software*. New York: Wiley.

Kao, H. Y., Liu, M. C., Huang, C. L., & Chang, Y. C. (2009). E-learning systems evaluation with data envelopment analysis and Bayesian networks. In *Proceedings of the 2009 Fifth International Joint Conference on INC, IMS and IDC*, (pp. 1207-1210). INC/IMS/IDC.

Karaboga & Akay. (2009). A comparative study of artificial bee colony algorithm. *Applied Mathematics and Computation*, *214*, 108–132. doi:10.1016/j.amc.2009.03.090.

Karaboga & Basturk. (2007). A powerful and efficient algorithm for numerical function optimization: Artificial bee colony algorithm. Berlin: Springer Science+Business Media B.V.

Karaboga. (2005). *An idea based on honey bee swarm for numerical optimization*. Technical Report-TR06.

Karam, M., Safa, H., & Artail, H. (2007). An abstract workflow-based framework for testing composed web services. In *Proceedings of the IEEE/ACS International Conference on Computer Systems and Applications, 2007. AICCSA*.

Kaufmann, A. (1975). *Introduction to the theory of fuzzy subsets*. New York: Academic Press.

Kaufmann, A. (1977). *Theorie des sous-ensembles flous (fuzzy set theory)*. Paris: Masson.

Kauppi, T., Kalesnykiene, V., Kamarainen, J.-K., Lensu, L., Sorri, I., Raninen A., ... Pietilä, J. (2006). *DIARETDB1 diabetic retinopathy database and evaluation protocol* (Technical report).

Kauppinen, M., & Kujala, S. (2001). Starting improvement of requirements engineering processes: An experience report. *Product Focused Software Process Improvement*, 196-209.

Kauppinen, M., Kujala, S., Aaltio, T., & Lehtola, L. (2002). Introducing requirements engineering: How to make a cultural change happen in practice. In *Proceedings. IEEE Joint International Conference on Requirements Engineering*, (pp. 43-51). IEEE.

Kauppinen, M., Vartiainen, M., Kontio, J., Kujala, S., & Sulonen, R. (2004). Implementing requirements engineering processes throughout organizations: Success factors and challenges. *Information and Software Technology*, *46*(14), 937–953. doi:10.1016/j.infsof.2004.04.002.

Kawahara, Y., & Furusawa, H. (1995). *An algebraic formatisation of fuzzy relations*. Paper presented at second International Seminar on Relational Methods in Computer Science. Rio de Janeiro, Brazil.

Kawahara, Y. (1990). Pushout-complements and basic concepts of grammars in topoi. *Theoretical Computer Science, 77*, 267–289. doi:10.1016/0304-3975(90)90171-D.

Kawahara, Y. (1995). Relational set theory. *Lecture Notes in Computer Science, 953*, 44–58. doi:10.1007/3-540-60164-3_19.

Kawahara, Y., & Mizoguchi, Y. (1992). Categorical assertion semantics in topoi. *Adv. in Software Sci. and Technol., 4*, 137–150.

Kawahara, Y., & Mizoguchi, Y. (1994). Relational structures and their partial morphisms in the view of single pushout rewriting. *Lecture Notes in Computer Science, 776*, 218–233. doi:10.1007/3-540-57787-4_14.

Kellner, M. I. Becker-Kornstaedt, Riddle, Tomal, & Verlage. (1998). Process guides: Effective guidance for process participants. In *Proceedings of the Fifth International Conference on the Software Process*, (pp. 11-25). IEEE.

Khalid. (2010). Activity classification and anomaly detection using m-mediods based modeling of motion patterns. *Pattern Recognition, 43*(10), 3636-3647.

Khalili, A. Badrabadi, & Khoshalhan. (2008). A framework for distributed market place based on intelligent software agents and semantic web services. In *Proceedings of the 2008 IEEE Congress on Services*. IEEE.

Khamesan, A., & Hammond, N. (2004). Synchronous collaborative concept mapping via ICT: Learning effectiveness and personal and interpersonal awareness. In *Proceedings of the First International Conference on Concept Mapping*, (pp. 385–392). IEEE.

Khan, M. T. Zia, Daudpota, Hussain, & Taimoor. (2006). *Integrating context-aware pervasive environments*. Paper presented at the 2nd International Conference on Emerging Technologies. Peshawar, Pakistan.

Kitchenham, B. A., & Mendes, E. (2009). Why comparative effort prediction studies may be invalid. In *Proceedings of the 5ᵗʰ International Conference on Predictor Models in Software Engineering* (pp. 4:1–4:5). Vancouver, Canada: IEEE.

Kitchenham, B., Mendes, E., & Travassos, G. H. (2006). A systematic review of cross-company vs. within-company cost estimation studies. In *Proceedings of the Evaluation and Assessment in Software Engineering,* (pp. 89 – 98). EASE.

Kitchenham, B. A. (2007). *Guidelines for performing systematic literature reviews in software engineering (version 2.3). Software Engineering Group.* School of Computer Science and Mathematics, Keele University and Department of Computer Science, University of Durham.

Koch, S. (2008). Effort modeling and programmer participation in open source software projects. *Information Economics and Policy, 20*(4), 345–355. doi:10.1016/j.infoecopol.2008.06.004.

Koch, S., & Schneider, G. (2002). Effort, co-operation and co-ordination in an open source software project: GNOME. *Information Systems Journal, 12*(1), 27–42. doi:10.1046/j.1365-2575.2002.00110.x.

Kohner, E. M., Aldington, S. J., Stratton, I. M., Manley, S. E., Holman, R. R., & Matthews, D. R. et al. (1998). United Kingdom prospective diabetes study, 30: Diabetic retinopathy at diagnosis of noninsulin-dependent diabetes mellitus and associated risk factors. *Archives of Ophthalmology, 116*(3), 297–303. doi:10.1001/archopht.116.3.297 PMID:9514482.

Komi-Sirvio & Tihinen. (2005). Lessons learned by participants of distributed software development. *Knowledge and Process Management, 12*(2).

Kopetz, H. (n.d.). *Real-time systems, design principles for distributed embedded applications*. Dordrecht, The Netherlands: Kluwer Academic Publishers.

Korel, B., & Laski, J. (1988, October). Dynamic program slicing. *Information Processing Letters*, 155–163. doi:10.1016/0020-0190(88)90054-3.

Koskinen, Pihlanto, & Vanharanta. (2003). Tacit knowledge acquisition and sharing in a project work context. *International Journal of Project Management*, *21*(4), 281–290. doi:10.1016/S0263-7863(02)00030-3.

Koznov, D., Malinov, V., Sokhransky, E., & Novikova, M. (2009). *A knowledge management approach for industrial model-based testing*. Setubal, Portugal: Academic Press.

Krinke, J. (2007). A study of consistent and inconsistent changes to code clones. In *Proceedings of WCRE*. IEEE.

Kumar, M., Paul, S., & Tadisina, S. (2005). Knowledge management practices in Indian software development companies: Findings from an exploratory study. *Asian Academy of Management Journal*, *10*(1), 59–78.

Ladan, M. (2010). Web services testing approaches: A survey and a classification. In *Proceedings of the International Conference on Networked Digital Technologies*, (pp. 70-79). Beirut, Lebanon: ICNDT.

Larsen, M., Godt, J., Larsen, N., Lund-Andersen, H., Sjolie, A. K., & Agardh, E. et al. (2003). Automated detection of fundus photographic red lesions in diabetic retinopathy. *Investigative Ophthalmology & Visual Science*, *44*(2), 761–766. doi:10.1167/iovs.02-0418 PMID:12556411.

Lee, Lee, Kingsley, Wang, & Russell, Klein, & Wanr. (2001). Comparison of diagnosis of early retinal lesions of diabetic retinopathy between a computer system and human experts. *Graefes Archive for Clinical and Experimental Ophthalmology*, *119*(4), 509–515. doi:10.1007/s004170100310 PMID:11296016.

Lee, Lee, & Wang, Klein, Kingsley, & Warn. (2005). Computer classification of nonproliferative diabetic retinopathy. *Archives of Ophthalmology*, *123*(6), 759–764. doi:10.1001/archopht.123.6.759 PMID:15955976.

Leung, K., Bhagt, R. S., Buchan, N. R., Erez, M., & Gibson, C. B. (2005). Culture and international business: Recent advances and their implications for future research. *Journal of International Business Studies*, *36*, 357–378. doi:10.1057/palgrave.jibs.8400150.

Lillesand, & Kiefer. (2008). *Remote sensing and image interpretation* (6th Ed.). New York: Wiley.

Li, M., & Gao, M. (2003). Strategies for developing China's software industries. *Information Technologies and International Development*, *1*(1), 61–73. doi:10.1162/itid.2003.1.1.61.

Lindvall, Rus, & Sinha. (2003). Software systems support for knowledge management. *Journal of Knowledge Management*, *7*(5), 137–150. doi:10.1108/13673270310505449.

Lipnack & Stamps. (1997). *Virtual teams: Reaching across space, time and organizations with technology*. New York: John Wiley & Sons.

Liu, Y., Wu, J., Liu, X., & Gu, G. (2009). Investigation of knowledge management methods in software testing process. In *Proceedings of the 2009 International Conference on Information Technology and Computer Science* (pp. 90-94). Washington, DC: IEEE Computer Society.

Liu, G. (2010). Spontaneous group decision making in distributed collaborative learning: Toward a new research direction. *MERLOT Journal of Online Learning and Teaching*, *6*(1), 279–296.

Lo, M., & Gandon. (2007). *Semantic web services in corporate memories*. Paper presented at the Second International Conference on Internet and Web Applications and Services (ICIW'07). New York, NY.

Lonchamp, J. (2005). Open source software development process modeling. In S. Acuna, & N. Juristo (Eds.), *Software Process Modeling* (pp. 29–64). New York: Springer. doi:10.1007/0-387-24262-7_2.

Long, III., & Srihann. (2004). Geoscience and remote sensing symposium. In Proceedings of Unsupervised and Supervised Classifications: Land Cover Classification using ERDAS Imagine, (vol. 4, pp. 20-24). IEEE.

Lunenburg, F. (2010). The decision making process. *National Forum of Educational Administration And Supervision Journal*, *27*(4), 1-12.

Lutz. (2009). Linguistic challenges in global software development: Lessons learned in an International SW development division. In *Proceedings of the 2009 Fourth IEEE International Conference on Global Software Engineering (ICGSE '09)*, (pp. 249–253). Limerick, Ireland: IEEE Computer Society.

Ma, Ni, & Sun. (2009). *Equilibrium species counts and migration model tradeoffs for biogeography based based optimization.* Paper presented at the Joint 48th IEEE Conference on Decision and Control and 28th Chinese Control Conference. Shanghai, China. Kennedy, J., & Eberhart, R. (1995). Particle swarm optimization. In *Proceedings of IEEE International Conference on Neural Networks,* (vol. 4, pp. 1942–1948). IEEE. Goel, Gupta, & Panchal. (2010). Hybrid ACO-BBO approach for predicting the deployment strategies of enemy troops in a military terrain application. In *Proceedings of the Second International Conference on Intelligent Systems and Nanotechnology.* IEEE.

Ma. (2010). An analysis of the equilibrium of migration models for biogeography-based optimization. *Information Sciences, 180,* 3444–3464.

Maddux, R. D. (1991a). Introductory course on relations algebras, finite-dimensional cylindric algebras, and their interconnections. *Colloq. Math. Soc., 54,* 361–392.

Maddux, R. D. (1991b). The origin of relation algebras in the developement and axiomatization of the calculus of relations. *Studia Logica, 50,* 421–455. doi:10.1007/BF00370681.

Mahemoff, M. J., & Johnston, L. J. (1999). The planet pattern language for software internationalisation. In D. Manolescu & B. Wolf (Eds.), *Proceedings of the 6th Annual Conference on the Pattern Languages of Programs.* IEEE.

Mahmood, Z., & Saeed, S. (2008). Software industry in Pakistan: An investigation into the CMMI practice of project planning, monitoring and control. In *Proceedings of the 9th International Conference IBIMA.* Morocco, Tunisia: IBIMA.

Mamdani, E. H. (1981). *Advances in the linguistic syntesis of fuzzy controllers in fuzzy reasoning and its applications.* London: Academic Press.

Mangia, L., & Paiano, R. (2003). MMWA: A software sizing model for web applications. In *Proceedings of the Fourth International Conference on Web Information Systems Engineering,* (pp. 53-63). IEEE.

Martin, D. Paolucci, McIlraith, Burstein, McDermott, McGuinness, ... Sycara. (2004). Bringing semantics to web services: The OWL-S approach. In *Proceedings of the First International Workshop on Semantic Web Services and Web Process Composition (SWSWPC 2004).* San Diego, CA: SWSWPC.

Martin, R. C. (2005). The test bus imperative: Architectures that support automated acceptance testing. *IEEE Software, 22*(4), 65–67. doi:10.1109/MS.2005.110.

Matayong, S., & Mahmood, A. (2011). KMS innovation decision making: The case study of oil and gas industry in Malaysia. In *Proceeding of* National Postgraduate Conference (NPC). Malaysia: NPC.

Maxwell, K., Wassenhove, L. V., & Dutta, S. (1999). Performance evaluation of general and company specific models in software development effort estimation. *Management Science, 45*(6), 77–83. doi:10.1287/mnsc.45.6.787.

McCall, H., Arnold, V., & Sutton, S. (2008). Use of knowledge management systems and the impact on the acquisition of explicit knowledge. *Journal of Information Systems, 22*(2), 77–101. doi:10.2308/jis.2008.22.2.77.

McGuinness, D. L., & Van Harmelen, F. (2004). OWL web ontology language overview. *World Wide Web Consortium (W3C).* Retrieved from www.w3.org/TR/owl-features

McIlraith, S., Son, & Zeng. (2001). Semantic web services. *IEEE Intelligent Systems, 16*(2), 46–53. doi:10.1109/5254.920599.

Mei, H., & Zhang. (2005). A framework for testing web services and its supporting tool. In *Proceedings of the IEEE International Workshop on Service-Oriented System Engineering.* IEEE.

Mendes, E. (2011a). Knowledge representation using Bayesian networks: A case study in web effort estimation. In *Proceedings of the World Congress on information and Communication Technologies (WICT 2011),* (pp. 310-315). WICT.

Mendes, E. (2011b). Building a web effort estimation model through knowledge elicitation. In *Proceedings of the International Conference on Enterprise Information Systems (ICEIS),* (pp. 128-135). ICEIS.

Mendes, E. (2012a). Using knowledge elicitation to improve web effort estimation: Lessons from six industrial case studies. In *Proceedings of the International Conference on Software Engineering (ICSE 2012)*, (pp. 1112-1121). ICSE.

Mendes, E., & Counsell, S. (2000). Web development effort estimation using analogy. In *Proceedings of the 2000 Australian Software Engineering Conference*, (pp. 203-212). ASEC.

Mendes, E., & Kitchenham, B. A. (2004). Further comparison of cross-company and within-company effort estimation models for web applications. In *Proceedings of IEEE Metrics*, (pp. 348-357). IEEE.

Mendes, E., Polino, C., & Mosley, N. (2009). Building an expert-based web effort estimation model using Bayesian networks. In *Proceedings of the 13th International Conference on Evaluation & Assessment in Software Engineering*, (pp. 1-10). IEEE.

Mendes, E. (2012b). An overview of web effort estimation. In M. Zelkowitz (Ed.), *Advances in Computers* (Vol. 78). London: Elsevier Academic Press.

Mendes, E., Mosley, N., & Counsell, S. (2001, January-March). Web metrics - Metrics for estimating effort to design and author web applications. *IEEE MultiMedia*, 50–57. doi:10.1109/93.923953.

Mendes, E., Mosley, N., & Counsell, S. (2003). Investigating early web size measures for web cost estimation. In *Proceedings of Evaluation and Assessment in Software Engineering*. EASE.

Mendes, E., Mosley, N., & Counsell, S. (2005a). Investigating web size metrics for early web cost estimation. *Journal of Systems and Software*, 77(2), 157–172. doi:10.1016/j.jss.2004.08.034.

Mendes, E., Mosley, N., & Counsell, S. (2005b). The need for web engineering: An introduction. In E. Mendes, & N. Mosley (Eds.), *Web Engineering* (pp. 1–26). Berlin: Springer-Verlag.

Menzies, T., Port, D., Chen, Z., Hihn, J., & Sherry, S. (2005). Validation methods for calibrating software effort models. In *Proceedings of the 27th International Conference on Software Engineering* (pp. 15–21). St. Louis, MO: IEEE.

Menzies, T., Chen, Z., Hihn, J., & Lum, K. (2006). Selecting best practices for effort estimation. *IEEE Transactions on Software Engineering*, 32(11), 883–895. doi:10.1109/TSE.2006.114.

MESSIDOR. (n.d.). Retrieved from http://messidor.crihan.fr/index-en.php

Mili, A. (1983). A relational approach to the design of deterministic programs. *Acta Inf.*, 315-328.

Mili, A., Desharnais, J., & Mili, F. (1987). Relational heuristics for the design of deterministic programs. *Acta Informatica*, 24(3), 239–276. doi:10.1007/BF00265990.

Mind Mapping. (n.d.). Retrieved Sep. 2012 from http://www.mind-mapping.org/blog/

Minevich, M., & Richter, F.-J. (2005). *Global outsourcing report*. Retrieved on July 08, 2012, from http://globalequations.com/Global%20Outsourcing%20Report.pdf

Mizoguchi, R., & Bourdeau, J. (2000). Using ontological engineering to overcome common AI-ED problems. *International Journal of Artificial Intelligence in Education*, 11(2), 107–121.

Mockus, A., Fielding, R., & Herbsleb, J. (2002). Two case studies of open source software development: Apache and Mozilla. *ACM Transactions on Software Engineering and Methodology*, 11(3), 309–346. doi:10.1145/567793.567795.

Mohammed, W., & Jalal, A. (2011). The influence of knowledge management system (KMS) on enhancing decision making process (DMP). *International Journal of Business and Management*, 6(8), 216–229. doi:10.5539/ijbm.v6n8p216.

Molven, A., Ringdal, M., Nordbo, A. M., Raeder, H., Stoy, J., & Lipkind, G. M. et al. (2008). Mutations in the insulin gene can cause MODY and autoantibody-negative type 1 diabetes. *Diabetes*, 57(4), 1131–1135. doi:10.2337/db07-1467 PMID:18192540.

Montironi, R., Whimster, W. F., Collan, Y., Hamilton, P. W., Thompson, D., & Bartels, P. H. (1996). How to develop and use a Bayesian belief network. *Journal of Clinical Pathology*, 49, 194. doi:10.1136/jcp.49.3.194 PMID:8675727.

Morgan, C. C., & Robinson. (1987). Specification statements and refinement. *IBM Journal of Research and Development, 32*(5), 546–555. doi:10.1147/rd.315.0546.

Morris, J. M. (1987). A theoretical basis for stepwise refinement and the programming calculus. *Theoretical Computer Science, 9*, 287–306.

Myers, M. D., & Tan, F. B. (2002). Beyond models of national culture in information systems research. *Journal of Global Information Management, 10*(1), 24–32. doi:10.4018/jgim.2002010103.

Natalya, F. N., & Deborah, L. M. (2001). Ontology development 101: A guide to creating your first ontology. Palo Alto, CA: Stanford.

Nguyen, V. (2010a). Improved size and effort estimation models for software maintenance. In *Proceedings of 26th International Conference on Software Maintenance*. Timisoara, Romania: IEEE.

Ni, J., Jiu, Y., & Ni. (2010). A practical development of knowledge management model for petrochemical product family. In *Proceedings of the 2011 International Conference on Information Management, Innovation Management and Industrial Engineering*. IEEE.

Nicholson & Sahay. (2001). Some political and cultural issues in the globalization of software development: Case experience from Britain and India. *Information and Organization, 11*(1), 25–43. doi:10.1016/S0959-8022(00)00008-4.

Niemeijer, van Ginneken, Russell, Suttorp-Schulten, & Abra'moff. (2007). Automated detection and differentiation of drusen, exudates, and cotton-wool spots in digital color fundus photographs for diabetic retinopathy diagnosis. *Investigative Ophthalmology & Visual Science, 48*(5), 2260-2267.

Niemeijer, van Ginneken, Staal, Suttorp-Schulten, & Abràmoff. (2005). Automatic detection of red lesions in digital color fundus photographs. *IEEE Transactions on Medical Imaging, 24*(5), 584-592.

Niemeijer, Ginneken, Cree, Mizutani, & Quellec, Sanchez, … Abramoff. (2010). Retinopathy online challenge: Automatic detection of microaneurysms in digital color fundus photographs. *IEEE Transactions on Medical Imaging, 1*(29), 185–195. doi:10.1109/TMI.2009.2033909 PMID:19822469.

Nikula, U., Sajaniemi, J., & Kälviäinen, H. (2000). *A state-of-the-practice survey on requirements engineering in small-and medium-sized enterprises*. Lappeenranta University of Technology.

Noll, Beecham, & Richardson. (2010). Global software development and collaboration: Barriers and solutions. *ACM Inroads, 1*, 66–78.

Nonaka, I., & Konno, N. (1998). The Concept of ba: Building a foundation for knowledge creation. *California Management Review, 40*(3), 40–54. doi:10.2307/41165942.

Nonaka, I., & Takeuchi, H. (1995). *The knowledge-creating company: How Japanese companies create the dynamics of innovation*. New York: Oxford University Press.

Nonaka, I., Toyama, R., & Konno, N. (2000). SECI, ba and leadership: A unified model of dynamic knowledge creation. *Long Range Planning, 33*(1), 5–34. doi:10.1016/S0024-6301(99)00115-6.

Novak, J. D., & Cañas, A. J. (2008). *The theory underlying concept maps and how to construct and use them (Technical Report IHMC CmapTools 2006-01 Rev 01-2008)*. Boca Raton, FL: Institute for Human and Machine Cognition.

Orzano, A., McInerney, C., Scharf, D., Tallia, A., & Crabtree, B. (2008). A knowledge management model: Implications for enhancing quality in health care. *Journal of the American Society for Information Science and Technology, 59*(3), 489–505. doi:10.1002/asi.20763.

Osareh, A., Mirmehdi, M., Thomas, B., & Markham, R. (2002). Comparative exudate classification using support vector machines and neural networks. In *Proceedings of the 5th International Conference on Medical Image Computing and Computer-Assisted Intervention*, (pp. 413-420). IEEE.

Panchal, V., Singh, P., Kaur, N., & Kundra, H. (2009). Biogeography based satellite image classification. *International Journal of Computer Science and Information Security, 6*(2), 269–274.

Paolucci, M., & Sycara. (2003). Autonomous semantic web services. *IEEE Internet Computing, 7*(5), 34–41. doi:10.1109/MIC.2003.1232516.

Parkinson, G. N. (1957). *Parkinson's law and other studies in administration.* Boston, MA: Houghton-Mifflin.

Parpinelli, Lopes, & Freitas. (2002). Data mining with an ant colony optimization algorithm. *IEEE Transactions on Evolutionary Computation, 6*(4), 321–332. doi:10.1109/TEVC.2002.802452.

Passino, K. M. (2002). Biomimicry of bacterial foraging for distributed optimization and control. *IEEE Control Systems Magazine, 22*(3), 52–67. doi:10.1109/MCS.2002.1004010.

Patel-Schneider, P. F., Hayes, P., & Horrocks, I. (2004). OWL web ontology language: Semantics and abstract syntax. *W3C Recommendation.* Retrieved from http://www.w3.org/TR/owl-semantics/

Pedrinaci, C. Domingue, Brelage, van Lessen, Karastoyanova, & Leymann. (2008). Semantic business process management: Scaling up the management of business processes. In *Proceedings of the IEEE International Conference on Semantic Computing* (pp. 546-553). IEEE.

Pedrycz, W., & Gomides, F. (1998). *An Introduction to fuzzy sets: Analysis and design.* Academic Press.

Peirce, C. S. (1880). On the algebra of logic. *American Journal of Mathematics, 3*, 15–57. doi:10.2307/2369442.

Peirce, C. S. (1885). On the algebra of logic: A contribution to the philosophy of notation. *American Journal of Mathematics, 7*, 180–202. doi:10.2307/2369451.

Piatrik & Izquierdo. (2006). Image classification using an ant colony optimization approach. *Lecture Notes in Computer Science, 4306*, 159–168. doi:10.1007/11930334_13.

Plotnick. (1997). *Concept mapping: A graphical system for understanding the relationship between concepts.* Retrieved from http://www.mind-mapping.org/seminal-papers-in-information-mapping/concept-mapping-overview.html

Polanyi, M. (1967). *The tacit dimension.* Chicago: University of Chicago Press.

Prakash, V., & Gopalakrishnan, S. (2011). Testing efficiency exploited: Scripted versus exploratory testing. In *Proceedings of the International Conference on Electronic Computer Technology.* IEEE.

Prasanth, Y., Sarika, Santhosh Anuhya, Vineela, & Ajay Babu. (2012). Framework for testing web services through SOA (service oriented architecture). *International Journal of Engineering Trends and Technology, 3*(2).

Pundt, H., & Bishr. (1999). Domain ontologies for data sharing-An example from environmental monitoring using field GIS. *Computers & Geosciences, 28*, 98–102.

Putnam, L. H. (1978). A general empirical solution to the macro software sizing and estimating problem. *IEEE Transactions on Software Engineering, 4*(4), 345–361. doi:10.1109/TSE.1978.231521.

Quellec, Lamard, & Josselin, Cazuguel, Cochener, & Roux. (2008). Optimal wavelet transform for the detection of microaneurysms in retina photographs. *IEEE Transactions on Medical Imaging, 27*(9), 1230–1241. doi:10.1109/TMI.2008.920619 PMID:18779064.

Quellec, Russell, & Abràmoff. (2011). Optimal filter framework for automated, instantaneous detection of lesions in retinal images. *IEEE Transactions on Medical Imaging, 30*(2), 523–533. doi:10.1109/TMI.2010.2089383 PMID:21292586.

Qwaider, W. (2011). Integrated of knowledge management and e- learning system. *International Journal of Hybrid Information Technology, 4*(4), 59–70.

Rajabally, E., Sen, P., Whittle, S., & Dalton, J. (2004). Aids to Bayesian belief network construction. In *Proceedings of the Intelligent Systems,* (pp. 457-461). IEEE.

Rajasekaran, P. Miller, Verma, & Sheth. (2004). Enhancing web services description and discovery to facilitate composition. In *Proceedings of SWSWPC 2004*, (pp. 55-68). SWSWPC.

Raj, P. (2012). Knowledge management – A road map for winning organization. *International Journal of Research in Economics & Social Sciences*, 2(2), 363–373.

Ramil, J. F. (2000). Algorithmic cost estimation software evolution. In *Proceedings of the 22nd International Conference on Software Engineering* (pp. 701–703). Limerick, Ireland: IEEE.

Raymond, E. S. (1999). The cathedral and the bazaar: Musings on Linux and open source by an accidental revolutionary. Sebastopol, CA: O'Reilly and Accociates Inc.

Reddy, C. S., & Raju, K. (2009). An improved fuzzy approach for COCOMO's effort estimation using Gaussian membership function. *Journal of Software*, 4(5), 452–459. doi:10.4304/jsw.4.5.452-459.

Reichle, M., & Hanft, A. (2006). The FLOSSWALD information system on free and open source software. [University of Hildesheim, Institute of Computer Science.]. *Proceedings of*, LWA2006, 229–233.

Reid, S. (2000). BS 7925-2: The software component testing standard. In *Proceedings 1st Asia-Pacific Conference on Quality Software* (pp. 139-148). IEEE.

Reifer, D. J. (2000, November-December). Web development: Estimating quick-to-market software. *IEEE Software*, 57–64. doi:10.1109/52.895169.

Remli, K., & Deris, B. (2012). *Automated biological pathway knowledge retrieval based on semantic web services composition and AI planning*. Paper presented at the International Conference on Information Retrieval & Knowledge Management. Kuala Lumpur, Malaysia.

Rentea, C., Schieferdecker, I., & Cristea, V. (2009). Ensuring quality of web applications by client-side testing using TTCN-3[C/OL]//. In *Proceedings of the 9th International Conference on Web Engineering*. San Sebastian, Spain: IEEE. Retrieved from http://sunsite.informatik.rwth-aachen.de/Publications-/CEUR-WS/Vol-561/paper1.pdf

Reza, Eswaran, & Hati. (2009). Automatic tracing of optic disc and exudates from color fundus images using fixed and variable thresholds. *Journal of Medical Systems*, 33, 73–80. doi:10.1007/s10916-008-9166-4 PMID:19238899.

Riege, A. (2005). Three dozen knowledge sharing barriers managers must consider. *Journal of Knowledge Management*, 9(3), 18–35. doi:10.1108/13673270510602746.

Robin & Uma. (2010). Ontology based semantic knowledge representation for software risk management. *International Journal of Engineering Science and Technology*, 2(10), 5611–5617.

Robin & Uma. (2011a). An intelligent ontology-based e-learning tool for software risk management. *International Journal of Education Economics and Development*, 2(4), 320–346. doi:10.1504/IJEED.2011.043830.

Robin & Uma. (2011e). Development of educational ontology for software risk ananlysis. In *Proceedings of the International Conference on Communication, Computing & Security- ICCCS2011*. ACM.

Robin & Uma. (2011f). An ontology based linguistic infrastructure to represent software risk identification knowledge. In *Proceedings of the International Conference & Workshop on Emerging Trends in Technology (ICWET '11)*. ACM.

Robin, & Uma. (2011b). Design and development of ontology suite for software risk planning, software risk tracking and software risk control. *Journal of Computer Science, 7*(3), 320-327.

Robin, & Uma. (2011c). An ontology driven elearning agent for software risk management. *International Journal of Academic Research, 3*(2), 30-36.

Robin, & Uma. (2011d). Design and development of SRI ONTO: An educational ontology representing software risk identification knowledge. *International Journal of Computer Applications, 15*, 5-13.

Robin, Hepzibah Miriam, & Uma. (2012). Design and development of an ontology for data structure. *Archives des Sciences, 65*(4), 74–85.

Rollett, H. (2003). *Knowledge management: Processes and technologies*. Dordrecht, The Netherlands: Kluwer Academic Publishers. doi:10.1007/978-1-4615-0345-3.

Ross, T. J. (2004). *Fuzzy logic with engineering applications*. Albuquerque, NM: University of New Mexico.

Rouhani, S., Asgari, S., & Mirhosseini, S. (2012). Review study: Business intelligence concepts and approaches. *American Journal of Scientific Research, 50*, 62–75.

Roy, C. K., & Cordy, J. R. (2007). *A survey on software clone detection research* (Technical Report 541). Kingston, Canada: Queen's University.

Ruhe, M., Jeffery, R., & Wieczorek, I. (2003). Cost estimation for web applications. In *Proceedings ICSE 2003*, (pp. 285-294). ICSE.

Russell Records, L. (2005). The fusion of process and knowledge management. *BPTrends*. Retrieved from www.bptrends.com

Saeed, S., Khawaja, F. M., & Mahmood, Z. (2012). A review of software quality methodologies. *Advanced Automated Software Testing: Frameworks for Refined Practice, 129*.

Sajeva, S., & Jucevicius, R. (2010). Determination of essential knowledge management system components and their parameters. *Social Sciences, 1*(67), 80–90.

Samuel, P., & Surendran, A. (2010). Forward slicing algorithm based test data generation. In *Proceedings of 3rd IEEE International Conference on Computer Science & Information Technology*. IEEE.

Sáncheza, Garcíaa, & Mayoc, Lópezb, & Horneroa. (2009). Retinal image analysis based on mixture models to detect hard exudates. *Medical Image Analysis, 13*(4), 650–658. doi:10.1016/j.media.2009.05.005 PMID:19539518.

Sandhawalia, B., & Dalcher, D. (2007). Knowledge support for software projects. In *Proceeding of IRMA International Conference*, (pp. 936-940). Vancouver, Canada: IRMA.

Scacchi, W. (2003). Issues and experiences in modeling open source software development processes. In *Proceedings of the 3rd ICSE Workshop on Open Source Software Engineering* (pp. 121-125). Portland, OR: ICSE.

Schmidt, G., Kahl, W., & Brink, C. (1997). *Relational methods in computer science*. Berlin: Springer.

Schmidt, G., & Ströhlein, T. (1985). Relations algebras: Concept of points and representability. *Disc. Math., 54*, 83–92. doi:10.1016/0012-365X(85)90064-0.

Schmidt, G., & Ströhlein, T. (1989). *Relationen und graphen*. Berlin: Springer-Verlag. doi:10.1007/978-3-642-83608-4.

Schmidt, G., & Ströhlein, T. (1993). *Relations and graphs*. Berlin: Springer-Verlag. doi:10.1007/978-3-642-77968-8.

Shannak, R. (2010). Knowledge-based systems support for strategic decisions. *European Journal of Economics, Finance and Administrative Sciences*, (21), 7-20.

Sharma, A. Hellmann, & Maurer. (2012). Testing of web services – A systematic mapping. In *Proceedings of the IEEE World Congress on Services (SERVICES 2012)*. Honolulu, HI: IEEE.

Showole, A., Sahibuddin, S., & Ibrahim, S. (2011). Layered approach to open source software development success. In *Proceedings of the Communications of the IBIMA, 2011*. IBIMA.

Siddiqi, J., & Shekaran, M. C. (1996). Requirements engineering: The emerging wisdom. *IEEE Software, 13*(2), 15–19. doi:10.1109/MS.1996.506458.

Simon, D. (2008). Biogeography based optimization. *IEEE Transactions on Evolutionary Computation, 12*(6). doi:10.1109/TEVC.2008.919004.

Singh, J. (2007). Open-source software and knowledge management in digital context: Issues and implications. In *Proceedings of the INFLIBNET's Convention*. INFLIBNET.

Singh, A. K., & Sharma, V. (2011). Key attributes of successful knowledge management: An empirical study in telecommunication and software industries. *International Journal of Business Information Systems*, 7(1), 78–92. doi:10.1504/IJBIS.2011.037298.

Sinthanayothin, Boyce, Williamson, Cook, & Mensah, Lal, & Usher. (2002). Automated detection of diabetic retinopathy on digital fundus images. *Journal of Diabetic Medicine*, 19, 105–112. doi:10.1046/j.1464-5491.2002.00613.x PMID:11874425.

Smith & Blanck. (2002). From experience: Leading dispersed teams. *Journal of Product Innovation Management*, 19(4), 294–304. doi:10.1016/S0737-6782(02)00146-7.

Sneed, H. M. (2004). A cost model for software maintenance and evolution. In *Proceedings of the IEEE International Conference on Software Maintenance* (pp. 264–273). Chicago, IL: IEEE.

Sneed, H. M. (2005). Estimating the cost of a reengineering project. In *Proceedings of the 12ᵗʰ Working Conference on Reverse Engineering* (pp. 111–119). Pittsburgh, PA: IEEE.

Software Design Patterns. (n.d.). Retrieved Sep. 2012 from http://www.oodesign.com/

Sommerville, I. (2004). *Software engineering* (8th ed.). Englewood Cliffs, NJ: Pearson Education.

Sommerville, I., & Kotonya, G. (1998). *Requirements engineering: Processes and techniques*. New York: John Wiley & Sons, Inc..

Song, L., Zhang, C., Wang, Y., & Lin, L. (2009). Knowledge Management in multi-party IS development teams: A case study at Fudan University. *International Journal of Management Innovation Systems*, 1(2), 1–14.

Sosnovsky & Gavrilova. (2005). Development of educational ontology for c-programming. In *Proceeding of XI International Conference on Knowledge - Dialogue - Solution*, (Vol. 1, pp. 127-131). IEEE.

Sowa, J. F. (2000). *Knowledge representation – Logical, philosophical, and computational foundations*. Pacific Grove, CA: Brooks/Cole.

Sowe, S., Stamelos, I., & Angelis, L. (2008). Understanding knowledge sharing activities in free/open source software projects: An empirical study. *Journal of Systems and Software*, 81, 431–446. doi:10.1016/j.jss.2007.03.086.

Staal, Abramoff, & Niemeijer, Viergever, & van Ginneken. (2004). Ridge-based vessel segmentation in color images of the retina. *IEEE Transactions on Medical Imaging*, 23(4), 501–509. doi:10.1109/TMI.2004.825627 PMID:15084075.

Straub, D., Loch, K., Evaristo, R., Karahanna, E., & Strite, M. (2002). Towards a theory-based measurement of culture. *Journal of Global Information Management*, 10(1), 13–23. doi:10.4018/jgim.2002010102.

Ströhlein, E. (1895). *Vorlesungen über die algebra der logik(exacte logik)*. Leipzig, Germany: Teubner.

Sun, C. Wang, Mu, Liu, Wang, & Chen, T.Y. (2011). Metamorphic testing for web services: Framework and a case study. In *Proceedings of the 2011 IEEE International Conference on Web Services (ICWS)*. ICWS.

Surendran, A., Samuel, P., & Jacob, K. P. (2011). Code clones in program test sequence identification. In *Proceedings of World Congress on Information and Communication Technologies*. IEEE.

Takahashi, Abiko, Negishi, Itabashi, Kato, Takahashi, & Shiratori. (2005). An ontology-based e-learning system for network security. In *Proceedings of the 19th International Conference on Advanced Information Networking and Applications*, (Vol. 1, pp. 197-202). IEEE.

Tamura, S., Higuchi, S., & Tanaka, K. (1971). Pattern classification based on fuzzy relations. *IEEE Transactions on Systems, Man, and Cybernetics*, 1, 61–66. doi:10.1109/TSMC.1971.5408605.

Tariq & Akram. (2010). An automated system for colored retinal image background and noise segmentation. In *Proceedings of the IEEE Symposium on Industrial Electronics and Applications (ISIEA 2010)*, (pp. 405-409). IEEE.

Tarski, A. (1941). On the calculus of relations. *J. Symb. Log.*, *6*(3), 73–89. doi:10.2307/2268577.

Tchier, F. (2002a). Demonic semantics by monotypes. In *Proceedings of the International Arab Conference on Information Technology* (Acit2002). University of Qatar.

Tchier, F. (2002b). Demonic relational semantics of compound diagrams. In J. Desharnais, M. Frappier, & W. MacCaull (Eds.), Relational Methods in computer Science: The Québec Seminar, (pp. 117-140). Methods Publishers.

Tchier, F. (2003). While loop demonic relational semantics monotype/residual style. In *Proceedings of the 2003 International Conference on Software Engineering Research and Practice (SERP'03)*. Las Vegas, NV: SERP.

Tchier, F. (1996). *Sémantiques relationnelles démoniaques et vérification de boucles non déterministes. (Theses of doctorat). Département de Mathématiques et de statistique.* Canada: Université Laval.

Tchier, F. (2004). Demonic semantics: Using monotypes and residuals. *International Journal of Mathematics and Mathematical Sciences*, *3*, 135–160. doi:10.1155/S016117120420415X.

Teodorović, & Dell'Orco. (2000). Bee colony optimization – A cooperative learning approach to complex transportation problems. *Advanced OR and AI Methods in Transportation*.

Thayer, R., & Dorfman, M. (1997). Software requirements engineering glossary. In Thayer & Davis (Eds.), Software requirements: Objects, functions, and states. Englewood Cliffs, NJ: Prentice-Hall, Inc.

The Theory Underlying Concept Maps and How to Construct and Use Them. (n.d.). Retrieved Aug. 2012 from http://cmap.ihmc.us/publications/researchpapers/theorycmaps/theoryunderlyingconceptmaps.htm

Trendowicz, A., Heidrich, J., Münch, J., Ishigai, Y., Yokoyama, K., & Kikuchi, N. (2006). Development of a hybrid cost estimation model in an iterative manner. In *Proceedings of the 28th International Conference on Software Engineering* (pp. 331–340). Shanghai, China: IEEE.

University of Iowa. (n.d.). *Retinopathy online challenge website*. Retrieved from http://roc.healthcare.uiowa.edu/results.php

Usher, Dumskyj, & Himaga, Williamson, Nussey, & Boyce. (2003). Automated detection of diabetic retinopathy in digital retinal images: A tool for diabetic retinopathy screening. *Diabetic Medicine*, *21*(1), 84–90. doi:10.1046/j.1464-5491.2003.01085.x PMID:14706060.

Van Vliet, H. (2008). *Software engineering: Principles and practice*. Chichester, UK: John Wiley & Sons.

Vila, M. A., & Delgado, M. (1983). On medical diagnosis using possibility measures. *FSS*, *10*, 211–222. doi:10.1016/S0165-0114(83)80116-X.

Walston, C. E., & Felix, C. P. (1997). A method of programming measurement and estimation. *IBM Systems Journal*, *16*, 54–73. doi:10.1147/sj.161.0054.

Walter, Klein, Massin, & Erginay. (2002). A contribution of image processing to the diagnosis of diabetic retinopathy—Detection of exudates in color fundus images of the human. *IEEE Transactions on Medical Imaging*, *21*(10), 1236–1243. doi:10.1109/TMI.2002.806290 PMID:12585705.

Walter, Massin, & Erginay, Ordonez, Jeulin, & Klein. (2007). Automatic detection of microaneurysms in color fundus images. *Medical Image Analysis*, *11*(6), 555–566. doi:10.1016/j.media.2007.05.001 PMID:17950655.

Wang, Y., Guo, D., & Shi, H. (2007). Measuring the evolution of open source software systems with their communities. *SIGSOFT Software Engineering Notes, 32*(6).

Wang, Jiang, Chia, & Tan. (2010). Wikipedia2Onto – Building concept ontology automatically, experimenting with web image retrieval. *Informatica*, *34*, 297–306.

Weber, R., Aha, D. W., & Becerra-Fernandez, I. (2001). Intelligent lessons learned systems. *International Journal of Expert Systems Research and Applications, 20*(1), 17–34. doi:10.1016/S0957-4174(00)00046-4.

Weiser, M. (1984). Program slicing. *IEEE Transactions on Software Engineering, 10*(4), 352–357. doi:10.1109/TSE.1984.5010248.

Whitehead, A. N., & Russell, B. (1910). *Principia mathematica* (Vol. I). Cambridge, UK: Cambridge Univ. Press.

Wiig, K. (1993). *Knowledge management foundations: Thinking about thinking: How people and organizations create, represent, and use knowledge.* New York: Schema Press.

Wirth, N. (1971). Program development by stepwise refinement. *Communications of the ACM, 14*(4), 221–227. doi:10.1145/362575.362577.

Woelk, D., & Lefrere. (2002). Technology for performance-based lifelong learning. In *Proceedings of the International Conference on Computers in Education (ICCE'02).* ICCE.

Wongthongtham, P., Kasisopha, N., Chang, E., & Dillon, T. A. (2008). Software engineering ontology as software engineering knowledge representation. In *Proceedings of the Third International Conference on Convergence and Hybrid Information Technology,* (pp. 668-675). IEEE.

Wu, D. Parsia, Sirin, Hendler, & Nau. (2003). Automating DAML-S web services composition using SHOP2. In *Proceedings International Semantic Web Conference (ISWC)* (LNCS), (vol. 2342). Berlin: Springer.

Wu, K. C., & Chiu. (2008). Toward tourist service integration and personalization with semantic web services: A case study in Hong Kong. In *Proceedings of the IEEE International Conference on e-Business Engineering.* IEEE.

Yazid, Arof, & Isa. (2011). Automated identification of exudates and optic disc based on inverse surface thresholding. *Journal of Medical Systems.* doi: doi:10.1007/s10916-011-9659-4 PMID:21318328.

Yu, L. (2006). Indirectly predicting the maintenance effort of open-source software. *Journal of Software Maintenance and Evolution: Research and Practice, 18*(5), 311–332. doi:10.1002/smr.335.

Zadeh, L. A. (1973). *The concept of a linguistic variable and its application to approximate reasoning.* Memorandum ERL-M 411 Berkeley.

Zadeh, L. A. (1965). Fuzzy sets. *Information and Control, 8,* 338–353. doi:10.1016/S0019-9958(65)90241-X.

Zadeh, L. A. (1971). Similarity relations and fuzzy orderings. *Information Sciences, 3,* 177–206. doi:10.1016/S0020-0255(71)80005-1.

Zadeh, L. A. (1975). Calculus of fuzzy restrictions. In Zadeh et al. (Eds.), *Fuzzy Sets and Their Applications to Cognitive and Decision Processes.* New York: Academic Press.

Zhang, Wu, & Yo, Li, & Karray. (2010). Detection of microaneurysms using multi-scale correlation coefficients. *Pattern Recognition, 43*(6), 2237–2248. doi:10.1016/j.patcog.2009.12.017.

Zhao, L., & Elbaum, S. G. (2003). Quality assurance under the open source development model. *Journal of Systems and Software, 66*(1), 65–75. doi:10.1016/S0164-1212(02)00064-X.

Zhu & Huo. Q. (2005). Developing a software testing ontology in UML for a software growth environment of web-based applications. In Software Evolution with UML and XML, (pp. 263-295). Hershey, PA: IDEA Group Inc.

Zhu, H. (2006). A framework for service-oriented testing of web services. In *Proceedings of the 30th Annual International Computer Software and Applications Conference.* COMPSAC.

Zimmermann, H. J. (1990). *Fuzzy set theory and its applications* (2nd ed.). Boston: Kluwer Academic Publishers.

Zouaq & Nkambou. (2008). Building domain ontologies from text for educational purposes. *IEEE Transactions on Learning Technologies, 1*(1), 49–62. doi:10.1109/TLT.2008.12.

About the Contributors

Saqib Saeed is an assistant professor at the Computer Science department at Bahria University Islamabad, Pakistan. He has a Ph.D. in Information Systems from University of Siegen, Germany, and a Masters degree in Software Technology from Stuttgart University of Applied Sciences, Germany. He is also a certified software quality engineer from American Society of Quality. His research interests lie in the areas of human-centered computing, computer supported cooperative work, empirical software engineering and ICT4D.

Izzat Alsmadi is an associate professor in the department of computer information systems at Yarmouk University in Jordan. He obtained his Ph.D degree in software engineering from NDSU (USA) and his second master in software engineering from NDSU (USA) and his first master in CIS from University of Phoenix (USA). He had a B.Sc degree in telecommunication engineering from Mutah University in Jordan. He has several published books, journals, and conference articles largely in software engineering and information retrieval fields.

* * *

Tamer Abdou is a PhD candidate in the Department of Computer Science and Software Engineering, Concordia University. He has experience in various software engineering roles such as a developer, team leader, and test manager. He currently works as a teaching assistant and supervises capstone projects. His research interests include agile methodologies, open source software process development, and software testing.

Sameer Abufardeh is assistant professor at department of computer science and operations research at North Dakota State University, USA. He received a PhD in Software Engineering from North Dakota State University, an MS in Computer Science from St. Cloud State University, USA, a BS in Computer Science from Southern Illinois University, USA, and an AS in Computer Programming and Systems Analysis from Palestine Polytechnic University. His areas of interest include software engineering information retrieval and data mining. He has more than 8 years of teaching experience and more than 8 years of industry experience.

Emad A. Abu-Shanab earned his PhD in business administration, majoring in MIS area in 2005 from Southern Illinois University – Carbondale, USA. He earned his MBA from Wilfrid Laurier University in Canada and his Bachelor in civil engineering from Yarmouk University (YU) in Jordan. He is an associate professor in MIS, where he taught courses like operations research, e-commerce, e-government, introductory and advanced courses in MIS, production information systems, and legal issues of computing. His research interests are in areas like E-government, technology acceptance, E-marketing and E-CRM, digital divide and E-learning. Published many articles in journals and conferences and authored two books in e-government area. Dr. Emad worked as an assistant dean for students' affairs, quality assurance officer in Oman, and the director of Faculty Development Center at YU.

M. Usman Akram received his PhD in computer engineering with specialization in medical imaging from National University of Sciences and Technology, Pakistan, in 2012. He is currently assistant professor at Bahria University, Pakistan. His research interests include medical image analysis, image processing, machine learning, and pattern recognition.

Huda Al Rashidi is a Ph.D student in Melbourne University. In 2010, she did her master in fuzzy demonic operators with Dr Fairouz Tchier.

Sascha Alda is a professor in software architecture at the University of Bonn-Rhein-Sieg (Sankt Augustin). He got a Dipl. Information degree from University of Koblen-Landau and Leiden University in 2000. In software architecture, his current research topics include: end-user customization, model-based management, and several related subjects in SOA. Other research topics include: architectural patterns for mobile devices, and workflow architectures for different applications.

Tayyaba Ayub is graduate student at Bahria Univesity. Her research interests include software development and evaluation.

Simon Baker Studied Software Engineering at the University of Auckland followed by a MSc research degree in Computer Science, where he focused on the applications of Bayesian Networks for Web cost estimation. He co-authored several publications in this area with his Supervisor at the time Professor Emilia Mendes. He is currently pursuing further postgraduate studies in Advanced Computer Science at the University of Cambridge Computer Laboratory. In addition to his academic work, he has several years of technical consultancy experience working for IBM, where worked with major clients in numerous sectors including energy (Ausgrid), aviation (Air New Zealand), manufacturing, construction, and the Australian Government.

Lavika Goel is a research scholar in the Department of Computer Engineering at Delhi Technological University (DTU), Delhi, India. She worked at Oracle India Private Ltd. for six months through campus recruitment and then left it to pursue research in the field of Nature Inspired Intelligence, her interest area. Securing a GATE percentile of 98.7%, she did her M.E. (Master of Engineering with *Distinction*) in Computer Technology & Applications from Delhi Technological University (formerly Delhi College of Engineering), Delhi, and B-Tech (with *Honours*) in Computer Science & Engineering from JSS Academy of Technical Education, U.P. Technical University and has always been among the top rank-holders of the university in these courses.

Peter Grogono has degrees from Cambridge University and Concordia University. Currently, he is a Professor in the Department of Computer Science and Software Engineering at Concordia University, which he joined in 1984. He is the author of several textbooks, including the best-selling *Programming in Pascal*. His areas of research include programming language design, artificial life, and computer graphics. More than 120 students have completed masters' or doctoral degrees under his supervision. He has long been interested in interdisciplinary uses of computers. He designed *Musys*, a prize-winning language for electronic music composition, and supervises students working in multimedia. He has made significant contributions to teaching and curriculum development. He coordinated the introduction of the first undergraduate and graduate Software Engineering programs in Quebec, and he has received awards for teaching from both the Faculty of Engineering and the President of Concordia, as well as awards from student organizations.

Ashi Iram is Master student at Bahria University Islamabad, Pakistan. He has a bachelor's degree in computer science and her research interest lie in the areas of software engineering and compiler construction. She is also working as lab engineer at Bahria Univesity.

Pankaj Kamthan has been teaching in academia and industry for several years. He has also served on the program committees of several international conferences and editorial boards of journals related to education, information technology, and resource management. His areas of teaching and research interests include conceptual modeling, requirements engineering, and software quality.

Shehzad Khalid graduated from Ghulam Ishaq Khan Institute of Engineering Sciences and Technology, Pakistan, in 2000. He received the M.Sc. degree from National University of Science and Technology, Pakistan, in 2003, and the Ph.D. degree from the University of Manchester, U.K., in 2009. He is currently an Assistant professor at the Bahria University of Management and Computer Sciences, Pakistan. His research interests include dimensionality reduction, indexing and retrieval, profiling and classification, trajectory-based motion learning profiling and classification, computer vision, and machine learning.

Rawan T. Khasawneh graduated from Yarmouk University with a Bachelor of Management Information Systems in 2011, and is a master degree student specializing in Management Information System at Yarmouk University in Jordan. Rawan has research interest in e-government topics like digital divide, security issues, and adoption of e-government. Also, she works on research projects in social media, E-marketing and E-CRM, knowledge management systems, and group decision support systems.

Emilia Mendes is Professor of Software Engineering at the Blekinge Institute of Technology, in the School of Computing (Karlskrona, Sweden). She has to date focused her research in three disciplines: Empirical Web Engineering, Empirical Software Engineering, and Computer Science/Web & Software Engineering education. To date this research has led to 170+ refereed publications, including two books (one edited, *Web Engineering* [2005] and one authored, *Cost Estimation Techniques for Web Projects* [2007]). These publications are particularly focused in the areas of Software & Web effort prediction, Software & Web measurement and metrics (quality, size metrics, productivity, and usability), Empirical studies (in areas such as maintainability prediction, process improvement and pair programming), Evidence-Based Research (systematic literature reviews, meta-analyses), and Software/Web engineering education (learning theories, collaborative learning). Her work has received over 2100 citations (including self-citations), with a h-index on Google Scholar of, and has obtained awards for best papers at several conferences.

D. Doreen Hephzibah Miriam is currently working as a Professor and Head at Loyola ICAM College of Engineering and Technology in the Department of Information Technology. She received her B.Tech in Information Technology from Madras University, Chennai, M.E in Computer Science and Engineering from Anna University, Chennai, and Ph.D in Computer Science and Engineering from Anna University. Her research interests include parallel and distributed computing, peer-to-peer computing and grid computing. Previous positions include Assistant professor at the Department of Computer Science and Engineering, Sri Venkateswara College of Engineering, Chennai and Teaching Research Associate at the Department of Computer Science, Anna University, Chennai. She has published about 20 papers in International Journals and Conferences. She is a life member of ISTE.

Kiran Nazeer is currently studying Master in Software Engineering at Bahria University Islamabad, Pakistan. Her research interests include software engineering and Web development.

V.K. Panchal is the Associate Director at Defense Terrain & Research Lab, Defense and Research Development Organization (DRDO), New Delhi, India. He is an Associate Member of IEEE (Computer Society) and Life Member of Indian Society of Remote Sensing. He is an Associate Member of IEEE (Computer Society) and Life Member of Indian Society of Remote Sensing. He is also the Vice-Chairman of the Indian Society of Remote Sensing, Delhi Chapter. He has done Ph.D in Computational Intelligence from Jawarharlal Nehru University, Delhi, and M.S. in Information Systems from BITS, Pilani, and is currently working as Scientist 'G' at DRDO, Delhi. His research interests are in the synthesis of terrain understanding model based on incomplete information set using bio-inspired intelligence and remote sensing. He has chaired sessions & delivered invited talks at many national & international conferences.

C.R. Rene Robin obtained his ME and PhD from Anna University, India in 2006 and 2011, respectively. He is currently working as Professor and Head of the Department of Computer Science and Engineering, Jerusalem College of Engineering, Chennai, India. His research interests include artificial intelligence, knowledge management, ontology, Semantic Web, and e-learning. He has published more than 40 papers in National/International Conferences and Journals. He is one of the recipients of IBM's 'Mentor Award' for The Great Mind Challenge 2011. He is a life member of ISTE. His lectures on "Ontological Engineering," "Role of Ontology in AI," have been well received. He is the President of Jerusalem Research Forum. He has published a book titled *Role of Ontology in Software Risk Management – KM Approach* with LAP Lambert Publishing House, Germany.

Philip Samuel is the head of Information Technology Division, SOE, Cochin University of Science & Technology. He is an eminent teacher with several publications to his credit. His areas of interest are software testing, computer networks, distributed systems, bioinformatics, etc.

Anupama Surendran is a research scholar in the Department of Computer Science, Cochin University of Science & Technology. Her areas of interest are software testing, search-based testing techniques, data mining, etc.

Fairouz Tchier was born in Setif, Algeria. She received BSc (Honors) in Mathematics and MSc in functional analysis from Université de Sherbrooke, Québec, Canada, in 1991, and PhD degree in Theoretical Computer Science from Université Laval in 1996. She is member of IEEE, ACM, and many associations. She taught at Université de Sherbrooke, and Université Laval. She is Associate Professor in mathematics at King Saud University. She is in charge with the implementation of the academic accreditation processes with NCAAA. She supervised about 30 BSc student projects, and 12 master students. Her research interests mainly concern discrete mathematics, software engineering, formal methods, and fuzzy logic. In 2009, she was awarded the best staff member in teaching. In 2012, she was awarded the best academic researcher in Higher Education conference. Dr. Fairouz received financial support for her research projects from King Saud University, Riyadh.

G.V. Uma received her ME from Bharathidasan University, India, in 1994, and her PhD from Anna University, Chennai, India, in 2002. She is currently working as Professor and Head of the Department of Computer Technology, Madras Institute of Technology, Chennai-44. She was the Founder Head of Department of Information Science and Technology in Anna University, Chennai-25. Her research interests include software engineering, genetic privacy, ontology, knowledge engineering and management and natural language processing. She is the recipients of Best Citizens of India Award 2011 by Indian Publishing House, New Delhi, Rashtriya Gaurav Award 2010 by India International Friendship Society, New Delhi and Tamil Nadu Young Women Scientist for the year 2003 by Science City, Govt. of Tamil Nadu, India. She has consulted to a number of industries and educational institutions on various IT and Software engineering projects. She has published a book titled "Essentials of Software Engineering."

Liguo Yu is an associate professor at Computer Science Department, Indiana University South Bend. He received his Ph.D. degree in computer science from Vanderbilt University in 2004. He received his MS degree from Institute of Metal Research, Chinese Academy of Science in 1995. He received his BS degree in Physics from Jilin University in 1992. Before joining Indiana University South Bend, he was a visiting assistant professor at Tennessee Tech University. His research areas include software coupling, software maintenance and software evolution, empirical software engineering, and open-source development. He is also interested in social network analysis, knowledge management, complex system, and mathematical modeling.

Index

A

Abstract State Machines (ASMs) 42
Aggregated Knowledge Map (AKMa) 73
Ant Colony Optimization 151-152, 154, 157, 172, 174-175
Artificial Intelligence (AI) 42
Artificial Intelligence in Education (AIED) 230

B

Bacterial Foraging Optimization 152, 174
Bayesian networks 83-84, 241-242, 248
Bee Colony Optimization (BCO) 151, 165
Biogeography Based Optimization 152, 161, 172, 175
black-box testing 59, 121
Business Process Execution Language (BPEL) 126
Business Process Management (BPM) 42

C

Capability Maturity Model Integration (CMM/CMMI) 8
Case-Based Reasoning (CBR) 146
Central Bank of Bahrain (CBB) 7
closed-source projects 87-90, 106
code clones 49, 52-55, 57-61
Community of Practice (CoP) 142
Computer Networks (CN) 229
Conditional Probability Table (CPT) 70
Cotton Wool Spots (CWS) 177, 184
Cryptography 229

D

DARPA Agent Markup Language (DAML) 38
DARPA Agent Markup Language for Services (DAML-S) 42

decision-making systems (DSS) 1
Decision Tree 241, 244-245, 247
demonic calculus 195
demonic fuzzy inclusion 213
Diabetic Retinopathy (DR) 176
Directed Acyclic Graph (DAG) 69
dynamic feedback model (DFM) 6
dynamic slicing 55-57

E

effort estimation 64-67, 69, 72-74, 82-85, 87-88, 107-108
Electronic Process Guide (EPG) 21
elementary theory of relations 199
embedded systems 49-52, 58, 60-61
error matrix 151, 156-159, 162-164, 168-169, 171-173
Explicit Knowledge 2, 11, 13, 16-18, 21, 140, 142, 145-146, 149

F

Field Of View (FOV) 187
fuzziness 196, 199
fuzzy c-means (fcm) 180
fuzzy demonic composition 213, 220-221
fuzzy logic 87, 107, 196-198, 205, 213, 221, 224
fuzzy set theory 196-197, 204-205, 223, 225

G

Global Software Engineering (GSE) 12-14, 33
Graphical User Interface (GUI) 124

H

Haemorrhages (HM) 177
Hard Exudates (HE) 177

Hofstede cultural model 27
Hue, Saturation and Intensity (HSI) 181

I

image clustering and heuristic method (HSI) 156, 160, 167, 169
Industrial Credit and Investment Corporation of India (ICICI) 6
internationalization (I18N) 20, 25, 34

J

Jet Propulsion Laboratory 110, 117

K

Knowledge Management (KM) 2, 12, 18
Knowledge Management Life Cycles (KMLCs) 142
knowledge management system 2, 6-7, 10-11, 47, 147, 226-228, 246-247

L

Learning Objects (LOs) 230
linear regression analysis 93-96, 98, 105
Linux kernel Branch 94-97, 99-104
localization (L10N) 20, 25, 34

M

Microaneurysms (MAs) 177
multi-variable models 95-98, 100-102, 105

N

nonfunctional requirements 117
Non-Proliferative Diabetic Retinopathy (NPDR) 177

O

Object Oriented Architecture (OOA) 121
ontology 36, 38, 40-43, 47, 123, 128, 142, 226-236, 239-240, 246-249
Open Source Initiative (OSI) 141
open-source projects 86-91, 106
Open Source Software (OSS) 135
Optic Disc (OD) 177, 183
optimization algorithm 152, 161, 165, 174-175

P

program slicing 49, 55, 58-62
Proposed Method (PM) 189
Punnet squares 198

Q

Quadratic Assignment Problem (QAP) 153
Quality Assurance (QA) 127
Quality of Service (QoS) 37

R

real-time systems 49, 51, 55, 57-62
refinement ordering 196
relational calculus 194-195, 199, 201, 204
Requirements Engineering (RE) 110
Requirements Management (RM) 110
Resource Description Framework (RDF) 37, 42
Retinopathy Online Challenge (ROC) 179
Rule Markup Language (RuleML) 41

S

Service Oriented Access Protocol (SOAP) 124
Service Oriented Architecture (SOA) 38, 120
single-variable models 93-96, 98-103, 105
Small and Medium Scale Enterprises (SMEs) 110
Software Development Life-Cycle (SDLC) 23
Software Engineering Body of Knowledge (SWE-BOK) 230
Software Engineering Ontology (SEONTO) 230
Software Risk Identification Ontology (SRIONTO) 231
Software Risk Management 230, 236, 239-240, 242, 247, 249
stakeholders 13, 21, 25, 27, 116-117, 145, 147
static testing 59, 137
stigmergy 154
Swarm Intelligence (SI) 151, 153
Swarm Particle Optimization 152

T

Tacit Knowledge 2, 13, 16-18, 20, 26-27, 29, 69, 85, 140, 142, 144-145, 149
Test Driven Development (TDD) 120, 127

Test Environment Set-Up 137, 147
Test Execution activity 137, 139
testing as a service (TAS) 122
Testing Knowledge Management (TKM) 135, 143, 149

U

Universal Data Description Interface (UDDI) 124
Unmanned underwater vehicles(UUV) 153

W

Web Ontology Language (OWL) 42, 232
Web Service Description Language (WSDL) 36, 38, 124
Web Service Modelling Ontology (WSMO) 41
Web services 35-38, 40-48, 119-122, 124-134, 248
Web Services Interoperability (WS-I) 133
white-box testing 59